Lecture Notes in Computer Science 15226

The series Lecture Notes in Computer Science (LNCS), including its subseries Lecture Notes in Artificial Intelligence (LNAI) and Lecture Notes in Bioinformatics (LNBI), has established itself as a medium for the publication of new developments in computer science and information technology research, teaching, and education.

LNCS enjoys close cooperation with the computer science R & D community, the series counts many renowned academics among its volume editors and paper authors, and collaborates with prestigious societies. Its mission is to serve this international community by providing an invaluable service, mainly focused on the publication of conference and workshop proceedings and postproceedings. LNCS commenced publication in 1973.

Luigi Carro · Francesco Regazzoni ·
Christian Pilato
Editors

Embedded Computer Systems: Architectures, Modeling, and Simulation

24th International Conference, SAMOS 2024
Samos, Greece, June 29 – July 4, 2024
Proceedings, Part I

Springer

Editors
Luigi Carro
Federal University of Rio Grande do Sul
Porto Alegre, Rio Grande do Sul, Brazil

Francesco Regazzoni
University of Amsterdam
Amsterdam, The Netherlands

Christian Pilato
Polytechnic University of Milan
Milan, Italy

ISSN 0302-9743 ISSN 1611-3349 (electronic)
Lecture Notes in Computer Science
ISBN 978-3-031-78376-0 ISBN 978-3-031-78377-7 (eBook)
https://doi.org/10.1007/978-3-031-78377-7

This Springer imprint is published by the registered company Springer Nature Switzerland AG
The registered company address is: Gewerbestrasse 11, 6330 Cham, Switzerland

Preface

SAMOS is a conference with a unique format. It brings together every year researchers from both academia and industry on the topic of embedded systems in the perfect setting of Samos island. The SAMOS 2024 keynotes covered a wide range of topics including embedded systems design aspects by Alberto Sangiovanni-Vincentelli (UC Berkeley, USA) and bioinspired techniques for autonomous robots by Theocharis Theocharides (University of Cyprus, Cyprus). A specific focus was been put on security through tutorials by Apostolos Fournaris (Industrial Systems Institute, Greece) and Francesco Regazzoni (Amsterdam University, The Netherlands).

The SAMOS 2024 proceedings comprise a selection of publications targeting either systems themselves - through their applications, architectures, and underlying processors - or methods created to automate their design. A total of 57 papers were submitted to the general track and 24 papers were selected by the program committee to be presented at the conference (42% Acceptance rate). Two special sessions were introduced in the program to respectively gather novel work on security and to report recent results of European projects. Finally, a poster session was organized to provide young researchers a chance to receive high-quality feedback from distinguished researchers from both academia and industry.

The SAMOS 2024 committee wants to acknowledge the generous support of the many reviewers who contributed to the quality of these proceedings. We hope that you enjoy reading them!

July 2024

Luigi Carro
Francesco Regazzoni
Christian Pilato

Organization

General Chair

Luigi Carro	Instituto de Informática UFRGS, Brazil

Program Chairs

Francesco Regazzoni	Università della Svizzera italiana, Switzerland and University of Amsterdam, The Netherlands
Christian Pilato	Politecnico di Milano, Italy

Special Session Chairs

Innovative Architectures and Tools for Security

Apostolos Fournaris	Industrial Systems Institute, Greece

Reports from European Research Projects

Giovanni Agosta	Politecnico di Milano, Italy
Dimitrios Soudris	NTUA, Greece

Poster Session

Carlo Galuzzi	TU Delft, The Netherlands
Georgi N. Gaydadjiev	TU Delft, The Netherlands

Tutorial Chairs

Apostolos Fournaris	Industrial Systems Institute, Greece
Francesco Regazzoni	Università della Svizzera italiana, Switzerland and University of Amsterdam, The Netherlands

Web Chair

Tom Slooff	Università della Svizzera italiana, Switzerland

Proceedings and Finance Chair

Carlo Galuzzi	TU Delft, The Netherlands

Submission Chair

Andy D. Pimentel	University of Amsterdam, The Netherlands

Publicity Chair

Rubén Salvador	CentraleSupélec, IRISA, Inria, France

Steering Committee

Shuvra Bhattacharyya	University of Maryland, College Park, USA and IETR, France
Holger Blume	Leibniz Universität Hannover, Germany
Ed F. Deprettere	Leiden University, The Netherlands
Nikitas Dimopoulos	University of Victoria, Canada
Carlo Galuzzi	Delft University of Technology, The Netherlands
Georgi N. Gaydadjiev	TU Delft, The Netherlands
John Glossner	Optimum Semiconductor Technologies, USA
Walid Najjar	University of California Riverside, USA
Andy D. Pimentel	University of Amsterdam, The Netherlands
Olli Silvén	University of Oulu, Finland
Dimitrios Soudris	NTUA, Greece
Jarmo Takala	Tampere University of Technology, Finland
Stephan Wong	TU Delft, The Netherlands

Program Committee

Giovanni Agosta	Politecnico Di Milano, Italy
Shuvra Bhattacharyya	University of Maryland, USA
Holger Blume	Leibniz Universität Hannover, Germany
Jeronimo Castrillon	TU Dresden, Germany

Ricardo Chaves	INESC-ID, Portugal
Francesco Conti	UniBo, Italy
Serena Curzel	Politecnico Di Milano, Italy
Karol Desnos	INSA Rennes, France
Vassilios V. Dimakopoulos	University of Ioannina, Greece
Giorgos Dimitrakopoulos	Democritus University of Thrace, Greece
Holger Flatt	Fraunhofer IOSB, Germany
Apostolos Fournaris	Industrial Systems Institute, Greece
Carlo Galuzzi	Delft University of Technology, The Netherlands
Georgi N. Gaydadjiev	Delft University of Technology, The Netherlands
Andreas Gerstlauer	University of Texas at Austin, USA
John Glossner	Rivier University, USA
Diana Göhringer	TU Dresden, Germany
Xinfei Guo	Shanghai Jiao Tong University, China
Said Hamdioui	TU Delft, Netherlands
Frank Hannig	Friedrich Alexander University, Germany
Christian Haubelt	University of Rostock, Germany
Jasmin Jahić	University of Cambridge, UK
Matthias Jung	University of Würzburg and Fraunhofer IESE, Germany
Pekka Jääskeläinen	Tampere University of Technology, Finland
Christoforos Kachris	InAccel, Greece
Georgios Keramidas	Aristotle University of Thessaloniki, Greece
Leonidas Kosmidis	BSC, Spain
Angeliki Kritikakou	Inria - Irisa, France
John McAllister	Queen's University Belfast, UK
Paolo Meloni	Università degli Studi di Cagliari, Italy
Alexandre Mercat	Tampere University of Technology, Finland
Chrysostomos Nicopoulos	University of Cyprus, Cyprus
Alex Orailoglu	UC San Diego, USA
Andrés Otero	Universidad Politécnica de Madrid, Spain
Anuj Pathania	University of Amsterdam, The Netherlands
Maxime Pelcat	INSA Rennes, France
Christian Pilato	Politecnico di Milano, Italy
Andy Pimentel	University of Amsterdam, Netherlands
Oscar Plata	University of Málaga, Spain
Dionisios Pnevmatikatos	NTUA, Greece
Francesco Regazzoni	University of Amsterdam, Netherlands
Marc Reichenbach	Universität Rostock, Germany
Ruben Salvador	CentraleSupélec, IETR, France
Cristina Silvano	Politecnico di Milano, Italy
Dimitrios Soudris	NTUA, Greece

Secondary Reviewers

Contents – Part I

Contents – Part II

FAA+RTS: Designing Fault-Aware Adaptive Real-Time Systems —From Specification to Execution—

Lukas Miedema[1(✉)], Dolly Sapra[1], Petr Novobilsky[2], Sebastian Altmeyer[3], Clemens Grelck[4], and Andy D. Pimentel[1]

[1] University of Amsterdam, Amsterdam, Netherlands
{l.miedema,d.sapra,a.d.pimentel}@uva.nl
[2] Q-media s.r.o., Prague, Czech Republic
pno@qmediacz.onmicrosoft.com
[3] University of Augsburg, Augsburg, Germany
altmeyer@uni-augsburg.de
[4] Friedrich Schiller University Jena, Jena, Germany
clemens.grelck@uni-jena.de

Abstract. Large-scale cyber-physical systems, such as those for subway transportation or air traffic control, are becoming increasingly complex and often need to operate without human intervention. At the same time, these systems are subject to high requirements on the timing behavior and fault-tolerance. Consequently, the detection and mitigation of both hard and soft errors is of high importance in the already complex systems design process. The main challenges towards fault-aware real-time systems is the overall system design, in which the sheer size of the state-space and the system's complexity exceeds the capacity of today's development tools. In this paper, we present a new holistic methodology called FAA+RTS, for designing fault-aware adaptive real-time systems. We cover the entire path from system specification using a coordination language, via design-space exploration and task scheduling to the adaptive fault-aware runtime environment. Mitigating both hard and soft errors addresses competing requirements. Improving soft error tolerance (through redundant execution) may accelerate the aging process of silicon, thus expediting hard error failures. FAA+RTS is a novel solution as it integrates previously-isolated methods for dealing with multiple constraints into a single framework, presenting a single overview of all possible trade-offs to the application designer. This integration ensures that all aspects of system design, from specification to execution, are cohesively addressed, resulting in a robust and reliable system. We exemplify FAA+RTS using industrial-sized autonomous subway transportation system as a use-case.

1 Introduction

Complex cyber-physical, e.g. controlling critical infrastructure, are subject to a wide array of functional and non-functional requirements, ranging from reliabil-

L. Carro et al. (Eds.): SAMOS 2024, LNCS 15226, pp. 1–17, 2025.
https://doi.org/10.1007/978-3-031-78377-7_1

ity and fault-tolerance to timeliness, energy usage and total system cost [15]. Availability combined with real-time reactivity is particularly challenging: Such systems must be available for years or even decades while always providing correct reactions within tight deadlines during their entire lifetime [7]. Yet, their long lifetime makes hardware faults, both soft and hard, inevitable [4]. Nevertheless, the system's functional and timing correctness must still persist.

Engineering correct and robust software systems is considered a challenging task in general. This general challenge is aggravated in our case in two ways. Firstly, the consequences of malfunctioning software in cyber-physical systems can be extremely serious up to the loss of lives. Secondly, the term correctness not only involves computational (or functional) correctness, i.e. computing correct results eventually, but expands to properties of program execution such as timing behavior and energy consumption. Computing the results within a given time period and energy budget can be as important for system correctness as their numerical values. Coordination languages such as TeamPlay coordination language [12] have been developed to alleviate the enormous software development burden by elevating coordination as a first-class citizen. The coordination layer enables the specification of application building blocks which can systematically be protected against hard and soft faults of hardware components, with the objective to ensure system integrity (functional results, time bounds, energy budgets) as long as possible despite faulting compute resources.

Autonomous adaptivity is a promising mitigation technique for hardware errors (both hard and soft) in the presence of real-time constraints. Limited over-provisioning of resources (extra cores, extra slack in the schedule) can be used effectively as the runtime system can respond to errors by rescheduling. However, competing constraints emerge, in particular as redundant execution to detect and mitigate soft errors increases system utilization, requires provisioning more hardware, increases energy consumption and accelerates silicon aging thus expediting the arrival of hard errors. To that end, Design-Space Exploration (DSE) offers a potent mechanism to help evaluate and reduce the number of design points. Many different System-on-Chip (SoC) designs can be explored, each offering a different amount of available computational resources to the application, and thus different degrees of room for adaptivity, fault-tolerance and thus different aging characteristics.

Contribution: In such a setting, we propose FAA+RTS: A new holistic methodology for designing fault-aware real-time systems. FAA+RTS encompasses the entire design flow from the application specification, multi-core system-on-a-chip (SoC) design, adaptive scheduling to mean time to failure (MTTF) analysis and the runtime environment. In FAA+RTS, adaptivity takes center stage as a driver of reliability to guarantee timing correctness even in case of partial system failure. The FAA+RTS runtime automatically reconfigures itself and reacts to hardware faults, using either re-execution (soft errors) or re-scheduling (hard errors) of critical components. FAA+RTS caters to the competing requirements of tolerance for soft errors and hard errors, of energy use and hardware utilization by recognizing that each solution is a compromise. Using design space exploration (DSE), we give the application designer full insight in the trade-off between the various competing constraints and the resulting lifetime reliability as mean-time-to-failure (MTTF). This holistic view enables the application designer to select a compromise best tailored to the unique requirements of their application.

2 Industrial Use Case

We both motivate and validate our FAA+RTS methodology by a case study revolving around the communication subsystem of a railway control system developed by QMedia s.r.o., as illustrated in Fig. 1. The application contains multiple tasks with precedence relations, has real-time constraints. It is a safety-critical application, thus reliability in the presence of both soft and hard errors must be considered. Consequently, the use-case exhibits a breadth of requirements benefiting from a holistic approach such as offered by FAA+RTS, making it ideally suited to evaluated our method.

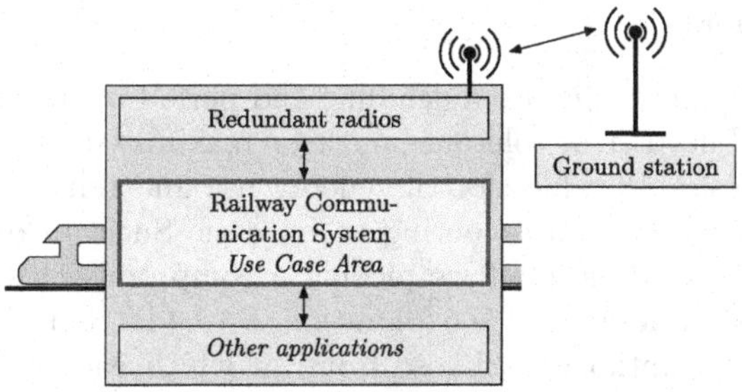

Fig. 1. Overview of the railway communication system

2.1 Description

The communication subsystem operates several different information flows between the ground system and the moving train(s). Each information flow is specific in purpose and criticality. It is necessary to establish independent communication channels for each of them. Under normal conditions each information flow has its own communication channel with allocated resources, but in case of incidents it is crucial to primarily keep up communication channels associated with the most critical information flows. Therefore, the system must be able to respond to various operating conditions (signal level, channel interference, HW-fault, line overload, etc.).

We show the parts of the software architecture of the use case in Fig. 2. The railway communication subsystem is composed of 7 computational modules and

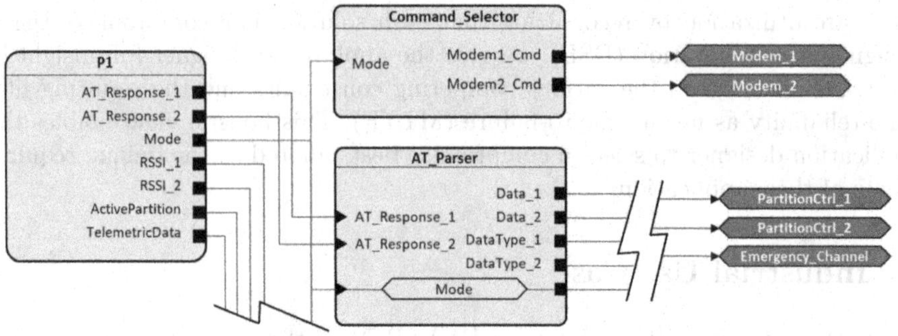

Fig. 2. Excerpt of the QMedia software architecture, showing 3 compute tasks and 5 sink tasks

9 sinks, for a total of 16 real-time tasks. Each module is responsible for a part of the independent communication channels: *P1*, for instance, reads data from physical channels, and the data is further processed by the *AT Parser*.

2.2 Requirements

The timing requirements dictate a deadline and period of 100 ms. Furthermore, the soft error and hard error tolerance must be maximized, while energy should be minimized. Desirable values for the energy use and reliability requirements are not static and instead are contingent on cost. Such an open formulation of requirements is ideal as it allows picking a compromise between the different factors. Through design space exploration, FAA+RTS gives the application designer a range of options to choose from, of which each such point can be subjected to cost-benefit analysis within the organization. The final process of narrowing the output of DSE down to a single option is out of scope for this paper.

3 Related Work

To the best of our knowledge, there is no other framework that addresses the fault-aware and adaptive aspect of real-time systems from specification all the way down to the execution and at the same time address both hard and soft errors. Several works address either soft errors [21] or hard errors [1] individually, but do not consider both together. Notably, some publications explore fault-tolerant scheduling techniques [18, 19], but these efforts constitute only a fraction of the broader framework proposed in our work.

Coordination is a well established computing paradigm with a plethora of languages, abstractions and approaches, surveyed in [5]. Yet, it lacks adoption in mission-critical cyber-physical systems, even more so in fault-tolerance contexts. Hume [8], a resource-aware language for real-time systems, offers guarantees on time and space. Similarly, AADL, the Architecture Analysis & Design Language [6] supports performance and reliability analyses in real-time system design. However, both lack resilience features. Fault-tolerant Linda [3] extends the Linda coordination language [17], based on a tuple-space in which messages can be shared between processes and the extensions focus mostly on making tuple-space operations safer and fault-tolerant.

The authors in [11] introduce utilization control as a technique to mitigate the core aging and core-failures (i.e. avoid hard-errors). This research focuses on the software aspect of embedded systems design and assumes the availability of specific hardware for improving lifetime reliability. Another similar work, [20] considers both hard and soft errors to extend the MTTF of a given hardware chip. In direct contrast, our framework delves into the bigger picture which include task scheduling and floorplan design of the SoC. A more powerful SoC design logically lowers utilization at the same redundancy levels, improving MTTF.

4 Integrated Methodology

We present an integrated methodology that cohesively links various stages of system design and execution, ranging from application specification to a fault-tolerant adaptive real-time runtime environment and a tailored multi-core SoC design.

Figure 3 outlines the proposed workflow.

Application Specification (Sect. 5) concerns the specification of the real-time application using the TeamPlay coordination language [12]. We leverage a coordination language to enable mechanical processing of the application code, its interdependencies and non-functional requirements in a robust and high-level manner.

Fault-Tolerant Adaptive Real-Time Scheduling (Sect. 6) is concerned with ensuring that all timing constraints are met under all conditions. Our approach is two-fold: (1) a scheduling bounds analyzer communicates with the iterative Design Space Exploration tool, while (2) offline schedules are produced for a range of degradation states from a particular design point.

Design Space Exploration (Sect. 7) identifies the SoC floorplan that optimizes lifetime reliability and power consumption in presence of errors. The tool generates a Pareto set from which an application designer selects a design point.

Our fault-tolerant, self-adaptive **Runtime Environment** *Artie* is linked with the compiled task code and runs the generated schedule set on the selected hardware. We discuss this aspect together with the validation of our industrial use-case in Sect. 8.

Each stage of our methodology is interconnected, ensuring that decisions made at one stage inform and enhance subsequent stages.

- The high-level application specification using the TeamPlay coordination language ensures robustness and clarity, feeding directly into the design space exploration.

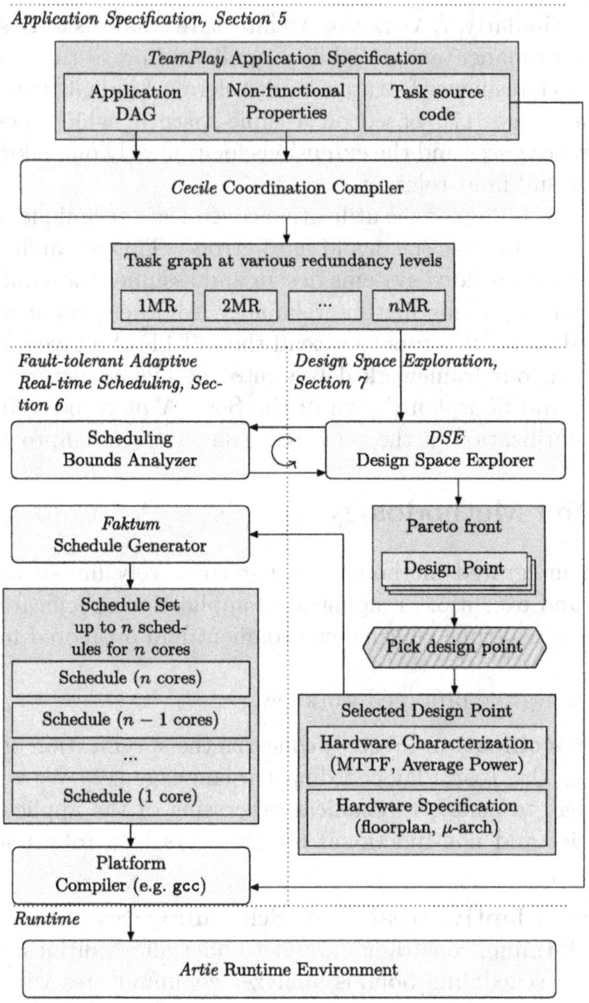

Fig. 3. FAA+RTS methodology overview

- The scheduling component interacts continuously with design space exploration to ensure that timing constraints are met under all conditions.
- The Design Space Exploration stage identifies optimal configurations, directly influencing the scheduling and runtime environment to balance reliability and power consumption effectively.
- The *Artie* runtime environment dynamically adapts based on the schedules and configurations identified, ensuring real-time system resilience.

This cohesive approach ensures that our methodology is more than just a collection of techniques; it is a unified framework designed to address the complexities of modern fault-tolerant real-time systems.

5 Application Specification

The combination of functional and non-functional requirements plus resilience against hardware failure creates an enormous software engineering complexity problem that we address by leveraging the TeamPlay coordination language [12]. TeamPlay is an exogenous coordination language [2] that naturally induces a two-layer software architecture: On the *component implementation layer* we leverage a standard programming language (usually C/C++) to implement software components with defined but manageable size and complexity along with determined non-functional behavior. On the *coordination layer* the TeamPlay language permits the high-level specification of integrating individual components into a complete (cyber-physical) system that guarantees non-functional requirements and optimizes for non-functional objectives, e.g. saving energy, depending on the application. Communication between components is facilitated via *channels*.

Access to a channel is exclusive: a sending component must always be scheduled in its entirety before a receiving component, ensuring absence of contention. The explicit modeling of communication enables task-level redundancy, as multiple jobs can be spawned within one epoch. Non-functional properties of individual components are predetermined across the range of available micro architectures and, where applicable, specific voltage and frequency settings. The information is provided to TeamPlay via a data-base, coined the *non-functional properties file* (see Fig. 3).

We leverage our two-layer, exogenous coordination design for further degrees of freedom in system design and integration. One example is *multi-versioning* where the component engineers provide multiple functionally exchangeable implementations of a component which differ in their non-functional properties, be it through competing implementation or through alternative compilation. Another example, prominently featuring in this work is the systematic and transparent introduction of redundancy to component execution for increased resilience against soft and hard hardware faults.

The FAA+RTS requires considerable flexibility of the application. Not only by requiring adaptivity to handle soft and hard errors, but also support for a range of platforms to enable effective Design Space Exploration. The component model, each with well-defined semantics, unlocks this flexibility without requiring dedicated support by the application developer. The Cecile coordination compiler serves as the front-end of the proposed FAA+RTS toolchain. As per Fig. 3, it ingests the TeamPlay coordination specification together with the non-functional properties file, and it produces a number of task graphs with different component replication levels in machine-readable form to be further processed by our subsequent toolchain.

6 Fault-Tolerant Adaptive Real-Time Scheduler

We implement fault-tolerance via redundancy: redundant cores compensate for hard errors and redundant executions compensate soft errors. At runtime, we adapt the schedule as dictated by the environment, i.e., the number of available cores and the presence of soft errors. In case of a hard error, we remap tasks of a failing core to available, healthy cores. Doing so decreases the number of available cores, and thus redundant execution may no longer be feasible. Consequently, hard errors may lead to an increased exposure to soft errors.

Soft Errors. We consider triple and dual modular redundancy at the task level as primary means of mitigating soft errors, but other techniques are also compatible with FAA+RTS, provided a sufficient schedulability test is available. Triple modular redundancy mitigates errors by means of majority voting, while dual modular redundancy detects errors that then are mitigated by re-execution of the erroneous actors. Note that the system's response time increases with the level of redundancy, but the system response time can still be statically derived given an upper bound on the number of faults [9].

Hard Errors. Adaptivity implies limited predictability due to system changes at run-time. Real-time scheduling, on the other hand, typically requires a high degree of predictability to enable derivation of real-time guarantees. Systems that are inherently unpredictable are unsuitable for a precise scheduling analysis. To overcome this contradiction, we resort to a set of statically precomputed schedules and a runtime environment that can dynamically switch between them.

To simplify remapping as a consequence of a hard error, we introduce *processing elements* as an abstract entity to which tasks are mapped. At runtime, cores are mapped to processing elements based on their availability. Hence, we do not need to compute schedule for all permutations of failed cores. Consequently, the number of schedules scales only linearly with the number of processing units. The size of each schedule scale linearly with the number of tasks. As such, for a system of n tasks and π processing units, we introduce a runtime memory complexity of only $\mathcal{O}(n \times \pi)$.

First, we prepare the task graph as encoded by the coordination language in two aspects: (a) transformation into a bipartite graph distinguishing between communication (data nodes) and computations (actor nodes); (b) partitioning the bipartite graph into sections that execute sequentially. Figure 4 shows such an extended graph, partitioned into two sections which can be scheduled independently. The sectioning of the graphs allows us to change redundancy levels in between. For each section, we derive a set of static schedules via HEFT-scheduling [14]. The HEFT-scheduler is slightly adapted to correctly account for redundant execution and to schedule, if feasible, redundant actors on different processing elements. The precomputed schedules per section differ in the number of available processing elements and the redundancy level of the actor execution (TMR, DMR, no redundancy, see Fig. 5).

Example. Figure 6 shows a sequence of hard errors. We assume a system of 6 cores. The actors are scheduled using triple-modular redundancy on 5 processing

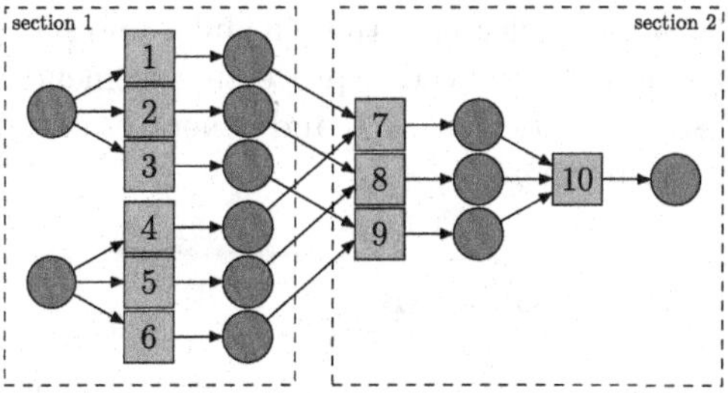

Fig. 4. Illustration of bipartite graph (example)

elements that are mapped to 5 of the 6 available cores, leaving one redundant core idle (a). In case of a hard error, i.e., a permanently failing core, processing element PE_3 is remapped to the spare core (b). In case a further core fails, the actors are mapped to only 4 processing elements using dual-modular redundancy. The switch from triple to dual-modular redundancy is necessary to meet the system requirements despite fewer processing elements. With the chosen scheduling, i.e., static section scheduling and adaptivity between sections, system's response time under x hard errors and y soft errors is merely a straight-forward combinatorial computation of maximal section lengths.

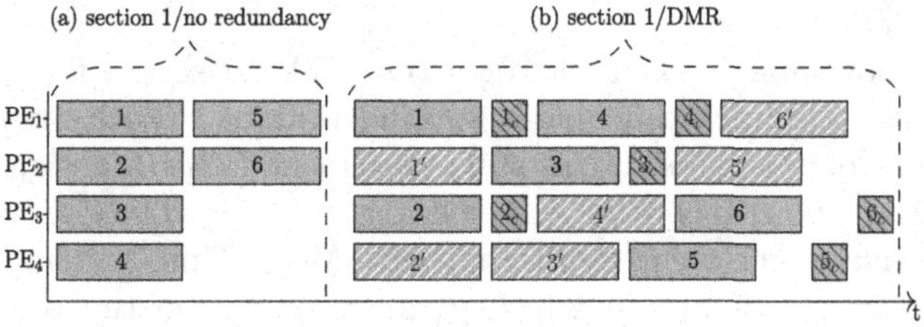

Fig. 5. Two schedules for Sect. 1 from Fig. 4, both with five processing elements, (a) without redundancy and (b) with dual modular redundancy.

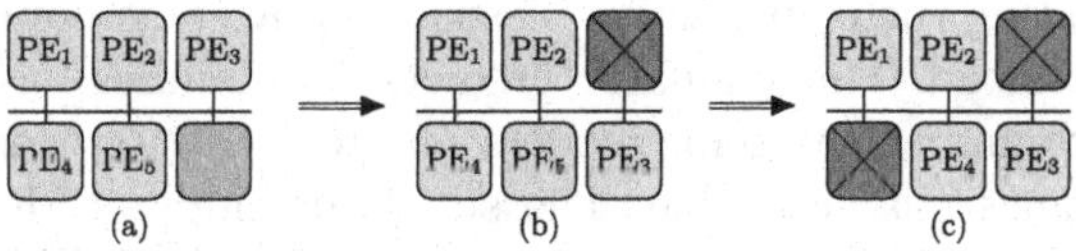

Fig. 6. Reaction to hard errors: Moving from TMR execution on 5 processing elements and one spare core (a) to TMR execution (b) to DMR execution on 4 processing elements.

Static Analysis. *Faktum* implements the scheduler and scheduling analysis. It provides lower/upper bounds on needed processing elements, serves as a quick schedulability analysis to be used in DSE and generates section schedules to be used in the runtime environment.

7 Design-Space Exploration

The objective of the Design-Space Exploration (DSE) tool [13] is to help designing a specific Multi-core System-on-Chip (SoC) for an application, implementing core based redundancy to safeguard against hard errors. The redundant cores on the SoC offer a safety net to the application, allowing for the remapping of a workload in the event that one of the processing cores fails. This approach ensures that task deadlines continue to be met, even with reduced core resources. However, the decision to integrate extra cores at the onset is not without consequences. It introduces added costs, not only in terms of the monetary expenditure but also in the physical space occupied on the chip and the increased power consumption. This raises a pivotal question: how many extra cores are truly necessary to balance reliability and cost-effectiveness?

Our analysis indicates that the number of extra cores required is dependent on the specific system requirements and workload characteristics. Detailed experimentation and results demonstrate the trade-offs between reliability, cost, and power consumption, providing a clear guideline for determining the optimal number of extra cores.

The DSE tool employs a Genetic Algorithm (GA) to explore floorplan designs for a fixed grid size microchip and a specific workload. Each arrangement of (different types of) cores on a grid style placement forms a design point. The maximum size of the grid is predetermined (e.g., Fig. 11). The GA is designed as a multi-objective search algorithm to optimize Mean-Time-To-Failure (MTTF) and average power consumption, which are inherently conflicting objectives. The optimization objective of average power consumption directly reflects the operational cost of the system and indirectly influences the physical cost through the required number of cores in the system. The framework produces a *Pareto Set* of design points, offering insights into floorplan choices that provide the trade-off between lifetime reliability (via MTTF) and power consumption. The framework evaluates design points using a simulator [16], which operates at a high abstraction level, estimating the chip's active lifespan and average power consumption for a specific workload. The simulator predicts core failures based on thermal, power and electro-migration ageing models, and redistributes workload until the application becomes unschedulable. The simulator employs Monte Carlo simulations with the stochastic fault models to predict the MTTF by averaging Time-To-Failures for each simulation and similarly computes the mean power usage.

Due to the significant computational requirements associated with performing numerous simulations per design point, the DSE tool continuously interacts with the *Scheduling Bounds Analyzer Faktum* to decrease the overall simulation count. When invoked, the *Scheduling Bounds Analyzer* provides information on the quality of the current floorplan specifically in terms of its potential to offer a valid and relaxed task schedule. The relaxation aspect suggests the capability of the floorplan to accommodate acceptable disruptions in the task schedule. Based on this analysis, the tool empirically categorizes the design point as good, bad or intermediate [13]. Given the costly nature of simulations, a higher number of simulations is reserved for design points that fall in the intermediate range. The intuition here is that these specific floorplans effectively illustrate the trade-offs between power consumption and MTTF. They are valuable as they do not represent extremes, offering neither the flexibility for any relaxation in the schedule nor an excessively relaxed one. In other words, these floorplans represent a critical middle ground where the intricate relationship between power efficiency and reliability is evident.

The DSE tool predicts the SoC's reliability by considering core failures, i.e. hard errors. Soft errors are addressed via redundant execution. The DSE tool can be configured to account for soft errors by pre-processing the application to incorporate redundant tasks. It is important to note that lifetime reliability is significantly influenced by the presence of redundancy. Executing each task multiple times increases the computational demand, resulting in higher power consumption and elevated core temperatures. This elevated temperature accelerates the aging process of cores, emphasizing the trade-off between redundancy and the associated increase in power consumption and core aging.

8 Validation

The first step is to model the application in the TeamPlay coordination language, as shown in Fig. 7. Following the specification of the non-functional requirements *period* and *deadline*, we can easily identify two sections in the code that describe the application's *components* and their interactions through *channels*, respectively. The specification of a component consists of a set of typed *inports* and a set of typed *outports*, using a syntax reminiscent of C structs. Typed channels connect outport to inports. TeamPlay supports the annotation of various further properties to components, e.g. the redundancy level for resilience [10]. For space reasons we cannot show them all here. Note that we use the latest syntax of TeamPlay here, which slightly diverges from the syntax used in [12].

The strength of the TeamPlay exogenous coordination approach is that we can model our use case pretty much one-to-one according to the architecture specification in Fig. 2. Component implementations do not need to be (re-)implemented, but can be adopted from existing software repositories. Port types, and thus channel types, are merely symbolic on the coordination layer, permitting integrity checks, but again are implemented at component implementation layer with programming language suited for that task, in the context of real-time software usually C.

This specification is converted to a bipartite graph split into sequential sections, composed of computing nodes (green) and data nodes (blue). Figure 8a

```
app Railway {
  period = 100ms;
  deadline = 100ms;
  components {
    P1 { outports { Str_t AT_Response1;
                    Str_t AT_Response2;
                    u16 Mode;
                    PST_TelemetricData_t TelemetricData; ... }}
    CommandSelector { inports  {u16 Mode;}
                      outports {ET_ModemCmd_t Modem1CMD;
                                ET_ModemCmd_t Modem2CMD;}}
    ... }
  channels {
    P1.Mode -> CommandSelector.Mode;
    P1.AT_Response1 -> AT_Parser.AT_Response1;
    P1.AT_Response2 -> AT_Parser.AT_Response2;
    P1.Mode -> AT_Parser.ModeIn;
    ...}
}
```

Fig. 7. Excerpt from use case TeamPlay coordination code

shows one such section of the railway application. Next, we produce redundant variants of this graph to handle soft-errors. This means that we need to introduce replicas and comparators (dual-modular redundancy) or voters (triple-modular redundancy). Due to space limitations, we only show the bipartite graphs for dual-modular redundancy in Fig. 8b.

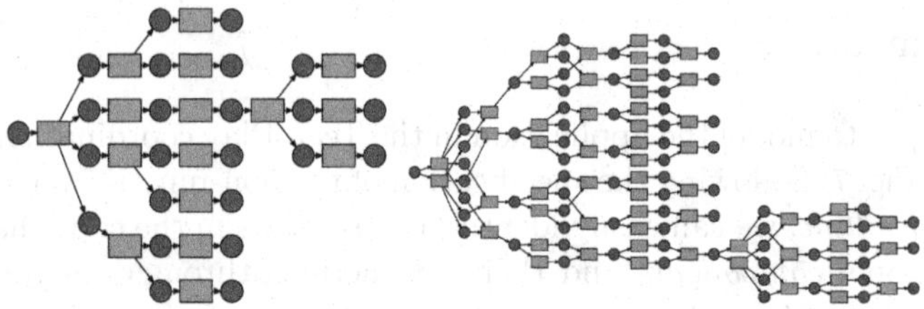

(a) no redundancy (b) dual-modular redundancy

Fig. 8. Task graphs for one section of the railway use-case.

The Design Space Exploration (DSE) tool is applied to the QMedia use-case without redundancy, along with a dual-redundant task graph. Figures 9a and 9b highlights all the design points explored by the GA for no-redundancy and with dual-redundancy, respectively. Each floorplan is represented by its average power consumption and MTTF (as estimated by the simulator). The Pareto Set, denoted in orange, emerges as the GA converges in both scenarios.

Furthermore, a direct comparison between the two Pareto Sets is demonstrated in Fig. 9c. It is noteworthy that the prospect of building safeguards against soft errors and hard errors incur a heavy cost in terms of operational power consumption of the SoC. Reduction in power consumption by curtailing the number of cores on the SoC shortens the lifetime reliability of the system.

Pareto Points #1, #2, and #3, illustrated in Fig. 9c highlight the cost of protecting the system against soft errors. Point #1, without redundancy, consumes 1.03 W on average with a predicted lifetime of ≈13.5 years. After introducing redundancy, Point #2 offers a similar predicted lifetime but with an increased power consumption of ≈2.25 W. Similarly, Point #3 operates at a comparable power level but is projected to have a shorter lifetime of ≈7 years. The significant contrast in lifetime reliability stems from the utilization of redundant schedules, wherein each task is executed multiple times. This leads to increased computational demands, higher power consumption, and overall, accelerates the aging process of the underlying microchip. Eventually, this framework provides valuable insights to the system designer to choose appropriate resources in creating a fault-aware adaptive real time system.

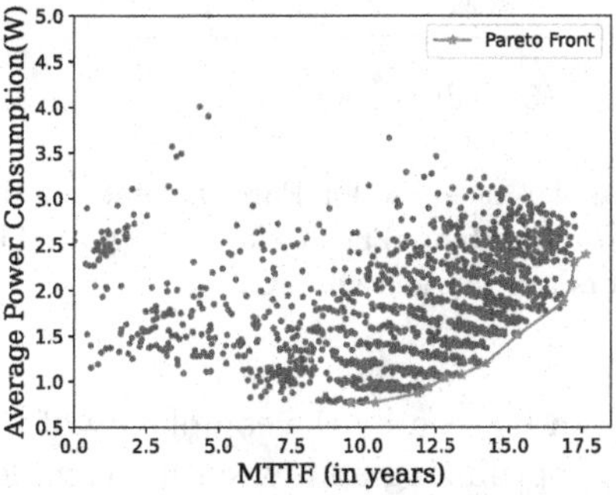

(a) No redundancy present

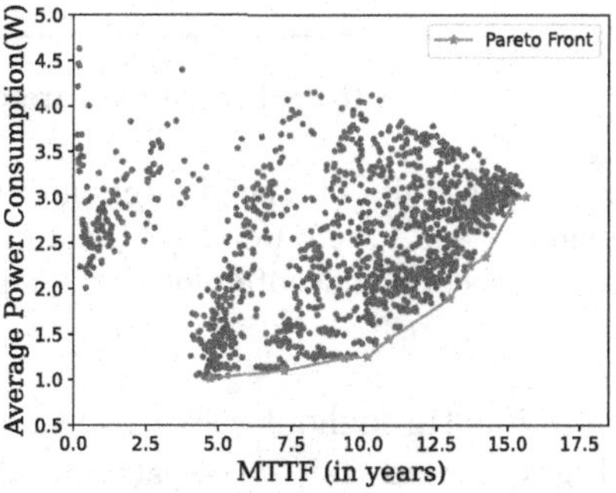

(b) Dual redundancy present

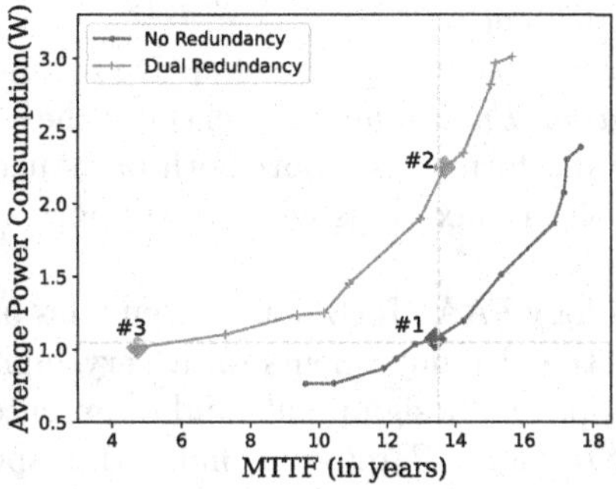

(c) Pareto Set comparison

Fig. 9. All design points explored by the DSE tool for no redundancy and dual redundancy modes. The orange line in (a) and (b) highlights the Pareto set. (Color figure online)

The schedules corresponding to Pareto Points #1 and #3 are shown in Fig. 10. Pareto Point #2 is omitted due to space limitations. In both the cases, the task graph offers only limited parallelism, see Fig. 8, so that many cores

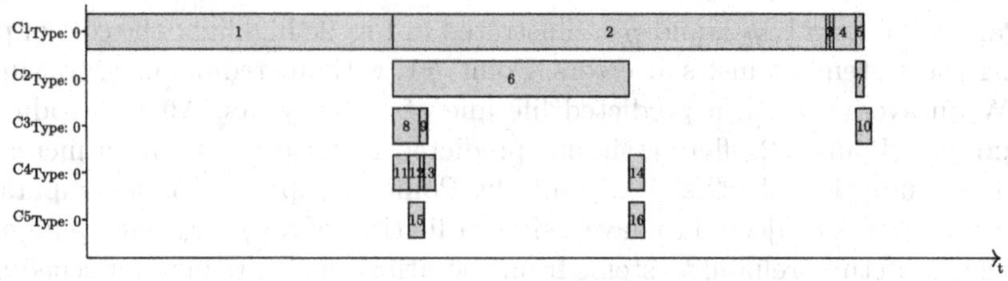

(a) Schedule for Pareto Point #1 (no redundancy)

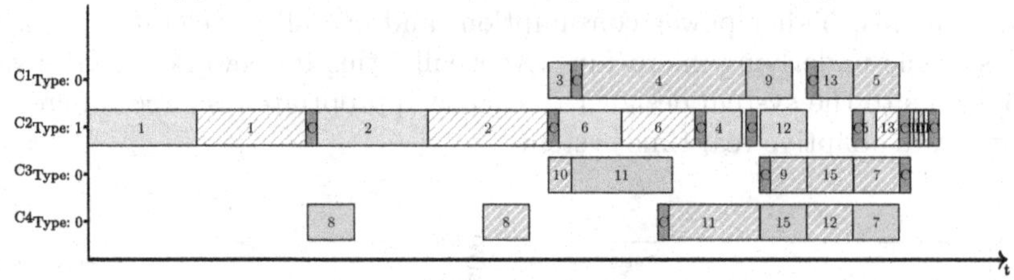

(b) Schedule for Pareto Point #3 (redundancy)

Fig. 10. Schedules of a single section of the railway use-case for Pareto Point #1 (no redundacy) and Pareto Point #3 (dual-modular redundancy) as marked in Fig. 11. The hatched executions denote replaces, comparators are marked with **C**.

remain idle throughout task execution. As can be seen by the complexity of the task graphs and the state-space, developing, optimizing and executing complex adaptive fault-aware real-time systems needs to be accommodated by suitable design-tools. Although all points from Fig. 11 are Pareto optimal, the floorplans and schedules differ significantly.

Furthermore, we have implemented the adaptive runtime environment *Artie*, short for *AROMA Runtime Environment*, to execute the schedules computed by *Faktum* on the selected platform. It support both bare-metal and pthread-based execution, for instance via Linux. This way, we support a large range of target architectures.

Our design methodology FAA+RTS not only enables us to specify the application and its non-functional requirements on a very high level of abstraction, but also to find Pareto-optimal design points and to execute the application with timing guarantees. The design is Pareto-optimal with respect to the mean-time-to-failure, cost and power consumption. Thus, we can execute the application in a fault-tolerant manner protecting us form hard and soft errors via self-adaptivity while meeting the stringent timing constraints.

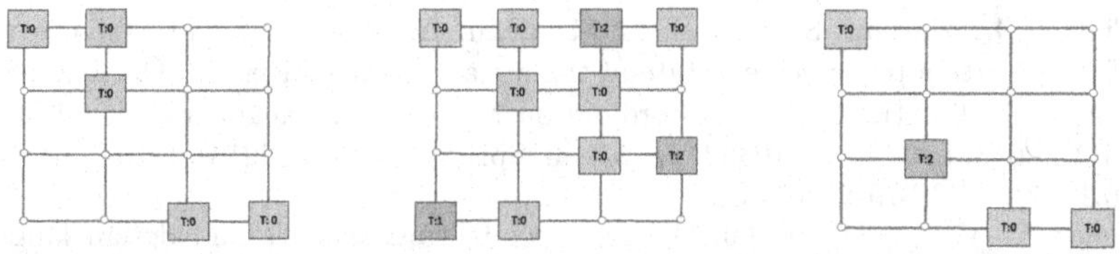

(a) Floorplan for Pareto Point #1 (no redundancy)

(b) Floorplan for Pareto Point #2 (redundancy)

(c) Floorplan for Pareto Point #3 (redundancy)

Fig. 11. Pareto Points #1, #2 and #3 as marked in Fig. 9c. Point #1 without redundancy, consumes ≈1.03 W on average and has predicted lifetime of ≈13.5 years. When redundancy is required, Point #2 provides similar predicted lifetime consuming ≈2.25 W. Similarly, Point #3 operates at similar power, but is predicted to have half the lifetime at ≈7 years.

9 Conclusion

In this paper, we have presented FAA+RTS, the first complete design methodology for the specification, development and execution of fault-tolerant adaptive real-time systems. We use a coordination language to model the application and its non-functional requirements. This specification is then input to Design-Space exploration, which searches for optimal system configurations and schedules. The scheduler provides a set of static schedules with varying levels of redundancy uses a variant of HEFT scheduling. The runtime system then switches between these schedules at runtime depending on the current number of hard and soft-errors.

FAA+RTS targets highly complex self-adaptive systems featuring a wide array of contradicting requirements, foremost fault-tolerance via adaptivity timeliness, power consumption and costs. We have validated FAA+RTS on a real railway use-case. The results show the immense design space and complexity that can only be mastered using automated methodologies such as FAA+RTS.

References

1. Abdi, A., Zarandi, H.: A meta heuristic-based task scheduling and mapping method to optimize main design challenges of heterogeneous multiprocessor embedded systems. Microelectron. J. **87**, 1–11 (2019)
2. Arbab, F.: Composition of interacting computations. In: Goldin, D., Smolka, S.A., Wegner, P. (eds.) Interactive Computation. Springer, Heidelberg (2006). https://doi.org/10.1007/3-540-34874-3_12
3. Bakken, D., Schlichting, R.: Supporting fault-tolerant parallel programming in Linda. IEEE Trans. Parallel Distrib. Syst. **6**(3), 287–302 (1995)
4. Bansal, S., Bansal, R., Arora, K.: Energy conscious scheduling for fault-tolerant real-time distributed computing systems. In: Pandey, S., Shanker, U., Saravanan, V., Ramalingam, R. (eds.) Role of Data-Intensive Distributed Computing Systems in Designing Data Solutions. EAI/Springer Innovations in Communication and Computing. Springer, Cham (2023). https://doi.org/10.1007/978-3-031-15542-0_1

5. Ciatto, G., Mariani, S., Louvel, M., Omicini, A., Zambonelli, F.: Twenty years of coordination technologies: state-of-the-art and perspectives. In: Di Marzo Serugendo, G., Loreti, M. (eds.) Coordination Models and Languages. COORDINATION 2018. LNCS, vol. 10852, pp. 51–80. Springer, Cham (2018). https://doi.org/10.1007/978-3-319-92408-3_3
6. Feiler, P., Gluch, D., Hudak, J.: The architecture analysis and design language (AADL): an introduction. Technical report. Carnegie-Mellon University, Pittsburgh, USA (2006)
7. Gunes, V., Peter, S., Givargis, T., Vahid, F.: A survey on concepts, applications, and challenges in cyber-physical systems. KSII Trans. Internet Inf. Syst. **8**(12), 4242–4268 (2014)
8. Hammond, K., Michaelson, G.: Hume: a domain-specific language for real-time embedded systems. In: Pfenning, F., Smaragdakis, Y. (eds.) GPCE 2003. LNCS, vol. 2830, pp. 37–56. Springer, Heidelberg (2003). https://doi.org/10.1007/978-3-540-39815-8_3
9. Kühbacher, C., Ungerer, T., Altmeyer, S.: Redundant dataflow applications on clustered manycore architectures. In: Hong, J., Bures, M., Park, J.W., Cerny, T. (eds.) SAC 2022: Proceedings of the 37th ACM/SIGAPP Symposium on Applied Computing, Virtual Event, 25–29 April 2022, pp. 226–235 (2022)
10. Loeve, W., Grelck, C.: Towards facilitating resilience in cyber-physical systems using coordination languages. In: Constantinou, E. (ed.) 13th Seminar on Advanced Techniques and Tools for Software Evolution (SATToSE 2020), vol. 2754. CEUR Workshop Proceedings (2020)
11. Ma, Y., Chantem, T., Dick, R., Hu, X.: Improving system-level lifetime reliability of multicore soft real-time systems. IEEE Trans. Very Large Scale Integr. VLSI Syst. **25**(6), 1895–1905 (2017)
12. Roeder, J., Rouxel, B., Altmeyer, S., Grelck, C.: Towards energy-, time- and security-aware multi-core coordination. In: Bliudze, S., Bocchi, L. (eds.) 22nd International Conference on Coordination Models and Languages (COORD 2020), Malta. LNCS, vol. 12134, pp. 57–74. Springer, Cham (2020). https://doi.org/10.1007/978-3-030-50029-0_4
13. Sapra, D., Pimentel, A.D.: Exploring multi-core systems with lifetime reliability and power consumption trade-offs. In: Silvano, C., Pilato, C., Reichenbach, M. (eds.) Embedded Computer Systems: Architectures, Modeling, and Simulation: 23rd International Conference, SAMOS 2023. Springer, Cham (2023). https://doi.org/10.1007/978-3-031-46077-7_6
14. Topcuoglu, H., Hariri, S., Wu, M.Y.: Performance-effective and low-complexity task scheduling for heterogeneous computing. IEEE Trans. Parallel Distrib. Syst. **13**(3), 260–274 (2002)
15. Villarreal Lozano, C., Vijayan, K.: Literature review on cyber physical systems design. Procedia Manuf. **45**, 295–300 (2020)
16. Wasala, S.M., Niknam, S., Pathania, A., Grelck, C., Pimentel, A.D.: Lifetime estimation for core-failure resilient multi-core processors. In: 16th IEEE International Symposium on Embedded Multicore/Many-core Systems-on-Chip (MCSoC 2023). IEEE (2023)
17. Wells, G.: Coordination languages: back to the future with Linda. In: 2nd International Workshop on Coordination and Adaption Techniques for Software Entities (WCAT 2005) (2005)
18. Youness, H., Omar, A., Moness, M.: An optimized weighted average makespan in fault-tolerant heterogeneous MPSoCs. IEEE Trans. Parallel Distrib. Syst. **32**(8), 1933–1946 (2021)

19. Zhang, L., Li, K., Li, C., Li, K.: Bi-objective workflow scheduling of the energy consumption and reliability in heterogeneous computing systems. Inf. Sci. **379**, 241–256 (2017)
20. Zhou, J., Hu, X., Ma, Y., Sun, J., Wei, T., Hu, S.: Improving availability of multicore real-time systems suffering both permanent and transient faults. IEEE Trans. Comput. **68**(12), 1785–1801 (2019)
21. Zhou, J., et al.: Resource management for improving soft-error and lifetime reliability of real-time MPSoCs. IEEE Trans. Comput.-Aided Design Integr. Circ. Syst. **38**(12), 2215–2228 (2018)

Experimental Assessment and Biaffine Modeling of the Impact of Ambient Temperature on SoC Power Requirements

Kameswar Rao Vaddina[1], Florian Brandner[1], Gérard Memmi[1], and Pierre Jouvelot[1,2(✉)]

[1] LTCI - Télécom Paris - Institut polytechnique de Paris, Palaiseau, France
[2] Mines Paris, PSL University, Paris, France
pierre.jouvelot@minesparis.psl.eu

Abstract. Based on fundamental physics-based considerations, we introduce the Biaffine Temperature-Voltage power model (BiTV) for SoC systems, which takes the influence of dynamic voltage, frequency, and ambient temperature conditions into account. Using an ARM-Cortex-based AM572x system operating in a temperature-controlled oven, we provide experimental evidence of the validity of the BiTV power model over a significant range of ambient temperatures (25 to 55 °C), voltages (0.98 to 1.23 V) and frequencies (100 to 1,500 MHz).

These experiments and the BiTV model provide quantitative elements to assess the impact of ambient temperature on systems' performance. Such insights could be of use to system designers and compiler writers, in particular when dealing with embedded systems operating in harsh conditions or under energy-critical constraints.

Keywords: Energy · temperature · energy profiling · monitoring infrastructure

1 Introduction

The laws of thermodynamics impose that the warmer the ambient temperature is, the more difficult it will be to cool down silicon-based processing devices, and thus the more energy these devices will consume. Many research works investigate the subtle interplay between energy, power, and temperature at a rather large system scale (see, for instance, among the recent ones, (Guermouche and Orgerie (2022))). The situation is, in fact, even more complex at a finer-grained level, where system-provided performance and environmental counters typically used in the above-mentioned lines of research might not provide the precision required. In particular, since many embedded systems are operated on energy-constrained batteries and in various mobile settings (cold remote outdoors, temperate indoors, hot engines, etc.) (Prakash et al. (2020)), a detailed understanding of how power requirements and energy consumption parameters

L. Carro et al. (Eds.): SAMOS 2024, LNCS 15226, pp. 18–33, 2025.
https://doi.org/10.1007/978-3-031-78377-7_2

evolve with respect to temperature is clearly needed to implement performance-increasing strategies.

If the system-on-chip (SoC) manufacturers provide tools such as Xilinx Power Estimator (Inc. (2018)) or Intel FPGA Power and Thermal Calculator (Intel (2020)) for power-related analysis, they are CPU-intensive and very complex to set up and use, thus being mostly dedicated to the design phase of SoCs. Our goal here is to come up with a simpler yet experimentally and physically validated model that could be used, say, within a compiler or an embedded run-time to take temperature-related power-management decisions. Such a model could be, for instance, used to decide when and how to increase the CPU frequency to meet real-time computational demands while taking into account the temperature conditions. This is a key element to ensure that the processor temperature is always maintained within its manufacturer-specified limits and thus that thermal runaways are avoided.

Unfortunately, setting up an experiment to inform such an issue is rather complex for a typical computer-oriented academic laboratory, which may explain the scarcity of related works in the domain (see Sect. 5), even though the application spectrum is rather vast, in particular when dealing with battery-equipped systems.

In this paper, we describe how we conducted such an experiment on one specific system, namely a Texas Instrument AM572x chip. Our contributions are (1) an experimental assessment of the impact of ambient temperature on the energy and power characteristics of a SoC system, and (2) the Biaffine Temperature-Voltage power model (BiTV), a physics-inspired and experimentally-validated analytical model of SoC system behavior with respect to both ambient temperature, dynamic voltage, and CPU clock frequency. Our experiments suggest that the BiTV power model provides a good approximation of the system behavior over a significant spectrum of temperatures, voltages, and frequencies.

These new results are a considerable improvement with regard to the previous work of (Skadron et al. (2003); Chandrakasan et al. (1996); Vaddina et al. (2017)), where all experiments were run at constant ambient temperature. Using a temperature-controlled oven, we report here on an extensive data-gathering run, from which a detailed analysis of how such a system behaves for various temperature points is performed. Even though we focus in this paper on one particular SoC system, we believe that the approach taken here and the corresponding results should be, thanks to their reliance on physics-informed concepts (see Sect. 2), similar for other SoC systems overall. Of course, future work will be needed to confirm this hypothesis.

The structure of the paper is as follows. In Sect. 2, we introduce the BiTV power model. In Sect. 3, we describe the experimental setup and protocol used to check the validity of BiTV. In Sect. 4, we present and analyze the data that support this model. Related work is presented in Sect. 5. We conclude and discuss future work in Sect. 6.

2 The BiTV Power Model

Even though transistor-level models exist to study how the various involved currents (gate leakage current, sub-threshold current, etc.) vary with respect to say temperature, voltage or technology-specific parameters such as channel length and width, scaling these models to the billions of transistors found in a typical chip is very difficult. Given the interplay between all these elements, power requirements for digital computing devices P_{cpu} are thus linked to many complex physical processes. A coarse definition for this power requirement is:

$$\begin{aligned} P_{cpu} &= P_{dynamic} + P_{static} \\ &= P_{dynamic} + P_{gate} + P_{subthreshold}, \end{aligned} \tag{1}$$

where the static power is considered to be the sum of two dominant components (Narendra and (eds.) (2006)): (1) the sub-threshold (leakage) power, of key importance, since it doesn't contribute to the integrated circuit's (IC) function and constitutes a significant fraction of IC energy consumption (Lucian (2011)), and (2) the usually smaller gate-leakage power.[1] Each power component P_i corresponds to a current component I_i, such that $P_i = V_{dd}I_i$, where V_{dd} is the supply voltage at drain. An approximate assessment of a component's energy consumption while running a device, E_i, can then be obtained as $P_i t$, where t is the time during which the system is run.

There exist analytical and numerical models for each of these components (see, for instance, Chandrakasan et al. (Chandrakasan et al. (1996)) or Skadron et al. (Skadron et al. (2003)). Even though these apply only to the smallest components of an actual SoC and thus cannot be used directly at the system level, one can still build upon them and Eq. 1. In particular, these observations suggest the following constraints to follow when designing a parameterized temperature-aware system-level analytical power model.

- $I_{dynamic}$ is linked to the actual running of programs, and can be deemed proportional (by a factor ϵ) to the frequency f of the processor and to V_{dd} (De Vogeleer et al. (2014a)):

$$I_{dynamic} = \epsilon f V_{dd}.$$

- $I_{subthreshold}$ is proportional to T^2 and to an exponential of a function of the temperature T and V_{gs}, the gate-to-source voltage:

$$I_{subthreshold} = \alpha T^2 e^{\beta(V_{gs}-V_{th})/T},$$

where V_{th} is the threshold voltage (Liu et al. (2007)). Since V_{gs} varies between 0 and V_{dd}, V_{th} being its minimum, we decide to approximate the voltage term $V_{gs} - V_{th}$ in the exponent by Taylor expansion around the minimum of the voltage range (which is narrow here, between 0.98 V and 1.23 V, see Sect. 3) to first order in V_{dd}. After rewriting αT^2 as $e^{\ln(\alpha T^2)}$ and adding

[1] The usually smaller short-circuit power dissipation effects are here ignored.

the exponents, we further simplify the model, since the considered ambient-temperature range is here, when expressed in Kelvins, narrow (from 25 °C to 55 °C, see Sect. 3), by approximating β/T and $\ln(\alpha T^2)$ by Taylor expansion around 273.15 K (0 °C) to first order in T. The resulting approximate exponent is then of the form $a + bV_{dd} + cT + dV_{dd}T$, where T is now expressed in °C.

– I_{gate} depends in a complex manner upon T and V_{dd}. However, since this term is most of the time very small when compared to $I_{subthreshold}$, we assume it to be 0, to simplify the model (Liu and Kursun (2007)).

We suggest thus to build upon this high-level analysis of the physical foundations behind the modeling of the power requirement, P_{cpu}, for a single CPU to generalize it for a whole SoC board, at least as far as CPU-bound tasks are concerned. Abstracting over the formal mathematical formulae introduced above, we introduce thus the *Biaffine Temperature-Voltage Power Model* (BiTV)[2] to approximate the power requirements of SoCs. It is specified as follows.

$$P_{BiTV} = V_{dd}(\epsilon f V_{dd} + e^{a+bV_{dd}+cT+dV_{dd}T}). \qquad (2)$$

The BiTV model parameters ϵ, a, b, c, and d are linked to the particularities of the system at hand such as the technology parameters or the actual code being run on the device (OS, user code, I/O, etc.). In the rest of this paper, we provide experimental evidence for the validity of the BiTV power model.

3 Experimental Setup

In order to validate BiTV under varying conditions, including benchmark characteristics, temperature, processor frequency, and supply voltage, we performed a campaign measuring the instantaneous power requirements of a SoC system. The setup for these measurement experiments is shown in Fig. 1.

3.1 Equipment

The central component of this setup is an oven that allows us to precisely control the ambient temperature inside the oven's chamber. The oven model is a UFP 400, produced by Memmert GmBH (Germany), which has a chamber volume of 53 l, a temperature range starting from 5 °C above room temperature (no cooling possible) up to 300 °C, and forced air convection. The temperature probes of the oven are located at the top of the chamber. We used the oven to heat the chamber to 25, 35, 45, and 55 °C. We refer to the temperature inside the oven's chamber as the *ambient temperature* for the experiments.

As a SoC system, we use an AM572x EVM development board manufactured by Texas Instruments. The board hosts a Sitara ARM SoC chip, 2 GB DDR3L

[2] BiTV is loosely called "biaffine" since it is affine in its exponent term with respect to each of its T and V_{dd} parameters when the other is held constant.

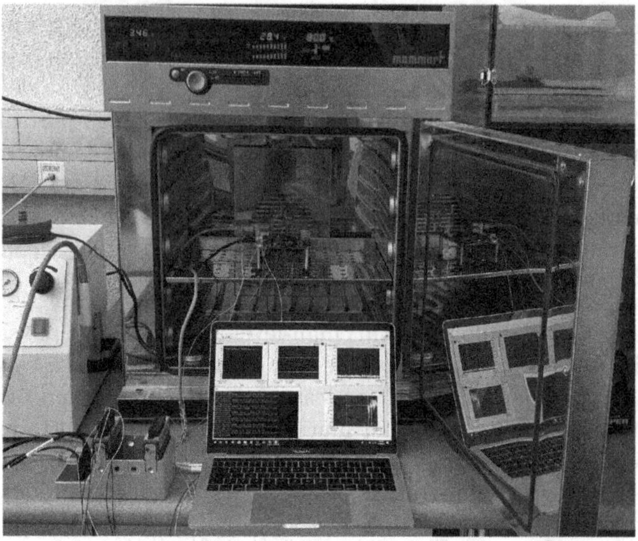

Fig. 1. Representative picture of the experimental setup. The AM572x board is inside the thermal oven. It is connected to the host system and NI cDAQ with its I/O modules NI 9215 and NI 9211. (Oven courtesy Centre des matériaux, Mines Paris, Evry)

memory, 4 GB of flash memory, a TPS659037 power management chip, and several connectors (audio, HDMI, Ethernet, USB, etc.). For our measurements, we are interested in monitoring the power of the microprocessors inside the Sitara SoC only. We thus modified the board to directly measure the power at the current-sense resistors of the microprocessor submodule, which are intended for high-precision power monitoring and thus allow measurements independent from other components on the board/SoC. The chip itself is fabricated using a 23-nm design process and contains two ARM Cortex A15 cores in the microprocessor submodule. During the experiments, only a single core was active, running the Linux operating system from Texas Instruments' Processor SDK (v.04).

We modified the setup of the Linux power management to allow us to manually control the microprocessor's clock frequency and voltage settings. The processor supports three voltage settings: `OPP_NOM` (0.98 V), `OPP_OD` (1.09 V), and `OPP_HIGH` (1.23 V).[3] The clock frequency can be controlled in steps of 100 MHz in the range from 100 to 1,500 MHz. However, the processor specification imposes a minimum voltage level for certain frequency settings, i.e., `OP_NOM`, up to 1,000 MHz, `OPP_OD`, up to 1,176 MHz, and `OPP_HIGH`, for higher frequencies. Note that it is possible to impose higher voltage levels; for our measurements, we nevertheless always use the lowest possible voltage level for a given frequency.

Power monitoring is semi-automatized using National Instruments LabVIEW software running on a separate host machine (a MacBook Pro running Win-

[3] Note that these voltage numbers are specific to a particular board and thus may slightly vary between different boards.

dows, in this case). The host machine is connected to a Compact DAQ data-acquisition module by National Instruments (NI cDAQ-9174) holding an I/O module NI 9215, in-turn connected to the aforementioned current-sense resistors on the microprocessor submodule[4] of the AM572x EVM development board. A second I/O module, an NI 9211, is connected to a temperature probe at the heatsink. The measured sensor data from both I/O modules are processed by the cDAQ module and sent to the host machine, where the data is annotated and recorded in a trace file. LabVIEW and the cDAQ equipment ensure a tight synchronization between the two measured data streams.

3.2 Protocol

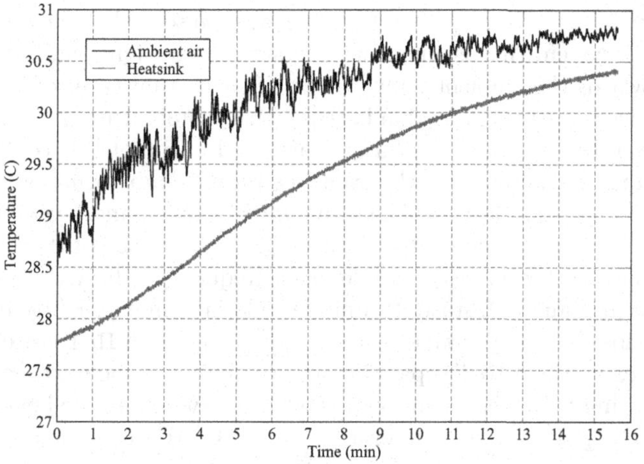

Fig. 2. Ambient air and heatsink temperatures when the system is shutdown.

The AM572x EVM development board is placed inside the oven at the 2nd of 4 levels of shelves in order to improve air circulation and minimize the time to reach the target temperature. Figure 2 provides an idea of the time needed to heat the oven's chamber with respect to a specified target temperature. In addition to the oven's temperature probes, we also placed, as mentioned above, a probe at the SoC's heatsink. This *heatsink temperature* is the best possible approximation of the actual temperature conditions of the transistors inside the chip that can be measured from the outside. More precisely, we compute this last so-called *junction temperature*, i.e., the temperature at the transistor

[4] This submodule hosts the 2 processor cores, the L1 and L2 caches, the boot ROM, the power management unit and the PLL.

level, from the thermal resistance of the heatsink (CTS Electronic Components (2006)) and the SoC chip (TI Inc. (2011); TI Inc. (2017); TI Inc. (2018)). Note that the chip itself also provides integrated temperature probes, but they are not very precise and reliable, e.g., reading temperature values from these sensors interferes with the execution of the current program.

For measurements, we consider 3 benchmark kernels: `Goldrader` (a bit-reversal algorithm), `Blowfish` (a symmetric block cipher), and `SHA` (a hashing function). These kernels are compute-bound and thus mostly stress the microprocessors, but do so with a different mix of instructions. Thus running these kernels for a short period (a couple of seconds) allows us to optimally control the actual temperature conditions at the transistor level of the chip, while monitoring power of a processor core in isolation. Given that these running times are rather short, we assume the chip-level temperatures to remain quasi-constant.

As can be seen in Fig. 2, it takes about 10 min to increase the ambient temperature from 28.5 °C to roughly 30.5 °C. It can also be seen that the heatsink temperature for a system that is shutdown follows with a slight lag, but eventually converges towards the ambient temperature. Heating times are considerable; the experiments were thus performed in batches with temperature strictly increasing within a batch. More precisely, a batch starts with a completely cooled oven (at room temperature); we then set the oven to a target temperature of 25 °C, while keeping the SoC system in an `IDLE` state. Once the oven and heatsink temperatures have both reached the target temperature, we run one of the short kernels as a benchmark at the lowest possible clock frequency (100 MHz) and put the system again into an `IDLE` state. Running the kernel might slightly increase the temperature inside the chip; we thus keep the system in an `IDLE` state for a while to allow any excess heat to dissipate before proceeding to the next measurement, i.e., by increasing the clock frequency by 100 Mhz, switching the benchmark kernel, or increasing the target temperature by 10 °C. We also made sure that all runs were using warm cache states.

We performed a series of experimental campaigns to gather physical data, namely power requirements for the three benchmark kernels running at different settings. The parameters under study were the following:

- benchmark B. One out of the three kernels `Goldrader`, `Blowfish`, or `SHA`;
- temperature T. Ambient temperatures of 25, 35, 45, or 55 °C in the oven;[5]
- frequency f. Clock frequency of the microprocessor module, varied in steps of 100 MHz from 100 to 1,500 MHz;
- voltage V_{dd}. Minimal voltage settings `OPP_NOM`, `OPP_OD`, or `OPP_HIGH`, depending on the requirements of the clock frequency.

[5] We limited the maximum ambient temperature to 55 °C, since going beyond this value would increase the on-chip temperature to more than 90 °C, at which point the CPU would experience a thermal emergency and shutdown. Cooling the board to less than 25 °C would require a refrigerating enclosure (see Sect. 6).

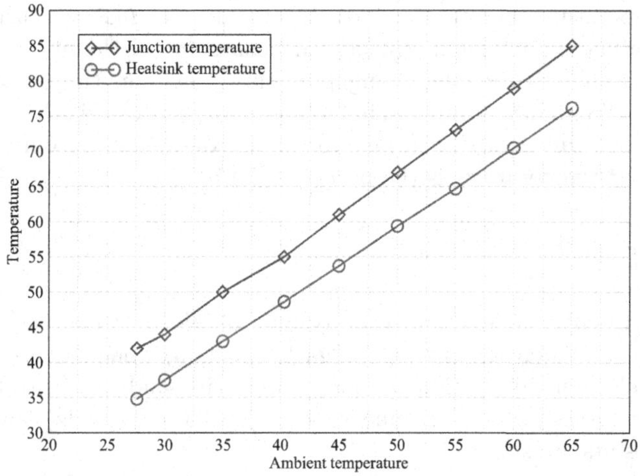

Fig. 3. Junction and heatsink temperatures with respect to ambient temperature (in °C). The system is running `IDLE`.

3.3 Temperature Calibration

The introduction of an oven to induce higher ambient-temperature conditions introduces a new constraint on heat transfer via the chip's heatsink. There are thus many different temperatures involved in the current experiment. The model in Eq. 2 relies on a temperature T that is, in fact, the junction temperature T_j, while what is controlled by the oven is the ambient temperature T_a. In addition, our temperature probe is mounted on the SoC chip's heatsink, thus providing us another temperature point T_h.

We compared these different temperatures as follows. As mentioned above, we derived T_j from T_h considering the thermal resistance parameters as specified for the heatsink (CTS Electronic Components (2006)) and the SoC chip (TI Inc. (2017)) using a standard manufacturer-provided formula (TI Inc. (2011)). An on-chip microprocessor-domain thermal sensor measures the approximate junction temperature, and their values can be retrieved from the command line using the *sysfs* pseudo file system, a feature provided by the Linux kernel. After allowing the board to soak for 5 min, the junction temperature T_j corresponding to each ambient temperature T_a has thus been recorded. Using the junction temperature model and θ_i parameters provided in (TI Inc. (2017)), we also checked for the consistency of our measurements with the modeled ones.

Figure 3 relates the data points for T_j, T_h, and T_a for a system in an `IDLE` state and running at the lowest voltage/frequency setting. For every degree increase in T_a, as long as the system is running `IDLE`, T_j increases by a factor of 1.135. The obtained numbers are consistent with measurements by Texas Instruments Incorporated, the manufacturer of the SoC (TI Inc. (2018)).

When assessing the validity of the BiTV model, one has thus to be careful to use the proper temperature variant. Note however that, since the relationships between temperatures are mostly linear when running `IDLE`, we surmised that using the biaffine model could still be valid using any of the above mentioned temperatures, the only impact being possible changes in the proportionality coefficients and parameters. This is, in fact, what we validate via the experiments described below. Unless otherwise mentioned, we consider thus from now on that T, the *ambient* temperature, is the parameter of interest here.

4 Results

Below we present the experimental results obtained using the previously described setup. Given the size of the gathered data, when discussing specific results, we select in this section the most interesting and/or illustrative subset of parameter values for B (benchmark index), T (°C), f (MHz), and V_{dd} (V). The other results are similar.

4.1 Measurements

In Fig. 4a is plotted the measured average power when running $B =$ `Goldrader` for various T and f (i.e., also V_{dd}). As expected, the power needs increase with f. Three different regimes can be noticed, clearly linked to the frequency boundaries of the 3 different supply voltage settings (V_{dd}) required by the Texas Instruments chip (see Sect. 3). The significant and non-linear impact of T on power requirements is clearly visible, in particular at high-frequency settings. The non-linearity of power with respect to V_{dd} can indirectly be seen at the mid-voltage setting, since the points for frequencies 1, 1.1 and 1.2 GHz, corresponding each to a different value of V_{dd}, are not aligned.

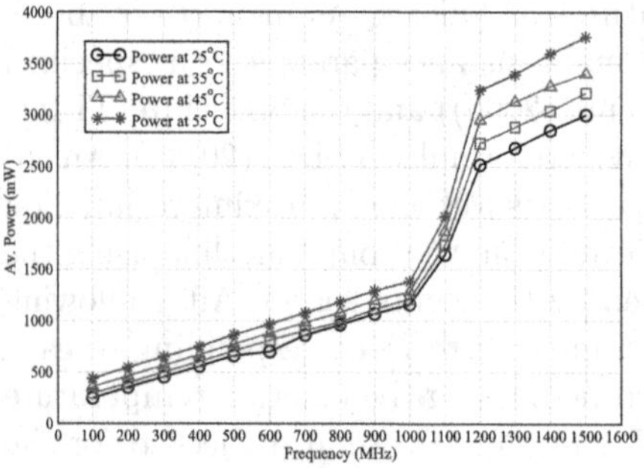

(a) `Goldrader`.

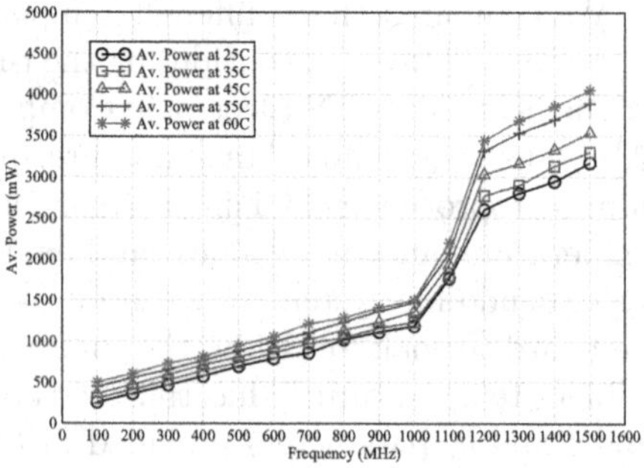

(b) `qsort`.

Fig. 4. Average power vs. frequency for `Goldrader` (a) and `qsort` (b).

The three core benchmarks B_i are rather small program kernels. They amount to about a dozen of lines of code each and run rather fast (depending on frequency, between 8 and 120 s for `Goldrader`, 21 and 331 s for `Blowfish`, and 43 and 683 s for SHA). Thus, we also decided to run some more significant programs to further explore the impact of the ambient temperature on the thermal behavior under complex load. Using typical benchmark examples, namely `susan`, `bitcount`, `basicMath`, and `qsort` from the MiBench benchmark suite for embedded systems Guthaus et al. (2001)), we obtained quite similar experimental results to those found for smaller benchmarks (see, for instance, Fig. 4b), suggesting that a unique generic model of power requirements could probably be designed, which is what we did with BiTV.

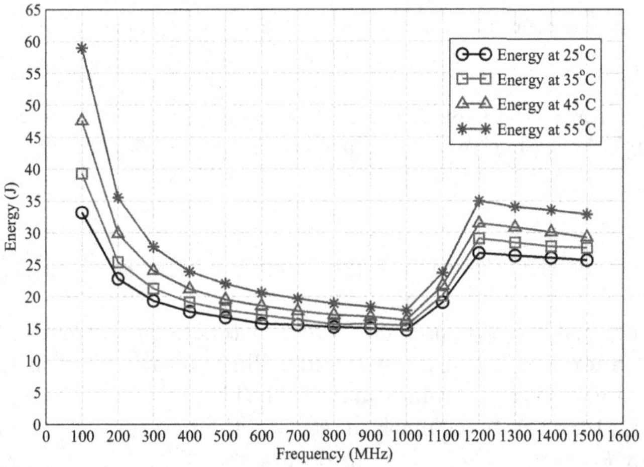

Fig. 5. Energy consumption vs. frequency and temperature (`Goldrader`).

Finally, when multiplying an average power value by the total running time of the corresponding program, one gets its energy consumption profile, e.g., for `Goldrader` in Fig. 5. One can clearly see the typical convex energy/frequency curve discussed by De Vogeleer et al. (De Vogeleer et al. (2014a)), although the characteristics of these convexity profiles vary for each of the three frequency intervals mentioned in Sect. 3. Notice that, in particular when running slowly, the energy consumption can vary by a quite significant factor with ambient temperature (almost 2, between 25 and 55 °C). Also, this graph suggests that the energy/frequency rule keeps being valid for each frequency interval when varying the ambient temperature, a property not experimentally checked until now.

4.2 BiTV Model Assessment

To assess the validity of BiTV, we performed a non-linear fitting of P_{BiTV} (Eq. 2) using the experimental power data gathered from running the `Blowfish` benchmark kernel. We used the default solver for non-linear problems SWARM from LibreOffice. The model parameters we obtained for BiTV that minimize the

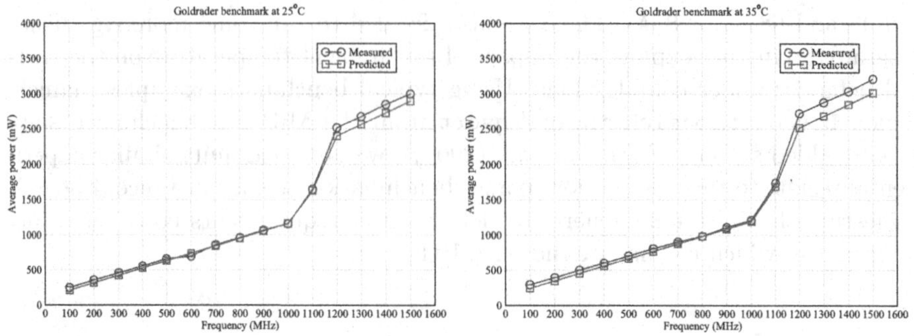

(a) Predicted and measured average power at 25 °C.

(b) Predicted and measured average power at 35 °C.

Fig. 6. Comparison of BiTV-predicted (red) and measured (blue) average power (in mW) at 25 and 35 °C while varying voltage and frequency (`Goldrader`). (Color figure online)

standard error for the `Blowfish` kernel are: $\epsilon = 1.10$, $a = -1.32$, $b = 4.44$, $c = 3.85 \times 10^{-2}$, and $d = -3.67 \times 10^{-4}$.

We then applied the obtained model parameters to the other two benchmark kernels `Goldrader` and `SHA`. Figures 6 and 7 illustrate the good fit between the measured average power (in blue) and the BiTV-predicted average power (in red) for the `Goldrader` benchmark at various temperature (T), voltage (V_{dd}), and frequency (f) settings. The best fit occurs at $T = 55\,°\text{C}$ (Fig. 7, right), while some divergence can be observed for all other settings – notably towards the high end of the frequency spectrum. Yet, the relative (with respect to the mean) standard errors of estimate (RSE) for these four temperature values are all below 2% for `Goldrader`.

Applying the model with the same parameter values (for ϵ, a, b, c, and d) to `SHA` yields similar results, which are not shown here. The RSE values vary slightly, but are still below 2% for all configurations. This suggests that the BiTV power model provides good accuracy even across the considered benchmark kernels and a wide range of temperatures.

As a final check, we compared the actual total energy consumed by `SHA` with a prediction based on the BiTV model, which is computed by multiplying the modeled power value (again using the same model-parameter values) for `SHA` by its actual running time. The results, for the temperatures (T) 45 and 55 °C and varying voltage and frequency settings (V_{dd} and f), are given in Fig. 8. One can observe a good fit between the related curves, albeit with a clearly visible gap. This gap can be explained by the fact that the model was not fit using the `SHA` power data, consequently leading to a slight error (recall that the RSE was small, below 2%, but not zero). In addition, we can observe an amplification of the absolute model error probably due to the multiplication with the benchmark's running time.

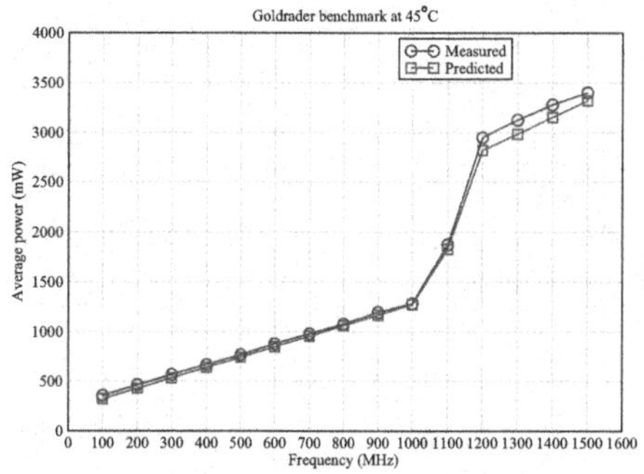

(a) Predicted and measured average power at 45 °C.

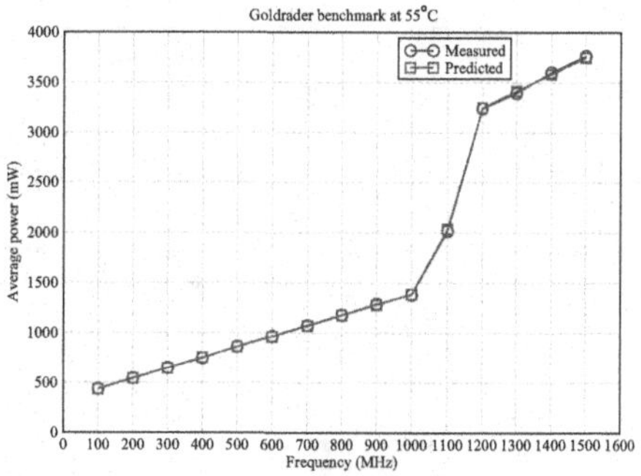

(b) Predicted and measured average power at 55 °C.

Fig. 7. Comparison of BiTV-predicted (red) and measured (blue) average power (in mW) at 45 and 55 °C while varying voltage and frequency (`Goldrader`). (Color figure online)

5 Related Work

The impact of ambient temperature on CPU power requirements and/or energy consumption is extensively studied at the large-grain level of data centers or HPC farms (see, for instance, (El-Sayed et al. (2012)) (Gupta et al. (2021))). Yet, research that focuses on more low-level devices, yet at a coarser level than Register Transfer Level (RTL), is rarer. A possible reason for this might be that experimental validation of analytical models is a complicated affair at such a small scale, requiring somewhat complex equipment and protocols.

Among significant related work, De Vogeleer et al. (De Vogeleer et al. (2014b)) introduce a temperature-aware power model for the Samsung Galaxy A7 and A15 processors. They experimentally confirm the exponential behavior of power w.r.t. temperature and equip an analytical model with parameters that are polynomial functions of temperature, frequency and number of cores. The use of an oven in our experiments allows for a much better controlled initial-temperature condition for the measurements. In particular, De Vogeleer et al. (De Vogeleer et al. (2014b)) manually forced heating, resulting in a less homogeneous environment for the device than in our experiments. Finally, the BiTV model is built on more physics-based foundations and is able to handle varying voltage.

Vaddina et al. (Vaddina et al. (2021)) proposed a workflow for energy and temperature profiling on high-performance systems running parallel applications. They carried out their experiments on Intel's X86-based multi-core processors, utilizing the NAS parallel benchmark suite. Their approach allows full and dynamic runtime control over the execution of applications, ensuring that the processors' frequency remains within a specified range. They demonstrated that the energy response to frequency scaling is greatly influenced by the characteristics of the workload and forms a convex function around the optimal frequency

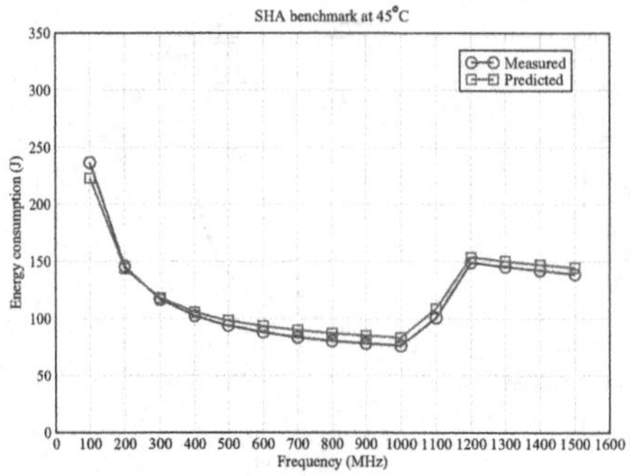

(a) Predicted and measured energy consumption at 45 °C.

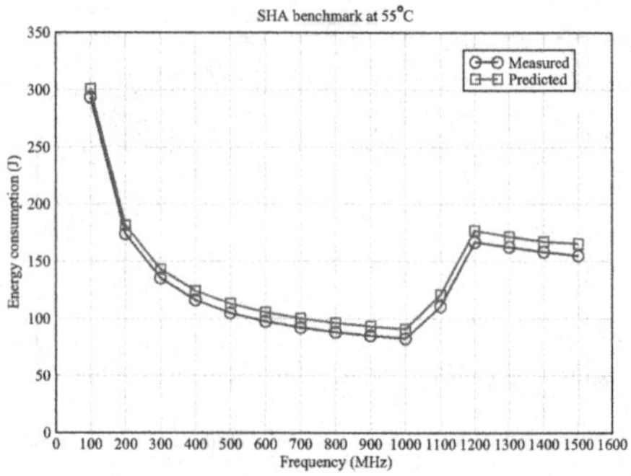

(b) Predicted and measured energy consumption at 55 °C.

Fig. 8. Comparison of BiTV-predicted (red) and measured (blue) total energy consumption at 45 and 55 °C while varying (voltage and) frequency, in MHz (`SHA`). The fit is similar at 25 °C (and thus omitted here), while the experimental data are missing at 35 °C, due to technical issues during the experiment. (Color figure online)

point. Despite this previous work by the same lead author, the present paper, attempting to tackle similar issues, focuses on a totally different architecture, which, by itself, justifies this new work. In addition to introducing the new BiTV model, it also demonstrates the universality of the taken approach, methodology and theoretical framework, which are thus relevant to different architectures.

Recent work by Texas Instruments (TI Inc. (2018)) as well as Intel/ARM (Singla et al. (2015), Bhat et al. (2018)) used a similar setup as ours, notably with a temperature-controlled oven.[6] The measurements by Texas Instruments are also based on an AM572x EVM board and are in line with our measurements (cf. Fig. 3), considering an `IDLE` system (TI Inc. (2018 (Fig. 1))). Other results are, however, not comparable, since they measured the power requirements of the entire SoC system using the `Drystone` benchmark. Yet, our measurements still follow the same overall trends. The biggest difference, though, is that Texas Instruments only provides measured data and does not introduce a power model that may be used for predictions.

The work supported by Intel and ARM uses different SoC systems based on the Odroid platform (Samsung Exynos 5410 and Exynos 5422) and aims at designing a Dynamic Thermal and Power Management (DTPM) algorithm (see (Singh et al. (2020)) for a survey). In the initial work (Singla et al. (2015)), the objective is to predict the evolution of the SoC system's temperature in the future and apply dynamic voltage and frequency scaling to control the temperature – even without cooling support by a fan. In more recent work, the algorithm was extended to incorporate a power model (Bhat et al. (2018)) whose parameters have been determined in a similar setup as ours. However, the power model itself is only compared to the measured data, but otherwise is not evalu-

[6] This research was performed independently of ours.

ated. Instead, the DTPM algorithm is evaluated; it performs runtime monitoring and, based on a mix of measured and predicted parameters, tries to find an optimal frequency setting when the SoC's temperature exceeds a certain threshold. Our work focuses on the power model itself. Notably, we introduce a simpler analytical power model, explain its link to physical foundations, and show its adequacy with experimental measurements across different benchmarks as well as temperature, frequency, and voltage settings.

6 Conclusion and Future Work

Based on physics-informed and experimental considerations, we modeled and quantified the influence of the ambient temperature on the power requirements of SoC systems at the microprocessor level. We believe these results must be considered in future system energy profiles, especially when running on batteries and dealing with energy-critical applications. We introduced a new ambient-temperature-, frequency- and voltage-aware power model, BiTV. Preliminary experiments on an ARM-based AM572x system suggest that it provides a very good fit with actual experimental data on a wide spectrum of temperature, voltage, and frequency settings even across benchmark kernels.

For future work, it would be interesting to experiment with and analyze the influence of the ambient temperature at levels lower (typically in the $[-30, 20]$ degree Celsius) than the ones used in the experiments presented in this paper, in order to cover the range of realistic outdoor temperatures and assess the generality of the BiTV model in this extended domain.

Another interesting venue for research would be to provide a more scientific grounding to the BiTV analytical model, in particular the values of its parameters, based on more fundamental physics taking into account aggregation effects. This is an important issue since, for now, the model parameters are learned from experimental data; the cost of such experiments can only be justified for products deployed in large numbers.

Finally, and even though we expect the physical grounding of BiTV to make it somewhat universal, extending the types of computer boards (and even studying the impact of the individual differences among boards of the same type) and benchmarks used to validate and/or extend it is needed. In particular, the test programs used in this paper are CPU-bound kernels. Studying how well BiTV can be adapted, via parameter changes or more fundamental generalizations, to programs that access different memory-cache levels or boards that use more recent SoCs or other silicon-manufacturing technologies is clearly warranted.

Acknowledgments. This work was supported in part by ANR under the France 2030 program, grant NF-NAI: ANR-22-PEFT-0003. We thank the Centre des matériaux (Mines Paris, PSL University) for allowing access to and providing assistance for their temperature-controlled oven and the reviewers for their useful comments.

References

Bhat, G., Singla, G., Unver, A.K., Ogras, U.Y.: Algorithmic optimization of thermal and power management for heterogeneous mobile platforms. IEEE Trans. Very Large Scale Integr. Syst. **26**(3), 544–557 (2018). https://doi.org/10.1109/TVLSI.2017.2770163

Chandrakasan, A., Yang, I., Vieri, C., Antoniadis, D.: Design considerations and tools for low-voltage digital system design. In: Proceedings of the 33rd Annual Design Automation Conference, (DAC 1996), pp. 113–118. Association for Computing Machinery (1996). https://doi.org/10.1145/240518.240540

CTS Electronic Components 2006. Cooling Critical Components. CTS Electronic Components. Application Note – AN1010 (2006)

De Vogeleer, K., Memmi, G., Jouvelot, P., Coelho, F.: The energy/frequency convexity rule: modeling and experimental validation on mobile devices. In: Wyrzykowski, R., Dongarra, J., Karczewski, K., Waśniewski, J. (eds.) Parallel Processing and Applied Mathematics, pp. 793–803. Springer, Heidelberg (2014a). https://doi.org/10.1007/978-3-642-55224-3_74

De Vogeleer, K., Memmi, G., Jouvelot, P., Coelho, F.: Modeling the temperature bias of power consumption for nanometer-scale CPUs in application processors. In: 2014 International Conference on Embedded Computer Systems: Architectures, Modeling, and Simulation (SAMOS XIV), pp. 172–180 (2014). https://doi.org/10.1109/SAMOS.2014.6893209

El-Sayed, N., Stefanovici, I.A., Amvrosiadis, G., Hwang, A.A., Schroeder, B.: Temperature management in data centers: why some (might) like it hot. In: Proceedings of the 12th ACM SIGMETRICS/PERFORMANCE Joint International Conference on Measurement and Modeling of Computer Systems (SIGMETRICS 2012). Association for Computing Machinery, New York, NY, USA, pp. 163–174 (2012). https://doi.org/10.1145/2254756.2254778

Guermouche, A., Orgerie, A.-C.: Thermal design power and vectorized instructions behavior. Concurr. Comput. Pract. Exp. **34**, 2 (2022). https://doi.org/10.1002/cpe.6261

Gupta, R., Asgari, S., Moazamigoodarzi, H., Down, D.G., Puri, I.K.: Energy, exergy and computing efficiency based data center workload and cooling management. Appl. Energy **299**(2021), 117050 (2021). https://doi.org/10.1016/j.apenergy.2021.117050

Guthaus, M.R., Ringenberg, J.S., Ernst, D., Austin, T.M., Mudge, T., Brown, R.B.: MiBench: a free, commercially representative embedded benchmark suite. In: Proceedings of the Fourth Annual IEEE International Workshop on Workload Characterization. WWC-4 (Cat. No. 01EX538), pp. 3–14 (2001). https://doi.org/10.1109/WWC.2001.990739

Xilinx Inc. Xilinx Power Estimator User Guide (2018)

Intel. Intel® FPGA Power and Thermal Calculator User Guide (2020)

Liu, Y., Dick, R.P., Shang, L., Yang, H.: Accurate temperature-dependent integrated circuit leakage power estimation is easy. In: Proceedings of the Conference on Design, Automation and Test in Europe, (DATE 2007). EDA Consortium, pp. 1526–1531 (2007)

Liu, Z., Kursun, V.: PMOS-only sleep switch dual-threshold voltage domino logic in Sub-65-Nm CMOS technologies. IEEE Trans. Very Large Scale Integr. Syst. **15**(12), 1311–1319 (2007). https://doi.org/10.1109/TVLSI.2007.903947

Lucian, S.: Leakage Power - it's worse than you think (2011). https://www.eetimes.com/leakage-power-its-worse-than-you-think/

Narendra, S.G., Chandrakasan, A.P. (eds.): Leakage in Nanometer CMOS Technologies. Springer, Heidelberg (2006)

Prakash, A., Wang, S., Mitra, T.: Mobile application processors: techniques for software power-performance optimization. IEEE Consum. Electron. Mag. **9**(4), 67–76 (2020). https://doi.org/10.1109/MCE.2020.2969171

Singh, A.K., Dey, S., McDonald-Maier, K., Basireddy, K.R., Merrett, G.V., Al-Hashimi, B.M.: Dynamic energy and thermal management of multi-core mobile platforms: a survey. IEEE Des. Test **37**(5), 25–33 (2020). https://doi.org/10.1109/MDAT.2020.2982629

Singla, G., Kaur, G., Unver, A.K., Ogras, U.Y.: Predictive dynamic thermal and power management for heterogeneous mobile platforms. In: Proceedings of the 2015 Design, Automation & Test in Europe Conference & Exhibition, (DATE 2015). EDA Consortium, pp. 960–965 (2015)

Skadron, K., Stan, M.R., Huang, W., Velusamy, S., Sankaranarayanan, K., Tarjan, D.: Temperature-aware microarchitecture. In: Proceedings of the 30th Annual International Symposium on Computer Architecture, (ISCA 2003), pp. 2–13. Association for Computing Machinery (2003). https://doi.org/10.1145/859618.859620

TI Inc. Understanding Thermal Dissipation and Design of a Heatsink. TI Inc. Application Report - SLVA462 (2011)

TI Inc. Thermal Design Guide for DSP and ARM Application Processors. TI Inc. Application Report - SPRABI3B (2017)

TI Inc. AM572x Thermal Considerations. TI Inc. Application Report - SPRAC53A (2018)

Vaddina, K.R., Brandner, F., Memmi, G., Jouvelot, P.: Experimental energy profiling of energy-critical embedded applications. In: 25th International Conference on Software SoftCOM, pp. 1–6 (2017). https://minesparis-psl.hal.science/hal-01625409v2/file/A-666-v2.pdf

Vaddina, K.R., Lefevre, L., Orgerie, A.C.: Experimental workflow for energy and temperature profiling on HPC systems. In: 2021 IEEE Symposium on Computers and Communications (ISCC), pp. 1–7. IEEE (2021)

EPIC-Q: Equivalent-Policy Invariant Comparison Enhanced Transfer Q-learning for Run-Time SoC Performance-Power Optimization

Anmol Surhonne(✉), Haitham S. Fawzi, Florian Maurer, Oliver Lenke, Michael Meidinger, Thomas Wild, and Andreas Herkersdorf

Technical University of Munich, Arcistrasse 21, 80333 Munich, Germany
anmol.surhonne@tum.de

Abstract. As power density becomes the main constraint of multicore systems, managing power consumption using DVFS while providing the desired performance becomes increasingly critical. Reinforcement learning (RL) performs significantly better than conventional methods in performance-power optimization under different hardware configurations and varying software applications. RL agents learn through trial-and-error by receiving rewards which is defined by an objective function (e.g. instructions-per-second (IPS)) within specified constraints (e.g. power budget). System and application requirements lead to changing objectives and constraints which in turn result in different reward functions. The RL agents adapt to these changing objectives and constraints (and hence reward functions). Equivalent-policy invariant comparison (EPIC) is a popular technique to evaluate different reward functions. EPIC provides a numerical score which quantifies the difference in two reward functions. In this work, we use this EPIC distance (score) to transfer knowledge and improve learning for changing reward functions. Experimental results using a DVFS enabled RISCV based system-on-chip implemented on an FPGA shows 16.2% lower power budget overshoots compared to a tabular Q-learning agent with direct transfer.

Keywords: EPIC · DVFS · reinforcement learning · reward functions · power management · transfer learning

1 Introduction

The power wall has become one of the primary challenges of managing modern computing systems. Meeting application objectives (e.g. IPS, FPS, response time etc.) within system constraints (e.g. power budget) is critical in managing these complex systems. The objectives and constraints are typically conflicting in nature (e.g. Instruction throughput vs power consumption) and hence call for performance-power optimization. Dynamic voltage and frequency scaling (DVFS) is one of the most widely used technique for performance-power

L. Carro et al. (Eds.): SAMOS 2024, LNCS 15226, pp. 34–45, 2025.
https://doi.org/10.1007/978-3-031-78377-7_3

optimization in CPU cores. It enables designers to design methods to set the voltage/frequency (V/F) levels of a CPU core by monitoring several CPU performance metrics (e.g. utilization, memory accesses) to meet the application objectives and system constraints. Several heuristics have been proposed in literature to perform performance-power optimization. However these methods are inefficient in the face of stochastic workloads and environments, varying application requirements and system constraints [11].

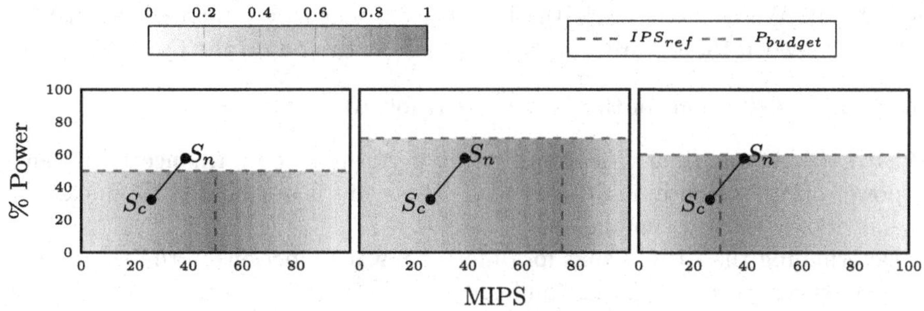

Fig. 1. Visual representation of 3 different reward functions showing an hypothetical state transition from S_c to S_n.

Reinforcement learning (e.g. Q-learning) is a model-free technique which has been proven to be better than heuristics for run-time power management. RL agents monitor the current state of the system and learn the best action to be taken in the state for a given reward function via trial-and-error. Q-learning maintains a table of Q-values for all states and actions and typically learns by exploration/exploitation in the state-action space as defined by the action selection strategy. The time taken to learn an optimal policy increases exponentially with the size of the state and action spaces. This can be accelerated by using the Experience Replay technique, where the past experiences are stored in a memory buffer and used in batches to speed-up learning.

A reward function is used to numerically quantify the effectiveness of an action taken in a particular state. The reward function is defined by the current objectives and constraints provided to the RL agent. The objective and constraint provided can change dynamically in run time resulting in different reward functions. A policy learnt by the RL agent for the source reward function is not always optimal for the target reward function i.e. the best action in a state for the source reward function might be sub-optimal for the target reward function and vice versa. The RL agent has to unlearn and relearn these sub-optimal state-action pairs which is inefficient and time-consuming. The rate at which the RL agent learns the new reward function can be improved by transfer learning. Equivalent Policy Invariant Comparison (EPIC) is an algorithm which allows us to evaluate the difference between two reward functions without learning the policy [4]. In this work, we propose to use the EPIC-distance as a metric to employ transfer learning in RL agents to improve its learning efficiency for a change in reward function.

Example 1. Consider the 3 different reward functions corresponding to 3 different combinations of IPS reference (IPS_{ref}) and Power budget (P_{budget}) as shown in Fig. 1. Consider the hypothetical state transition as shown from the state S_c to S_n by applying an action a. We can clearly see that the reward achieved by the RL agent for the above transition is different for the different reward functions. The agent has to learn by trial-and-error the Q-value for the state action pair (S_c, a). We can accelerate the learning efficiency by evaluating the EPIC distance between the reward functions and use it to update the Q-value.

The main contributions of this paper are as follows:

- EPIC-Q: A run time Q-learning agent performing performance (IPS) and power optimization in multi-core SoC. The agent is augmented by an experience replay (ER) technique.
- Determining the EPIC scores for different reward functions in run time using experiences stored in the ER buffer.
- Using the EPIC scores to modify the Q-values of states and actions to accelerate learning and improve performance.
- Empirical analysis of performance, number of power budget overshoots and resource utilization of EPIC-Q as a DVFS controller for a RISC based system-on-chip implemented on an FPGA.

2 Background and Related Work

2.1 Q-learning

Q-learning is a type of reinforcement learning where the agent learns the Q-value of an action in a particular state via trial-and-error. It uses the rewards given by the environment to learn hence model-free. Q-learning agents can handle problems with stochastic transitions and rewards. Tabular Q-learning (QT-DT) is one of the most popular forms of Q-learning where the agent keeps a Q-value for every state-action pair in a table. The Q-value depicts the learned expected reward when an action is applied in a particular state. At each learning epoch t, the Q-value is updated by the following equation:

$$Q(s,a) \leftarrow (1-\beta)Q(s,a) + \beta(R + \gamma maxQ(s',a')) \quad (1)$$

where, $Q(s,a)$ is the Q-value, s is the current state, a is the action, s' is the next state, β is the learning rate, γ is the discount factor and R is the reward.

2.2 Experience Replay

Experience replay (ER) is a memory replay technique used in reinforcement learning where we store the experiences of the agent at each time-step [14].

Experience replay speeds up the learning process of RL agents by reusing the stored experiences. An experience (e_t) added into the ER buffer at any epoch t is a tuple: $e_t = (s, a, R, s')$. The experiences are stored in a fixed-size memory buffer of size N_{ER}. The ER buffer is typically implemented as a FIFO with uniqueness property. FIFO implies that the most recent experiences are stored in the ER buffer and uniqueness implies that no two experiences in the buffer are identical. The experiences stored in the ER buffer are randomly sampled in each iteration and are used to update the Q-values of the experience's state and action using the experience's reward (using Eq. 1).

2.3 EPIC: Equivalent-Policy Invariant Comparison [4]

Quantifying the dissimilarity between different reward functions in Reinforcement Learning can be very useful in gaining information about the learning process, analyzing the learned parameters, and optimizing the agent's behavior in the environment. Most work on quantifying the difference between reward functions evaluated the policies associated with the learned reward. This is time consuming and is sensitive to environment changes. Equivalent Policy Invariant Comparison (EPIC) distance is an elegant metric that can be used to directly quantify the difference between the reward functions without having to resort to their associated policies making it a more robust and invariant metric to the changes in the environment.

EPIC distance is calculated in two key steps. Firstly, the reward functions are canonically shaped (normalized) by evaluating the expectation of the rewards over some arbitrary distributions of the state-action spaces. Such canonicalization ensures that the reward function is independent of the initial state distribution and the transition dynamics within the environment. Secondly, the EPIC distance is calculated as the Pearson distance between the two canonically shaped rewards.

Definition 1. *Canonically shaped reward: Let $R : SxAxS \to \mathbb{R}$ be a reward function. Given distributions D_S and D_A over the states and actions, let X and X' be random variables independently sampled from D_S and A sampled from D_A. The canonically shaped reward is defined as:*

$$C_{D_S,D_A}(R)(s,a,s') = R(s,a,s') + \mathbb{E}[\gamma R(s',A,X') - R(s,A,X') - \gamma R(X,A,X')] \quad (2)$$

Definition 2. *Pearson distance: The Pearson distance between two random variables X and Y is defined as:*

$$D_p(X,Y) = \sqrt{1 - p(X,Y)}/\sqrt{2} \quad (3)$$

where, $p(X,Y)$ is the Pearson correlation between X and Y defined as

$$p(X,Y) = \frac{\mathbb{E}[(X - \mu_x)(Y - \mu_y)]}{\sigma_x \sigma_y} \quad (4)$$

where, (μ_x, σ_x) and (μ_y, σ_x) are the mean and standard deviation of the variables X and Y respectively.

Definition 3. *EPIC Distance: Given two canonically shaped rewards $C_{D_S,D_A}(R_A)$ and $C_{D_S,D_A}(R_B)$ over some distributions D_S and D_A (which are distributions over states S and actions A respectively), the EPIC distance between two rewards R_A and R_B is:*

$$D - EPIC(R_A, R_B) = D_p(C_{D_S,D_A}(R_A), C_{D_S,D_A}(R_B)) \tag{5}$$

2.4 Related Work on RL Based Performance-Power Optimization

Reinforcement learning based SoC performance-power optimization is a well studied topic in the community. Tabular Q-learning based approaches are proposed in [7,9,16]. Classifier system based approaches are proposed in [3,13]. Neural network approaches using Deep Q-learning and Imitation learning are described in [5,10,11]. Many transfer learning techniques have been applied to RL based performance-power optimization. Chen et al. proposed a batch-update method to accelerate convergence of learning of the RL agent by using the reward received for a particular state to update all the other dominated states [2]. Jenkus et al. proposed intra-state (ISLT) and intra-task (ITLT) learning transfer which enhances the standard Q-learning to improve learning [8]. Chen et al. presented a Smart Knowledge Transfer Technique (STQL) which introduces a contradiction checking mechanism to speed up the learning process between two tasks by evicting inappropriate knowledge transfer [1]. All these methods transfer knowledge between states or tasks but for a given fixed reward function. This work proposes a transfer learning technique applied to changing reward functions. Transfer learning between states or tasks can be applied to this work to further improve learning which will be addressed in future work.

3 EPIC-Q Based CPU Performance-Power Optimization Using DVFS

3.1 Working of Q-Learning Based DVFS

Figure 2 shows the block diagram of the EPIC-Q based CPU performance-power optimization. The Q-learning agent operates periodically with a time period t_Q. At every iteration, the QL-agent reads the current state of the system (s) and recommends an action (a) to the CPU based on the action-selection strategy. In the next iteration, the reward (R) is used to update the Q-value of the state-action pair (s, a) using Eq. 1. The Q-learning agent is augmented with an experience replay buffer. The ER buffer holds the previous experiences seen by the Q-learning agent. Each experience is tuple made up of the state, action, reward and next state (s, a, R, s'). The ER buffer implements the FIFO principle with the uniqueness property as described in Sect. 2.2. The states, actions, action selection strategy, objectives and rewards are defined as follows:

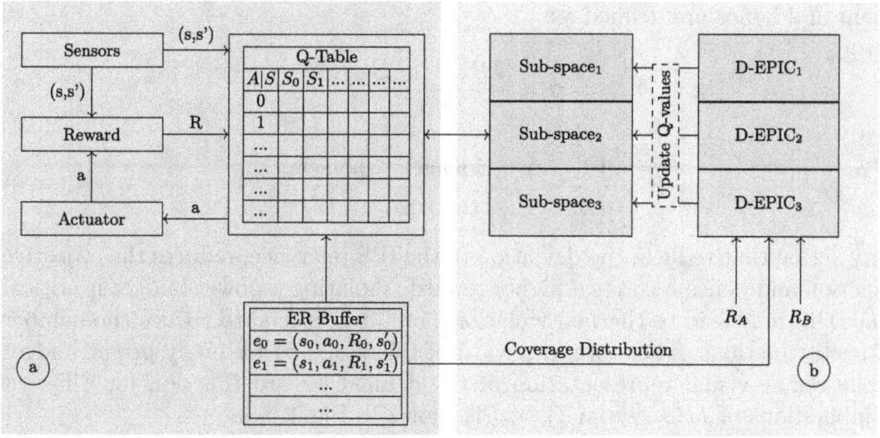

Fig. 2. Working of EPIC-Q: ⓐ Tabular Q-learning using an ER buffer ⓑ Dividing the state-action space into sub-spaces, evaluating EPIC distances for the sub-spaces and using them to update the Q-values.

States and Actions. The states and actions of our work are defined as follows:

- The current frequency (f), CPU utilization (u) and instructions-per-second (IPS) constitute the input state of the EPIC-Q agent i.e. $X = \{f, u, IPS\}$. The CPU utilization is calculated as:

$$u = 1 - \frac{\#cycles\_cpu\_stalled}{\#cycles\_total} \tag{6}$$

  where, $\#cycles\_cpu\_stalled$ is the number of cycles the CPU was stalled due to cache or branch misses. $\#cycles\_total$ is the number of cycles in the time period t_{lct} at maximum CPU frequency.
- The frequency, utilization and IPS are binned into 8, 16 and 16 bins.
- The actions which can be applied by the EPIC-Q agent are increase (+2, +1) or decrease (−2, −1) or do nothing (±0) in frequency of the processor by a unit step. The voltage level is scaled proportionally w.r.t. the frequency.

Objective and Reward Function. EPIC-Q agent is deployed as a low-level controller performing DVFS to optimize the performance (IPS) and power of a core. The objectives (goals) and constraints of the EPIC-Q agent are provided by a software supervisor. The objective of the EPIC-Q agent is to learn to efficiently control the frequency of the core to provide a reference IPS throughput (IPS_{ref}) with a power budget (P_{budget}). These two are conflicting objectives since increasing the frequency increases the IPS throughput and the power budget. The EPIC-Q agent has to provide the closest possible IPS to the IPS reference while minimizing the number of power budget overshoots. The objective (Δ) and reward functions (R) are used to enforce this behavior in the EPIC-Q agent and hence are defined as:

$$\Delta = \frac{|IPS - IPS_{ref}|}{IPS_{max}} \tag{7}$$

$$R = \begin{cases} 1 - \Delta, & \text{if } power \leq power_{budget} \\ 0, & \text{otherwise} \end{cases} \tag{8}$$

Any action that reduces the deviation to the IPS reference, reduces the objective function and hence receives a higher reward. Violating a power budget is critical since this may lead to thermal violations, and it is crucial to reduce the number of such violations. Therefore, a reward of 0 is assigned for every power budget violation. A visual representation of the defined reward function for different combinations of IPS_{ref} and P_{budget} is shown in Fig. 1.

3.2 Transfer Learning Using EPIC Distance

A change in the objective (IPS_{ref}) or the constraints (P_{budget}) leads to a change in the reward function. The supervisor changes the objective and/or constraint adhering to application and system requirements. EPIC-Q is applied every time there is a change in the reward function. Let R_A be the current reward function and R_B be the new reward function. EPIC-Q works in two stages. First, the state-action space is divided into sub-spaces ($sub - space_n$). Secondly, the EPIC distances ($D - EPIC_n$) is calculated using R_A, R_B and coverage distribution supplied by the ER buffer.

State-Action Space Division. We first divide the state-action space into smaller sub-spaces. Figure 1 shows the reward function for different combinations of IPS_{ref} and P_{budget}. We observe that the reward functions are similar in certain states and different in other states. Determining the EPIC distance for the complete state-action space and using this value for updating the Q-values is inefficient. Let ($IPS_{ref\,A}$,$P_{budget\,A}$) and ($IPS_{ref\,B}$,$P_{budget\,B}$) be the objectives and constraints for the reward functions R_A and R_B respectively. We can then divide the state-space using these metrics are boundaries to get the sub-spaces.

Updating Q-values Using EPIC Distances. Once the sub-spaces are established, we find the EPIC distances for each sub-space using the reward functions R_A, R_B and the ER buffer. The ER buffer holds a list of most recent and unique experiences faced by the Q-learning agent. We use this as coverage distribution for calculating the EPIC distances as defined in Section. The EPIC distance quantifies the difference in the two reward functions for the different sub-spaces based on the experiences stored in the ER buffer. We use the EPIC distance as a factor to forget some knowledge learned for the reward function R_A to accelerate the learning of the reward function R_B. An EPIC distance of 0 indicates no change in the sub-spaces and an EPIC distance of 1 indicates a complete contradiction in the reward functions. The EPIC distances of the different sub-spaces are used to then modify the Q-values of the state-action (s, a) pairs of the respective sub-spaces as:

$$Q(s,a) \leftarrow (1 - D - EPIC) * Q(s,a) + (D - EPIC * Q_0) \tag{9}$$

where, Q_0 is the value used for initialization of the Q-learning agent.

Zero Padding Experiences in EPIC Calculations. The performance of EPIC-Q is directly influenced by the size of the ER buffer and the number of experiences stored in it corresponding to the individual sub-spaces. In run time learning, the inputs to the learning agent are not uniform. The states visited by EPIC-Q is influenced by the objectives and constraints, the applications being run on the processing core and also the number of iterations the agent has been called. The number of experiences corresponding to a sub-space is also influenced by the size of the sub-space itself. In case the number of experiences for a sub-space is lower than a threshold $\theta_{\#exp}$, we perform zero padding while calculating the EPIC distance for the sub-space. This prevents a limited number of experiences to dominate the EPIC distance of the whole sub-space.

4 Experimental Setup and Results

4.1 Experimental Setup

We evaluate our methodology on an Xilinx Virtex 7 FPGA implementing the PULP RISC-V based system-on-chip [12]. The SoC implements a 3-core system and uses the general purpose configuration provided by the PULP platform. The SoC runs on the FPGA with a maximum frequency of 30MHz. Each core in the SoC is controlled by an EPIC-Q agent running as a software process on the same core. We use benchmarks from the MiBench benchmark suite [6] to constitute workloads for our experiment. The MiBench benchmarks have different compute and memory characteristics and we randomly schedule the benchmarks in sequential order to get workload with varying CPU intensiveness. We average each set of experiments over 50 randomly generated workloads. The reward function is changed every 25–30 s in our setup. The EPIC-Q agent has a time period t_Q of 5 ms, ER buffer size of 100, zero padding threshold ($\theta_{\#exp}$) of 10 and the initial Q-value (Q_0) is 0.125. The learning rate (β) is 0.125 and the discount factor (γ) is 0.1.

4.2 Sweeping EPIC Distances Vs Performance

Firstly, to see the benefits of transfer learning for a change in reward function using Eq. 9, we first train the Q-learning agents for a source domain reward function. We then change the reward function and update the learnt Q-values with different EPIC distance values. The EPIC distances are obtained by linearly sweeping from the range [0,1]. Figure 3 shows the number of power budget overshoots achieved by the different sweeping EPIC distances for two different scenarios of changes in reward functions. In both scenarios, we maximize the performance under different power budgets i.e. $IPS_{ref} = IPS_{max}$. We initially train the agents in the source domain with a power budget of $0.8P_{max}$. In the first scenario, we change the power budget from $0.8P_{max}$ to $0.6P_{max}$ whereas in the second scenario we change it from $0.8P_{max}$ to $0.4P_{max}$. The EPIC distances calculated in the two scenarios are 0.38 and 0.58 respectively. We can clearly observe that the performance of EPIC-Q by updating the Q-values using Eq. 9 improves within the range [0,1]. We also observe that the performance improvement using the calculated EPIC distance is close to the best achieved improvement. This proves that the calculated EPIC distance is a good metric to update Q-values for a change in reward function.

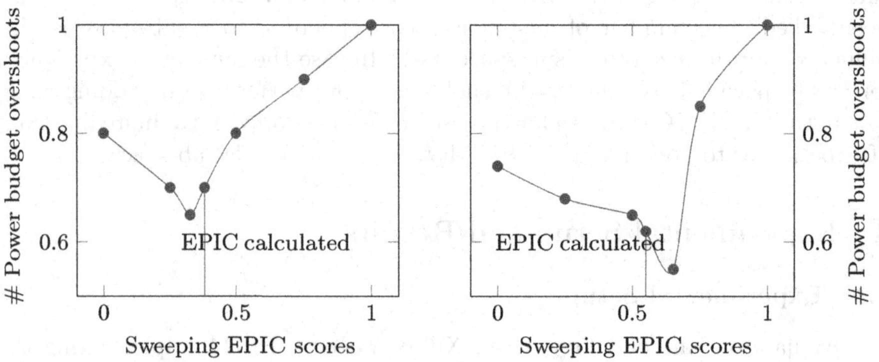

Fig. 3. Sweeping EPIC distance vs number of power budget overshoots where EPIC-Q is used to maximize the performance ($IPS_{ref} = IPS_{max}$) under changing power budgets. The Q-values are updated using Eq. 9

4.3 Results

EPIC-Q based transfer learning is applied when there is a change in reward function (i.e. change in objective IPS_{ref} and/or power budget). We evaluate the effectiveness of our approach against the performance of a standard Q-learning agent with direct transfer (i.e. the Q-values are transferred from the source domain to target domain without modification) and a Q-learning agent from scratch (i.e. the q-values are reset for a change in reward function). Figure 4 summarizes the results of our work. We use ① the IPS difference ($|IPS - IPS_{ref}|$) and ② number of power budget overshoots as metrics to evaluate our work. We set IPS_{ref} to IPS_{max} where the agents are required to maximize performance under a power budget. We use three different power budgets ($0.4P_{max}$, $0.6P_{max}$, $0.8P_{max}$) for the source and target domains which gives us 6 different transitions or reward function changes. The bottom left set of graphs in Fig. 4

depict a decrease in power budget whereas the top right set of graphs depict an increase in power budget.

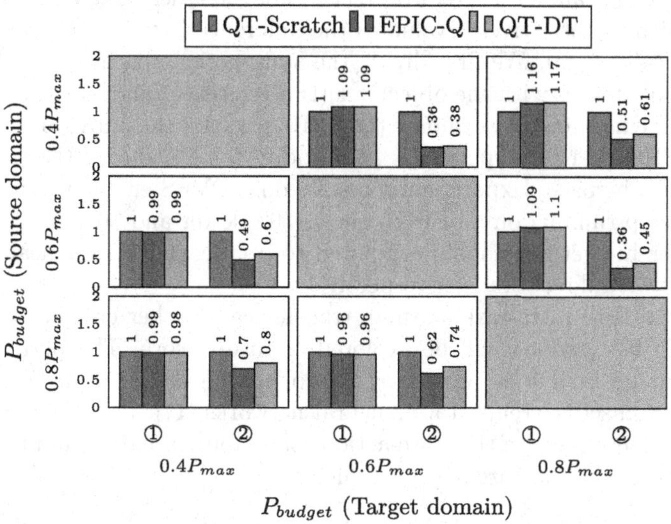

Fig. 4. Results comparing the performance of EPIC-Q, Q-table with direct transfer (QT-DT) and Q-table from scratch (QT-Scratch). ① IPS difference and ② Number of power budget overshoots as metrics.

For an increase in power budget, EPIC-Q achieves 59% lower and 17.2% lower power budget overshoots which achieving 11.35% higher and 1% higher IPS difference relative to the QT-Scratch and QT-DT respectively. For a decrease in power budget, EPIC-Q achieves 39.67% lower and 15.67% lower power budget overshoots which achieving 2% lower and 0% lower IPS difference relative to the QT-Scratch and QT-DT respectively. In both the scenarios, EPIC-Q reduces the number of power budget overshoots significantly while trying to maximize the IPS throughput of the CPU core.

Overhead. EPIC-Q is used when there is a change in the objective or constraints i.e. the reward function. This in our experimental setup is done every 25–30 s. The calculation of the EPIC distances and updating the Q-values for the different sub-spaces requires less than 1 ms in our experimental setup which is negligible. The time complexity increases exponentially w.r.t the size of the state-action space. It increases linearly w.r.t the number of sub-spaces.

5 Conclusion

In this work, we proposed EPIC-Q: A Q-learning agent enhanced with Equivalent Policy Invariant Comparison (EPIC) based transfer learning for run time SOC performance-power optimization. The Q-learning agent is augmented with an experience replay feature which accelerates the learning process by batch training. EPIC-Q based transfer learning is applied when there is a change in the objective or constraints (i.e. reward function) of the Q-learning agent. EPIC is a method which quantitatively evaluates the difference between two reward functions (EPIC-distance). We first divide the state-action space of the Q-learning agent into sub-spaces with the objectives (IPS reference) and constraints (power budget) as the margins. We evaluate the EPIC-score for the individual sub-spaces using the ER buffer for experiences and modify the Q-value of the state-action pairs in the sub-space. Experimental results on a DVFS enabled RISC-V based system-on-chip running on an FPGA shows 50% lower and 16.435% lower number of power budget overshoots compared to a Q-learning agent learning from scratch and with direct transfer respectively.

Intra-state and Intra-task learning transfer can further enhance the performance of EPIC-Q which will be explored as future work. The performance of EPIC-Q can be further improved by approximating the state-action space as done in LCS based systems [15] or neural networks [17]. Future work can also address the intersection of the state-action space approximation and EPIC based transfer learning to increase learning efficiency.

Acknowledgements. We would like to thank our colleagues from the Chair of Integrated Systems at TU Munich, our partners in the IPF project: Rolf Ernst (TU Braunschweig, Germany), Nikil Dutt (UC Irvine, USA) and Fadi Kurdahi (UC Irvine, USA) and acknowledge the financial support from the DFG under Grant HE4584/7-2.

References

1. Chen, L., Li, X., Jiang, F., Li, C., Xu, J.: Smart knowledge transfer-based runtime power management. In: 2023 Design, Automation & Test in Europe Conference & Exhibition (DATE) (2023)
2. Chen, Z., Marculescu, D.: Distributed reinforcement learning for power limited many-core system performance optimization. In: 2015 Design, Automation & Test in Europe Conference & Exhibition (DATE) (2015)
3. Donyanavard, B., et al.: SOSA: self-optimizing learning with self-adaptive control for hierarchical system-on-chip management. In: Proceedings of the 52nd Annual IEEE/ACM International Symposium on Microarchitecture (2019)
4. Gleave, A., Dennis, M., Legg, S., Russell, S., Leike, J.: Quantifying differences in reward functions. arXiv preprint arXiv:2006.13900 (2020)
5. Gupta, U., Mandal, S.K., Mao, M., Chakrabarti, C., Ogras, U.Y.: A deep q-learning approach for dynamic management of heterogeneous processors. IEEE Comput. Archit. Lett. **18**, 14–17 (2019)
6. Guthaus, M.R., Ringenberg, J.S., Ernst, D., Austin, T.M., Mudge, T., Brown, R.B.: MiBench: a free, commercially representative embedded benchmark suite. In: Proceedings of the fourth annual IEEE International Workshop on Workload Characterization, WWC-4 (Cat. No. 01EX538) (2001)
7. Iranfar, A., Shahsavani, S.N., Kamal, M., Afzali-Kusha, A.: A heuristic machine learning-based algorithm for power and thermal management of heterogeneous MPSoCs. In: 2015 IEEE/ACM International Symposium on Low Power Electronics and Design (ISLPED) (2015)

8. Jenkus, D., Xia, F., Shafik, R., Yakovlev, A.: Runtime energy minimization of distributed many-core systems using transfer learning. In: 2022 Design, Automation & Test in Europe Conference & Exhibition (DATE) (2022)
9. Liu, W., Tan, Y., Qiu, Q.: Enhanced q-learning algorithm for dynamic power management with performance constraint. In: 2010 Design, Automation & Test in Europe Conference & Exhibition (DATE 2010) (2010)
10. Mandal, S.K., Bhat, G., Patil, C.A., Doppa, J.R., Pande, P.P., Ogras, U.Y.: Dynamic resource management of heterogeneous mobile platforms via imitation learning. IEEE Trans. Very Large Scale Integr. (VLSI) Syst. **27**(12), 2842–2854 (2019)
11. Rapp, M., et al.: MLCAD: a survey of research in machine learning for cad keynote paper. IEEE Trans. Comput.-Aided Des. Integr. Circ. Syst. (2021)
12. Rossi, D., et al.: Pulp: a parallel ultra low power platform for next generation IoT applications. In: 2015 IEEE Hot Chips 27 Symposium (HCS) (2015)
13. Surhonne, A., Doan, N.A.V., Maurer, F., Wild, T., Herkersdorf, A.: GAE-LCT: a run-time GA-based classifier evolution method for hardware LCT controlled SOC performance-power optimization. In: International Conference on Architecture of Computing Systems (2022)
14. Surhonne, A., Maurer, F., Wild, T., Herkersdorf, A.: LCT-DER: LCT with dynamic sized experience replay for runtime SOC performance-power optimization. In: Proceedings of the Genetic and Evolutionary Computation Conference Companion (2023)
15. Surhonne, A., Maurer, F., Wild, T., Herkersdorf, A.: LCT-TL: learning classifier table (LCT) with transfer learning for runtime SOC performance-power optimization. In: 2023 IEEE 16th International Symposium on Embedded Multicore/Many-core Systems-on-Chip (MCSoC) (2023)
16. Wang, Z., et al.: Modular reinforcement learning for self-adaptive energy efficiency optimization in multicore system. In: 2017 22nd Asia and South Pacific Design Automation Conference (ASP-DAC) (2017)
17. Zhuang, F., et al.: A comprehensive survey on transfer learning. Proc. IEEE **109**(1), 43–76 (2020)

Accelerating Depthwise Separable Convolutions on Ultra-Low-Power Devices

Francesco Daghero(✉), Alessio Burrello, Massimo Poncino, Enrico Macii, and Daniele Jahier Pagliari

Politecnico di Torino, Corso Castelfidardo 39, 10129 Turin, Italy
{francesco.daghero,alessio.burrello,massimo.poncino,enrico.macii, daniele.jahierpagliari}@polito.it

Abstract. Depthwise separable convolutions are a fundamental component in efficient Deep Neural Networks, as they reduce the number of parameters and operations compared to traditional convolutions while maintaining comparable accuracy. However, their low data reuse opportunities make deploying them notoriously difficult. In this work, we perform an extensive exploration of alternatives to fuse the depthwise and pointwise kernels that constitute the separable convolutional block. Our approach aims to minimize time-consuming memory transfers by combining different data layouts. When targeting a commercial ultra-low-power device with a three-level memory hierarchy, the GreenWaves GAP8 SoC, we reduce the latency of end-to-end network execution by up to 11.40%. Furthermore, our kernels reduce activation data movements between L2 and L1 memories by up to 52.97%.

Keywords: Deep Learning · Edge Platforms · TinyML · MCUs

1 Introduction

A popular trend for AI-based IoT applications consists of performing computations directly on sensing devices, thus avoiding or at least reducing the dependency on a network connection, making applications more secure, energy-efficient, and responsive. Consequently, much research has been done to devise HW platforms, algorithms, or new operators to enable fast and energy-efficient Deep Neural Networks (DNNs) inference on IoT nodes [6,9]. One notable example is represented by *depthwise separable convolutions*, which have progressively become core components of several efficient DNN architectures [4,10,17], thanks to their reduced number of parameters and operations w.r.t. standard convolutions, at the cost of limited or 0 accuracy drops. On the other hand, these primitives are challenging to accelerate, as they are characterized by a lower data reuse w.r.t. standard convolutions.

At the same time, edge-oriented hardware architectures are starting to include more complex memory hierarchies, with a smaller but faster L1 memory, where the whole network does not fit, and a bigger but slower L2 memory.

L. Carro et al. (Eds.): SAMOS 2024, LNCS 15226, pp. 46–58, 2025.
https://doi.org/10.1007/978-3-031-78377-7_4

These memories are often software-controlled scratchpads to get rid of energy-expensive caches. Moving data between different memory levels requires a significant amount of energy. Layer fusion [3, 18] has been introduced to lessen the memory transfers, where two or more layers are merged into one. This approach avoids moving intermediate tensors back and forth from L1 to L2, thus avoiding time-consuming transfers at the cost of additional overhead in terms of peak memory usage. However, most fusion optimizations are limited to the simple case of one convolution and an elementwise operator (e.g. Pooling, ReLU, etc.) [14].

Table 1. Notation

Dimension	Abbreviations
Input (rows,columns,channels)	IX/IY/C
Output (rows,columns,channels)	OX/OY/K
Weights (filter height/width, channels in/out)	FX/FY/C/K
Padding/Stride	P/S
Fused dimension	FD

In this work, we propose instead a set of efficient fusion alternatives for depthwise and pointwise convolution sequences aimed at maximizing the data reuse of each primitive while minimizing the data transfers and re-organizations between different memory levels. Our kernel library is released as open-source at: https://github.com/eml-eda/depthwise-separable-fusion. Our main contributions are as follows:

- We propose and benchmark *six new fused kernels*, each leveraging different data layouts and data processing patterns. On the GreenWaves GAP8 SoC [7], considering 36 blocks with different input/output sizes and n. of channels, our most effective solution has a median computational overhead of as low as 5.13%, when not considering memory transfers.
- We expand the open-source AI-compiler DORY [2] to support fused kernels, adding an engine that chooses which layer to fuse based on graph analysis with pre-defined constraints. Using our kernels as backend and GAP8 as target, we reduce the inference latency of end-to-end Deep Neural Networks (DNNs) execution by up to 11.40% while reducing activation memory transfers by 27.26%. When minimizing the number of transfers, we achieve a reduction of up to 52.97% while reducing the inference latency by 2.64%.

2 Background and Related Works

2.1 Depthwise Separable Convolutions

Table 1 reports the notation used in the paper for convolution hyperparameters. Depthwise separable convolutions factorize a standard convolution into two parts: a DepthWise convolution (DW) and a 1×1 convolution called PointWise (PW). Their equations can be written as follows:

$$O^{DW}_{k,h,w} = \sum_{i,j}^{F_x,F_y} I_{k,x+i,y+j} \cdot W_{k,i,j} \quad O^{PW}_{k,x,y} = \sum_{c}^{C} I_{c,x,y} \cdot W_{k,c}$$

where I, W, and O denote input, weights, and output tensors for a pixel at height x, width y, and channel c/k. Note that the DW computation is applied to each channel independently. As an example, a convolution with $C = 32$, $K = 64$, $OX = OY = 56$, $FX = FY = 3$, and $S = 2$ requires 14.5M multiply-and-accumulate (MAC) operations, while the corresponding depthwise separable block (DW + PW) only 1.8M, with a reduction of 7.9×. Memory is reduced by the same factor, from 18.4 kB to 2.3 kB.

However, DW is characterized by a significantly lower data reuse compared to standard convolutions, requiring careful handling to maximize its efficiency. Libraries such as CMSIS-NN [12] and PULP-NN [8], implementing state-of-the-art primitives for deep learning, respectively, on ARM and RISC-V SoCs, propose either specific implementations to be selected depending on the kernel dimension, or implementations that require data re-organization before execution. In particular, PULP-NN converts the input data layout from Height-Width-Channel (HWC), used for all other library layers, to Channel-Height-Width (CHW) for DW, significantly improving the data locality but requiring an additional data re-organization step. Therefore, the efficiency of such layers remains low: considering the same hyper-parameters of the previous example, the DW layer accounts for only 12.3% of the total operations of the DW+PW block but requires 59.9% of the total latency when executed with the PULP-NN library on GAP8 [7].

2.2 Depth-First Tiling and Layer-Fusion

Data movement between memory levels is a critical problem for deep learning models [11], as given modern networks' size, even single layers may not fit in L1 [2]. A key method to solve this problem is *tiling*, which divides layers into sub-operations, each using only a portion of the inputs/weights and/or computing a portion of the output, but fitting entirely in L1 [2]. Clearly, the overhead of tiling is an increase in the required data transfers. For instance, the same input might be loaded multiple times in different tiles to compute different output channels.

Several works [5,13] have proposed ways to alleviate this problem, by performing the execution in a "depth-first" fashion, that is, processing the same tile over successive layers, rather than completing the execution of all the tiles of a layer before starting with the next one. The authors of [13] show that, on a MobilenetV2 architecture with an input resolution of 224 × 224, depth-first tiling reduces the peak memory usage by up to 8×. However, this comes at the cost of a computational overhead (around 3%) due to the redundant computations to recalculate intermediate pixels included in the receptive fields of multiple contiguous tiles. The authors of [5] propose a depth-first inference method too, but compared with [13], instead of square tiles, they use *row* tiles, always splitting the layer on the IY/OY dimension. Further, they buffer in L1 the intermediate pixels that should be recomputed between adjacent tiles to contain the computational overheads. They reduce memory transfers by up to 5.2x with a small 0.3% overhead in terms of computations.

In this work, we take inspiration from the row-based inference of [5], combining it with another popular approach to reduce the data movements, i.e., layer fusion. Most of the currently employed deep learning backends such as CuDNN [3], Triton [18], and ONNX runtime [15] support fusion between convolutions and elementwise operators (e.g., ReLU or BatchNorm). However, more complex fusion patterns, such as the one between DW and PW proposed in this work, are less explored. To the best of our knowledge, we are the first to release an open-source library for depth-first DW+PW fusion targeted for edge devices.

2.3 IoT Edge Nodes

Thanks to their energy efficiency, heterogeneous platforms have become increasingly popular as IoT edge nodes. They comprise multiple cores or processing elements covering specific tasks, such as I/O, optimized digital signal processing (DSP), or matrix multiplication acceleration, and they usually employ a multi-level hierarchy of software-controlled memories, with lower levels (L1) featuring fast access but small size, and higher levels being slower but bigger. Examples of these architectures are already commercialized by NXP[1], STM[2], and GreenWaves [7]. In particular, GreenWaves proposes the GAP8 SoC, which features a single RISC-V core to handle I/O and sensor interfaces and an 8-core RISC-V processor cluster used to speed up DSP. GAP8 features 64 kB of L1, 512 kB of L2, and an optional external L3 memory, with Direct Memory Access (DMA) controllers to handle data transfers.

3 Materials and Methods

3.1 Fused Kernel Design

This section describes several alternatives to fuse the DW and PW layers, designed to produce different constraints and memory-latency trade-offs. For all versions, we use S and FX/FY to denote the stride and the filter size of the DW (since all three values are equal to 1 for PW). The inner kernels that we fuse are written in C language, and are slightly modified versions of the PULP-NN primitives for GAP8 [8]. Therefore, all our kernels target multi-core platforms with 8-bit SIMD extensions. We consider fusing both DW-PW sequences and PW-DW sequences. All our fused kernels use intermediate buffers to avoid recomputation since this solution guarantees lower latency [5].

[1] https://www.nxp.com/products/processors-and-microcontrollers/arm-microcontrollers/general-purpose-mcus/lpc4300-cortex-m4-m0.

[2] https://www.st.com/en/microcontrollers-microprocessors/stm32h7-series.html.

Depthwise-Pointwise. When fusing the DW-PW sequence, we tile on a per-row basis to limit the overlap between contiguous tiles and, therefore, the additional memory transfers. Specifically, we divide the layers into blocks of FD rows (we show $FD = 3$ in Fig. 1). In the fused kernel, we first apply the DW operator on each tile, followed by the PW one, as shown by the lowermost set of arrows in the figure. Given that the PW layer has a receptive field of 1, this fusion naturally avoids recomputation. On the other hand, it has two limitations. First, it incurs a memory overhead caused by the intermediate buffer of dimension $C \cdot OX \cdot FD$. Noteworthy, optimal values of FD depend on the parallelization employed by the pointwise kernel. In PULP-NN, each core computes half of an output feature map row, therefore yielding sub-optimal performance if FD is not a multiple of $\frac{N_{cores}}{2}$. As a second limitation, all input channels of the PW must be stored in the intermediate buffer to compute a single output, given that moving partial outputs (in high precision) to L2 would be highly sub-optimal, as explained in [2]. Consequently, all DW output channels for the same pixel have to be computed before the PW (since $K_{DW} = C_{PW}$), limiting the available tiling options.

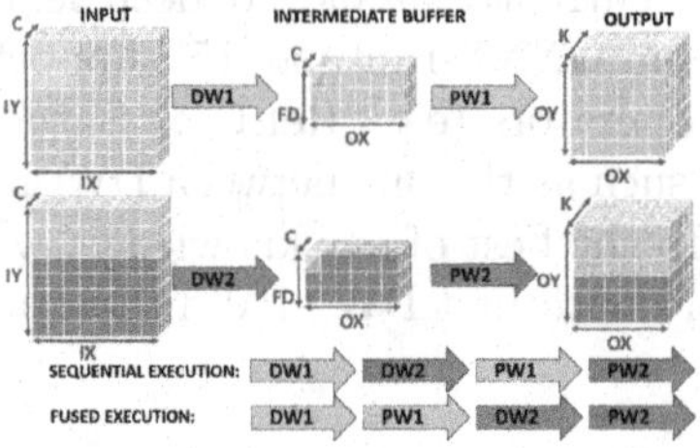

Fig. 1. Execution flow for standard and fused DW-PW sequences, for a layer with $FD = 3$, and $IX/IY = 8$.

Pointwise-Depthwise. For the PW-DW sequence, we propose two fused implementations, exploring both a row-wise tiling of the input (as for DW-PW) and a channel-wise one.

a) Channel-wise execution: The left part of Fig. 2 provides a high-level overview of the channel-wise tiling, comparing it to an unfused execution. This kernel leverages the independence of the different channels in the DW. Accordingly, we process FD channels per tile using an intermediate buffer of size $FD \cdot IX \cdot IY$. Compared to the previous kernel, this version's main advantage is that it enables flexibility in tiling layers also along the channel dimension. Moreover, recomputation is avoided by having an intermediate buffer that includes all spatial locations of the feature map. On the other hand, the intermediate buffer overhead may become substantial for large feature maps, potentially limiting the utility of this kernel. For this solution, optimal values of FD are determined by the DW primitive, which is parallelized over the channels in PULP-NN, leading to performance degradations for FD not multiple of N_{cores}. Another limitation arises from the increased number of input loads required in the PW. In fact, input reuse can no longer be leveraged fully to produce all K output channels, but only a subset of size FD.

b) Row-wise execution: We also implement a row-wise fused kernel for the PW-DW sequence, shown in the right part of Fig. 2. Similarly to the DW-PW fusion, and contrarily to the channel-wise PW-DW, this kernel maximizes input data reuse. Furthermore, it maintains the benefits of the channel-wise PW-DW in terms of tiling freedom, given that the channel dimension is not constrained. However, this fusion requires special care to avoid recomputation: indeed, to execute two adjacent blocks, the DW kernel reuses $FY - 1$ rows of its input. Accordingly, as depicted in Fig. 2, we shift the intermediate buffer after the completion of each tile, moving the last $FY - 1$ rows of the buffer to the beginning. Despite the additional memory movements caused by the shift operation, this solution outperforms one that recomputes PW output rows.

The memory overhead for this kernel is $C \cdot IX \cdot FD$, where a requirement is that $FD \geq FY$, as we need enough rows in the buffer to produce at least one DW output, that is, a number greater or equal to the filter's vertical receptive field. Above this lower bound, optimal values of FD come from the parallelization of the PW kernel, which as explained in Sect. 3.1 requires $\frac{N_{cores}}{2}$ rows for maximum throughput. As each tile needs $FD - (FY - 1)$ new input rows, FD must be a multiple of $\frac{N_{cores}}{2} + FY - 1$ to ensure the maximum efficiency of the PW.

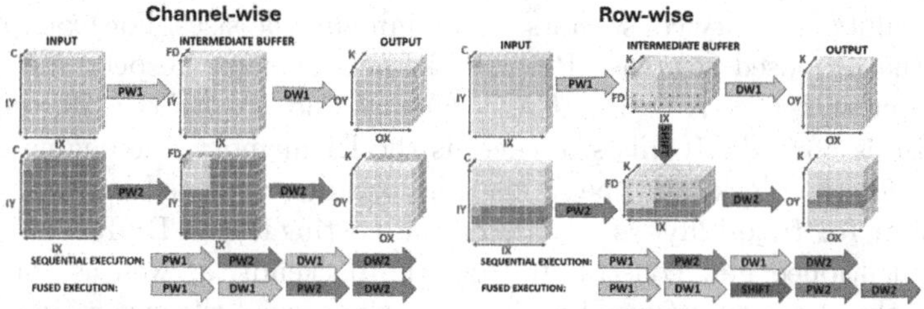

Fig. 2. Execution flow for standard and fused PW-DW sequences for a layer with $FD = 4$ and $K = 8$ with channel-wise (left) or row-wise (right) tiling.

3.2 Data Layout Selection

To implement our kernels in C, we enhance PULP-NN to have, for both PW and DW, four alternative "single-layer" primitives, using all possible combinations of CHW and HWC data layouts for the input and output buffers. From these, we then create the fused kernels, selecting only combinations that use the same data layout for input and output activations, to ensure that burdensome data re-organization steps are eliminated between concatenated kernels of the same type. Since we consider fused kernels for both DW-PW and PW-DW sequences (the latter with two different tiling alternatives), we initially have a pool of 12 kernels. Based on the findings of [8], we then remove layout combinations already identified as suboptimal, such as using CHW for both PW input and DW output in the PW-DW approach, ending up with 6 kernels. Lastly, we profile these 6 kernels running entirely in L1 on our target platform. Thanks to this profiling, we further restrict the set, considering only the kernels with the lowest latency for each sequence type (2 in total) in end-to-end DNN deployments. The details of this last selection step are reported in Sect. 4.2.

3.3 End-to-End Network Deployment

In addition to the kernels, a memory management engine, a tensor allocation engine, and a translator from high-level descriptions (e.g., ONNX) to C kernel function calls are also required to deploy real DNNs on hardware. For this purpose, we leveraged the open-source framework DORY [2] that comprises all these components, including a tiler that automatically partitions the layers into sub-nodes whose tensors fit entirely in L1 memory.

In particular, we extended DORY to support our kernels with three key innovations: i) a fusion engine, which enables block fusion given an input method (PW-DW or DW-PW) and its constraints; ii) a new tiler for fused kernels, and iii) a post-processing optimizer that, given a profiled execution of every single layer in a network with multiple kernels alternatives, selects the optimal combination to minimize the latency or the number of memory transfers.

The **fusion engine** determines whether block fusion is possible, given backend constraints, memory constraints, and minimum tile sizes. For example, considering the proposed row-wise PW-DW kernel, we must respect $FD \geq FY$. With a layer with $C = K = 512$, $FX = FY = 3$ and $IX = IY = 16$, the smallest tile size is 66.6 kB. If this size exceeds the L1 memory, the engine disables the fusion for the block, and the unfused kernels are employed instead.

The **tiler for fused layers** is based on the existing tiler in DORY, integrating the aforementioned new constraints from the backends, as well as constraints related to the geometry of fused layers (e.g., the spatial tile size ratio of input, intermediate, and output tiles has to be compatible), and heuristics related to the optimal FD values, as detailed in Sect. 3.1.

Lastly, the **post-processing optimizer** receives an input flag to select between minimizing the number of cycles or the memory transfers. Below, we detail how the min-latency mode works, but the reasoning is analogous for min-memory. First, three versions of the complete network, enabling DW-PW fusion, PW-DW fusion, or disabling all fusions, are executed, and the latencies of every layer are collected. For this, we only consider the "optimal" combination of fusion type and data layout for each sequence, selected as explained in Sect. 3.2. Subsequently, two steps are performed: first, we consider DW-PW and PW-DW separately, comparing the latency of the corresponding fused blocks with the unfused execution of their composing layers, and selecting the lowest latency alternative for each block. Then, the two resulting *partially-fused* graphs are compared with each other. With an exhaustive search, the fusion option that minimizes latency is selected for each block. Noteworthy, this search has complexity 2^M, where M is the maximum number of fused blocks (e.g., 13 for a MobileNetV1), which is manageable for edge DNNs.

4 Experimental Results

4.1 Experimental Setup

To benchmark the ideal performance of each kernel in L1, we initially employed the GVSoC virtual platform [1], which allows to simulate a modified version of GAP8 with an increased L1 memory size (1 MB in our experiments), thus forcedly avoiding memory transfers between memory levels. End-to-end neural networks are instead deployed on the actual GAP8 hardware, using the modified DORY compiler described in Sect. 3.3 to handle the layers' fusion, tiling, and memory allocations. We use the GAPuino board with the GAP8 SoC and an external 8 MB flash memory for benchmarking. Memory transfers, cycles, and latency are measured using hardware performance counters at a frequency of 100 MHz.

For assessing the effectiveness of the proposed fused kernels on end-to-end DNN execution, we considered three architectures: i) MobilenetV1 (MV1) [10], whose 29 layers include an initial standard convolution followed by 13 depthwise separable blocks, and final pooling and fully connected layers; ii) MobilenetV2 (MV2) [17], with a sequence of 16 *bottleneck blocks* (i.e., PW-DW-PW blocks with residual additions) for a total of 65 layers; iii) DSCNN [19], composed of 4 DW-PW blocks and 9 total layers. For both MV1 and MV2, we use a width multiplier of 0.25 and benchmark both on 224 $\times$ 224 and 128$\times$128 inputs, as in the original papers. Furthermore, we also consider the MV1 variant proposed in the MLPerf Tiny Suite, which uses a 96 $\times$ 96 input for a visual wakeword task.

4.2 Kernel Analysis

First, we benchmark the performance of individual kernels with all tensors stored in L1 memory and, therefore, neglecting the overhead of memory transfers and memory re-organization steps between layers. With an infinite L1, fused and unfused latencies should ideally be identical. Therefore, this experiment allows us to analyze non-idealities related to the implementation of each kernel, e.g., due to strided memory accesses, control flow overheads, etc.

Figure 3 reports the median cycles over 36 DW-PW/PW-DW blocks with different geometries for our six fused kernel variants and for the two unfused baselines, as a function of the FD value. We consider $IX = IY \in [32, 64, 128]$, $S \in [1, 2]$, $C \in [32, 64, 128]$ and $K \in [C, 2C]$. Violin plots show the distribution of the performance over the 36 geometries at the minimum FD that allows the full exploitation of the multi-core parallelization on GAP8.

The legend uses a compact string to identify each kernel. For instance, *PW-DW Channels HWC/CHW/HWC* denote PW-DW fused kernels with tiling on

Table 2. Mobilenets-like architectures deployed on the GAP8 platforms. Abbreviations: B. Baseline, LL/LMT Lowest Latency/Memory Transfer, L Latency, WM Weights Memory, AMT Activation Memory Transfers

Model	Method	MACs	Tot.Cycles [#]	L [ms]	WM [B]	AMT [#]
MV1-224	B	41.0M	10.0M	100.6	463.6k	2.9M
	LL		8.9M [−11.16%]	89.4		2.75M [−5.39%]
	LMT		11.4M [+12.87%]	113.6		1.64M [−43.56%]
MV1-128	B	13.57M	3.08M	30.83	463.6k	879.0k
	LL		2.73M [−11.40%]	27.31		639.4k [−27.26%]
	LMT		3.07M [−0.23%]	30.76		491.9k [−47.74%]
MV1-96	B	7.49M	2.20M	22.04	208.1k	497.03k
	LL		2.02M [−8.43%]	20.18		343.81k [−30.83%]
	LMT		2.03M [−8.03%]	20.27		270.09k [−45.66%]
MV2-224	B	37.20M	14.89M	148.88	1.51M	5.83M
	LL		13.27M [−10.85%]	132.72		3.51M [−39.84%]
	LMT		13.43M [−9.73%]	134.38		3.28M [−43.80%]
MV2-128	B	13.01M	6.76M	67.62	1.51M	2.47M
	LL		6.33M [−6.43%]	63.27		1.72M [−30.39%]
	LMT		6.58M [−2.64%]	65.83		1.16M [−52.97%]
DSCNN	B	2.66M	686.25k	6.86	22.01k	144.67k
	LL		685.79k [−0.07%]	6.86		128.67k [−11.06%]
	LMT		761.42k [+10.95%]	7.61		80.67k [−44.24%]

the channels, using HWC as input/output data layout and CHW for the intermediate buffer. Overall, for PW-DW fusion, the top-performing kernel is *Rows HWC/CHW/HWC*, with a cycles' overhead of 7.15% at $FD = 20$. This is because the overhead of the shift operation becomes negligible compared to the execution of the whole kernel with large FD values. On the other hand, large values of FD are often unfeasible when considering a realistic L1 size, as the memory overhead of the intermediate buffer would reduce the available L1 memory for input, output, and weights tensors. Restricting to $FD < 10$, the *Channels HWC/CHW/HWC* at $FD = 8$ achieves the lowest overhead of 19.27%. Note that 8 is the smallest value of FD that leads to fully utilizing the 8 cores of GAP8. This kernel is superior to the version that uses an HWC intermediate data layout because a CHW input to the DW avoids strided loads, which would incur a higher latency overhead than strided stores of the PW output.

Concerning the DW-PW fusion, the top performing kernel across all FD values is *Rows CHW/HWC/CHW*. The minimal overhead of 5.13% is attained for $FD = 16$. Similarly to the PW-DW fusion, the optimal layout combination favors strided stores of the output over strided loads of the input. It's worth noting that this outcome aligns with the inherent structure of the PULP-NN functions. In

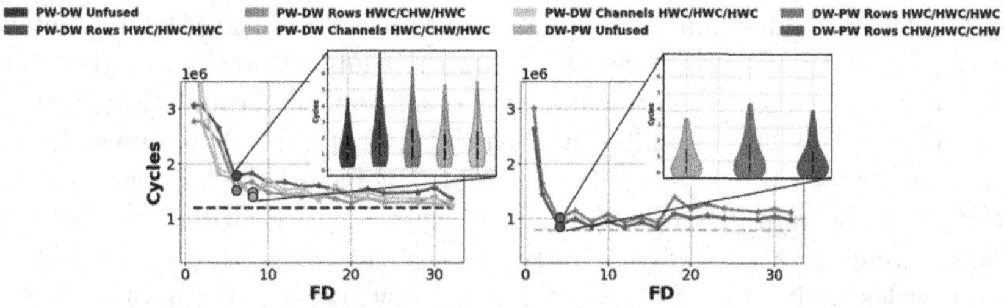

Fig. 3. Median execution cycles in L1 when changing the dimension of the intermediate buffer (*FD*).

fact, given the kernels' output stationary dataflow, each output is written only once, whereas inputs are reused for multiple convolution channels and/or multiple output spatial locations. Consequently, overheads associated with loading input data are more detrimental than those related to storing outputs. We also notice that at $FD = 4$ the kernel achieves an overhead of 11%, just 4% higher compared to the one obtained at $FD = 8$, while halving the memory overhead.

As a result of these analyses, we employ the *Channels HWC/CHW/HWC* fusion for PW-DW blocks and the *Rows CHW/HWC/CHW* one for the DW-PW blocks, to minimize the optimization complexity when deploying end-to-end neural networks, as anticipated in Sect. 3.3. For both kernels, FD is set to the minimal value that ensures utilization of all cores, i.e., $FD = 8$ and $FD = 4$.

4.3 End-to-End Network Deployment

Table 2 reports the performance of end-to-end networks with three different configurations: the un-fused Baseline, the fused combination that minimizes the latency, and the one that minimizes the number of memory transfers (which are a good proxy for energy consumption). We achieve the largest latency reduction on MV1-128 (11.40%), simultaneously reducing the memory transfers by 27.26%. Despite being characterized by more memory transfers (2.9M vs. 879k), MV1-224, achieves a slightly lower latency improvement of 11.16%, with a reduction in the number of transfers of only 5.39%. Interestingly, we also notice that by setting our post-processing optimizer to min-memory mode, while we can cut the number of transfers by roughly the same amount on MV1-128 and MV1-224, the former has a latency comparable to the baseline, while the latter incurs a 12.87% latency increase. While counter-intuitive, this result stems from the higher resolution of the input feature map, which forces the layers' tiles to be bigger on spatial dimensions. In fact, each fused tile is constrained to include either a whole number of rows or a whole number of complete feature maps, depending on the chosen kernel. This in turn, reduces the tile size on the output channels and, consequently, the input data reuse. The MV1-96 variant achieves a slightly lower latency reduction of 6.43%, with a memory transfer reduction of 45.66%. This seems to contradict the previous observation but is a consequence of a significantly reduced number of transfers compared to the MV1-128 network (497.03k vs. 879k), which in turn diminishes their impact on the overall network latency, thereby reducing the possibility of optimization through layer fusion.

Concerning the MV2 architecture, the MV2-224 variant achieves the best latency savings w.r.t. the baseline (10.85%). By fusing the kernels, both this network and the min. transfer one avoid expensive activation transfers from L3, thus reducing latency significantly. Nonetheless, MV2-128 also achieves a relevant cycles' reduction of 6.43% and a memory transfer saving of 52.97%.

Finally, DSCNN achieves the lowest gains in terms of latency, 0.07%. This is due to the large size of the intermediate features maps, caused by a large number of channels, which creates problems both with the DW-PW intermediate channels' constraint and with the PW-DW input data reuse. When the goal is minimizing memory transfers, we achieve a reduction of 44.24%.

To exemplify the energy gains from memory transfer reductions, we refer to the energy benchmarking of [16], on a chip with the same architecture of GAP8, albeit on a different technology node. Using those numbers to estimate the energy for computing, L2-L1 transfers, and L3-L2 transfers, and using our results on MV2-224, we obtain an estimated energy reduction of 90.94%. Savings are high in this case as the original network involves expensive L3 accesses, but this depends on the target's memory hierarchy, which is orthogonal to our approach.

a) End-to-End Network Analysis: Figure 4 depicts the fusion strategies selected by DORY for the "Lowest Latency" MV1-224 deployment. A first important consideration is that the engine combines unfused kernels and both types of fused sequences, demonstrating that all three strategies are relevant and that the choice between them strongly depends on the layer's geometric parameters.

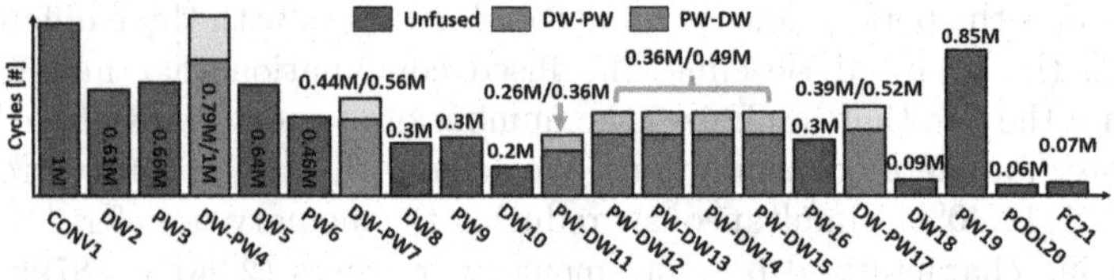

Fig. 4. Layer-by-layer execution cycles and memory transfers of the MV1-224 "Lowest Latency". The lighter colors show the improvement compared to the unfused execution.

In the early layers of the network, the (row-wise) DW-PW fusion is advantageous, as it allows the computation of all output channels without re-loading the input multiple times. Note that, as shown in Sect. 4.2, this fusion is also the one causing the lowest computational overhead. PW-DW fusion becomes more favorable in the network's core, where the number of channels increases. Indeed, this kernel effectively addresses the tiling issue stemming from the DW-PW kernel's constraint of storing all intermediate channels in L1, which negatively impacts performance by leading to small spatial tiles. Lastly, in the final stages of the network, DW-PW fusion is again employed once. This decision by the optimizer is prompted by a 4× reduction in spatial feature map size, rendering spatial tiling unnecessary, and therefore making the DW-PW the best alternative again.

5 Conclusions

Layer fusion is a well-known strategy to reduce the number of data transfers in DNNs. However, common DNN frameworks apply it only between convolutions and elementwise operators. This work proposes several efficient fusion strategies for DW-PW and PW-DW blocks. After extensive benchmarking, we integrate the best-performing fused kernels into an open-source framework for end-to-end network deployment. With experiments on 6 different networks and on the GAP8 SoC, we achieve a latency reduction of up to 11.40% and a maximum reduction of memory transfers of up to 52.97%.

Acknowledgments. This work has received funding from the Key Digital Technologies Joint Undertaking (KDT-JU) under grant agreement No 101095947. The JU receives support from the European Union's Horizon Europe research and innovation program.

Disclosure of Interests. The authors have no competing interests to declare that are relevant to the content of this article.

References

1. Bruschi, N., et al.: GVSoC: a highly configurable, fast and accurate full-platform simulator for RISC-V based IoT processors. In: IEEE ICCD (2021)
2. Burrello, A., et al.: DORY: automatic end-to-end deployment of real-world DNNs on low-cost IoT MCUs. IEEE TECS Comput. **70**(8), 1253–1268 (2021)
3. Chetlur, S., et al.: cuDNN: efficient primitives for deep learning. arXiv preprint arXiv:1410.0759 (2014)
4. Chollet, F.: Xception: deep learning with depthwise separable convolutions. In: CVPR, pp. 1251–1258 (2017)
5. Colleman, S., Verhelst, M.: High-utilization, high-flexibility depth-first CNN coprocessor for image pixel processing on FPGA. IEEE VLSI **29**(3), 461–471 (2021)
6. Daghero, F., et al.: Energy-efficient adaptive machine learning on IoT end-nodes with class-dependent confidence. In: IEEE ICECS (2020)
7. Flamand, E., et al.: GAP-8: a RISC-V SoC for AI at the edge of the IoT. In: IEEE ASAP. IEEE (2018)
8. Garofalo, A., et al.: PULP-NN: accelerating quantized neural networks on parallel ultra-low-power RISC-V processors. Philos. Trans. R. Soc. (2020)
9. Han, S., et al.: Deep compression: compressing deep neural networks with pruning, trained quantization and Huffman coding. arXiv preprint arXiv:1510.00149 (2015)
10. Howard, A.G., et al.: MobileNets: efficient convolutional neural networks for mobile vision applications (2017)
11. Ivanov, A., et al.: Data movement is all you need: a case study on optimizing transformers. MLSys **3**, 711–732 (2021)

12. Lai, L., et al.: CMSIS-NN: efficient neural network kernels for arm Cortex-M CPUs. arXiv preprint arXiv:1801.06601 (2018)
13. Lin, J., et al.: MCUNetV2: memory-efficient patch-based inference for tiny deep learning. arXiv preprint arXiv:2110.15352 (2021)
14. Niu, W., et al.: DNNFusion: accelerating deep neural networks execution with advanced operator fusion. In: ACM PLDI 2021, pp. 883–898 (2021)
15. ONNX-Runtime-developers: ONNX runtime (2021). https://onnxruntime.ai/
16. Rossi, D., et al.: Vega: a ten-core SoC for IoTa endnodes with DNN acceleration and cognitive wake-up from MRAM-based state-retentive sleep mode. IEEE JSSC **57**(1), 127–139 (2022)
17. Sandler, M., et al.: MobileNetV2: inverted residuals and linear bottlenecks (2018)
18. Tillet, P., et al.: Triton: an intermediate language and compiler for tiled neural network computations. In: ACM PLDI, pp. 10–19 (2019)
19. Zhang, Y., et al.: Hello edge: keyword spotting on microcontrollers. arXiv preprint arXiv:1711.07128 (2017)

It's All About PR
Smart Benchmarking AI Accelerators Using Performance Representatives

Alexander Louis-Ferdinand Jung(✉), Jannik Steinmetz, Jonathan Gietz, Konstantin Lübeck, and Oliver Bringmann

Embedded Systems, University of Tübingen, Tübingen, Germany
{a.jung,jannik.steinmetz,jonathan.gietz,konstantin.luebeck, oliver.bringmann}@uni-tuebingen.de

Abstract. Statistical models are widely used to estimate the performance of commercial off-the-shelf (COTS) AI hardware accelerators. However, training of statistical performance models often requires vast amounts of data, leading to a significant time investment and can be difficult in case of limited hardware availability.

To alleviate this problem, we propose a novel performance modeling methodology that significantly reduces the number of training samples while maintaining good accuracy. Our approach leverages knowledge of the target hardware architecture and initial parameter sweeps to identify a set of *Performance Representatives* (PR) for deep neural network (DNN) layers. These PRs are then used for benchmarking, building a statistical performance model, and making estimations. This targeted approach drastically reduces the number of training samples needed, opposed to random sampling, to achieve a better estimation accuracy.

We achieve a Mean Absolute Percentage Error (MAPE) of as low as 0.02% for single-layer estimations and 0.68% for whole DNN estimations with less than 10 000 training samples. The results demonstrate the superiority of our method for single-layer estimations compared to models trained with randomly sampled datasets of the same size.

Keywords: Performance Estimation · Benchmarking · AI Hardware Accelerators · Statistical Modelling · Deep Neural Networks

1 Introduction

Deep Neural Networks (DNNs) are being used in various tasks ranging from time series and image classification to natural language processing. As these models become part of more and more AI-assisted edge devices, there is an abundance of commercial off-the-shelf AI accelerator hardware. Determining which accelerator to use for a specific AI application is difficult, as real hardware might not yet be available and simulations tend to be very time-consuming. Therefore, it is important to be able to estimate the performance of a DNN mapped onto an accelerator platform.

L. Carro et al. (Eds.): SAMOS 2024, LNCS 15226, pp. 59–75, 2025.
https://doi.org/10.1007/978-3-031-78377-7_5

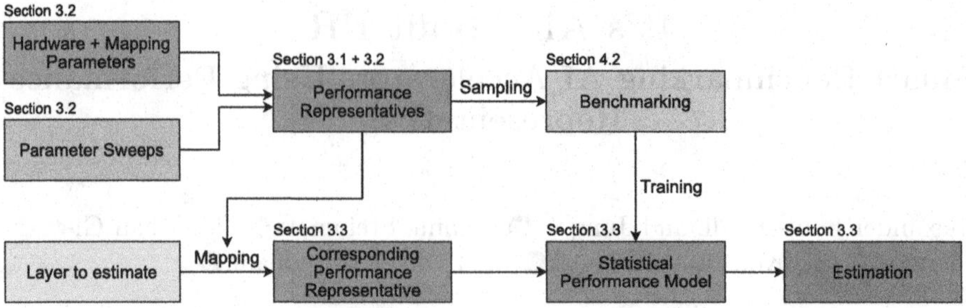

Fig. 1. The proposed performance modeling methodology and benchmarking strategy.

Another area where performance estimation models are needed is Neural Architecture Search (NAS). Especially for hardware-aware NAS targeting embedded platforms, a trade-off between a high DNN accuracy and the execution time has to be considered. However, measuring all possible DNN candidates can be extremely time-consuming. Therefore, an efficient performance estimator is needed to accelerate the optimization loop [4].

Statistical estimation models have been shown to have high accuracy for execution time estimation if a sufficient amount of training samples is obtainable [2,11,13]. Analytical models, on the other hand, require detailed knowledge about the architecture to yield accurate estimations [8,10].

Vendors of commercial off-the-shelf (COTS) accelerators often only provide a slow functional and timing simulator. Gathering a sufficiently large amount of training samples for statistical estimation models with these simulators is infeasible. Another problem with COTS platforms is, that often only general specifications such as the available functional units, and the memory bandwidth are publicly known. An accurate analytical performance model cannot be created from such limited information. But these known hardware characteristics can indicate interesting behavior with specific DNN layer parameters, e.g., which tile-sizes yield a good utilization.

This paper proposes a performance modeling methodology paired with a benchmarking strategy to select significant data points to reduce measurement runs and consequently measurement time. Depending on the amount of knowledge that is available for a platform, the known hardware characteristics can be used to find DNN layer parameters that are representative of the execution time behavior. If there is not much information about a platform, these *Performance Representatives* need to be determined empirically in an initial benchmark phase. An overview of the proposed approach is depicted in Fig. 1.

This paper makes the following contributions: (1) We describe a methodology to determine the Performance Representatives of a specific hardware platform. (2) We then use these Performance Representatives to carry out benchmarks on the hardware platform under consideration and then use these representative data points to train statistical models which can then be used to estimate the execution time of single-layers and whole DNNs. (3) We also show how the amount of training samples impacts the accuracy when using our approach compared to random sampling the same amount of data points.

2 Related Work

In ANNETTE [11] they use micro-kernel and multi-layer benchmarks of DNN layers to create machine learning estimation models. These Random Forest models are then combined with the well-known Roofline model [12] to better capture the regular execution time behavior of these platforms. They evaluate their mixed models on two hardware platforms (an FPGA and an ASIC accelerator) and achieve a mean absolute percentage error (MAPE) of as low as 12.71 % for single-layer estimations and 3.47 % for whole networks. Per platform and per layer 35 000 measurements were conducted.

Bouzidi et al. [2] compare five different machine learning methods for performance estimation on the NVIDIA Jetson AGX Xavier and TX2 GPUs. They measured around 200 000 whole DNN inferences, by using the execution times of the executed GPU kernels reported by NVIDIA's profiling tools. The MAPE of the best estimation model ranges between 7.67 % and 14.73 %.

The authors of Blackthorn [7] specifically exploit the very regular execution time behavior of the NVIDIA Jetson TX2 and the Jetson Nano to create their performance estimation models. They define a set of step-wise functions and reduce this set of functions gradually by measuring more and more data points. Each function that cannot explain the new data point is removed from the function set, resulting in one final step-wise function that is then used for estimating the performance. This requires around 15 000 measurements for the Convolution layer, resulting in a Root-Mean-Square-Percentage-Error (RMSPE) of 7.57 % for Convolution layers and an error between 0.45 % and 6.68 % for complete DNN execution time estimation.

In nn-Meter [13] DNN execution kernels are benchmarked, which contain multiple fused layers and are used for estimating the execution time of various DNNs by summing the estimated times for the contained kernels. They obtain up to 39 968 benchmark points for e.g. the Convolution execution kernel. These samples are then used for training Random Forest models, which yield a RMSPE between 1.3 5% and 22.25 % depending on the DNN and hardware platform.

The presented estimators require a vast amount of training samples to achieve the reported estimation accuracies. Additionally, the usage of step-wise functions by Blackthorn has some drawbacks. Firstly, a function pattern that describes the execution time behavior needs to be defined. Secondly, the step-wise function describing the execution time behavior must be covered by the parameter space of the function set. This is a prerequisite so that the approach finds a matching function. We address these shortcomings by, on the one hand, reducing the number of training samples, and on the other hand, determining the step width algorithmically instead of choosing from a set of pre-defined functions for an accurate execution time estimation.

3 Smart Benchmarking and Modeling

The execution time behavior of an AI accelerator platform often exhibits a very regular pattern. This is due to how AI accelerators compute the layers of a DNN.

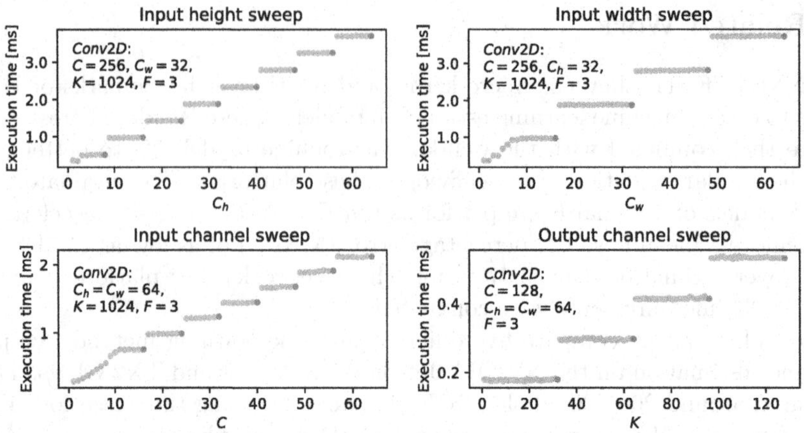

Fig. 2. Step-wise execution time behavior of the 2D-Convolution observed for different parameter sweeps, run on the NVIDIA Jetson AGX Xavier GPU. Performance Representatives are highlighted in red (last point on step). The parameters of the 2D-Convolution are described in Eq. 3 and its explanation. (Color figure online)

For example, the UltraTrail accelerator [1] always processes 8×8 output and input channels in one activation of the multiply accumulate (MAC) array. Therefore, the execution time behavior takes the shape of a step-wise function while increasing only the input channel parameter or the output channel parameter of the 1D-Convolution. We call these types of benchmarks *parameter sweeps*. But also other hardware platforms, like the NVIDIA Jetson AGX Xavier GPU exhibit a similar behavior, as can be seen in Fig. 2.

This also means, that many of the data points in fine-grained measurements do not contain new information about the execution time behavior of the platform. The aim of this work is to reduce the number of measured data points for building statistical performance models, while maintaining good accuracy when estimating the execution time of a single layer as well as of whole DNNs.

3.1 Performance Representatives (PR)

In our work, we combine the findings of [7] and [11]. Exploiting the regular execution time behavior to guide the selection of benchmark points, consequently reducing the number of points that need to be measured. These measurements are then used to train statistical models for execution time estimation. The idea is to only measure one representative data point for a step. We call this a **Performance Representative (PR)**. We algorithmically determine the last point of a step as our PR, as these are generally the points with optimal utilization of the AI accelerator architecture.

3.2 Hardware and Mapping Parameters

How the PRs of the execution time behavior can be derived heavily depends on how much knowledge about the accelerator architecture is available. We classify the amount of available architecture knowledge for the accelerators used in this work ranging from white-box to black-box. This spectrum is depicted in Fig. 3.

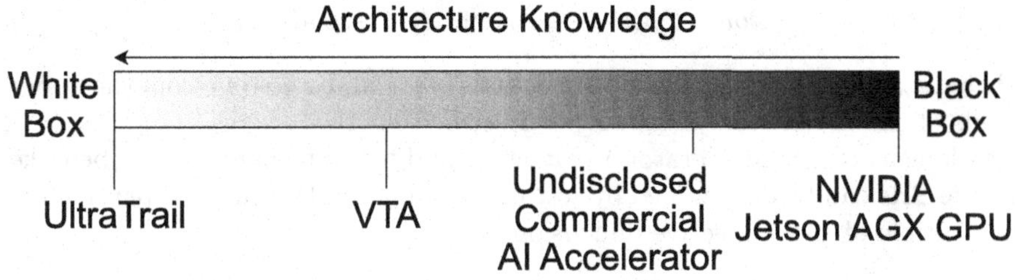

Fig. 3. Accelerator classification on the white-box to black-box spectrum.

White-box accelerators are architectures where all the needed information about how the accelerator works and DNN layers are mapped is publicly available so that the execution time behavior of the architecture can be derived, for instance from the number of processing elements (PEs) in each dimension and how the layer is unrolled onto the architecture.

At the other end of the spectrum are the **black-box accelerators**. For those architectures, almost no information is available and therefore, an execution time behavior cannot be determined without measurements.

When some information about the AI accelerator architecture is available, but not enough to accurately determine the execution time behavior, we speak of **gray-box accelerators**. For this category, it is necessary to use the available information to guide the selection of benchmarks that will help to either confirm the expected PRs or to determine the execution time behavior from which the PRs will be identified. Depending on the category, the accelerator belongs to, the process of finding the PRs differs:

As stated above, for **white-box accelerators**, all the necessary information is available, and the PRs can be determined from it. To illustrate this, we use the UltraTrail accelerator by Bernardo et al. [1] as an example. In the standard configuration, it only supports 1D-Convolutions:

$$Conv1D(C, C_w, K, F, s, pad) \tag{1}$$

with input channels C, input feature width C_w, output channels K, kernel size F, stride s and padding pad. In [1], the UltraTrail accelerator is described in detail so that it is possible to determine the hardware and mapping characteristics:

```
operation: Conv1D
operation_params: [C, C_w, K, F, s, pad]
dims: [8, 8]
mapping: [C, K]
```

This hardware and mapping description specifies that the parameters C and K of the Conv1D layer are mapped and unrolled on the two spatial dimensions of the UltraTrail accelerator, each with a size of eight. From this information, the PRs can be determined as:

$$Conv1D_R(x_C \cdot 8, C_w, x_K \cdot 8, F, s, pad) \tag{2}$$

with $x_C, x_K \in \{1, 2, ..., 7\}$. The upper bounds of x_C and x_K stem from the upper bounds of the parameters C and K as described in [1].

As long as the AI accelerator architecture and mapping can be described like this, the PRs can be determined by setting the values of the unrolled parameters to a multiple of the respective dimensions.

In the category of **black-box accelerators**, we have AI accelerator architectures, for which there is almost no information available. Therefore, the PRs can only be determined from measurements. To illustrate this, we look at the NVIDIA Jetson AGX Xavier GPU. E.g. we do not know how the TensorRT[1] backend maps the Convolution layer

$$Conv2D(C, C_h, C_w, K, F_h, F_w, s, pad) \tag{3}$$

with input channels C, input feature height C_h and width C_w, output channels K, kernel height F_h and width F_w, stride s and padding pad onto the Jetson AGX Xavier GPU. Therefore, we need to perform initial sweep benchmarks over the parameters $P = \{C, C_h, C_w, K, F_h = F_w\}$, that influence the execution time behavior the most. We only consider quadratic kernel sizes, as those are most commonly used in state-of-the-art DNNs.

We use the procedure described in Algorithm 1 to determine the step width $w_p \in W$ of each parameter $p \in P$ from the performed sweeps. In general, the PRs of the Conv2D layer can be determined from the step width w_p as follows:

$$\begin{aligned} Conv2D_R(&x_C \cdot w_C, x_{C_h} \cdot w_{C_h}, x_{C_w} \cdot w_{C_w}, \\ &x_K \cdot w_K, x_{F_h} \cdot w_{F_h}, x_{F_w} \cdot w_{F_w}, s, pad) \end{aligned} \tag{4}$$

where $x_p \in \mathbb{N}$ are the factors which determine each step (as an integer multiple of the step width). x_p might have an upper bound depending on the capabilities of the AI accelerator. If Algorithm 1 detects a linear influence of a parameter, it sets the step width $w_p = 1$. The described procedure works analogously for other layer types as well.

Although we performed parameter sweeps on the NVIDIA Jetson AGX GPU for Fully-Connected, Pooling, and activation layers as well, only the following layers exhibited a non-linear execution time behavior from which the following PRs could be determined:

- $Conv2D_R(x_C \cdot 8, x_{C_h} \cdot 8, x_{C_w} \cdot 16, x_K \cdot 32, F_h, F_w, s, pad)$ with $F_h = F_w \geq 3$
- $PointwiseConv2D_R(x_C \cdot 8, x_{C_h} \cdot 4, x_{C_w} \cdot 4, x_K \cdot 32, F_h = F_w = 1, s, pad)$
- $DepthwiseConv2D_R(x_C \cdot 8, C_h, C_w, K = 1, F_h, F_w)$ with input channels C, input height and width C_h and C_w, depthwise multiplier K and $F_h = F_w \geq 3$

[1] https://developer.nvidia.com/tensorrt, last accessed 03/26/2024.

Algorithm 1 Determine PRs from DNN layer parameter sweeps.

```
Require: S : P → (x, y) ← Sweep measurements over relevant layer parameters P,
         threshold_linear : ℝ+
function TestLinearBehavior(x, y, threshold_linear)
    y_min ← min(y), y_max ← max(y)            ▷ Get min and max of the values in y
    x_min ← min(x), x_max ← max(x)            ▷ Get min and max of the values in x
    slope_avg ← (y_max − y_min)/(x_max − x_min)   ▷ Compute average slope over the sweep measurements
    ŷ ← slope_avg · x + x_min                 ▷ Linear erstimation of the execution time behavior
    rmse ← RMSE(y, ŷ)                         ▷ RMSE between measured and linear estimation
    if rmse < threshold_linear then
        return True                           ▷ Parameter has linear influence on execution time
    else
        return False
function ExecutionTimeDelta(y)
    deltas ← [ ]
    for all y_i, y_{i+1} ∈ y do               ▷ Pairs of consecutive data points
        deltas.append(y_{i+1} − y_i)
    return deltas
W : P → ℕ          ▷ Step widths with which the parameters influence the execution time
for all p, (x, y) ∈ S do ▷ Layer parameter p with corresponding sweep over values x and measured execution time y
    if TestLinearBehavior(x, y, threshold_linear) then
        W[p] ← 1
    else
        deltas ← ExecutionTimeDelta(y)
        indices ← FindPeaks(deltas)           ▷ E.g. scipy.signal.find_peaks()
        w_p ← PeakDistance(indices)           ▷ Distance between peaks is the step width
        W[p] ← w_p
return W
```

Gray-box accelerators is the category that falls in between the two extremes, for which we provide two example AI accelerator architectures. The first one is an undisclosed commercial AI accelerator, for which the vendor provided us with a timing simulator under a non-disclosure agreement. We determined the execution time behavior by running initial sweep benchmarks and used Algorithm 1 to find the step widths. We found a non-linear execution time behavior for the following layers, resulting in the PRs:

- $Conv2D_R(C, x_{C_h} \cdot 8, x_{C_w} \cdot 8, x_K \cdot 16, F_h, F_w, s, pad)$
- $DepthwiseConv2D_R(C, x_{C_h} \cdot 8, x_{C_w} \cdot 8, K = 1, F_h, F_w)$ with input channels C, input height C_h, input width C_w, depthwise multiplier K and $F_h = F_w \geq 3$
- $FullyConnected_R(1, in, x_{out} \cdot 64)$ with inputs in and outputs out
- $AveragePool2D_R(C, x_{C_h} \cdot 8, x_{C_w} \cdot 8, F)$ with input channels C, input height, C_h, input width C_w, and pooling kernel size F

From the information that is available to us, we additionally know that this AI accelerator contains two separate functional units (FU). One optimized for big Convolution and Fully-Connected operations and one for different activation functions, Max- and Average-Pooling, and smaller Convolutions. These FUs can execute consecutive layers in a DNN in an overlapping fashion. We therefore constructed multi-layer benchmarks, similar to those in [11], to verify this specific behavior. This information is used to improve multi-layer and whole DNN estimations.

The second example is the Versatile Tensor Accelerator (VTA) [9] that is part of the Apache TVM project[2]. In this case, an expert could theoretically

[2] https://tvm.apache.org/, last accessed 03/26/2024.

retrieve all the required information from the open-source Chisel implementation. But most of the time, working with only semi-detailed information is necessary due to practical limitations. To illustrate our methodology, we assume that we only know the following about VTA: The supported operations are 2D-Convolution, general matrix multiplication (GeMM), Fully-Connected, and element-wise matrix operations. In the used configuration of the VTA hardware, the GeMM core can compute a $(1,16) \times (16,16)$ matrix-matrix multiplication per cycle. Furthermore, the documentation suggests that for a multiplication of matrices A and B, the columns of A, as well as the columns of B have to be an integer multiple of 16 or padding needs to be applied. Analogously, for the 2D-Convolution, the parameters input channels C and output channels K have to be integer multiples of 16 or again padding is necessary. To confirm these PRs, we performed sweeps for the GeMM and the 2D-Convolution operation, which revealed that the PRs are indeed:

$$Conv2D_R(x_C \cdot 16, C_h, C_w, x_K \cdot 16, F_h, F_w, s, pad) \quad \text{and} \tag{5}$$

$$FullyConnected_R(1, x_{in} \cdot 16, x_{out} \cdot 16) \tag{6}$$

3.3 Performance Estimation Using Performance Representatives

As our goal is to systematically reduce the number of benchmark points for training an estimator while still maintaining a good estimation accuracy, we use Random Forest Regression to build the estimator as they have been shown to be very accurate for DNN execution time estimation as described in [11,13] but other machine learning methods would also have been applicable [2].

After determining the PRs of an accelerator, we perform measurements using only data points from the set of PRs. Most of the time, even this constrained set of layer configurations is too large to be benchmarked completely. E.g. the set of PRs of the *Conv1D* operation supported by UltraTrail, still contains 1493520 possible configurations (the complete parameter space contains 95585280 data points). Consequently, we need to sample from the set of PRs. In this study, we explore the accuracy of our approach, without aiming for a specific target accuracy of the estimation. However, the benchmark sampling and model training could easily be used in an optimization loop until the desired estimation accuracy is achieved.

A relevant aspect to consider when using Random Forests is that this type of model cannot extrapolate, but only estimate in the range of values it has seen during training. Therefore, it is important to know for which DNN and, consequently, for which layer parameters a model should be able to make estimations and ensure that the range of benchmark points covers the area of interest.

Single-Layer Execution Time Estimation. When it comes to making an estimation for a layer, we first map the layer configuration in question to the corresponding PR by selecting the next larger integer multiple of the step width w_p for every parameter. For the *Conv2D* operation, this looks like this:

$$
\begin{aligned}
&Conv2D(C, C_h, C_w, K, F_h, F_w, s, pad) \rightarrow \\
&Conv2D_R(x_C \cdot w_C, x_{C_h} \cdot w_{C_h}, x_{C_w} \cdot w_{C_w}, \\
&\qquad x_K \cdot w_K, x_{F_h} \cdot w_{F_h}, x_{F_w} \cdot w_{F_w}, s, pad)
\end{aligned} \tag{7}
$$

$$
\text{with} \quad x_p = \left\lceil \frac{p}{w_p} \right\rceil \text{for } p \in P. \tag{8}
$$

We then make the estimation for this representative layer configuration. Note that for all parameters which have a linear influence on the execution time behavior the step width is $w_p = 1$ and, therefore, $x_p = p$ for $p \in P$.

This approach is effective because for the observed step-wise execution time behavior of the accelerators in question, all configurations within the same step exhibit very similar execution times.

Multi-layer and Network Execution Time Estimation. To be able to make execution time estimations for whole DNNs, we opted to take a similar approach to [11] and [13]. The authors of ANNETTE use two different types of so called 'multi-layer benchmarks' to capture layer fusion, while Zhang et al. call a set of operators that are typically fused during model deployment an 'execution kernel'. When estimating whole DNNs in both papers, the authors search for those subgraphs in the complete model graph, make estimations for the subgraphs and sum the individual estimated execution times.

We also use the most common building blocks of DNNs for which we want to make an estimation as multi-layer benchmarks. As those building blocks typically contain a type of Convolution (Conv2D, DepthwiseConv2D, PointwiseConv2D), we will again sample from the corresponding set of PRs to determine the parameters of the Convolution, select the resulting shapes of the remaining layers in the building block and carry out our benchmarks. These measurements are then used to determine how the runtime of a complete building-block behaves compared to the sum of individual execution times of the contained layers.

In the estimation phase for a whole DNN we, firstly, determine which building blocks are contained in the network and the layers and parameters inside the building block. Secondly, we map the configuration of the building block's convolutional layers to the corresponding PRs as described in Eq. 7. And, thirdly, we use those PRs to make estimations for the contained layers.

Depending on the platform, the estimation for a building block can differ. For the undisclosed commercial AI accelerator with two separate FUs which can execute certain layers in parallel, we estimate the execution time t_b of a building block b as follows:

$$
t_b = \begin{cases} \max\{t_l \text{ for } l \in b\} & \text{if } b \in \{PWConv2D(DWConv2D(x)), \\ & \qquad FullyConnected(Pool(x))\} \\ \sum_{l \in b} t_l & \text{else} \end{cases} \tag{9}
$$

Note that the undisclosed commercial AI accelerator fuses all ReLU layers with the preceding layers. Therefore, ReLU layers do not need to be considered in the sum of execution times.

In the case of the NVIDIA Jetson AGX Xavier GPU, we observed that the runtime of a building block is shorter than the sum of the individual runtimes of the contained layers. Therefore, we measured about 500 configurations per building-block to determine a so called fusing factor. The individually estimated layer execution times will be summed, corrected by this fusing factor, resulting in the execution time of a building block:

$$t_b = \sum_{l \in b} t_l - f_\beta(b) \tag{10}$$

The fusing factor $f_\beta(b)$ is calculated by a linear model for each type of building block β (see multi-layer benchmarks in Sect. 4.2) according to Eq. 11. The weights w_β and c_β are fitted to the measured multi-layer benchmarks. $\#ops(b)$ denotes the total number of operations in a block b.

$$f_\beta(b) = \#ops(b) \cdot w_\beta + c_\beta \tag{11}$$

The execution time of the whole DNN is the sum of the contained building blocks' execution times:

$$t_{DNN} = \sum_{b \in B} t_b \tag{12}$$

For DNN layers where we did not observe a step-wise execution time behavior, we sample up to 9 000 data points and use these data points to train a Random Forest model for usage in the estimation of a building block's execution time.

4 Evaluation

We evaluate our methodology for reducing the number of samples needed for training statistical estimation models for the UltraTrail accelerator (white-box), the VTA accelerator (gray-box), the undisclosed commercial AI accelerator (gray-box), and the NVIDIA Jetson AGX GPU (black-box).

4.1 Experimental Setup

We use the open-source tool ANNETTE[3] for generating single-layer and multi-layer benchmarks, which we extended to use PyTorch instead of TensorFlow models. These models are then deployed to the different platforms using different backends. For UltraTrail we use the custom C-interface of the accelerator together with the RTL simulation. As VTA is part of the Apache TVM (version 0.15.0-dev0) project, we use TVM to deploy our models on the accelerator and the Verilator RTL simulation to determine the execution time. The measurements for the undisclosed commercial AI accelerator are performed using the timing simulator provided by the vendor. Lastly, for deployment on the NVIDIA Jetson AGX Xavier GPU running CUDA 11.4, we also use TVM with the TensorRT 8.5.2 backend and record the execution times reported by TVM.

[3] https://github.com/embedded-machine-learning/annette, last accessed 03/26/2024.

4.2 Benchmarks

As the NVIDIA Jetson AGX Xavier GPU and the undisclosed commercial AI accelerator support a very broad range of operators, we ran **single-layer benchmarks** for the layers that are contained in the DNNs we use for the whole DNN evaluation. Namely, Conv2D, Depthwise Conv2D, Pointwise Conv2D, Average-Pooling, Max-Pooling, and Fully-Connected. For UltraTrail we ran the supported Conv1D and for VTA we benchmarked the two supported layers, Conv2D and Fully-Connected (via the general matrix multiplication). All benchmarks were sampled from the respective set of PRs.

As **multi-layer benchmarks** we selected recurring building-blocks of layers, which form the majority of our DNNs used for whole DNN evaluation.

- Depthwise Convolution followed by Pointwise Convolution, each followed by ReLU (also known as Depthwise Separable Convolution), as used in MobileNet [6]:

$$ReLU(PWConv2D(ReLU(DWConv2D(x))))$$

  Note that for the Jetson AGX GPU the influence of the ReLU layer on the execution time was negligible. Therefore, no dedicated estimation models were needed for ReLU on this platform.
- A block of two Convolutions with a shortcut connection followed by an element-wise addition with ReLU, as used in ResNet [5]:

$$ReLU(Add(x, Conv2D_1(ReLU(Conv2D_0(x)))))$$

- A block of two Convolutions with a shortcut connection that contains another Convolution, followed by an element-wise addition with ReLU, as used in ResNet [5]:

$$ReLU(Add(Conv2D_2(x), Conv2D_1(ReLU(Conv2D_0(x)))))$$

- A Max- or Average-Pooling layer followed by a Fully-Connected layer:

$$FullyConnected(Pool(x))$$

  The execution time behavior of Max- and Average-Pooling was identical on the undisclosed commercial AI accelerator and the Jetson AGX GPU. Therefore, a combined Pooling model could be used. This multi-layer benchmark was only performed for the undisclosed commercial AI accelerator, in order to verify the parallel execution on the two separate FUs.

4.3 Test Set and Sampling Strategy Comparison

To show that the models we build from the PRs can actually estimate the layer execution times of state-of-the-art DNNs we chose the layers from the Keras model zoo[4] to build our test set. These layer parameters have not been seen during training of our estimation models and will be used for evaluating the

[4] https://keras.io/api/applications/, last accessed 03/26/2024.

estimation accuracy. For the UltraTrail accelerator, we use the Conv1D layers of the TC-ResNet8 [3] as our test set.

To compare our method for selecting benchmark points against an uninformed approach, we sampled different data set sizes randomly from the set of PRs and randomly from the complete parameter space. We then trained Random Forest estimation models using both sampling methods and evaluated the accuracy of the prediction using the test set. If not otherwise specified, we report the mean absolute percentage error (MAPE) of the estimation over all the test set layers. An overview of the results is depicted in Table 1 as well as the mean measurement time of a single benchmark point on the different platforms. In case of the NVIDIA Jetson AGX Xavier GPU we performed each measurement 500 times and used the median in order to mitigate the influence of the first few slower runs, which were due to setup overhead. As the other measurements were performed using simulators, there was no need to perform multiple runs of the same benchmark point.

Table 1. Overview of the dataset size and RMSPE for the best MAPE results for all AI accelerators and layer types for which the PR sampling and mapping was applied. The last column shows the mean measurement time of a single benchmark point for the different platforms. For the Jetson AGX we performed 500 runs for each benchmark.

AI Accelerator	Layer Type	Dataset Size	RMSPE	MAPE	Mean Meas. Time [s]
UltraTrail	Conv1D	9000	0.51%	0.33%	0.38 ($SD = 0.07$)
VTA	Conv2D	8000	4.49%	7.09%	220.74 ($SD = 549.60$)
	Fully-Connected	9000	0.44%	0.02%	2.21 ($SD = 1.65$)
Undisclosed Commercial AI Accelerator	Conv2D	9000	9.93%	7.35%	5.34 ($SD = 0.36$)
	Depthwise Conv2D	4000	11.59%	3.44%	5.29 ($SD = 0.22$)
	Fully-Connected	5000	0.34%	0.35%	5.36 ($SD = 0.12$)
	2D Average Pooling	4000	6.09%	2.09%	5.29 ($SD = 0.05$)
NVIDIA Jetson AGX GPU	Conv2D	8000	27.06%	13.13%	47.59 ($SD = 13.29$)
	Pointwise Conv2D	9000	29.99%	13.84%	46.00 ($SD = 11.22$)
	Depthwise Conv2D	9000	11.43%	7.37%	65.12 ($SD = 40.65$)

4.4 UltraTrail (White-Box)

Figure 4 shows how the estimation accuracy develops when using different amounts of training data. In this case, sampling a dataset of only 9 000 layers from the set of PRs, yields an excellent MAPE of only 0.33%. This stems from the fact that the execution time behavior of the UltraTrail accelerator is extremely regular and the measurements of the RTL simulation do not contain any noise. Training the estimation model with the same amount of randomly sampled data points only reaches an accuracy of 10.98%.

We do not present whole DNN estimations for UltraTrail because the execution time of multiple layers is the sum of the single layer execution times [1].

4.5 VTA (Gray-Box)

Looking at the results of VTA, one of the gray-box accelerators, in Fig. 5 one can clearly see that our approach achieves a lower MAPE for the execution time

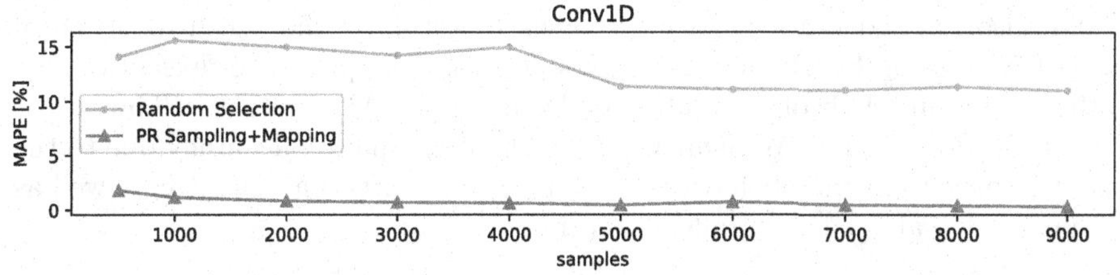

Fig. 4. Comparison of the estimation accuracy when sampling from the set of PRs vs. random sampling from the complete parameter space for the Conv1D layer on the UltraTrail accelerator.

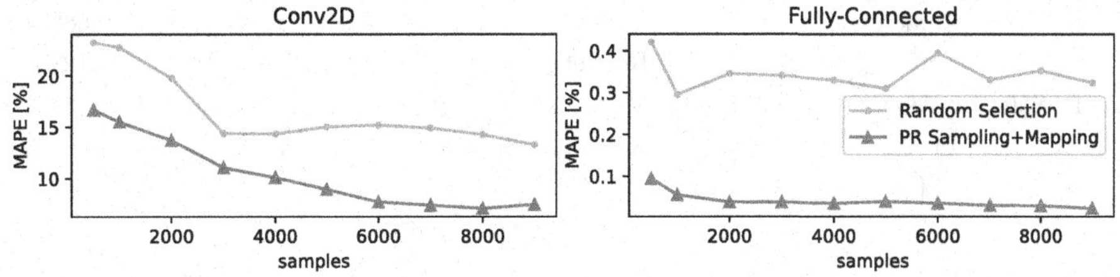

Fig. 5. Comparison of the estimation accuracy when sampling from the set of PRs vs. random sampling from the complete parameter space for the Conv2D and Fully-Connected layer on the VTA accelerator.

estimation of Conv2D and Fully-Connected layers compared to random sampling from the complete set of layer parameters. For this accelerator, we achieved our top result for the Conv2D layer of only 7.09% MAPE and the Fully-Connected layer of only 0.02% MAPE.

4.6 Undisclosed Commercial AI Accelerator (Gray-Box)

When comparing PR sampling and mapping against random sampling in Fig. 6, one can again see that our method results in a better estimation accuracy overall, but additionally the MAPE decreases much faster when increasing the training dataset size. Only for the Fully-Connected layer, our method does not outperform the random selection. But as we can see, the MAPE is always below 1%, meaning that the execution time of the Fully-Connected layer is straightforward to estimate even with very few training samples.

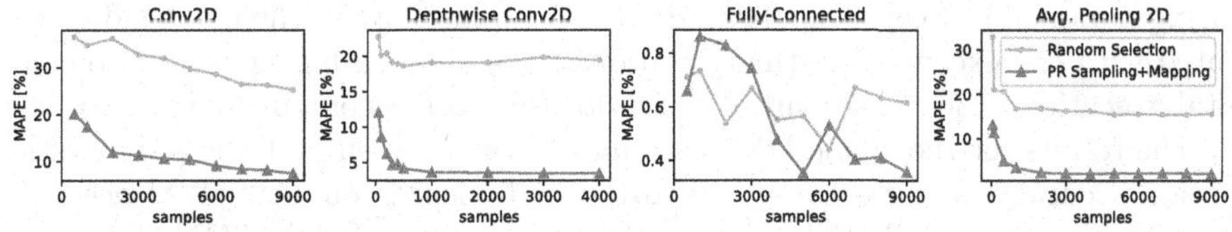

Fig. 6. Comparison of the estimation accuracy when sampling from the set of PRs vs. random sampling from the complete parameter space for different layers on the undisclosed commercial AI accelerator.

We also applied our estimation models to estimate the execution time of whole DNNs using Eqs. 9 and 12 to account for overlapping layer execution due to the two distinct FUs of the undisclosed commercial AI accelerator. The results are displayed in Table 2. We achieve an excellent estimation accuracy due to the step-wise execution time behavior of several layers on this accelerator as well as our knowledge about the parallel execution.

Table 2. Whole DNN estimation results for the undisclosed commercial AI accelerator and the NVIDIA Jetson AGX Xavier GPU.

AI Accelerator	DNN	Meas. time [ms]	Est. time [ms]	% Error
Undisclosed Commercial AI Accelerator	MobileNet [6]	2.95	2.93	0.68%
	ResNet18 [5]	4.88	4.63	5.12%
NVIDIA Jetson AGX GPU	MobileNet [6]	1.79	2.14	19.55%
	ResNet18 [5]	2.90	3.47	19.66%

4.7 NVIDIA Jetson AGX Xavier GPU (Black-Box)

The NVIDIA Jetson AGX Xavier GPU is not a highly specialized accelerator, but an embedded GPU. We still wanted to show that our approach can be used with this kind of computing device.

In Fig. 7 we see the MAPE of the single-layer estimations using PR sampling and mapping, and random sampling from the complete parameter space. The estimation accuracy is generally worse for the AGX Xavier GPU compared to the other AI accelerators, which can be explained by the fact that for this black-box accelerator we have almost no information to guide the sweep benchmarks or the selection of the PRs. Moreover, the complexity of an embedded GPU is generally higher than for specialized accelerators. Still, for Conv2D our approach yields better results compared to random sampling from such a small training dataset. For the Pointwise Conv2D and the Depthwise Conv2D our approach does not outperform the random selection.

This can be attributed to the fact that only one parameter (input channels C) has a step-wise influence on the execution time behavior of the Depthwise Conv2D, resulting in a set of PRs that is similar to the complete set of layer configurations. For the Pointwise Conv2D this can be explained by the overall very short execution times of this layer type (longest observed execution time during parameter sweeps was 0.28 ms). For such fast layers, the overhead associated with the execution of the operations amounts to a bigger portion of the total execution time, while our approach focuses on the computational part.

The results for the whole DNN estimations can be seen in Table 2. The estimation accuracy is worse compared to the undisclosed commercial AI accelerator. This can be attributed again to the fact that the Jetson AGX GPU is a black-box accelerator, for which we have almost no information, especially when it comes to how multiple layers are mapped onto the GPU architecture together.

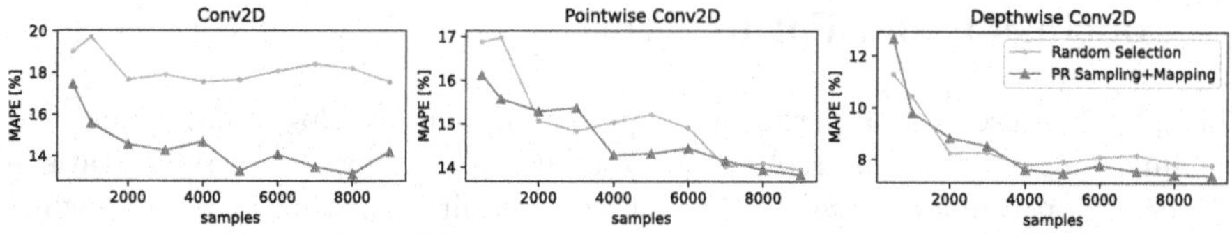

Fig. 7. Comparison of the estimation accuracy when sampling from the set of PRs vs. random sampling from the complete parameter space for different layers on the NVIDIA Jetson AGX Xavier GPU.

4.8 Comparison to State-of-the-Art

A comparison to other state-of-the-art (SOTA) execution time estimation approaches is presented in Table 3. If not otherwise stated, it shows the literature reported RMSPE and MAPE values of the approaches presented in Sect. 2 Related Work. Note that often only one of the metrics is available. Our approach has comparable accuracy to the other SOTA methods, while needing much fewer training samples, especially compared to the best approach for estimating execution time on the NVIDIA Jetson AGX Xavier GPU by Bouzidi et al. [2] who used approximately 200 000 whole DNN benchmarks for training their estimator.

Table 3. Comparison with SOTA execution time estimation methods.

Work	Type	Platform	Dataset Size	RMSPE	MAPE
ANNETTE [11]	Conv2D Layer	NCS2	35 000 per platform	42.60%	15.57%
		ZCU102		10.55%	12.71%
	Whole DNN	NCS2	36 570	–	7.44%
		ZCU102	37 812	–	3.47%
Blackthorn [7]	Conv2D Layer	Jetson Nano	15 000 per platform	5.89%	–
		Jetson TX2		6.10%	–
	Whole DNN	Jetson Nano	no multi-layer models	1.71%[a]	2.95%[a]
		Jetson TX2		3.06%[a]	4.29%[a]
Bouzidi et al. [2]	Whole DNN	Jetson AGX	~200 000 DNNs per platform	–	7.67%
		Jetson TX2		–	8.37%
nn-Meter [13]	Whole DNN	Cortex-A76	15 824[b]	2.76–5.54%[c]	–
		Adreno 640	14 040[b]	1.35–5.32%[c]	–
		NCS2	39 968[b]	4.26–22.25%[c]	–
This	Conv2D Layer	Undisclosed	9000	9.93%	7.35%
		Jetson AGX	8000	27.06%	13.13%
	Whole DNN	Undisclosed	max. 9000[d] + max. 500[e]	4.53%	2.90%
		Jetson AGX		20.17%	19.60%

[a]values were computed from the reported times, [b]size of the dataset for the Conv+bn+relu execution kernel, [c]the authors reported RMSPE separately for each DNN, [d]per layer type, [e]per building-block for the fusing factor on the AGX

5 Conclusion and Future Work

This paper presented a performance modeling methodology and associated benchmarking strategy to reduce the number of training samples for statistical performance models, and thus reduce the required measurement time while maintaining comparable estimation accuracy to state-of-the-art estimators. We leverage knowledge about the AI accelerator architecture and mapping to determine Performance Representatives (PR) algorithmically for the benchmarking and, later, estimation phase. We evaluated our approach for four different AI accelerators and, depending on the available hardware architecture knowledge, achieved an execution time estimation MAPE between 0.02–13.84% for single-layers and 2.90–19.60% for whole DNNs.

As future work, we plan to use the PRs of an AI accelerator as a search space constraint in hardware-aware NAS and to extend the PRs to additionally include the memory characteristics of the AI accelerator.

Acknowledgments. This work has been funded by the German Federal Ministry of Education and Research (BMBF) under grant number 16ES0876 (GENIAL!).

Disclosure of Interests. The authors have no competing interests to declare that are relevant to the content of this article.

References

1. Bernardo, P.P., Gerum, C., Frischknecht, A., Lübeck, K., Bringmann, O.: Ultra-Trail: a configurable ultralow-power TC-ResNet AI accelerator for efficient keyword spotting. IEEE Trans. Comput. Aided Des. Integr. Circuits Syst. **39**(11), 4240–4251 (2020)
2. Bouzidi, H., Ouarnoughi, H., Niar, S., Cadi, A.A.E.: Performance prediction for convolutional neural networks on edge GPUs. In: Proceedings of the 18th ACM International Conference on Computing Frontiers, CF 2021. ACM, May 2021
3. Choi, S., et al.: Temporal convolution for real-time keyword spotting on mobile devices (2019)
4. Gerum, C., Frischknecht, A., Hald, T., Bernardo, P.P., Lübeck, K., Bringmann, O.: Hardware accelerator and neural network co-optimization for ultra-low-power audio processing devices. In: 2022 25th Euromicro Conference on Digital System Design (DSD). IEEE, August 2022
5. He, K., Zhang, X., Ren, S., Sun, J.: Deep residual learning for image recognition (2015)
6. Howard, A.G., et al.: MobileNets: efficient convolutional neural networks for mobile vision applications (2017)
7. Lechner, M., Jantsch, A.: Blackthorn: latency estimation framework for CNNs on embedded Nvidia platforms. IEEE Access **9**, 110074–110084 (2021)
8. Lübeck, K., Jung, A.L.F., Wedlich, F., Bringmann, O.: Work-in-progress: ultra-fast yet accurate performance prediction for deep neural network accelerators. In: 2022 International Conference on Compilers, Architecture, and Synthesis for Embedded Systems (CASES). IEEE, October 2022

9. Moreau, T., et al.: A hardware-software blueprint for flexible deep learning specialization (2019)
10. Parashar, A., et al.: Timeloop: a systematic approach to DNN accelerator evaluation. In: 2019 IEEE International Symposium on Performance Analysis of Systems and Software (ISPASS). IEEE, March 2019
11. Wess, M., Ivanov, M., Unger, C., Nookala, A., Wendt, A., Jantsch, A.: ANNETTE: accurate neural network execution time estimation with stacked models. IEEE Access **9**, 3545–3556 (2021)
12. Williams, S., Waterman, A., Patterson, D.: Roofline: an insightful visual performance model for multicore architectures. Commun. ACM **52**(4), 65–76 (2009)
13. Zhang, L.L., et al.: nn-Meter: towards accurate latency prediction of deep-learning model inference on diverse edge devices. In: Proceedings of the 19th Annual International Conference on Mobile Systems, Applications, and Services, MobiSys 2021. ACM, June 2021

Travel Time-Based Task Mapping for NoC-Based DNN Accelerator

Yizhi Chen, Wenyao Zhu, and Zhonghai Lu(✉)

KTH Royal Institute of Technology, Stockholm, Sweden
{yizhic,wenyao,zhonghai}@kth.se

Abstract. Network-on-Chip (NoC) based architectures are recently proposed to accelerate deep neural networks in specialized hardware. Given that the hardware configuration is fixed post-manufacture, proper task mapping attracts researchers' interest. We propose a travel time-based task mapping method that allocates uneven counts of tasks across different Processing Elements (PEs). This approach utilizes the travel time recorded in the sampling window and implicitly makes use of static NoC architecture information and dynamic NoC congestion status. Furthermore, we examine the effectiveness of our method under various configurations, including different mapping iterations, flit sizes, and NoC architectures. Our method achieves up to 12.1% improvement compared with even mapping and static distance mapping for one layer. For a complete NN example, our method achieves 10.37% and 13.75% overall improvements to row-major mapping and distance-based mapping, respectively. While ideal travel time-based mapping (post-run) achieves 10.37% overall improvements to row-major mapping, we adopt a sampling window to efficiently map tasks during the running, achieving 8.17% (sampling window 10) improvement.

Keywords: Task mapping · DNN accelerator · Network-on-Chip

1 Introduction

Deep Neural Networks (DNNs) have emerged as one of the hottest topics in both academic and industry circles [10,21]. Due to the high computational complexity of DNN, hardware acceleration abstracts significant interest among researchers.

Notably, Network-on-Chip-based (NoC-based) accelerators [18,22] offer a balance between performance and flexibility, establishing a new paradigm in design approaches. Furthermore, NoCs have demonstrated remarkable potential in facilitating efficient on-chip data communication for operating neural networks [21].

With the specific hardware solutions being fixed after manufacturing, the subsequent challenge is efficiently mapping a DNN layer to the NoC platform [10]. The prevalent method, even mapping in [6], distributes tasks equally across

The research has been supported in part by Vetenskapsrå(Swedish Research Council) through the LearnPower project (2020-03494).

L. Carro et al. (Eds.): SAMOS 2024, LNCS 15226, pp. 76–92, 2025.
https://doi.org/10.1007/978-3-031-78377-7_6

all available Processing Elements (PEs) in a single iteration and repeats this process until task allocation is complete. However, even mapping does not consider the variance between different PEs, such as the distance to memory, and the run-time status of the NoC, leading to an unbalanced time consumption.

Our research aims to enhance the efficiency of accelerators by mapping different numbers of tasks among PEs, due to their inherent differences and varying running status. By allocating fewer tasks to slower PEs, we aim to balance the NoC workload, minimize idle time, and thereby improve overall performance.

The contributions of our work are summarized as follows:

- We propose a travel time-based mapping strategy to unevenly distribute tasks to PEs and reduce time consumption by balancing workload in NoC-based DNN accelerators.
- We investigate the impact of different NN layers, communication protocols, and hardware platforms by analyzing the performance of a layer under various conditions of mapping iterations, packet size, and NoC architecture. Additionally, we evaluate our method on a complete DNN model, LeNet [11].
- We propose an on-the-fly travel time-based mapping with a sampling window. We discuss the influence of various sampling window lengths.

In Sect. 2, we discuss the related work. In Sect. 3, we introduce the state-of-the-art task mapping methods and then present our travel time-based mapping method in Sect. 4. In Sect. 5, we show the experimental results to validate our approach. In Sect. 6, we conclude this paper.

2 Related Work

Strategically placing application tasks on processing cores has emerged as a crucial component in the design of NoC-based MPSoCs (Multi-processor System-on-Chip) for optimal performance [2]. Many works focus on non-DNN tasks including Best Neighbor mapping [4] for MPEG-4 and multiwindow display (MWD) tasks, [19] for synthetic traffic and MPEG-4 applications, L-shape isolated (Liso) mapping [17] for PARSEC and SPLASH-2 benchmarks. The mapping of such applications and benchmarks usually needs to consider diverse task dependencies, which leads to non-regular traffic patterns in NoC.

DNNs mapping deals with significantly different data traffic patterns from that in conventional MPSoCs [12]. GAMMA [9] introduces a specialized genetic algorithm performing a search in the massive mapping space. Autonomous Optimal Mapping Exploration (AOME) [21] leverages two reinforcement learning algorithms to efficiently explore optimal hardware mapping. ZigZag [13] extends the normal design space exploitation by introducing uneven mapping opportunities. These methodologies, prioritizing the exploration, are time-consuming.

Dense mapping [5] incorporates an input-sharing mechanism to reuse input data, thereby conserving resources. Similarly, Neu-NoC [12] aims to minimize redundant data traffic within neuromorphic acceleration systems and improve data transfer capabilities between adjacent layers. Configuring their nodes to transmit data to other computation nodes executing adjacent layers instead of directly to memory nodes makes the hardware complex. [16] uses integer linear programming to map the DNN layer, but it still maps the tasks evenly.

Load balancing, aiming to ensure equitable utilization in NoC, could be used for DNN tasks. [14] develop a static weight redistribution method for graph neural network inference using a PE array. Their approach focuses on maximizing the reuse of cached data. Work-stealing [3] is a dynamic load-balancing strategy that allows idle PEs in the network to actively seek tasks from busier PEs to optimize resource utilization and improve overall performance. Girao *et al.* [7] explores work-stealing mapping policies to determine whether a task migration between the cores should take place. It is flexible but frequently collecting the real-time workload status from other PEs is a large overhead for DNN tasks. Time-based partitioning is also introduced in [18], but it only considers communication latency and requires an initial execution. Additionally, it does not explore the effects of varying configurations on the partitioning.

Our method leverages travel time within a sampling window to unevenly distribute DNN tasks. It effectively balances the workload using a simple control algorithm and does not require an extra run.

3 Task Mapping Methods

3.1 DNN Tasks and Mapping to NoC

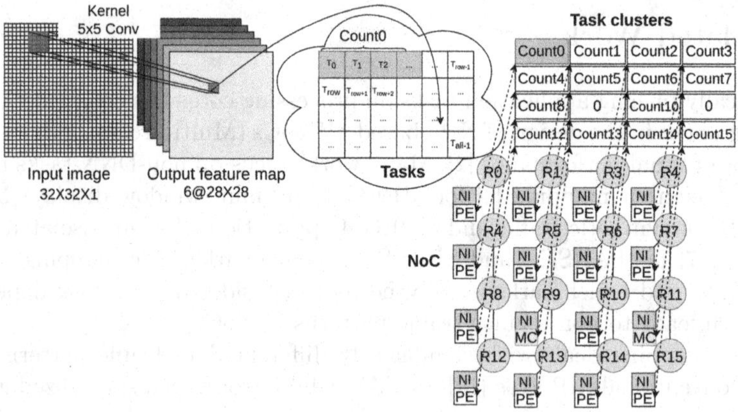

Fig. 1. Tasks mapping

We introduce the tasks to be mapped from a DNN model on the left side of Fig. 1, using the first layer of LeNet as an example. This layer processes a 32×32 padded input image through a 5×5 kernel convolution. This convolution operation constitutes a computation task and yields a pixel in the output feature map.

Mapping to NoC involves assigning these computation tasks in the cloud-shaped area in Fig. 1 to specific hardware resources. While a 4×4 NoC serves as an example, mapping is to allocate tasks to 16 clusters. For example, the first cluster on the right side, highlighted in blue, contains *Count*0 tasks, correspondingly color-coded in blue among all tasks within the cloud-shaped figure. Memory controller (MC) nodes are not assigned any tasks as they contain MCs rather than PEs.

3.2 Even Task Mapping

DNN tiling strategies generally allocate an equal amount of work to each available resource, until the final mapping iteration for tail tasks, where the remaining tasks may be not enough for all PEs. Allocating tasks to the entire NoC at once constitutes one mapping iteration.

We present the row-major strategy in Fig. 2. The left side shows $Count_{\text{even}} \times$ PENum green tasks, which constitute the main portion, along with the tail tasks. These tasks are evenly mapped across the PEs following the row order.

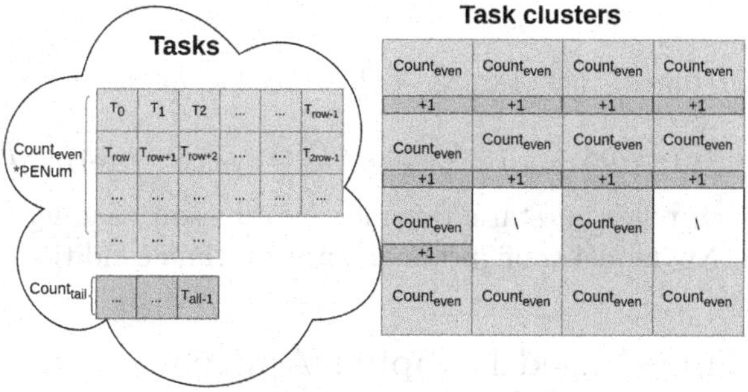

Fig. 2. Even mapping

However, even mapping lacks sensitivity to crucial information such as NoC architecture, and the real-time status of network congestion.

3.3 Distance-Based Task Mapping

To utilize the NoC architecture information, we explore the mapping according to different distances to memory nodes. A node is categorized as "distance 1" if it directly surrounds an MC node, as shown in Fig. 3. Similarly, nodes further from the MC are classified as "distance 2" and "distance 3" and colored.

Inspired by longer distances leading to longer time consumption, we distribute fewer tasks to far nodes as shown in Eq. (1). The total number of tasks is calculated by multiplying the number of nodes by the task count per node, as shown in Eq. (2). Combining Eq. (1)and Eq. (2), we can compute the task number for each node and map these tasks accordingly.

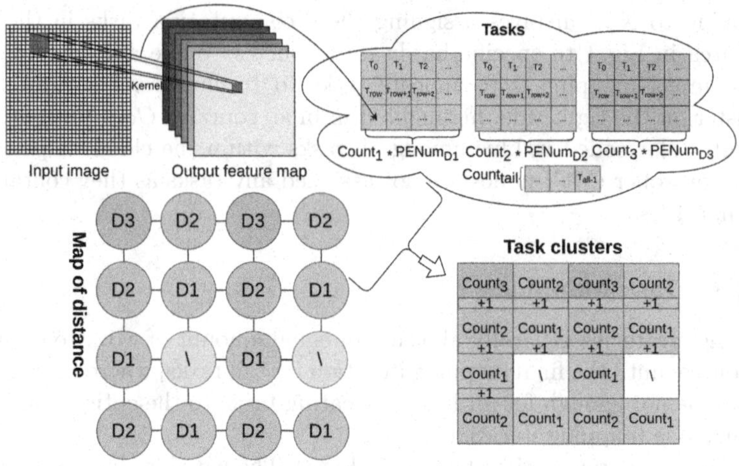

Fig. 3. Distance-based mapping

$$Task_{count1} * Distance1 = Task_{count2} * Distance2 = Task_{count3} * Distance3 \quad (1)$$

$$Task_{all} = Num_{D1} * Task_{count1} + Num_{D2} * Task_{count2} + Num_{D3} * Task_{count3} \quad (2)$$

This approach relies on static distance information, leading to fixed ratios despite varying NN model configurations and run-time conditions.

4 Travel Time-Based Mapping Approach

We propose a travel time-based mapping strategy for determining task allocation ratios in various scenarios. We explore the use of static latency, post-run recorded latency, and run-time travel time within a sampling window.

4.1 Travel Time

As shown in Fig. 4, travel time consists of different components. The first step is to send a request packet from the PE node to the MC node to gather data as the brown path in Fig. 4. This packet contains a compact payload such as the source ID and the index of the data needed, comprising only one single flit.

There is a memory access delay for complex DNN models that have high data demands. We present the time as a light yellow path in Fig. 4.

After picking up data, the MC node sends out a response packet, carrying the required inputs and weights, back to the PE node. By dividing the packet size by the bit count of a single flit, larger kernels generate packets containing more flits, leading to a longer travel time in NoC. The trajectory is tracked from

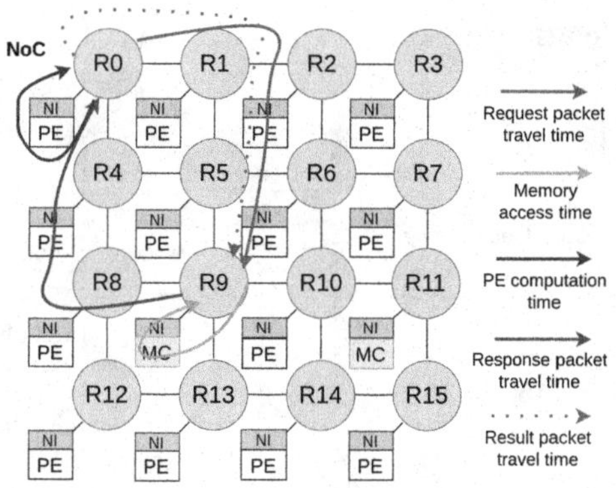

Fig. 4. Travel time in NoC

the moment the first flit leaves the MC node's NI until the last flit arrives at the requesting PE's router's VC buffer. This travel path is the purple path in Fig. 4.

Computation time for one task is obviously important and it is determined by kernel sizes which specify the required operations and the available hardware resources. Computation time, the dark green path in Fig. 4, varies across different layers due to different kernel sizes but is constant in the same layer.

The last step is to deliver the result packet to MC. PE will generate the next request packet while previous results are on the way. To highlight the feature of this overlap and avoid counting this overlapped travel time twice, we plot the result packet travel path by a dotted line.

We present the travel time used in our proposed mapping method in Eq. (3). The NoC congestion status is not directly but implicitly included in T_{req} and T_{resp}.

$$T_{travel} = T_{req} + T_{memaccess} + T_{resp} + T_{compu} \tag{3}$$

4.2 Travel Time-Based Task Mapping

Ideally, the overall latency is balanced by allocating different task counts in Eq. (4). The overall task count is shown in Eq. (5). By solving solve Eq. (5) and Eq. (4), we compute the task counts for the corresponding task cluster. Travel time-based mapping shown in Fig. 5 is to allocate task clusters according to different PEs.

$$Task_{count1} * T_{travel1} = Task_{count2} * T_{travel2} = ... = Task_{countN} * T_{travelN} \tag{4}$$

$$Task_{all} = Task_{count1} + Task_{count2} + ... + Task_{countN} \tag{5}$$

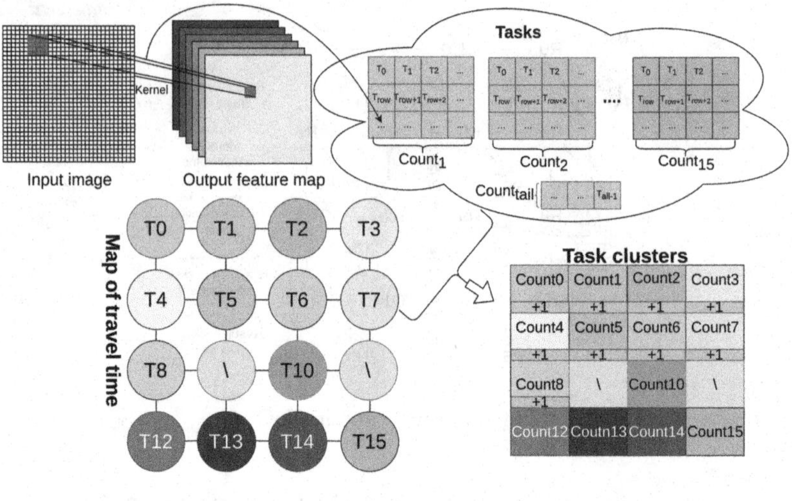

Fig. 5. Travel time-based mapping

Static-Latency-Based Task Mapping. Without running on NoC, we can compute the static latency (SL) in Eq. (6) according to static and model information. The PE computation time is derived from the workload divided by the available MAC count. The memory access time also depends on the workload and the bandwidth. By dividing the data size by bandwidth, we can compute the delay caused by memory access. Estimating time spent in NoC is challenging, but it will at least equal the product of distance and link delay. If multiple flits are involved, the latency between the head and tail flits must also be considered. Additionally, there are fixed overheads such as packetization latency.

$$T_{SL} = T_{compu} + T_{memaccess} + (D * T\_link + (FlitNum - 1) * T_{flit}) + T_{fixed} \quad (6)$$

Post-Run Travel Time-Based Mapping. Travel time is precisely recorded during a complete run, and mapping is performed afterward. This method yields accurate travel time data for use in Eq. (4), but necessitates an additional run.

Sampling Window in Travel Time-Based Mapping. To do the mapping during runtime, we propose a travel time-based mapping method utilizing a sampling window without an extra run. We divide the mapping process into two different routes in Fig. 6. The left route is for a small layer without enough samples and a row-major mapping is directly used. For a layer with enough tasks, we employ a short sampling window to estimate travel times rather than recording accurate time after one complete run. The sampling window length, *SamplingWindowLength*, determines the sampled task number for one PE. After sampling, we recorded travel time and computed the task number to be allocated for each node.

This travel time obtained is not the precise travel time used in Eq. (4), but is the sampled time, T_s, in Eq. (7). Additionally, the scope of task mapping shifts from encompassing all tasks to focusing on the residual tasks, as delineated in Eq. (8). Combining Eq. (7) and Eq. (8), we can compute the task number allocated to each PE after sampling.

$$Task_{count1} * T_{s1} = Task_{count2} * T_{s2} = ... = Task_{countN} * T_{sN} \tag{7}$$

$$(Task_{all} - Task_{sampled}) = Task_{count1} + Task_{count2} + ... + Task_{countN} \tag{8}$$

5 Experiments

The performance difference in DNN accelerators could be modeled by three main factors: NN structure, communication protocol, and hardware platform. We abstract the difference between these three parts and configure three variables separately: mapping iteration, packet size, and NoC hardware architecture.

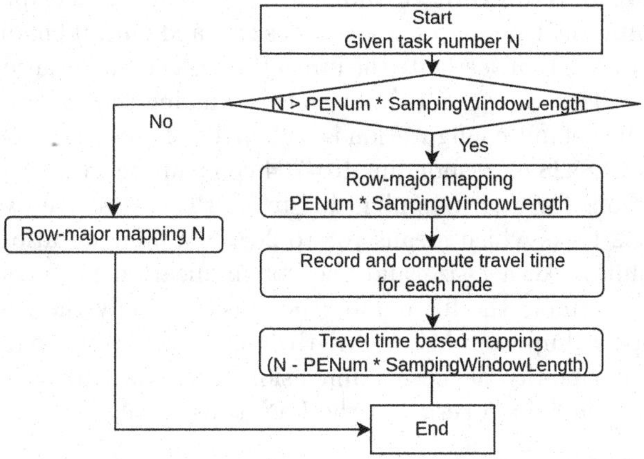

Fig. 6. Flowchart of travel time-based task mapping with sampling window

- Mapping iterations/packet number: determined by different DNN input feature map sizes, DNN output channels, and DNN kernel sizes.
- Packet size/flit number: determined by DNN kernel size and communication protocol which specifies the bits utilized by a single flit.
- NoC architecture: PE and MC nodes' varying numbers and positions.

5.1 Experiment Setup

Simulation Platform. First of all, we introduce the simulation platform, a cycle-accurate CNN-NoC accelerator simulation environment based on a behavior-level NoC simulator as outlined in [20]. The NoC consists of a VC network derived from Gem5-Garnet [1], utilizing the widely used X-Y routing algorithm. Each physical connection between routers comprises four virtual channels, with each VC containing a four-flit buffer. The NoC's operating frequency is set at 2 GHz, following the specifications in [20], while the PEs are configured to function at 200 MHz, as detailed in [8]. These configurations were selected due to their widespread acceptance in the field.

The nodes are labeled as PE nodes and MC (Memory controller) nodes, as shown in Fig. 1. Each PE contains 64 Multiply-Accumulate (MAC) units, mirroring the 64 MACs per PE configuration in the Simba [18] architecture. The computation delay is calculated by dividing the required MAC operations by 64. For example, a convolution requiring 25 MAC operations consumes one PE cycle and 128 MAC operations consume 2 PE cycles. The two nodes connected to MC have a memory bandwidth of 64 GB/s, emulating a DDR5 device [15]. One data of weight or input is one 16-bit fixed point number which is two Bytes. Hence, one data consumes $\frac{1}{32*10^9}s = 0.0625$ router cycles, and the memory access delay is determined by the data number.

Configuration for Different Scenarios. It is common that different models have varying input feature map sizes, kernel sizes, and output channels, affecting the number of tasks. To investigate the impact of task count variations, we extend the task count with ratios from 0.5x to 8x by adjusting the output channel from 3 to 48, while the default configuration is 6 (1x). The first layer of LeNet contains an output of 6 × 28x28 corresponding to 4704 convolution tasks. This means 336 mapping iterations for even mapping due to 14 PE nodes. We explore a range of 2352 to 37632 tasks which means 168 to 2688 mapping iterations.

The convolution kernel size and the communication protocol's bit-per-flit configuration determine the flit number per task. As only the response packet contains data picked up from MC nodes, the request and result packets' sizes are not impacted. We modify the kernel dimensions from 1×1 to 13×13 in **Tab.** 1, including the original 5×5 kernel in the LeNet first layer.

Table 1. Different kernel size and packet size

Input	Kernel size	Padding	Mapping iterations	Packet size in flits
28 × 28	1 × 1	0	336	1
	3 × 3	1		2
	5 × 5 (original)	2		4
	7 × 7	3		7
	9 × 9	4		11
	11 × 11	5		16
	13 × 13	6		22

Our investigation also extends to two different NoC architectures: one with two MCs and the other with four MCs.

We not only compare different methods but also evaluate the performance of our methods with different sampling windows. Unless otherwise specified, we use a sampling window of 10 in travel time-based DNN task mapping.

5.2 Experiment Results of Unevenness

Unevenness. We introduce the unevenness between task complementing time in Eq. (9). The unevenness ρ is the difference between the maximum delay by the slowest node and the minimum latency by the fastest node divided by the maximum latency. Our analysis focuses on minimizing the maximum time consumption because it, rather than average time overhead, determines the final inference time for a layer.

$$\rho = \frac{T_{max} - T_{min}}{T_{max}} \tag{9}$$

Unevenness Under Row-Major Mapping. We present the unevenness in Fig. 7a , showing the average time overhead for an end-to-end DNN task. To present the results more effectively, we arrange the results of the 14 PE nodes in an order of increasing distances. The end-to-end completion time for one DNN task ranges from 57.69 to 77.88 cycles, showing an unevenness of 25.92%.

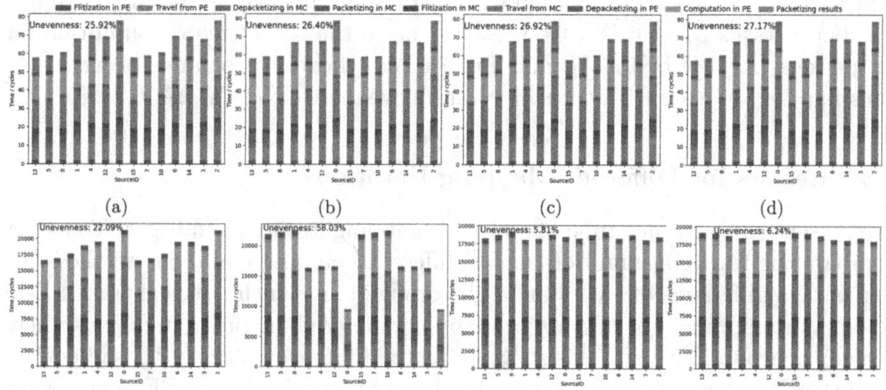

Fig. 7. Results of unevenness (a)Average results for row-major mapping (b)Average results for distance-based mapping (c)Average results for travel time-based mapping (sampling window 10) (d)Average results for travel time-based mapping (post-run) (e)Accumulated results for row-major mapping (f)Accumulated results for distance-based mapping (g)Accumulated results for travel time-based mapping (sampling window 10) (h)Accumulated results for travel time-based mapping (post-run)

Due to the overlap, we present partially accumulated time consumption in Fig. 7e, where the travel times of result packets and subsequent delays are excluded. Within the same PE, a response packet is always generated after the request packet. Although packets from different PEs may interleave within the network, they are processed sequentially within their respective PEs. Consequently, we depict them stacked in Fig. 7e. The unevenness in the partially accumulated time consumption is 22.09%, showing that the fastest PE—represented by the lowest bar in Fig. 7e—is idle for 22.09% time in this layer while the slowest PE is continuing its operation. This scenario highlights the inefficiency in resource usage and underscores the necessity for uneven mapping strategies.

Unevenness in Distance-Based Mappings. From Fig. 7b, we observe that travel time is significantly influenced by the NoC architecture, more exactly, the distances. Nodes 13, 5, and 8 are the fastest as they have only one distance, and nodes 1, 4, and 12 consume moderate time as their distances are two. Node 0 has the longest distance, three, and requires the most time. However, simply allocating the task following the ratio of distance, leads to the unevenness of 58.03% in Fig. 7f. This reveals that we need a better mapping method to set the ratio rather than simply adopting the distances as ratios.

Unevenness in Travel Time-Based Mapping The outcomes of travel time-based mapping with a sampling window of 10 tasks in Fig. 7c and post-run travel time-based mapping in Fig. 7d, also identify three stages of travel times across different PEs, which are associated with distance groups. By allocating a variable number of tasks to each PE, we nearly equalize the total time consumption for all packets per PE in Fig. 7g and Fig. 7h. We effectively balance overall time consumption on each PE and achieve an unevenness of 5.81% and 6.24%.

5.3 Results for Different Mapping Iterations

We present the inference time of different mapping iterations in Fig. 8. To better compare the time consumption across different mapping methods, we show the percentage difference of each bar to the orange bar, which is the slowest PE in row-major mapping. For row-major mapping, under all mapping iterations, there is a gap of around 21% and this shows potential to improve as one PE is idle while the other PE is working. In distance-based mapping, the fastest PE operates for a shorter duration compared to its counterpart in row-major mapping, while the slowest PE works for a longer period. This outcome illustrates the challenge and complexity of achieving effective uneven mapping.

Our proposed travel time mapping significantly narrows the gap between the low bar and high bar in the same mapping method from 21.2% to around 5%. Compared with row-major mapping, the total time consumed for processing a single layer is dominated by the slowest PE, and our method achieves notable improvement around 9.7%.

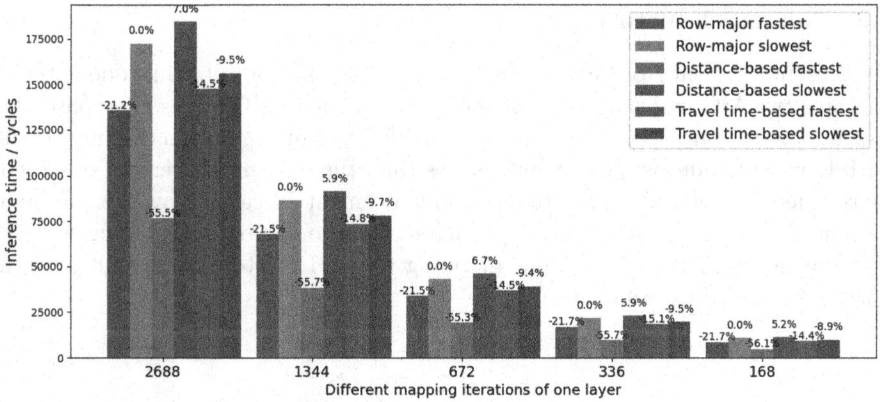

Fig. 8. Different mapping iterations

5.4 Results for Different Packet Sizes

Figure 9 reveals that unevenness exists across different packet sizes. All distance-based mapping worsens the situation by increasing the unevenness together with the final latency dominated by the slowest PE. Static-latency-based mapping achieves high performance while the flit number is small. However, as the number of flits increases, more flits are injected into the NoC, and the exclusion of congestion and queuing delays in the static latency calculations leads to decreased performance. Our proposed method enhances the latency for one single layer, reducing the time consumption of one layer up to 12.1%. This demonstrates the complexity of setting the ratio for uneven mapping and validates the effectiveness of our proposed method.

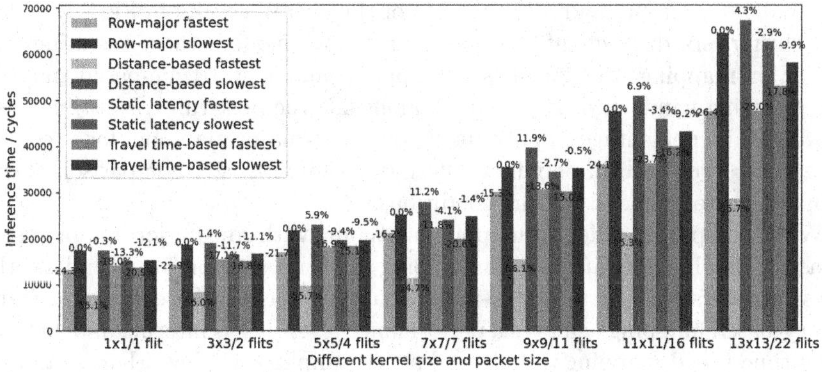

Fig. 9. Inference time for one layer with varying kernel size and packet size

5.5 NoC Architecture

We present different NoC architectures in Fig. 10a and Fig. 10b while one of them contains two MC nodes and one of them contains four MC nodes. Compared to row-major mapping, the enhancement provided by our method in configurations with four MC nodes is 5.6%, which is less than the 9.5% improvement observed in the default settings. This reduced enhancement is caused by the minimal variance in distances among nodes, which lowers the gap between the fastest PE and the slowest PE in row-major mapping from 21.7% to 9.3%, resulting in a narrower space for optimization.

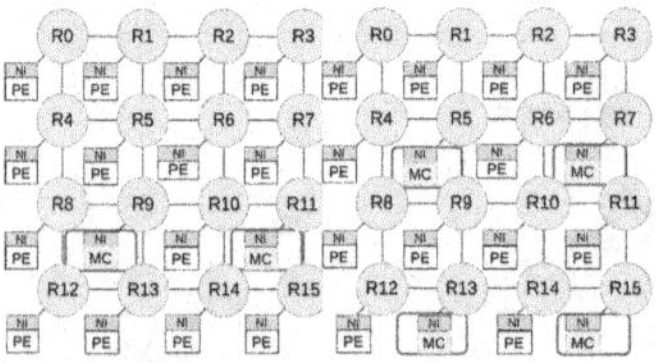

(a) 4x4 NoC with two MC nodes (b) 4x4 NoC with four MC nodes

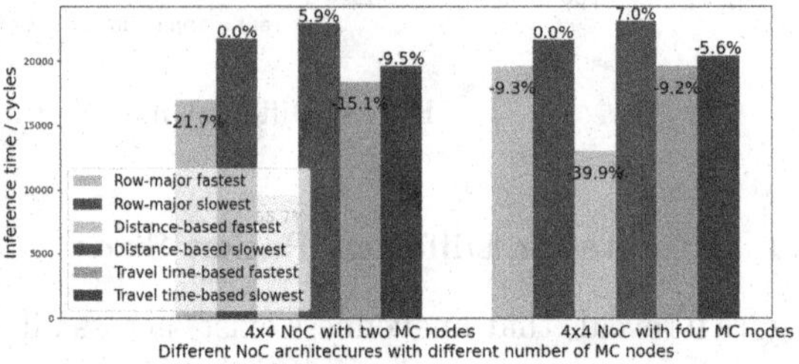

(c) Inference time under two NoC architecture

Fig. 10. Results of different NoC architectures

5.6 Experiment Results of Mapping Whole NN Model with Different Sampling Windows

We present the inference times across eight clusters, each representing one of the 7 individual layers and an aggregate of the overall results in Fig. 11. Within each cluster, six distinct inference times are documented: those resulting from row-major mapping, distance-based mapping, and travel time-based mapping with sampling windows of 1, 5, and 10, alongside the post-run travel time-based mapping. The percentage improvements over row-major mapping, for each cluster, are also presented in polylines, offering a comprehensive comparison of each mapping strategy under varying conditions.

When comparing different mapping methods, with row-major mapping serving as the baseline, distance-based mapping sometimes outperforms and at other times gets worse results than row-major mapping across different layers. Static-latency-based mapping achieves a performance level that is intermediate between travel time-based mapping of long and short sampling windows. For a sampling window of 1, performance drops are observed in layers 3, 5, and 6 due to the extremely few sampling packets. With a sampling window of 5, the performance is improved and only layer 6 shows a decrease compared to row-major mapping. It may be caused by the small packet count of 84 in layer 6; the minor loss is

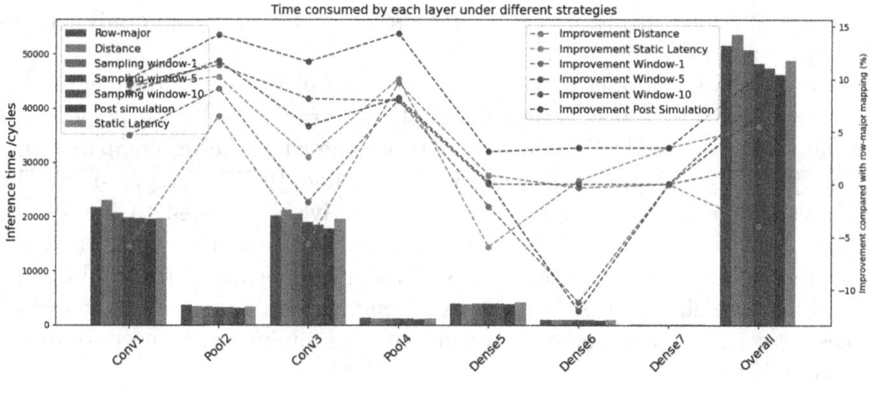

Fig. 11. Inference time for LeNet

just 105 cycles. With a longer sampling window of 10, the performance no longer worsens compared to row-major mapping in any layer.

All travel time-based mappings show improvement over row-major mapping and over distance-based mapping for the whole time consumption. With an increased sampling window length from 1 to 10, the overall improvement increases from 1.78% to 8.17%, approaching the ideal post-run travel time-based mapping of 10.37%.

5.7 Summary and Discussion

We summarize the experiment results as itemized below:

- Unevenness exists in even mapping, across various configurations including mapping iterations, packet size, and NoC architecture. Our proposed mapping consistently outperforms both row-major and distance-based mapping by dynamically determining the task ratio according to the travel time.
- A post-run travel time-based mapping invariably offers the best performance in all layers and the whole model, compared with row-major mapping, distance-based mapping, and travel time-based mapping with a sampling window. However, it needs one additional run to collect accurate travel time, resulting in extra time and energy consumption.
- Utilizing a sampling window during operation time provides sampled rather than precise travel times for mapping, eliminating the need for an extra run. Larger windows tend to offer better approximations as more samples are recorded. A sampling window of 10 offers an effective trade-off between performance and sample number, achieving an 8.17% improvement for a whole NN model, closely approaching the ideal post-run gain of 10.37%.

The superior results of post-run travel time-based mapping are derived from three main factors: 1) Enhanced accuracy as it tracks all packets rather than several samples; 2) Ability to work in smaller layers lacking sufficient tasks for sampling; 3) Unlike adjusting ratio after sampling, which benefits only leftover tasks, post-run mapping benefits all tasks.

The choice of sampling window length is crucial. For a window length of 1, the travel time has a bias compared to the accurate travel time in post-run, leading to varying final delay improvement for the whole LeNet compared with row-major mapping, from 1.78% for window 1 and 10.37% for post-run. This indicates that a too-small sample size is ineffective. Compared to the 10.37% improvement achieved by the ideal post-run outcomes, our implementation of a 10-task sampling window achieves an 8.17% improvement over row-major mapping. This high effectiveness is due to the repetitive nature of NN tasks, which makes network activities similarly predictable and minimizes the need for extensive sampling.

6 Conclusion

We have proposed a dynamic, travel time-based mapping strategy to mitigate the issue of uneven time consumption across PEs due to imbalanced task mapping, which leads to inferior performance. We compare our approach with traditional even mapping and distance-based mapping strategies. The results indicate that relying solely on the distance information is inadequate, thereby validating the significance of our method. Additionally, we examine the effects of different mapping iterations, packet sizes, and NoC architectures—factors corresponding to varying neural network models, communication protocols, and hardware platforms. Beyond collecting information from extra running, we proposed a technique for sampling travel time information during runtime and evaluated the impact of different window lengths.

The findings reveal a 22.09% unevenness in row-major mapping, which our method reduces to 5.81%. Consequently, we achieved a maximum 9.7% improvement in latency for varying mapping iterations, 12.1% for different packet sizes, and 9.7% for diverse NoC architectures. With post-run travel time-based mapping, our method obtains an enhancement of 10.37% for the whole LeNet. By implementing dynamic window lengths, we were able to estimate improvements without additional simulations, achieving 1.78%, 6.62%, and 8.17% improvements for sampling window lengths of 1, 5, and 10, respectively. This reveals that using more samples achieves a performance more similar to the ideal result with post-run.

In our future work, our proposed approach should be compared with other adaptive NoC mapping approaches to assess the power and area overheads. In addition, since wiring and thermal management will directly affect the NoC performance, their impact when applying our solution is worth investigating.

References

1. Agarwal, N., Krishna, T., Peh, L.S., Jha, N.K.: GARNET: a detailed on-chip network model inside a full-system simulator. In: 2009 IEEE International Symposium on Performance Analysis of Systems and Software, pp. 33–42. IEEE (2009)

2. Amin, W., et al.: Performance evaluation of application mapping approaches for network-on-chip designs. IEEE Access **8**, 63607–63631 (2020). https://doi.org/10.1109/ACCESS.2020.2982675
3. Blumofe, R.D., Leiserson, C.E.: Scheduling multithreaded computations by work stealing. JACM **46**(5), 720–748 (1999)
4. Carvalho, E.L.D.S., Calazans, N.L.V., Moraes, F.G.: Dynamic task mapping for MPSoCs. IEEE Des. Test Comput. **27**(5), 26–35 (2010). https://doi.org/10.1109/MDT.2010.106
5. Chen, K.C.J., Wang, C.C., Tsai, C.K., Liang, J.W.: Dynamic mapping mechanism to compute DNN models on a resource-limited NoC platform. In: 2021 International Symposium on VLSI Design, Automation and Test (VLSI-DAT), pp. 1–4 (2021). https://doi.org/10.1109/VLSI-DAT52063.2021.9427320
6. Chen, Y.H., Yang, T.J., Emer, J., Sze, V.: Eyeriss v2: a flexible accelerator for emerging deep neural networks on mobile devices. IEEE J. Emerg. Sel. Top. Cir. Syst. **9**(2), 292–308 (2019)
7. Girão, G., Santini, T., Wagner, F.R.: Exploring resource mapping policies for dynamic clustering on NoC-based MPSoCs. In: 2013 Design, Automation & Test in Europe Conference & Exhibition (DATE), pp. 681–684. IEEE (2013)
8. Hu, X., et al.: High-performance reconfigurable DNN accelerator on a bandwidth-limited embedded system. ACM Trans. Embed. Comput. Syst. (2022)
9. Kao, S.C., Krishna, T.: GAMMA: automating the HW mapping of DNN models on accelerators via genetic algorithm. In: 2020 IEEE/ACM International Conference On Computer Aided Design (ICCAD), pp. 1–9 (2020)
10. Kwon, H., Chatarasi, P., Sarkar, V., Krishna, T., Pellauer, M., Parashar, A.: MAESTRO: a data-centric approach to understand reuse, performance, and hardware cost of DNN mappings. IEEE Micro **40**(3), 20–29 (2020)
11. Lecun, Y., Bottou, L., Bengio, Y., Haffner, P.: Gradient-based learning applied to document recognition. Proc. IEEE **86**(11), 2278–2324 (1998). https://doi.org/10.1109/5.726791
12. Liu, X., Wen, W., Qian, X., Li, H., Chen, Y.: Neu-NoC: a high-efficient interconnection network for accelerated neuromorphic systems. In: 2018 23rd Asia and South Pacific Design Automation Conference (ASP-DAC), pp. 141–146 (2018). https://doi.org/10.1109/ASPDAC.2018.8297296
13. Mei, L., Houshmand, P., Jain, V., Giraldo, S., Verhelst, M.: ZigZag: enlarging joint architecture-mapping design space exploration for DNN accelerators. IEEE Trans. Comput. **70**(8), 1160–1174 (2021). https://doi.org/10.1109/TC.2021.3059962
14. Mondal, S., Manasi, S.D., Kunal, K., Sapatnekar, S.S.: GNNIE: GNN inference engine with load-balancing and graph-specific caching. In: Proceedings of the 59th ACM/IEEE Design Automation Conference, pp. 565–570 (2022)
15. Neda, N., Ebel, A., Reynwar, B., Reagen, B.: CiFlow: dataflow analysis and optimization of key switching for homomorphic encryption. arXiv preprint arXiv:2311.01598 (2023)
16. Russo, E., Palesi, M., Ascia, G., Patti, D., Monteleone, S., Catania, V.: Memory-aware DNN algorithm-hardware mapping via integer linear programming. In: Proceedings of the 20th ACM International Conference on Computing Frontiers, pp. 134–143 (2023)
17. Sadeghi, M.S., Sarmadi, S.B., Hessabi, S.: Toward on-chip network security using runtime isolation mapping. ACM Trans. Archit. Code Optim. **16**(3), 1–25 (2019)
18. Shao, Y.S., et al.: Simba: scaling deep-learning inference with multi-chip-module-based architecture. In: Proceedings of the 52nd Annual IEEE/ACM International Symposium on Microarchitecture, pp. 14–27 (2019)

19. Stuijk, S., Basten, T., Geilen, M., Ghamarian, A.H., Theelen, B.: Resource-efficient routing and scheduling of time-constrained streaming communication on networks-on-chip. J. Syst. Architect. **54**(3–4), 411–426 (2008)
20. Wang, B., Lu, Z.: Flexible and efficient QoS provisioning in AXI4-based network-on-chip architecture. IEEE Trans. Comput. Aided Des. Integr. Circuits Syst. **41**(5), 1523–1536 (2021)
21. Xue, Y., et al.: AOME: autonomous optimal mapping exploration using reinforcement learning for NoC-based accelerators running neural networks. In: 2022 IEEE 40th International Conference on Computer Design (ICCD), pp. 364–367. IEEE (2022)
22. Zhu, W., Chen, Y., Lu, Z.: Activation in network for NoC-based deep neural network accelerator. In: 2024 International VLSI Symposium on Technology, Systems and Applications (VLSI-TSA/VLSI-DAT), pp. 1–4. IEEE (2024)

HW-EPOLL: Hardware-Assisted User Space Event Notification for Epoll Syscall

Lars Nolte[1(✉)], Tim Twardzik[1], Camille Jalier[2], Jiyuan Shi[2], Thomas Wild[1], and Andreas Herkersdorf[1]

[1] Chair of Integrated Systems, Technical University of Munich, Munich, Germany
{lars.nolte,tim.twardzik,thomas.wild,herkersdorf}@tum.de
[2] Huawei Technologies, Grenoble, France
{camille.jalier,shijiyuan}@huawei.com

Abstract. In Linux, numerous applications use the epoll() kernel functionality as an efficient mechanism for being notified when one out of multiple events occurs. However, as epoll() can only notify of operating system mechanisms, a costly syscall is required for notifying about an event in user space. To mitigate this, we propose HW-EPOLL, which allows generating events purely in user space. In HW-EPOLL, the generated event is written into a kernel/user space shared data structure, and the notification of a sleeping thread about the occurred event is offloaded to a hardware unit. This results in a 90% CPU cycle reduction for user space event generation while still supporting multiple event sources.

Keywords: Event notification · Linux · Gem5 · Epoll

1 Introduction

Event-driven programming is widely used in modern multi-threaded applications, enabling the decoupling of different services by utilizing events to indicate state changes and trigger specific functionalities [8]. Among the various event notification mechanisms available, epoll() has emerged as a powerful solution, particularly on Linux-based systems. Epoll() (event poll) is a syscall designed to concurrently monitor multiple event sources, typically file descriptors, to see if events occur [5,9]. Upon detecting events, the syscall selectively returns them; otherwise, it blocks the thread, causing it to sleep until an event is triggered. This functionality is particularly useful in applications such as web servers that listen to multiple sockets or message brokers that distribute work among multiple microservice threads.

One performance insufficiency of the existing epoll() implementation lies in the cost of triggering events once the event source is in the user space. This overhead originates from the need to utilize an OS mechanism to generate an event that epoll() can wait for. For instance, using the eventfd() mechanism or executing a dummy write() syscall to a pipe() or socket() can generate an event. Regardless of the chosen mechanism's simplicity, issuing a syscall to trigger the

L. Carro et al. (Eds.): SAMOS 2024, LNCS 15226, pp. 93–107, 2025.
https://doi.org/10.1007/978-3-031-78377-7_7

event imposes a minimum of 4000 CPU cycles. Moreover, this syscall prolongs the time for the event to become receivable by the other thread, increasing the likelihood of the waiting thread entering a sleep state.

We propose HW-EPOLL, an approach to hardware assist event notification from user space in epoll(), eliminating the need for a syscall. By extending the existing epoll() implementation with a shared data structure between the kernel and user space, events can be directly generated for user space in HW-EPOLL. The notification about new events is offloaded to the hardware unit presented in HW-FUTEX. The hardware unit manages a wait queue of threads for an epoll() instance and triggers thread wake-ups when necessary, thereby offloading event notifications. This integration can reduce the CPU overhead for event generation, improving the responsiveness of epoll()-based applications.

The remainder of this paper is organized as follows: In Sect. 2, we provide an overview of the existing implementations and optimizations for event notification mechanisms in Linux, highlighting its strengths and limitations. Section 3 discusses the design principles and key features of our proposed HW-EPOLL. We present experimental results and performance evaluations in Sect. 4, demonstrating the effectiveness and benefits of our approach. Finally, we conclude the paper in Sect. 5 with a summary of our contributions and directions for future research.

2 Related Work

Various mechanisms can wait for multiple event sources or generate events in user space, such as futex2 and io_uring. Futex2, introduced by André Almeida in 2021, extends the futex() mechanism to allow waiting on multiple futexes simultaneously [1]. While futex2 enables event generation in user space, it only allows waiting for 32-bit user-space mutexes (futex) and indicates that at least one futex has changed without specifying which one. In contrast, epoll() provides specific information about which event has occurred, making it a more versatile mechanism for waiting on multiple events. Therefore, HW-EPOLL integrates the HW-FUTEX concept into epoll() instead of futex2 to support waiting on futex-like objects and more complex mechanisms in user space and the kernel.

Io_uring is a kernel mechanism proposed by Jens Axboe for performing asynchronous I/O operations [2]. It employs two shared rings between user space and the kernel: one for submitting work from user space, processed asynchronously by a kernel thread [4], and another for pushing results back to user space upon completion. Although beneficial in certain use cases, io_uring cannot replace epoll() or HW-EPOLL in all scenarios due to the different programming paradigms. Io_uring requires applications to be designed for asynchronous operations, with notifications for operation completions to process the results. In contrast, epoll() informs the application when a specific operation can be executed synchronously, allowing for different application designs and use cases.

An optimization for epoll() was proposed by Roman Penyaev called user epoll (uepoll()) [15]. This enhancement is visualized in Fig. 1, comparing the vanilla epoll() implementation (two leftmost diagrams) and the uepoll() optimization for epoll() (second from the right). For all these cases, we differentiate between two scenarios (not all shown in Fig. 1): 1. **With ready events (WRE)**: thread B generates an event before thread A wants to consume it; 2. **Without ready events (NRE)**: thread B generates an event after thread A wants to consume it. An event can be, for instance, a write syscall on an eventfd(), a 64-bit counter in the kernel that tracks events. When no ready events are available, both epoll() and uepoll() cause thread A to block in an epoll_wait() syscall. If ready events are available, epoll() collects them via an epoll_wait() syscall, as it stores occurred events in a kernel private data structure. Uepoll() improves this by introducing a shared ring data structure between the kernel and user space, storing occurred events. This allows collecting ready events directly from user space, making the epoll_wait() syscall necessary only when no events are available and the thread needs to block. Consequently, uepoll() enhances performance for collecting ready events (Thread A), and this optimization is also used in HW-EPOLL. However, uepoll() does not address scenarios without ready events, which is where HW-EPOLL provides further improvements.

The previous approaches rely only on software changes, while some related works require hardware changes. HW-EPOLL leverages the HW Unit from HW-FUTEX, making the closest related approaches those proposed by Nolte *et al.* in HAWEN [12] and HW-FUTEX [14]. HAWEN offloads event notification to a hardware unit that asynchronously wakes up threads, but this offload can only be triggered within the kernel, needing a syscall for event generation, unlike HW-EPOLL. HW-FUTEX extends HAWEN by integrating it into the fast user-level mutex (futex()) syscall. In futex, the event generation is moved to user space while the kernel manages wait queues for different futexes. In HW-FUTEX, this wait queue management is offloaded to a hardware unit, eliminating the need for a futex() syscall for the event-generating thread. However, HW-FUTEX is limited by the constraints of futex, which is primarily used for implementing efficient locks in user space. HW-EPOLL overcomes these limitations by leveraging HW-FUTEX in combination with epoll().

Apart from the concepts underlying HW-EPOLL, a similar approach was proposed by Intel in 2021, known as UserIPI (User-space Interrupts) [11,17]. UserIPI allows a running user space thread to receive interrupts without switching to kernel space. These special interrupts can be raised by another user space thread or the kernel via a new instruction, enabling the event-generating thread to send notifications with a single instruction. Comparing the event notification aspects, UserIPI outperforms HW-EPOLL in terms of overhead for the event-generating thread and latency, assuming the receiving thread is active. This advantage originates from UserIPI's specialized hardware architecture integrated directly into the CPU. However, HW-EPOLL differs from UserIPI by also managing waiting threads in hardware for software instances like epoll or futex. This waitlist management facilitates easier integration into existing mechanisms and avoids the need for changes to CPU core architecture. As Intel does not offer a platform combining an FPGA with CPUs that support UserIPI, a quantitative comparison between HW-EPOLL and UserIPI is currently not feasible.

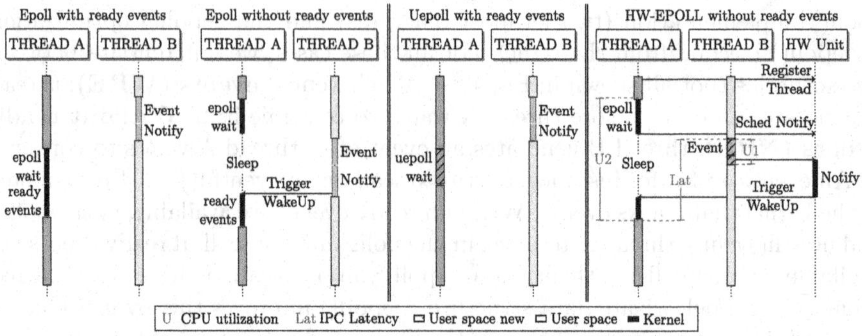

Fig. 1. Message sequence chart comparing three implementations: the original implementation using epoll(), the related work approach uepoll(), and HW-EPOLL. The epoll() diagrams (the two most left diagrams) show scenarios where thread B generates an event before thread A intends to consume it (with ready events) and when thread B generates it after (without ready events). The next diagram illustrates changes made for uepoll(), while the case without ready events remains the same. Finally, we introduce HW-EPOLL (most right diagram), emphasizing the scenario without ready events, given its similarity to uepoll in cases with ready events. On the most right, the concept of HW-EPOLL is presented, focussing on the without ready events case as the with ready events case is the same with uepoll().

3 HW-EPOLL Concept

The concept of HW-EPOLL is visualized in a message sequence chart shown in Fig. 1 comparing the epoll() implementation (two most left diagram), the uepoll() optimization for epoll() (second from the right), and the proposed HW-EPOLL concept on the right. For hardware assistance in HW-EPOLL, the hardware unit (HW Unit) of HW-FUTEX is embedded into the uepoll() mechanism. However, applying HW-FUTEX to uepoll() alone would not enable generating events from user space, as thread B still has to issue a syscall for event generation in uepoll(). To avoid this syscall in HW-EPOLL, uepoll() was extended by the capability of writing occurred events directly from user space to the uepoll() ring. Additionally, this new function interacts with the HW Unit whenever threads are sleeping to let the HW Unit asynchronously wake them up. Hence, with HW-EPOLL a syscall can be saved for the event generation for thread B, drastically reducing the overhead for communicating between the threads. This integration of HW-EPOLL does not turn off the existing functionality of generating events in the kernel, resulting in a mechanism that can be used to wait on multiple kernel and user space events. As HW-EPOLL improves the scenario without ready events, only this scenario is shown in Fig. 1. The scenario with ready events is the same as with uepoll().

To enable HW-EPOLL, software changes must be made, and the hardware architecture has to be extended by the HW Unit proposed in HW-FUTEX. The paper focuses primarily on the software changes described in Sect. 3.1, while an overview of the HW Unit is given in Sect. 3.2.

3.1 Required Software Changes

The changes required for uepoll() itself are considered present in the code and are not described in this paper. On the kernel side, the existing HW Unit's device driver has to be extended by new functions to be integrated into the kernel code of uepoll(). The user space implementation of uepoll() is enhanced to interact with the HW Unit directly from user space. Additionally, a new event generation mechanism in user space is needed. We implemented ueventfd() as an exemplary user space event generation mechanism. Ueventfd() is designed to function as a replacement for eventfd() implementations in existing applications.

Linux Kernel - Device Driver: The device driver of the HW Unit provides the interface to communicate with the hardware component. During bootup, the HW Unit is initialized. Afterward, each thread that wants to utilize HW-EPOLL registers itself at the HW Unit to be woken up when required (Register Thread in Fig. 1). A scheduler notification (Sched Notify in Fig. 1) is sent whenever a thread utilizing HW-EPOLL went to sleep. This message is mandatory to track an HW Unit's internal thread state. Mainly, two new functionalities extended the existing device driver. First, a function to add the calling thread to the wait list in the HW Unit (add_me_to_hw_wait_que()) and second, a function to wake up all sleeping threads in one waitlist (clear_hw_wait_que()).

```
ep_poll()
  [...]
+ if (file->f_flags & O_HW_WAKEUP)
+   threads_asleep = 1;
+   add_me_to_hw_wait_que();
+ else
    add_me_to_sw_wait_que();
  schedule_hrtimeout_range();
  [...]

ep_add_event_to_uring()
  [...]
  add_event_to_ring[...];
+ if (threads_asleep)
+   threads_asleep = 0;
+   clear_hw_wait_que();
  [...]
```

Listing 1.1. Required source code modification for *epoll()* mechanism to use HW-EPOLL in pseudo code diff [18]. Lines starting with "+" are added.

Uepoll() extensions: The existing user space and kernel implementation of uepoll() has to be slightly extended for HW-EPOLL. On the kernel side, we have to ensure that the thread that goes to sleep calls the add_me_to_hw_wait_que()

instead of using a kernel waitlist. This is accomplished by differentiating in the ep_poll() function in which wait queue the calling thread enqueues itself (l. 3 - 7 in List. 1.1). The ep_poll() function blocks the execution of the thread by calling schedule_hrtimeout_range (l. 8 in List. 1.1). In addition, as the sleeping threads are no longer stored in the kernel, the HW Unit has to be notified via clear_hw_wait_que() whenever the event-generating thread adds an event to the ring. A new event is added to the uepoll() ring in the function ep_add_event_to_uring(). To trigger clear_hw_wait_que() only if necessary, a new variable indicates whether a thread is asleep. This variable is set in ep_poll() whenever a thread adds itself to the hardware wait queue (l. 4 in List. 1.1) and is unset before the wait queue is cleared in hardware (l. 15 in List. 1.1).

In user space, the existing uepoll() implementation was extended by the function ep_add_event_to_uring(), which is taken from the kernel to add events to the ring from the user space without any kernel involvement.

```
1 write_ueventfd(*buf)
2    [...]
3    fetch_add(count, *buf);
4    ep_add_event_to_uring();
```

Listing 1.2. Pseudo code for *write_ueventfd()* including the counter modification and event notification via the uepoll() functionality.

Ueventfd(): To use ueventfd(), a uepoll() instance must first be created to notify about events on the ueventfd(). Afterward, a new ueventfd() can be created with ueventfd(), which allocates a data structure in user space and opens an eventfd() file descriptor to leverage kernel functionality when setting up uepoll(). With write_ueventfd() and read_ueventfd(), an eventfd() like 64-bit counter in user space can be modified. In eventfd(), this counter tracks events and has the same functionality in ueventfd(). Hence, this counter modification is taken from the kernel eventfd() implementation. The pseudo-code for the write_ueventfd() can be found in List. 1.2. One of the first steps is the incrementation of the user space counter by the value given by the calling function (line 3 in List. 1.2). Then the newly generated event is notified by calling ep_add_event_to_uring() in user space, which adds the event to the uepoll() ring and notifies sleeping threads if needed (line 4 in List. 1.2). At the end of the application, close_ueventfd() can be called to free the initially allocated data structure and close the eventfd().

3.2 Hardware Unit

The major components of the HW Unit are shown in Fig. 2, which are three FSMs decoupled via FIFOs. A memory-mapped bus follower interface initializes the HW Unit and is used to offload commands. The initiator bus interface interacts with the system to wake up threads. Each FSM manages a data structure stored in internal resources. The Wait FSM organizes queues, storing the waiting threads for one epoll instance (wait queue). When the software offloads an event

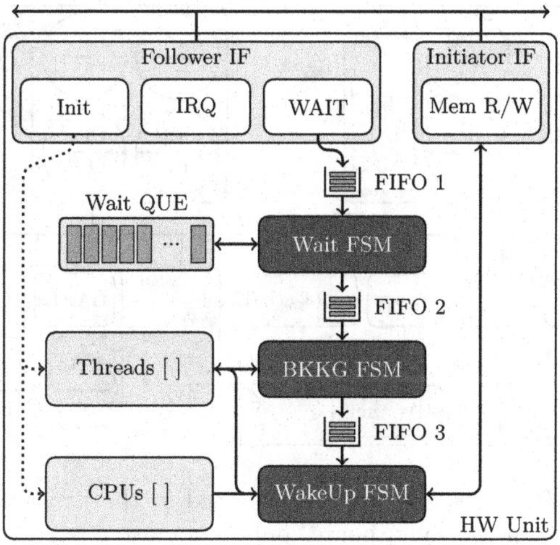

Fig. 2. The hardware unit's (HW Unit) internal structure as presented in [14].

notification to the HW Unit, the corresponding queue is emptied and forwarded to the Bookkeeping (BKKG) FSM. The BKKG manages the HW Unit's private thread state, forwarding only sleeping threads to the WakeUp FSM. This is mandatory as the WakeUp FSM is designed to only wake up sleeping threads. However, the Wait FSM might forward threads that are still transitioning to sleep, so the BKKG FSM buffers these threads until they are asleep and can be forwarded to the WakeUp FSM. To initiate a thread wake-up, the WakeUp FSM writes the to-be-woken-up thread into a linked list shared with a kernel. The HW Unit then triggers the kernel with an interrupt to perform the thread wake-up on a specific CPU core.

Since the data structures are stored in internal resources, their dimensions must be determined at design time. The key parameter is the number of threads ($\#Thd$) that the HW Unit should manage, indicating the maximum number of threads that can wait using HW-EPOLL. This parameter is independent of the number of event sources an epoll() instance monitors, as these are stored in a software-allocated data structure that can be dynamically resized [14]. The overall size of the three data structures in the HW Unit is shown in Eq. (1), where $\#CPUs$ is the number of CPUs in the system.

$$\begin{aligned} Data_{size} &= Wait\ QUE_{size} + Threads[\,]_{size} + CPUs[\,]_{size} \\ &= 6 \cdot \Big(\frac{\lceil log_2(\#Thd) \rceil}{8} B + 35B \Big) + \#Thd \cdot 21B + \#CPUs \cdot 16B \end{aligned} \tag{1}$$

The FIFOs generate back pressure to the preceding FSM or the CPUs to ensure that requests are never dropped. With this capability, FIFO 1 can have a depth of $\#CPUs$ (accommodating simultaneous requests from every CPU), which is sufficient under normal conditions. Under very rare conditions, back pressure will be generated. For FIFO 2 and FIFO 3, although the theoretical maximum

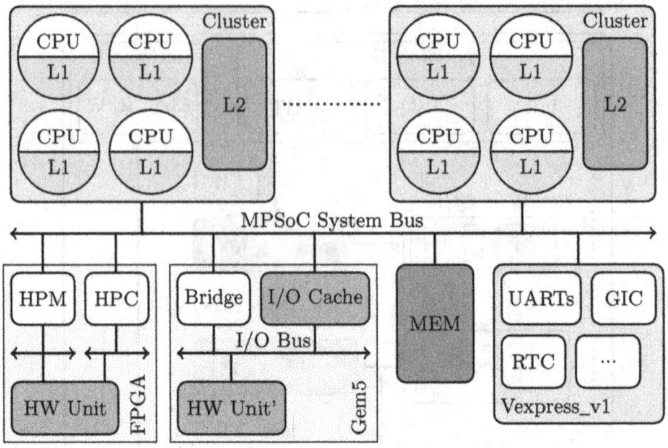

Fig. 3. Overview of the system architecture used in the two prototyping platforms as presented in [14]. On the Zynq board, only one cluster is available, and the block labeled with FPGA is used. In the Gem5 simulation, the number of cores and clusters can be configured, while the Gem5 block is effective.

depth is $\#Thd - 1$, we observed that a depth of 16 was never fully utilized on our prototyping platform.

4 Experimental Evaluation

Two prototyping platforms are used for the experimental evaluation: a simulated one and an FPGA-based hardware implementation. As a simulator, the Gem5 Full-System simulator [3] is used. A Zynq UltraScale+ MPSoC ZCU102 Evaluation Kit was chosen for the hardware implementation, combining dedicated ARM CPU cores with an FPGA extension. While the simulation platform is used for a scalability analysis and a more in-depth timing analysis, the hardware implementation is used to test a more extensive input set and to have a more accurate I/O. The MPSoC's hardware architecture of both platforms is shown in Fig. 3. For the Zynq platform, only one cluster with 4 CPU cores and the HW Unit in the FPGA box is valid. In Gem5, we simulated a design with 32 CPU cores in 8 clusters and the HW Unit in the box labeled with Gem5.

Zynq Setup: The CPU cores on the Zynq board are four ARM Cortex-A53 CPU cores running on 1.2GHz with a dedicated 32kB L1 data and 32kB L1 instruction cache. All cores share a 1MB L2 cache and 4GB of DDR4 memory. The HW Unit operates at 250 MHz and is connected via the High-Performance Master (HPM) port to the HW Unit's follower port, while the High-Performance Coherency (HPC) port is used for memory accesses through the initiator port. The hardware resources utilized by the HW Unit are detailed in Tab. 1, using Vivado version v2021.1 for synthesis. The design parameters for the HW Unit include $\#Thd = 64$ and a FIFO depth 16 for all FIFOs. The three data structures and the FIFOs are mapped to Block RAM (BRAM).

Gem5 Setup: In Gem5, the system parameters were chosen to be comparable to those on the Zynq platform. Therefore, the same frequencies and cache

Table 1. Hardware resources that are used to implement the HW Unit on the Zynq platform (as presented in [14]). These resources are compared with the resource consumption by a Microblaze soft core [19].

HW Module	CLB	LUT	REG	MUX	BRAM
Follower Memory interface	674	1486	1935	246	0
Initiator Memory interface	139	318	176	0	0
FIFOs	97	238	133	0	5.5
Internal data structures	194	420	182	0	17
Futex FSM	160	678	354	0	0
BKKG FSM	111	184	77	0	0
WakeUp FSM	130	731	432	0	0
HW Unit	1080	4051	3289	246	22.5
MBlaze Linux MMU 64bit		4802	4497		18

dimensions were used in Gem5. The simulated CPU model is an in-order Armv8-A model called HPI, and a DDR4 2400 4×16 memory model was used. A bus bridge connects the MPSoC System Bus with the I/O Bus, the counterpart for the HPM port on the Zynq board. To perform cache coherent memory accesses by the HW Unit, a cache is required and is configured to be between the I/O bus and the MPSoC System Bus. To be highlighted is that the HW Unit does not profit from the cache behavior but is used to perform coherency protocol-compliant memory accesses on the MPSoC System Bus. For accurate, in-depth timing analysis, GLS Tracing [13] is used as a low intrusive software tracing mechanism. GLS Tracing offloads via pseudo instructions the expensive tracepoint recording to Gem5 and reduces the burden added to the simulated system by the software tracing.

Software Setup: On both prototyping platforms, a Linux kernel based on version 5.10 [18] is executed with the same device driver for the HW Unit. On the Zynq board, a few additional drivers were required to operate the board. All applications were built with a compiler/cross-compiler based on gcc-10.2.0 [6], including a custom Glibc v2.32 [7], which is used to abstract the added software changes in user space.

For evaluation purposes, we developed a library to easily compare different mechanisms against each other. With this library, different test scenarios can be represented. One exemplary scenario is visualized in Fig. 4. The library provides a message pool (MPool) implementation, which is used as a pre-allocated pool of messages in shared memory to exchange efficiently data between threads. The other important part of the library is the Notification Engine. This engine implements lockless queues in shared memory and custom functionality to block whenever the queue is empty or full. Different mechanisms can be chosen for this blocking functionality. In the following five configurations are compared: standard epoll() + eventfd() (epoll-origin), epoll() with HAWEN optimization + eventfd() (HAWEN), uepoll() + eventfd() (Uepoll), futex() with HW-FUTEX optimiza-

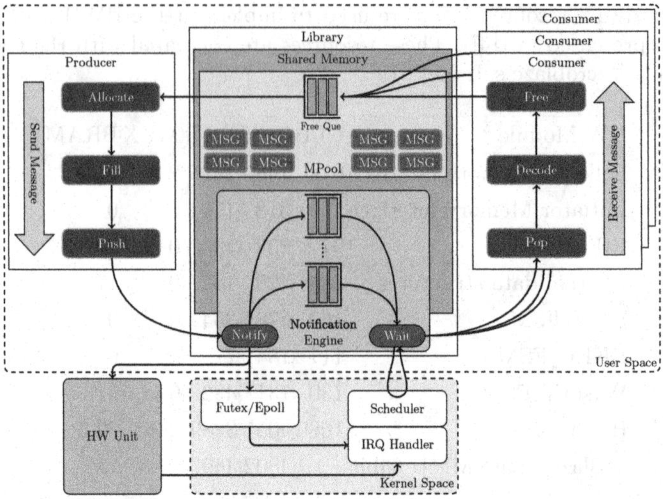

Fig. 4. Architecture of the test application as presented in [14].

tion (HW-FUTEX), and HW-EPOLL. Whenever a thread wants to monitor only one queue at a time, futex() is the most performant option, but epoll()/uepoll() can be used. If a thread wants to monitor multiple queues (e.g., a consumer thread can receive from multiple queues work), only epoll()/uepoll() can be used. A scenario shown in Fig. 4 is used where one producer thread generates messages for a variable number of consumer threads. Each producer-consumer pair has its dedicated queue in the Notification Engine, and the producer sends messages to the different consumers in a round-robin order.

This scenario is chosen to be able to compare HW-EPOLL and HW-FUTEX. The presented results might raise the question of why HW-EPOLL is required in addition to HW-FUTEX as the results are often better or similar with HW-FUTEX. With HW-EPOLL the limitation of HW-FUTEX to wait only on one event source can be overcome while achieving very comparable performance. Hence, as soon as the application has to be more generic by waiting on multiple event sources, HW-FUTEX cannot be used anymore, and HW-EPOLL is mandatory. Additionally, the event generation and collection in epoll()/uepoll() are designed to be independent of the number of event sources monitored. This is also indicated by the often-discussed complexity of O(1) for epoll() [10]. Hence, the kernel knows which event was generated and does not have to check all monitored event sources. For this reason, even though the results in Sect. 4.1 and Sect. 4.2 show a scenario with only one event source, they are also representative of the use case with multiple use cases (except for HW-FUTEX).

4.1 High-Level Application Analysis

A high-level analysis compares the application's performance using different blocking mechanisms. As a performance measure, I/O operations per second (IOP/s) is used, while one I/O operation is considered one message (32 bytes)

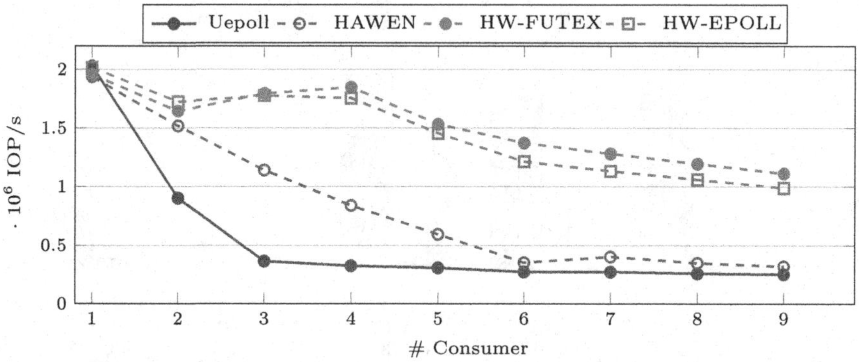

Fig. 5. I/O operations per second (IOP/s) in test application executed on the Zynq board comparing different mechanisms. The native input set is used, and the number of consumer threads is adjusted (shown on the x-axis).

generated by the producer thread. The IOP/s for the different mechanisms depending on the number of consumer threads is shown in Fig. 5. While the producer thread exclusively runs on one core, the consumer threads must share the remaining three cores. This results in multiple threads sharing CPU cores with more than three consumer threads.

Independent of the used mechanism, the highest IOP/s rate that can be achieved is about 2 MIOP/s in a configuration with one consumer. The reason for the decrease of the IOP/s when using more consumers is that they block due to an empty queue, resulting in a notification that has to be sent by the producer. The worst rate is achieved with Uepoll (same results for epoll-origin) as a syscall is required to trigger an event, and the software performs the notification. An improvement can be seen by offloading the event notification in the kernel to a hardware assist (HAWEN), especially when using less than two consumer threads per core. From six consumer threads onwards, Uepoll and HAWEN are very similar, indicating that the time to generate the event in the kernel becomes the dominating factor. An even bigger performance improvement can be achieved when this event generation and notification can be executed entirely in user space (HW-FUTEX, HW-EPOLL). The rate still depends on the number of consumers because more consumer threads result in more notifications that have to be sent by the producer but with way less burden. What can also be seen is that even though HW-EPOLL is a generic approach to waiting for multiple event sources, almost the same rates can be achieved as with the futex() mechanism, which is highly optimized to notify about only one event. The difference between HW-EPOLL and HW-FUTEX is that the functions executed are mostly a bit slower in HW-EPOLL (more details in Sect. 4.2). This is beneficial for configurations where only one consumer is running on the CPU cores (less or equal to 3 consumers), resulting in fewer occasions in which no event is available for a consumer. However, with more than three consumers, the blocking syscalls on thread A side are very similar (not shown in the plot), and the slower execution times result in fewer IOP/s.

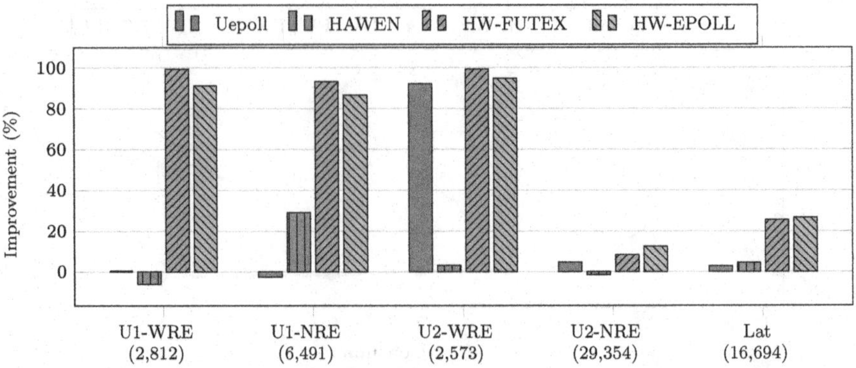

Fig. 6. Average CPU cycle reduction for the selected mechanisms in different phases (U1, U2, Lat). The reduction is given in percent while using the epoll-origin implementation as the baseline. The values in brackets represent CPU cycles of epoll-origin.

4.2 In-Depth Analysis

In addition to the high-level application evaluation, an in-depth analysis is conducted where the different steps in the mechanisms are compared using epoll-origin as the baseline. For the analysis, three metrics are defined and described in the following. The metrics are visualized in Fig. 1 (U1, U2, Lat) and were measured with GLS Tracing in Gem5. The improvements (CPU cycle reduction) compared to epoll-origin are visualized in Fig. 6.

Metric 1 (*U1* in Fig. 1) indicates the number of CPU cycles spent by thread B to generate an event and send out the notification if required. As the notification is only needed if another thread (thread A) waits for an event to be notified, two cases are differentiated. First, *U1* when Notify is performed (*U1-NRE*) and second, *U1-WRE* without the Notify step.

The results for *U1* shown in Fig. 6 indicate that when the event generating thread does not have to send an event notification, HAWEN and Uepoll perform similarly to epoll-origin. This can be explained by all the mechanisms using an eventfd() syscall to generate the event, executing almost the same code. However, with HW-FUTEX and HW-EPOLL the syscall is no longer needed to generate an event, resulting in a CPU cycle reduction of over 90%. HW-FUTEX reduces the required time to about 21 CPU cycles as only one atomic operation is needed.

If an event notification has to be sent (*U1-NRE*), Uepoll still does not see a performance improvement as uepoll() only targets a faster event reception when ready events already exist. With HAWEN an improvement of 30% can be achieved by offloading the event notification within the kernel to a hardware assist. HW-EPOLL performs lightly worse than HW-FUTEX due to the uepoll() ring handling, which is required to support waiting on multiple events.

Metric 2 (*U2* in Fig. 1) is the counterpart to *U1* on the event receiving side (thread A). If ready events are available, thread A does not have to go to sleep

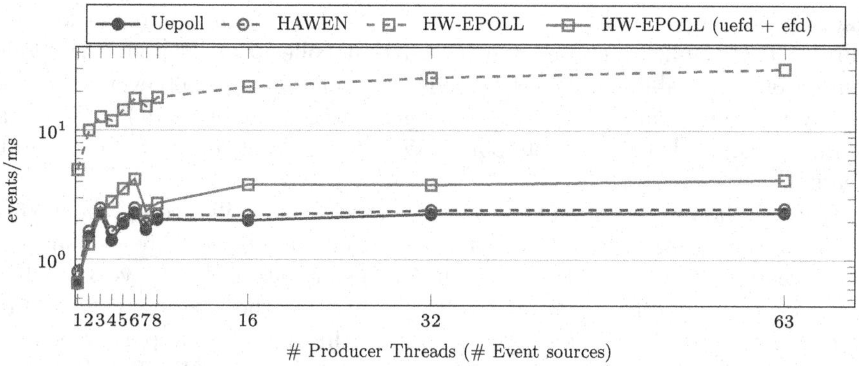

Fig. 7. Generated events per millisecond (shown on the y-axis using a logarithmic scale) in the Uepoll test application [16] executed on the Zynq board comparing different mechanisms. The number of event-generating threads is adjusted (shown on the x-axis) while each thread generates 1000000 events. The HW-EPOLL (uefd + efd) variant uses half of the threads to generate events in user space and the other half in the kernel.

(*U2-WRE*) and only blocks when no ready events are available (*U2-NRE*). For *U2-NRE*, the sleeping time of the thread is not considered but only the time to put the thread to sleep and wake it up again.

For *U2-WRE*, the advantages of uepoll() can be seen as ready events can be collected quickly with the uepoll() ring. As HW-EPOLL leverages uepoll() to collect the events, a similar improvement of more than 90% can be achieved. HW-FUTEX can be even faster as futex() has to perform only one atomic operation to collect ready events.

None of the mechanisms is designed to improve *U2-NRE*; therefore, only marginal differences exist here. HW-EPOLL and HW-FUTEX can achieve an improvement of around 10%. However, this metric is dominated by scheduling functions and context switches. HW-FUTEX performs slightly worse than HW-EPOLL because a different syscall is used to put the thread to sleep, which costs more CPU cycles.

Metric 3 (*Lat* in Fig. 1) depicts the latency, so the time it takes after the event generation until the waiting thread continues its execution. As thread A has to sleep for *Lat*, only the scenario without ready events has to be considered.

The Latency cannot be improved with HAWEN and Uepoll, but with HW-FUTEX and HW-EPOLL it can be reduced by 25%. The improvement is because the thread wake-up can be triggered earlier with hardware assistance as the offload to the HW Unit is triggered directly from the user space, which saves the time usually required to enter the kernel.

4.3 Multi-event Source Analysis

The previously presented results showcase a scenario where only one event source is montiored by the used mechanisms. This subsection uses an application published by Roman Penyaev [16] to use HW-EPOLL to wait for multiple event sources. This application uses one thread that collects via uepoll() or epoll() events from a variable number of threads that generate 1000000 events each. In the default configuration, the events are generated using eventfd(). This application was extended to also support HW-EPOLL using ueventfd to generate events.

Figure 7 shows the number of events generated per millisecond (events/ms) executing the application on the Zynq board. The number of threads that generate events is shown on the x-axis, and the event rate is on the y-axis, which uses a logarithmic scale. The mechanisms tested are the ones used in the previous measurement except for HW-FUTEX as this does not support waiting on multiple events. Additionally, one test scenario was added (HW-EPOLL (uefd + efd)) where half of the event sources are in the kernel (eventfd()) and the other half is generated in the user space (ueventfd()). It can be seen that HAWEN is slightly better than Uepoll. This is unexpected as Uepoll does not need a syscall to collect events, and the application is designed to rarely put a thread asleep. However, as the application is using eventfd() as a counter that is incremented to generate an event, the counter may be incremented multiple times while only one event notification via epoll()/uepoll() is sent out. Hence, using a slower epoll() syscall to collect occurred events can result in fewer epoll() syscalls and a slightly higher event rate. Generating all the events directly in user space with HW-EPOLL results in a vast improvement. This improvement cannot be profited from as noticeable in the scenario using kernel and user space event sources. The limiting factor here is that the threads using the kernel event sources are not faster with HW-EPOLL.

5 Conclusion and Outlook

This paper presents HW-EPOLL, a novel approach for hardware-assisted event notification in epoll(), enabling event generation and notification from user space without a syscall. Therefore, hardware assistance is integrated into uepoll(), an epoll() optimization which utilizes a ring data structure shared between kernel and user space to store occurred events. For HW-EPOLL uepoll() is extended to facilitate direct event writing from user space into the uepoll() ring. Upon event generation, the hardware unit from HW-FUTEX is triggered to asynchronously wake up all sleeping threads waiting for events on the uepoll() instance. This approach significantly reduces the burden on the event-generating thread, reducing CPU cycles by approximately 90% compared to the original epoll() implementation.

HW-EPOLL extends HW-FUTEX to support concurrently waiting on multiple events while reducing the burden on the event-generating thread. In the future, we envision generating events directly from a hardware component. This would save expensive upcalls to the kernel whenever an event is generated directly in a hardware component.

References

1. Almeida, A.: futex2: add wait on multiple futexes syscall (2021). https://lwn.net/Articles/869137/
2. Axboe, J.: Efficient IO with io_uring (2024). https://kernel.dk/io_uring.pdf
3. Binkert, N., et al.: The gem5 simulator. SIGARCH Comput. Archit. News **39**(2), 1–7 (2011). https://doi.org/10.1145/2024716.2024718
4. Corbet, J.: Ringing in a new asynchronous i/o API (2024). https://lwn.net/Articles/776703/
5. Epoll - Linux manual page. https://man7.org/linux/man-pages/man7/epoll.7.html. Accessed 1 Nov 2022
6. GCC: The GNU compiler collection (version 10.2.0) (2023). https://ftp.gnu.org/gnu/gcc/gcc-10.2.0/gcc-10.2.0.tar.gz
7. Glibc: The GNU C library (version 2.32) (2023). https://sourceware.org/git/glibc.git
8. Hugh, M.: Event-Driven Architecture: How SOA Enables the Real-time Enterprise. Addison-Wesley Professional (2009)
9. Kerrisk, M.: The Linux Programming Interface: A Linux and UNIX System Programming Handbook, 1st edn. No Starch Press, USA (2010)
10. Klitzke, E.: Blocking i/o, nonblocking i/o, and epoll (2024). https://eklitzke.org/blocking-io-nonblocking-io-and-epoll
11. Mehta, S.: x86 user interrupts support (2021). https://lwn.net/Articles/869140/
12. Nolte, L., et al.: HAWEN: hardware accelerator for thread wake-ups in Linux event notification. In: 2023 60th ACM/IEEE Design Automation Conference (DAC) (2023)
13. Nolte, L., et al.: GLS tracing: gem5-based low-intrusive software tracing. In: 2022 IEEE Nordic Circuits and Systems Conference (NorCAS), pp. 1–6. IEEE (2022)
14. Nolte, L., et al.: HW-FUTEX: hardware-assisted futex syscall. In: IEEE Transactions on Very Large Scale Integration (VLSI) Systems (2023). https://doi.org/10.1109/TVLSI.2023.3317926
15. Penyaev, R.: epoll: support pollable epoll from userspace (2023). https://lkml.org/lkml/2019/1/9/628
16. Penyaev, R.: userpolled epoll microbenchmark (2024). https://github.com/rouming/test-tools/blob/master/userpolled-epoll.c
17. Sankaran, R., Neiger, G., Shanbhogue, V., Koufaty, D.: User timer directly programmed by application, US Patent App. 17/212,977 (2022)
18. The Linux Kernel Organization: Linux kernel source tree (Linux 5.10) (2023). https://github.com/torvalds/linux
19. Xilinx: Performance and resource utilization for MicroBlaze v11.0 (2022). https://www.xilinx.com/htmldocs/ip_docs/pru_files/microblaze.html

SIZALIZER: Multilevel Analysis Framework for Object Size Optimization

Andreas Hager-Clukas(✉), Jonathan Schröter, and Stefan Wallentowitz

Hochschule München University of Applied Sciences, München, Germany
andreas.hager-clukas@hm.edu

Abstract. Due to the resource constraints and the increasing environmental impact of embedded systems, the development of frameworks to optimize the footprint of instruction set architectures becomes critical. This paper presents *SIZALIZER*, a multi-layer analysis framework for the co-design of embedded C/C++ applications and RISC-V instruction set extensions. SIZALIZER embodies a novel approach by automating analysis across three layers: LLVM intermediate representation, executable binary code, and runtime instruction execution using techniques such as data flow graph, static binary, and dynamic execution analysis. The analysis performed with the Embench benchmark demonstrates SIZALIZER's potential to identify optimization opportunities for both static and dynamic code sizes. The framework's unique architecture enables it to distill actionable insights from complex software structures and guide size-optimizing ISA improvements. The proposed improvements result in a calculated static and dynamic improvement of approximately 30 %.

Keywords: Static Analysis · Code Size · Instruction Set Architecture.

1 Introduction

Designers of embedded systems face tight resource constraints [10], and those systems contribute significantly to emissions [7]. Optimized memory footprints and power profiles require frameworks for efficient hardware and software development. One way to reduce the memory footprint is an optimized instruction set architecture (ISA) with improved code density. As embedded systems are often optimized to execute applications from one domain, there is a long tradition in hardware/software-codesign of domain-specific processors [8]. RISC-V has revived the research on domain-specific ISA optimization recently and the need for optimized platforms steadily increases. In order to tailor existing ISAs such as RV32, we need a deep insight into the current requirements from the software side. However, there is a lack of fully integrated, easily accessible and holistic frameworks that analyze existing software in the embedded domain and presents the results for a productive ISA optimization.

We propose SIZALIZER, an open-source framework suitable for the automated analysis of C/C++ applications targeting ISA based code size optimizations. RV32 with all extensions was chosen as the hardware target for the analysis, because it is open and extensible. SIZALIZER analyzes the target application

L. Carro et al. (Eds.): SAMOS 2024, LNCS 15226, pp. 108–121, 2025.
https://doi.org/10.1007/978-3-031-78377-7_8

on different levels, especially in terms of static and dynamic code size. As a main goal it looks for and evaluates patterns in the application, such as control flow patterns. In addition, the optimization potential for some ISA improvements is statically estimated. To validate our framework we present a case study using the *Embench* benchmark as an example [1] and validate it on the Musl libc as well as on the Linux kernel.

Specific contributions of the paper are:

- Development of a unique software analysis framework for ISA improvement.
- New combination of different analysis techniques on multiple layers.
- Results specific for ISA enhancement.
- Exemplary evaluation of the Embench benchmark, validation with Musl libc and Linux kernel.

2 Foundations

SIZALIZER analyzes an application at the Intermediate Representation (IR) in the compiler, the executable code in the binary, and the executed instructions. Each of these levels requires different representations and tools to extract and evaluate useful information. Instead of reinventing the wheel, SIZALIZER utilizes other available open source tools to perform its analysis. Before going into details of our approach, we first introduce the foundations of the class of tools before reviewing related work.

The LLVM Intermediate Representation (IR) is a well-defined abstract assembly language in the Static Single Assignment (SSA) format [2]. It is more typical and based on low-level operations, but is still abstract enough, so that various concrete instruction implementations do not affect the structure. It is therefore a suitable source for a structural evaluation of an application.

The structure of the IR can be analyzed using the Control Flow Graph (CFG) and the Data Flow Graph (DFG). Both directed graphs are defined as $G = (V, E)$. Where V is the set of nodes and E is the set of edges, where all elements in E are a two-tuple of elements from V. Thus, each edge has a direction from the first to the second element of the tuple. In the DFG, the individual IR instructions form the set V. The edges of the set E, on the other hand, are formed by the register-based data flows between the instructions. For the CFG, the basic blocks (BB) of the application form the nodes. The control flows between the BBs connect these two nodes and thus define their edges.

A higher layer of analysis is based on the binary Executable and Linkable Format [5]. The ELF header contains information about its sections such as the *.text* segment. This contains the binary encoded executable code of the application and therefore determines the static code size. The value can be read out with the tool *readelf*.

To evaluate the application code, the binary code must be converted back into assembly. In principle, all instructions are read statically in binary and translated back into mnemonics. A tool that can do this is *objdump*.

3 Related Work

Table 1. Comparison of SIZALIZER and related solutions.

	Open Source	DFG	Static	Dynamic
Data-Flow Analysis for MPI Programs [15]	○	●	○	○
Sharlit [16]	○	●	○	○
BitBlaze [14]	○	●*	●*	●
RISC-V Code-size Analysis Script [4]	●	○	●	○
PIN [11]	●	○	○	◑
Valgrind [13]	●	○	○	◑
DynamoRIO [6]	●	○	○	◑
SIZALIZER	●	●	●	●

○: Not supported
◑: Supported as platform
●: Fully supported
* Not sufficient for our purpose

Strout et al. have addressed dataflow analysis for code optimization in their paper [15]. They focus on Single-Program, Multiple-Data (SPMD) parallel programs that communicate with each other using message passing via the Message Passing Interface (MPI). Like SIZALIZER, they use an interprocedural CFG. However, they extend it with message passing edges between send and receive calls to model the data flows between threads. With the results of these analyses, you can significantly reduce the code size for the specific use case. SIZALIZER, on the other hand, is intended as an analysis framework for ISA improvements. Thus, the structure and general goal of the analysis is similar, only the specific use case and thus the DFG adaptation is not applicable.

A tool for building optimizers named Sharlit is intruced by Tjiang et al. [16]. The main target of the tool is helping with the contruction of data-flow analysis as well as the transitions using data-flow analysis informations. The tool is implemented in C++ and depicts different data-flow analysis from iterative, symbolic to interval ones. In comparison to SIZALIZER, the tool does not provide the same code size analysis capabilities. Aditionally it only delivers a static DFG analysis to work with.

Static and dynamic binary analysis is widely used in computer security. Song et al. have developed a binary analysis platform using *BitBlaze* [14]. It consists of the components *Vine*, *TEMU* and *Ruddler*. These subtools perform the static binary, dynamic analysis and symbolic execution. However, since the tool is designed for programs without access to the source code, the DFG must be generated from the binary to provide as accurate binary information as possible for. This is done by lifting the back-translated assembly code into an IR. This is not necessary for SIZALIZER because it has access to the LLVM IR. Symbolic execution is also not necessary for SIZALIZER as it is a functional analysis. In contrast, this is necessary for BitBlaze to investigate the purpose and potential maliciousness or vulnerability. The tool is motivated by different applications and therefore not suitable for the purpose of SIZALIZER.

A script for the analysis of code-size for RISC-V can be found in the RISC-V github archive [4]. This script provides a possibility of illustrating the code saving that could be achieved with `Zce` instruction extension. It recieves the disassembly, static and dynamic symbol table for a submitted ELF file. For this it uses objdump. The executable disassembly is then parsed and written into the instruction record, which contains the instructions found in the previoulsy mentioned ELF file and the parsed RISC-V instructions for each function. When the instruction record is completely populated, the script searches for the branch targets. The found targets are then marked with a special key to identify them as block heads. The instruction record is used to perform different analysis tasks. Compared to SIZALIZER, it provides only a static analysis and is only focused on the `Zce` extensions. In contrast to that SIZALIZER is usable for a general purpose by looking at all existing and new instructions and provides a wider approach to this topic.

There are a number of platforms for dynamic analysis [6,11,13]. *PIN*, *Valgrind* and *DrMemory* are analysis and instrumentation tools that act as middleware between the application and the system. Unfortunately, they do not support RV32, and adapting them to do so is relatively complex. Therefore they are not suitable for the use case of SIZALIZER. *ETISS* is an ISA simulator [12]. It can be easily extended for all RISC CPUs and already supports RV32.

4 Analysis Framework

SIZALIZER is designed to perform a fully automated analysis of applications. The primary recipients of the information gathered are human analysts and developers, who can leverage these insights for further hardware and software development. For the purpose of enhanced clarity and expedited comprehension, the results are represented graphically, as will be elucidated in the subsequent section.

We validate the framework with a case study on the Embech benchmark suite, which covers a wide range of application characteristics in the embedded space. Throughout this section, the framework will be described and applied to Embech.

4.1 Architecture

The analysis process commences by taking C/C++ source code as the analysis target. This is processed by the SIZALIZER, which subsequently generates statistics, graphical representations, and detailed information pertaining to the code under examination.

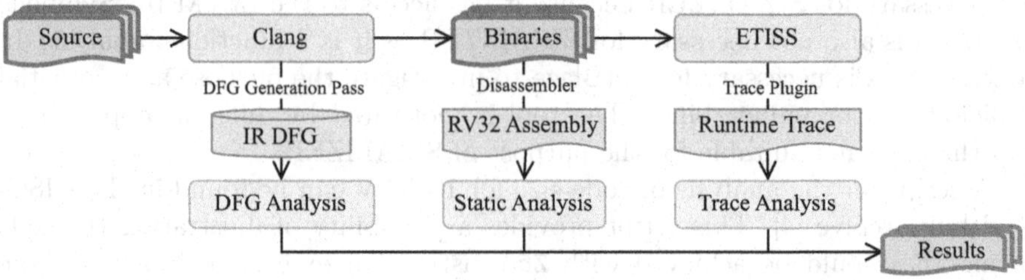

Fig. 1. Framework Architecture.

The architecture of SIZALIZER is stratified into three levels of analysis, which corresponds to the compilation and execution process. This multi-tier structure is illustrated by the columns depicted in Figure 1. Each row in the figure represents the extraction of information at respective stages of the process. Within the figure, the source and build artifacts are indicated in red, the analysis modules are highlighted in yellow, and the persistent representations are colored blue. These persistent representations facilitate reproducibility and the extensibility of the analysis process, as well as ensure verifiability and auditability.

The analysis is based on three different levels. Firstly, the highest level is the interprocedural data flow of the whole program. It is represented in a DFG, which is generated from the LLVM-IR by an analsis pass, while compiling source with the C/C++ compiler clang. Then stored in the graph database *Memgraph* [3]. *Memgraph* is suitable for this task because it has an C++ interface. This is necessary because the DFG generation pass in LLVM is written in C++. It also provides a superior performance compared to other graph databases like Neo4j [9]. The DFG is then analyzed by a separate program interfacing *Memgraph* producing statistics and structures about analysis target. With the advantage of being able to match patterns and structures in the DFG with the graph query language *Cypher*. This introduces an extensibility of the static analysis, because the Interface is standardized and the client is replaceable.

Secondly, the static machine code level, which is stored in executable binary programs called *Binaries*. The binary analysis is based on the target ISA RV32. It takes a binary in the ELF format and processes it. Including the extraction of the static code size, the code itself and an entropy analysis of the code. Only the assembly is suited for persisting it in a separate file in the Intel syntax. It is generated with the *objdump* tool, as described in Sect. 2. The assembly file is then parsed and analyzed by the static analyzer.

Thirdly, the execution investigated with the instruction set simulator ETISS. It is used because every ISA can be simulated and on instruction level analyzed. The binaries are executed with the simulator and every instruction along with its register values are stored in a runtime trace. This trace is then stored in a file and further analyzed by the trace analyzer.

4.2 IR DFG

The analysis conducted with the DFG is based on LLVM-IR. LLVM-IR and RV32 assembly have small differences, such as the separation of value selecting *phi* nodes and compare and branch instructions into two nodes in the IR DFG. However, the *phi* nodes are eliminated in the lowering to RV32. Furthermore, there are different nodes used for compare and branch instructions, such as *branch equals* or *branch greater than* instructions. However, these differences are not significant for the structural analysis of the data flow, and the functional flow remains consistent.

Algorithm 1. Build DFG and CFG.

```
1: procedure BuildCDFG(M: Module)
2:    session: DBSession ← connectToDB(IP, PORT)
3:    for all F: Function in M do
4:       for all BB: BasicBlock in F do
5:          for all sucBB: BasicBlock in successors(BB) do
6:             subgraph: SubGraph ← connectNodes(BB, sucBB, Type.CFG)
7:             session.push(subgraph)
8:          end for
9:          for all I: Instruction in BB do
10:             for all O: Operator in I do
11:                srcInst: Instruction ← getDataSourceInst(I, O)
12:                subgraph: SubGraph ← connectNodes(srcInst, I, Type.DFG)
13:                session.push(subgraph)
14:             end for
15:          end for
16:       end for
17:    end for
18:    session.close()
19:    return PreservedAnalyses::all()
20: end procedure
```

The DFG is generated with the Algorithm 1 in mind and executed during compilation of the target code. The DFG is then stored in the graph database *Memgraph*. A connection to the database is established in line 2, which is then closed again in line 18. The loop in line 10 iterates over all operators of all instructions in the module *M*. Then the source instruction that sets the value of the operator is searched for the operator *O* for the instruction *I*. There is a unique data source that cannot be changed again in the program flow, because this instruction is in the SSA. The two instructions are then connected in line 12 via a directed data flow path and henceforth referred to as nodes. This subgraph of the entire DFG is saved to the database in line 13. There is a new and previously non-existent path for each push. Since it is possible that the source or destination node already exists, they are only saved when non existent.

The analysis module relies on the concept of functional equality. Two nodes are considered as functionally equal, if they execute the same instruction, regardless of the registers they use. However, immediate instructions are not equal to register based ones. It is important to note that equality of instructions and nodes indicates functional equivalence. In contrast, instructions and nodes are considered identical only if they have the same function, registers, and immediate values (if applicable).

Algorithm 2. Match DFG.

```
MATCH p1=(x_11)-[:DFG]->...-[:DFG]-> (x_1N)
MATCH ...
MATCH pM=(x_M1)-[:DFG]->...-[:DFG]-> (x_MN)
WHERE SpecialCond(x_11, ..., x_1N) AND ... AND SpecialCond(x_M1, ..., x_MN)
RETURN p;
```

The Algorithm 2 performs a pattern matching on the DFG. The parameter N can be used to specify the length of the subgraph. For example, the width of parallel instructions can be set to 0 for $M = 1$, making it a single dependent data flow. However, it can be expanded to M parallel data flows. The complexity increases linearly with the dependent matching, whereas it increases quadratically in the parallel approach. SIZALIZER contains a generator for these queries. The parameters can be configured with various values for both N and M. Additionally, a list of values for N can be passed with the length of M.

Each structurally matched pattern is processed by the function *SpecialCond*. It is a function that maps a set of subgraphs to boolean values. Every pattern that resolves to false gets filtered. There are two types of filters. Firstly, node individual exclusive and inclusive filters. For instance, a filter can exclude all *phi* nodes or enforce a specific one to be a *st*. Secondly, there are structural filters, specifying structural properties of the subgraph to be matched. For example, a filter may require all terminating nodes to be equal. By using type of filter in conjunction with the specification of the *MATCH* commands, the logical structure of the data flows to be searched for can be completely predefined. This structure is predefined for a few common patterns. But, for special use cases, it needs to be defined by the user. These queries are also applicable to the CFG when using specific implementations of the *specialCond* function and the relationship type *:CFG*.

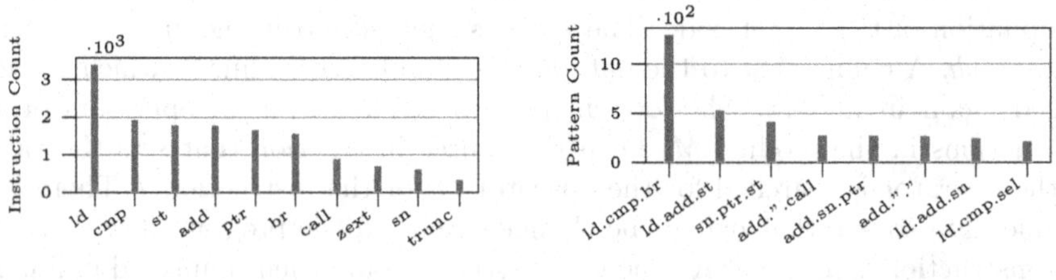

(a) Instruction Count. (b) Chain instruction Pattern.

Fig. 2. DFG Analysis Example.

The straightforward metric is to evaluate the number of similar nodes. The filter *SpecialCond* only filters *Const* and *phi* nodes as they are eliminated during lowering process. This results in the statistics shown in Fig. 2a. Using this metric, the most relevant instructions can be extracted, which have the greatest impact when implemented with smaller or faster instructions. The evaluation reveals that operations such as *ld* and *st*, control flow operations such as *cmp* and *br*, and arithmetic operations such as *add*, are used most frequently in the program. Therefore, these instructions also offer the greatest potential. It is also to be expected that a combination of these instructions will be used in the further data flow analysis.

More complex patterns can be identified by matching similar subtrees in the DFG. This can be done in two different ways. First, the size of the subtree can be specified. This results for the length of 3 in the example of *Embench* in the frequency plot Fig. 2b. This indicates that replacing the *ld cmp br* chain could have a significant impact on the size and possibly on the performance of the target. Another promising sequence is *laod add st*. This corresponds to the expected node distribution. Alternatively, one can specify the start and/or the end node of the subtree. Longer patterns provide more complex functionalities which could than be encoded in 48 bit instructions. The patterns are parameterized and encoded in *Cyper* queries, making them easy to use and to extend with custom patterns special for other targets and interests.

4.3 Binary Analysis

Binary analysis is a more heterogeneous process, i.e. it uses different approaches. The process starts with reading the segment information from the ELF header. This includes the static size of the entire binary as well as the individual segments. These values represent the static size and are therefore the key metric for static memory optimization.

Then, using the start and the size of the *.text* segment, the entropy graph is generated from the application code. Entropy measures the randomness of values, normalized between 0 and 1. Thus, if each value has the same probability of occurring, the entropy value is the highest. In the case of ISA encoding, this means that the more bits are used, the higher the entropy value is for each different instruction. From this the potential for further compression can be deduced. If the entropy is very high, i.e. a value between 0.8 and 1, there is not much prospect of a significant improvement in further compression. However, if the value is lower, there be structures in the code that can be found and exploited. In addition, the search space for further improvements may be limited spatially, since the indices show where the entropy is particularly low. For *Embench* compiled with *-Os*, the typical range is between 0.6 and 0.9. This is also suitable as a metric for evaluating the impact of new compression techniques.

Unlike the more abstract DFG analysis, the binary analysis can exclude optimizations that have already been made. For example, there are already many implementations of *cmp br* instructions such as *blt*. All of this can be recognized here, and thus unnecessary redundancy can be avoided when planning new optimizations.

The main part of the static analysis is the assembly analysis. A list of filenames from the assembly files to the binaries is passed to the analysis module. These are all first read in individually and parsed linearly. This results in a processable intermediate representation for each file, which can be analyzed individually for each binary. In addition, this information can be evaluated across files for global statistics.

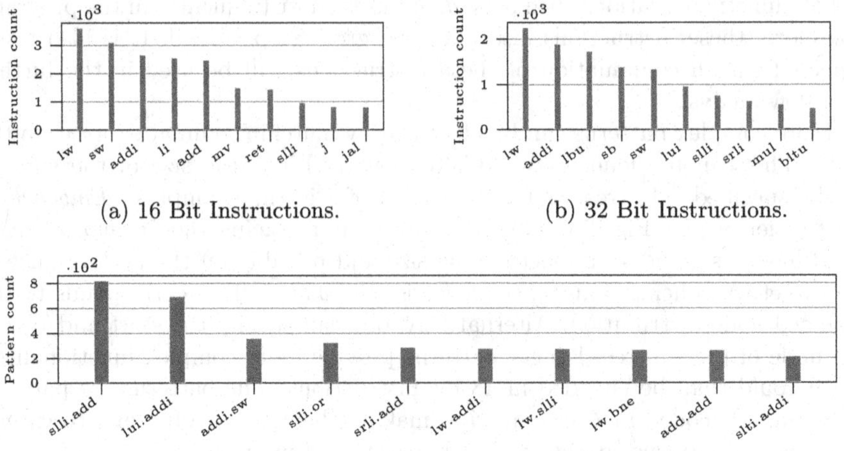

(a) 16 Bit Instructions.

(b) 32 Bit Instructions.

(c) Frequent instruction pairs.

Fig. 3. RISC-V Instruction Distribution Bitwith comparison.

First, an instruction distribution of compressed and uncompressed instructions is calculated for each analysis target individually and in total over all targets. The results for *Embench* are visualized in the Figs. 3a and 3b. It is particularly noticeable that the *ld word* statements appear particularly frequent in both the 16 and 32 bit codes. The compressed variant is only used for a limited range of values. It follows that it is worth extending this range for further values in order to be able to compress more instructions. With the same argument, it offers the *add immediate* instructions for further optimization.

The assembly analysis also evaluates instruction pairs that are directly connected by the data flow of a register. However, for performance reasons, this is only done locally without generating a global DFG, due to beeing structurally similar to the LLVM-IR DFG. The advantage of instruction pairs is that they combine instructions that have already been specifically implemented, thus reducing the effort required to plan a new instruction. However, the disadvantage of this representation is a distortion of the representation and the frequency, since *ld cmp st* is the most frequent in the IR DFG analysis, for example. Here, however, an implementation of the combination with *lw bne* only ranks 8th. This can be deduced form the different implementations depending on the specific function and so the one frequent combination spreading over many less frequent ones. From Fig. 3c it is evident, that combinations of add variants with memory or shift operations, such as a *shift left add* operation, can have a significant impact on code size. Which corresponds with the previous analyses.

4.4 Trace Analysis

Dynamic analysis examines the execution of the target application. This is done using runtime traces that are generated and saved by *ETISS*. These traces contain all executed instructions together with their memory address, opcode and register values. As with the other analysis, this is then used to generate evaluations that are related to the previous ones in such a way that the execution represents a special path through the DFG. Thus, the results are not expected to be fundamentally different from the previous two, but a different focus is set, so that not all the code is executed with the same frequency. For example, for Embench, less than 1 % of the source code is executed 99 % of the time for most test cases. These redundancy values are particularly high in this case because these are benchmarks and there is a main loop with an algorithm that is being benchmarked. The exception is nbody, where 60 % of the instructions are executed 99 % of the time. This is because the code in question is very small with 688 instructions, and the majority of them are executed regularly.

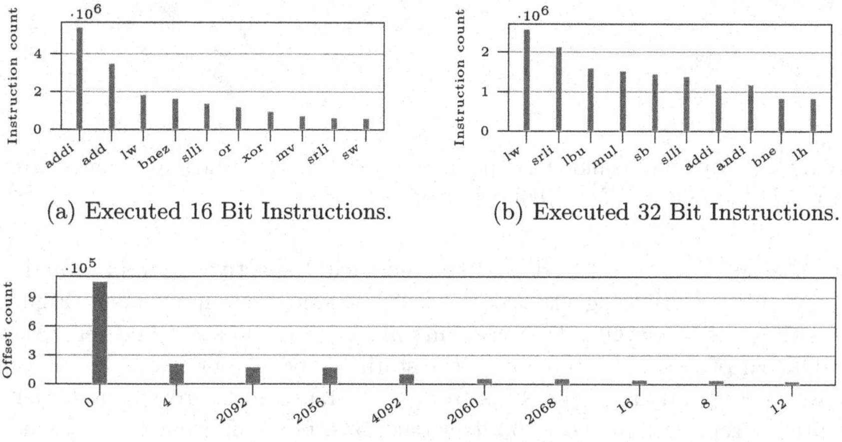

(a) Executed 16 Bit Instructions.

(b) Executed 32 Bit Instructions.

(c) LW Immediate value Distribution.

Fig. 4. Dynamic Results.

An instruction distribution is then calculated for all traces of the benchmarks individually and in total. This is shown in the Fig. 4. The instructions that have the greatest impact on runtime behavior and dynamic size can be deduced from this, since they are actually executed most frequently. For example, among the 16 bit instructions, the compressed *add* variants with and without immediate stand out. Among the 32 bit instructions, the *ld and logical shift right* instructions lead the way. For this analysis, many orders of magnitude more data has to be evaluated. This also corresponds to the fact that the trace files are significantly larger than the actual binary programs. This results in higher performance requirements for dynamic than for static analysis.

The big advantage of dynamic analysis is that further exploration is possible, since most frequent values are also evaluated. Figure 4c contains the most frequent register values for the 32-bit immediate ld word instruction. The 0 is by far the most common value, followed by the 4 by a wide margin. However, these values can also be represented with fewer bits in an immediate field of a

16-bit instruction. With SIZALIZER, this type of evaluation can be extended to all instructions with very little effort.

Dynamic instruction pairs linked by data flows are also evaluated. These enhance the power of the static ones and provide a more concrete view of the relevant ones. In the Embench example, the combination of *andi cadd* stands out. This combination requires 48 bits to encode and if you encode it with 32 bits you would save about 500 kb in dynamic size.

4.5 Suggested Instructions and Size Improvement

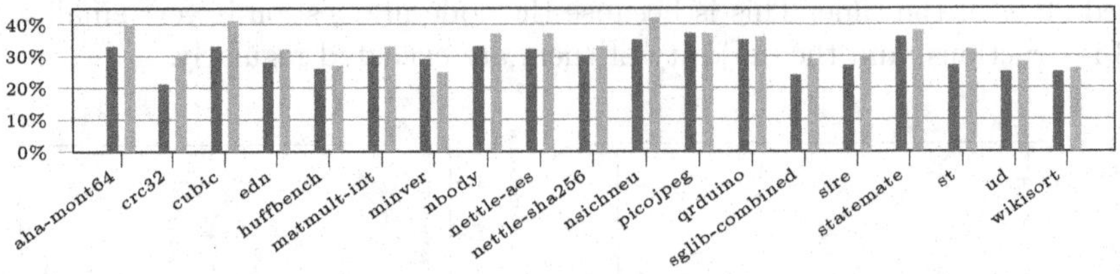

Fig. 5. Calculated Static and Dynamic Improvement (blue: static improvement, green: dynamic improvement) (Color figure online)

With the previously described analysis and their respective results in mind, we are now able to derive suggestion for instruction and size improvement. Figure 5 shows the possible amount for improving instruction and size in percent. While the blue bar of the diagram refers to the static analysis from Sect. 4.3, the green bar refers to the dynamic analysis from Sect. 4.4. The improvement potential for directly replacing 32 with 16 bit instructions, resulting from the static analysis, is also calculated statically. This is calculated individually for each binary, shown in Fig. 5. In addition to the individual improvement percentages, an average improvement percentage was calculated. The average improvement, which amounts to about 30% for all binaries, represents a significant value. Note, that all instructions must be mapped one-to-one to 16-bit instructions. This is a simple model for an estimate, but it is not completely true for all binaries. For example, there can be full 32 bit immediate values, that are not in the range of the compressed immediate instruction, and therefore require multiple instructions to encode. This value is therefore only an upper bound on the potential for improvement. The potential improvement resulting from the dynamic analysis results in an average percentage of 34%, which is also an upper bound.

4.6 Validation

The case study of SIZALIZER is validated on the larger projects, the Musl libc (v1.2.5) and the Linux kernel (v6.8.9). Both pieces of software are built and analyzed automatically by SIZALIZER. Both targets show the greatest potential with the *auipc jalr* function call (*e.call*). As well as with the *lui addi* instruction combination, used to load 32 bit immediate (*e.li*). This could be implemented in

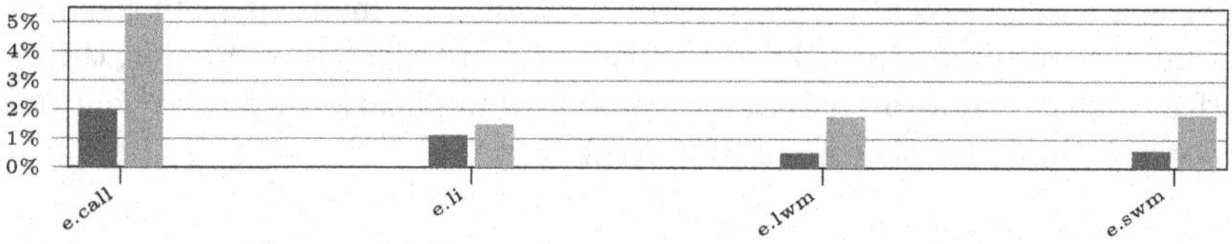

Fig. 6. Calculated Static Improvement (blue: Linux, green: Musl) (Color figure online)

a 48 bit instruction, as a full 32 bit immediate value can be encoded in both cases. In addition, both have great potential for optimization with grouped memory operations on the stack. This can be exploited by an operation that can read multiple values from the stack into registers (*e.lwm*) or write from registers to the stack (*s.swm*). Such an instruction would be easy to implement with 48 bits, as 31 destination and one source register could be encoded. The calculated code size reduction in % of each suggested instruction for the targets is shown in Figure 6. Musl shows for all found improvements an overall improvement potential of 30 % and the Linux kernel of 31%. This is close to the potential of Embench and thus shows that the basic software structures are self-similar, although some frequencies of patterns as seen in the function calls vary between the examples.

4.7 Discussion

The instruction suggestions of SIZALIZER are logical and functional. However, the framework does not have the ability to provide a real implementation, since it depends greatly on the actual processor architecture. This means that SIZALIZER can't specify any hardware overhead for the implementation of additional instructions. However the strengths of the tool lie in assisting the hardware architect in selecting new instructions through assessing the relevance of improvements based on the target software.

It is important that the analysis target is defined beforehand, due to the possibility of predefined forms or forms needing to be defined by the user. Since, for example, the power set of the DFG could be a target, which is not considered here due to being too large and issues with the mapping of instruction combinations to assembly instructions.

The resulting static and dynamic size optimizations are calculated upper bounds. Thus, there may be cases and/or values for which the estimate is not applicable, and therefore the actual value of the improvement is less than the given value. However, this value is correct in the order of magnitude and has an error in only one direction. It therefore gives a good indication of the potential for a particular improvement.

Embench was selected as the target application in the paper. This is not a complete application and the individual benchmarks contain only one algorithm, which leads to very small binaries and only contains 25 thousand nodes. These also have a special execution path where most of the time is spent in the area to be examined. In total, many different structures are covered. Moreover, these are algorithms that can also be found in embedded applications. So the benchmark is a good example for the use of SIZALIZER.

5 Future Work

As an improvement to SIZALIZER, the CFG will be merged with the DFG to form an intra-procedural Control Dataflow Graph (CDFG). This will have the advantage that structures consisting of more than one building block can be better analyzed. In addition, building block boundaries and chains can be analyzed explicitly.

The different layers of analysis will be more tightly coupled. This means that the executed instructions should be mapped with those in the binary and those in the DFG. This would make the synergies between the different analyses more prominent. SIZALIZER will be applied extensively to signal processing workloads. The RV32 command set will then be adapted based on these results. Special attention will be paid to the extension of the 16 bit compressed extension.

The more complex structures and small functions will be extracted from a representative set of real software. These will then be used to create meaningful instructions for a new RISC-V 48-Bit instruction set. This should run efficiently and software functions should be mappable to it in such a way that the static and dynamic size is smaller than that of an implementation using 16 and 32 bit instructions.

Another task is the implementation of metrics to measure the performance of the application under investigation. A desired result would be to measure the changes in runtimes and latency times in the event of a proposed improvement. In addition, it is planned to use a memory model for dynamic analysis to measure cache miss rates and their performance impact.

6 Conclusion

SIZALIZER represents a significant step forward in analysis on optimizing object size for embedded C/C++ applications on RV32 architectures, providing a comprehensive multi level analysis that automates the analysis process across the LLVM intermediate representation, executable binary code, and runtime instruction execution. The framework's novel approach provides developers and analysts with a vital tool for size optimization by identifying dominant patterns. As demonstrated by the Embench benchmark, SIZALIZER showcases its utility in suggesting optimization opportunities that can lead to ISA enhancements, thereby facilitating encoding efficiencies that result in reduced memory footprint. Future developments include extending the analysis capabilities, integrating a CDFG, enhancing the connection between analysis layers, targeting signal processing applications, and exploring the potential of RISC-V's 16-bit compressed instruction extensions. With the goal of improving the performance and sustainability of embedded systems, SIZALIZER is setting the pace for continued ISA refinement, which is essential to meet the economic and environmental challenges of the growing embedded microprocessor landscape.

References

1. Embench^{TM}: A modern embedded benchmark suite. https://www.embench.org/
2. LLVM language reference manual. https://llvm.org/docs/LangRef.html
3. Memgraph. https://memgraph.com/
4. RISC-V code-size analysis script. https://github.com/riscvarchive/riscv-code-size-reduction/tree/main/benchmarks
5. Tool Interface Standard (TIS) Executable and Linking Format (ELF) Specification. Standard, TIS Committee (1995). https://refspecs.linuxfoundation.org/elf/elf.pdf
6. Bruening, D., Amarasinghe, S.: Efficient, transparent, and comprehensive runtime code manipulation (2004)
7. Freitag, C., Berners-Lee, M., Widdicks, K., Knowles, B., Blair, G.S., Friday, A.: The real climate and transformative impact of ICT: a critique of estimates, trends, and regulations. Patterns **2**(9) (2021)
8. Hennessy, J., Patterson, D.: A new golden age for computer architecture: domain-specific hardware/software co-design, enhanced. In: ACM/IEEE 45th Annual International Symposium on Computer Architecture (ISCA) (2018)
9. Javor, A.: Memgraph vs. Neo4j: a performance comparison. https://memgraph.com/blog/memgraph-vs-neo4j-performance-benchmark-comparison
10. Lee, S., Shin, I., Kim, W., Lee, I., Min, S.L.: A design framework for real-time embedded systems with code size and energy constraints. ACM TECS **7**(2), 1–27 (2008)
11. Luk, C.K., et al.: Pin: building customized program analysis tools with dynamic instrumentation. ACM SIGPLAN Notices **40**(6), 190–200 (2005)
12. Mueller-Gritschneder, D., et al.: The extendable translating instruction set simulator (ETISS) interlinked with an MDA framework for fast RISC prototyping. In: 2017 International Symposium on Rapid System Prototyping (RSP), pp. 79–84 (2017)
13. Nethercote, N., Seward, J.: Valgrind: a framework for heavyweight dynamic binary instrumentation. ACM SIGPLAN Notices **42**(6), 89–100 (2007)
14. Song, D., et al.: BitBlaze: a new approach to computer security via binary analysis. In: Sekar, R., Pujari, A.K. (eds.) Information Systems Security, pp. 1–25. Springer, Berlin, Heidelberg (2008)
15. Strout, M.M., Kreaseck, B., Hovland, P.D.: Data-flow analysis for MPI programs. In: 2006 International Conference on Parallel Processing (ICPP'06), pp. 175–184. IEEE (2006)
16. Tjiang, S.W.K., Hennessy, J.L.: Sharlit—a tool for building optimizers. In: Proceedings of the ACM SIGPLAN 1992 Conference on Programming Language Design and Implementation, pp. 82–93. PLDI '92, Association for Computing Machinery, New York, NY, USA (1992). https://doi.org/10.1145/143095.143120

SafeFloatZone: Identify Safe Domains for Elementary Functions

Markus Krahl[1,2](✉), Matthias Güdemann[1], and Stefan Wallentowitz[1]

[1] Hochschule München University of Applied Sciences, Munich, Germany
{markus.krahl,matthias.guedemann,stefan.wallentowitz}@hm.edu
[2] TASKING Germany GmbH, Munich, Germany
markus.krahl@tasking.com

Abstract. Formal verification of embedded system software can profoundly influence both safety and security, and has the potential to alter the development process substantially. However, the complexity of formal verification, along with stringent time-to-market and resource constraints of embedded systems, has posed significant barriers to its adoption. Moreover, ensuring the accessibility of formal methods in the design and implementation of embedded systems remains a major challenge. In our paper, we evaluate formal methods and demonstrate the accessibility and benefits within a critical area of many industries: IEEE754 floating-point values are widely used and due to their fixed size, they can only approximate real numbers. For the most part, their behavior aligns with programmer expectations; however, certain corner cases exist in which they are susceptible to value cancellation, rounding errors, and deviations from standard mathematical rules. Such discrepancies can be problematic when calculated results diverge from software developer expectations, potentially leading to fatal errors. We propose `SafeFloatZone` which allows for the identification of safe domains for algorithms utilizing IEEE754 floating-point numbers. The approach is rooted in formal verification, leveraging modern, efficient Satisfiability Modulo Theories (SMT) solvers to deduce preconditions for functions, thereby providing stronger guarantees of correctness. In this work we demonstrate how `SafeFloatZone` can readily benefit embedded system developers and show that it is transferable to a variety of algorithms based on IEEE754 floating-point numbers.

Keywords: Embedded Systems · IEEE754 Floating-Point · Formal Verification

1 Introduction

Embedded systems often control safety-critical processes, such as advanced driver assistance systems (ADAS) in the automotive domain. It is imperative that such systems are carefully designed, implemented, and tested to comply

L. Carro et al. (Eds.): SAMOS 2024, LNCS 15226, pp. 122–137, 2025.
https://doi.org/10.1007/978-3-031-78377-7_9

with the relevant standards. It must be assured that unintended behavior of the embedded software never endangers the safety of the whole system.

In order to adequately react to and control the physical operation, the processing of real numbers is required. Because of the limitations of computer memory and processing power, calculations do generally not use infinite precision real numbers; instead, the finite set of floating-point (FP) numbers is used to approximate and represent real numbers. Currently, most processors conform to the FP-implementation defined by the IEEE754 Standard and are frequently equipped with a dedicated floating-point unit (FPU). When writing software that relies on the calculation of FP numbers, it must be considered that FP numbers only approximate real values and do not fulfill mathematical rules, e.g., associativity of addition.

Accordingly, when critical embedded systems depend on the correct computation of FP numbers, adequate techniques must be applied to verify that none of the possible input arguments to the FP algorithm lead to an incorrect result. However, there is a risk of systematic errors due to the nature of FP numbers, which are often system-dependent and difficult to identify [21]. This makes testing FP functions challenging.

As the main contribution of this paper, we present `SafeFloatZone`, a tool that leverages a combination of model checking and model counting to automatically determine safe input domains for FP algorithms such that the result corresponds to a user-defined set of properties. This method is designed to automatically identify which inputs from designated FP ranges will or will not lead to violations of the properties of the function being analyzed. `SafeFloatZone` uses binary search to pinpoint an interval for FP inputs that satisfies given Satisfiability Modulo Theories (SMT) equations using FP theory.

To demonstrate the practical applicability of `SafeFloatZone`, we evaluate its performance on a trigonometric FP algorithm used in industry and compare it against a purely enumeration based approach in a case study. We use the C Bounded Model Checker (CBMC) [19] to generate constraint problems in SMTLIB2 [6] format and solve these with `SafeFloatZone` by employing different SMT solvers. Additionally, to perform the enumeration based approach, the C sources are natively compiled and iteratively executed with all possible FP values until one of the stated assertions is violated.

The paper is structured as follows. In Sect. 2 we contend that existing testing techniques exhibit limitations in verifying FP algorithms, particularly with respect to the domain of supported input values. The algorithm of `SafeFloatZone` is described in Sect. 3. A case study to evaluate `SafeFloatZone` in comparison with a brute-force approach is conducted in Sect. 4.

2 Motivation and Background

FP numbers in the IEEE754 format are widely implemented in CPUs and are commonly provided in programming languages. Most often these are realized as 32-Bit wide single-precision `float` and 64-Bit wide double-precision `double`. Due to the fixed width bit size, they can only approximate real numbers. Therefore calculations are subject to value cancellation and rounding errors. Various special values exist which can lead to surprising results if one is not careful [18]. Still, IEEE754 numbers are extremely useful in many application areas, in particular physical calculations.

2.1 IEEE754 Floating Point

The following table shows the format of IEEE754 binary FP numbers. For a d bit format it contains an explicit sign bit, then e bits for the *exponent* and finally $m = d-1-e$ bits for the *mantissa*. The most common formats are $e = 8, m = 23$ for 32-Bit `float` and $e = 11, m = 52$ for `double`.

sign bit	exponent	mantissa
b_{d-1}	$b_{d-2} \cdots b_{d-2-e+1}$	$b_{d-2-e} \cdots b_0$

For specific bit patterns there exist special values like an explicit ± 0 (two different values) and $\pm\infty$. Special not-a-number (NaN) values indicate a calculation that did not give a valid result, e.g., the result of $\frac{0}{0}$.

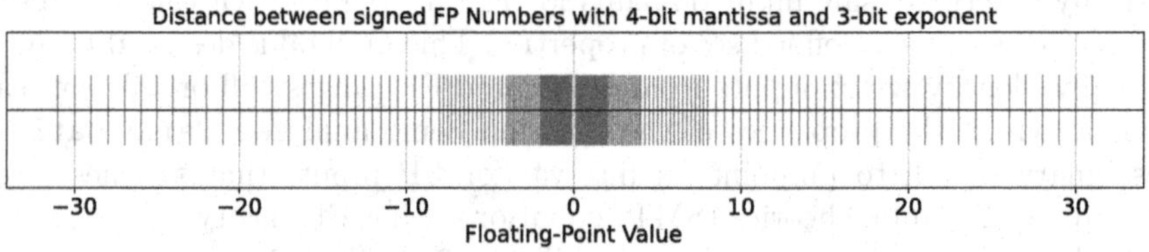

Fig. 1. Exemplary distance variation between consecutive FP numbers

Due to the fixed number of bits, the precision of IEEE754 calculation is limited. The distance between consecutive FP numbers can vary based on the magnitude of the exponent e as displayed in Fig. 1 for exemplary 8-bit FP numbers compliant to IEEE754. This implies that in regions where the gap to the next successive FP number is larger, there is an increased likelihood of bigger absolute rounding errors, as compared to FP intervals with smaller differences to the next FP number. Still, IEEE754 FP numbers are designed in a way that for the majority of FP numbers the computation behave very close to the theoretical results in $\mathbb{R}$.

But for some edge cases it results in imprecise or even mathematically wrong results which are not expected by the programmer. These outliers or intervals of problematic FP numbers have to be recognized since they might unintentionally disturb the safety-critical processes controlled by an embedded system, and in the worst-case scenario, lead to harm or danger to human life. Especially in the automotive domain, there are currently millions of vehicles on the road, resulting in millions or even billions of driving hours in total. Therefore, it must be recognized that, due to the long operation time of the embedded systems within these vehicles, errors that might theoretically occur with very low probability and under rare conditions could actually arise in reality.

2.2 Requirements for Software in Safety Critical Domains

There exist different strategies for the validation and verification of FP algorithms. Currently, testing-based approaches are widely used, e.g., unit testing to achieve a certain code coverage, or sample-based testing to evaluate the function under test against a predefined set of inputs. In the automotive domain, with respect to the ISO 26262 standard, specific requirements for performing software unit verification have to be fulfilled. To ensure thorough examination of relevant code, a certain level of code coverage must be achieved during testing. This is particularly critical for software units that require the highest Assurance Safety Integrity Level, ASIL D, for which reaching Modified Condition/Decision Coverage (MC/DC) is recommended. This criterion mandates that for each condition in a decision statement, its effect on the outcome of the decision is demonstrated independently [12]. MC/DC coverage is also required for highly critical airborne software, according to the DO-178C standard.

However, solely relying on a set of unit tests that achieve combined MC/DC coverage for FP algorithms may not be sufficient to ensure its correct functionality. In particular, the ISO 26262 standard strongly advocates the application of further measures for software unit verification. The executed unit tests should be derived from an analysis of the requirements, from equivalence classes, or from boundary values. Besides, it highly recommends additional static software unit verification, such as applying static analysis to examine the source code without executing it.

In requirements based testing of FP functions, it is challenging to ensure that the specified properties are verified across the entire set of potential FP input values. Testing based on the boundaries of representable FP numbers would demonstrate the behavior of the FP algorithm only in edge cases and not within ordinary ranges. Also, specifying equivalence classes would mandate the consideration of multiple different FP approximations within the interval of all possible FP values. It appears that developing unit tests based on these methods may not be sufficient to determine whether the FP implementation behaves as expected or to identify which ranges of FP numbers are supported.

The ISO 26262 standard includes formal verification as a method for static analysis. Given the intricate behavior of FP numbers in complex computations, there is promising potential for applying formal verification methods to ensure the correctness of FP operations in software units.

3 SMT-Based Evaluation of FP Computations

In this section, we present `SafeFloatZone`, an algorithm based on formal verification that automatically determines FP ranges for which the specified properties of the analyzed FP algorithm hold. First, we provide a brief overview of the most common formal verification techniques. Subsequently, we describe how `SafeFloatZone` employs bounded model checking to ascertain the potential results of FP computations for a given FP input interval. We demonstrate how `SafeFloatZone` iteratively applies the results obtained from model checking to further refine the analyzed FP intervals.

3.1 Overview of Formal Methods

There exist different approaches for formal analysis of programs. They differ mainly in the required effort for verification, degree of automation, precision of the analysis and resource requirements. The approaches are complementary, each with its own advantages and disadvantages.

Abstract interpretation presents an effective method for automatically detecting runtime errors in program code, such as the overflow of FP numbers and computations that result in NaN, or rounding errors [14]. In terms of deductive verification, available interactive theorem provers enable the manual creation of precise and reliable proofs for FP operations [3,9]. Additionally, there exists the analysis framework Frama-C [2] with its Weakest Precondition (WP) plugin [7] which automatically performs deductive verification of annotated C source code.

With regard to model checking, applying the C Bounded Model Checker (CBMC) [19] provides an interesting approach. Accordingly, the desired properties that should be maintained during program execution are inserted into the program code via `assert` statements. CBMC translates these source files into a Boolean satisfiability (SAT) or SMT formula, which is then submitted to a solver program.

This translation is done in such a way that if the formula is satisfiable, there exists a variable assignment that leads to an assertion violation. Properties for the FP algorithm can be specified within the program code using assertions written in native C. Furthermore, CBMC, commonly used in the industry, enables the analysis of nearly all standard-conforming program constructs, and supports multiple SAT and SMT solvers as backends.

Besides, SMT solvers are already employed in various program verification tools to efficiently find solutions for constraints in first-order logic. The SMTLIB, an initiative to define standards for SMT solvers, was extended with a theory for FP arithmetic in accordance with the IEEE754 standard [24]. This might further increase the potential to analyze FP operations with state-of-the-art solvers, such as Z3 [16], MathSAT [13], CVC5 [5] or bitwuzla [22].

3.2 SafeFloatZone

In the following, we introduce `SafeFloatZone`, a method to identify safe input domains for functions using FP numbers. It uses CBMC to generate an SMTLIB2 model and iteratively refines this initial model. The results obtained in this analysis are used to guide the refinement, the intermediate constraint problems are solved using current state-of-the-art SMT solvers that support the FP theory.

In many scenarios, FP algorithms perform as expected only for FP values within a specific range. For FP numbers outside of this designated interval, the precision of the computed result may diminish to a level that is not acceptable in critical domains. When analyzing an FP function to identify such outliers, relying solely on model checking with an SMT solver might not be sufficient. In the event that a property does not hold, the SMT solver outputs only a single FP number that violates the corresponding assertion.

In such cases, model counting techniques could be used for determining the total number of models—or variable assignments—that satisfy the derived SMT equations. Even though there are promising methods available for performing model counting of SAT problems, current approaches to reasoning about the number of solutions for SMT equations are still in an early development phase [10].

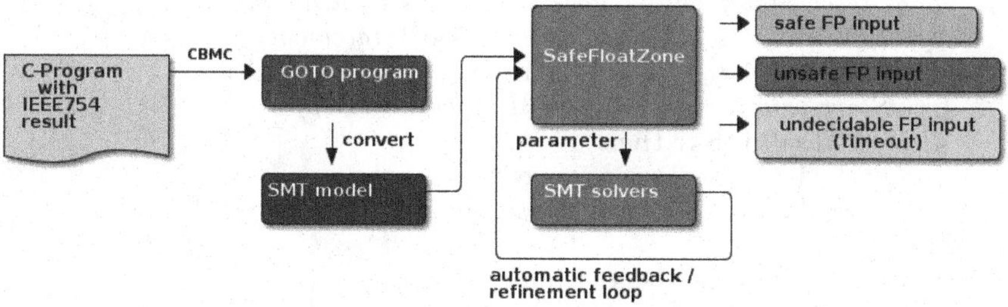

Fig. 2. Overview of the `SafeFloatZone` approach

Instead of utilizing enumerative model counting that merely aggregates any discovered FP values without considering their sequence, `SafeFloatZone` introduces a novel approach. The algorithm aims to identify the largest possible interval of FP values that ensures to be free of any FP value representing a counterexample. Thus, the values within this interval are confirmed as safe input for the evaluated FP function.

To make this analysis efficient, we leverage the exponents of FP numbers to modify the width of the currently analyzed input domain. To achieve this, we add a constraint to the SMT equation which requires the solution to be an FP number with an exponent that falls within an interval defined by minimum and maximum exponent values exponent. If the SMT solver can find a solution within a specified timeout period, we refine the range of permissible exponents by narrowing the bounds, and this updated restriction is then applied to the original SMT formula. A binary search technique is utilized to effectively adjust the scope of potential exponents throughout the execution of the algorithm.

`SafeFloatZone` is sound in that it reliably identifies FP exponents that produce FP values representing valid counterexample. If the employed SMT solver returns UNSAT, it is also sound in assuring that the current FP interval bounded by two FP exponents, does not contain a solution and is therefore safe for use as input. Should the SMT solving process be aborted by a timeout, the conclusion drawn by `SafeFloatZone` regarding the currently investigated FP interval would be considered unsound. Similarly, if the solver consistently returns SAT or UNSAT for the given input, the final result returned by `SafeFloatZone` would be deemed complete; otherwise it will be regarded as incomplete.

Algorithm 1. SafeFloatZone

```
1: (startExp, currentExp) ← (0, maxExponentSize − 1)
2: (satExponents, unsatExponents, timeoutExponents) ← emptyList
3: smtCommands ← parseSMTFile(filePath)
4: (privStart, privCurrent) ← (startExp, currentExp)
5: while privStart ≠ privCurrent do
6:     lowerBound ← FP(bitSign, startExp, emptyMantissa)
7:     upperBound ← FP(bitSign, currentExp, fullMantissa)
8:     rangeAssertStatement ← (lowerBound ≤ searchedSolution ≤ upperBound)
9:     AppendToList(smtCommands, rangeAssertStatement)
10:    solverResult, solution ← CallSMTSolver(smtCommands)
11:    (privStart, privCurrent) ← (startExp, currentExp)
12:    if solverResult is SAT then
13:        AppendToList(satExponents, currentExp)
14:        currentExp ← startExp + ⌊(currentExp − startExp)/2⌋
15:    else
16:        if solverResult is UNSAT then
17:            AppendToList(unsatExponents, currentExp)
18:        else
19:            AppendToList(timeoutExponents, currentExp)
20:        end if
21:        if isEmpty(satExponents) then
22:            break
23:        else
24:            startExp ← currentExp
25:            lastSatExp ← getLastElement(satExponents)
26:            currentExp ← startExp + ⌊(lastSatExp − startExp)/2⌋
27:            if solverResult is UNSAT then
28:                startExp ← startExp + 1
29:            end if
30:        end if
31:    end if
32: end while
```

The pseudocode of `SafeFloatZone` is presented in Algorithm 1. In lines 1 – 4 all relevant variables are initialized. Especially, *startExp* holds the FP exponent representing the lower bound of the current search interval whereas *currentExp* holds the exponent for the upper bound. The lists *satExponents*, *unsatExponents*, and respectively the *timeoutExponents* are used to gather the upper bound of the search interval depending on the status of the solver.

All original SMT-statements included in the provided SMT-file are parsed into the *smtCommands*-list. The content of this list will serve as input for the SMT-solver. *privStart* and *privCurrent* shall hold the values of *startExp* and *currentExp* from the previous iteration of the algorithm.

The while loop in lines 5 – 32 represents the core of the algorithm. It terminates when *privStart* equals *privCurrent*, indicating that *startExp* and *currentExp* were equal in the previous search. At the beginning, from lines 6 – 9 the *smtCommands*-list is appended with an assert-statement. This ensures that the solution lies within the interval determined by two bounds: a lower bound, which is the FP number denoted by *startExp* with an empty mantissa (all zero), and an upper bound, which is the FP number represented by *currentExp* with a full mantissa (all ones). Based on the return status of the SMT solver on the submitted *smtCommands*, *startExp* and *currentExp* are modified and the value of *currentExp* is added to different lists: to *satExponents* if the status is SAT (line 13), to *unsatExponents* if it is UNSAT (line 16), and to *timeoutExponents* when a timeout was encountered (line 19).

In case the solver returns SAT, the search interval is narrowed by setting *currentExp* to the result of adding half the previous distance between *startExp* and *currentExp* to the *startExp*, as seen in lines 14. If the solver returned UNSAT or a timeout was reached, the interval is shifted by initially setting *startExp* to *currentExp*. Subsequently, *currentExp* is updated to the sum of its current value and half the distance between its current value and the last known *currentExp* value for which the solver returned SAT, as shown in 24 – 26. If the solver result was UNSAT, the current *startExp* had previously been the upper bound of an interval that certainly did not contain a counterexample. Therefore, the *startExp* is incremented by one (line 28) to avoid evaluating an FP exponent twice. In the event that there is no previous value for *currentExp* for which the solver returned SAT, the loop is canceled, as seen in line 22.

Even though possible solutions may exist, we treat the occurrence of a timeout similar to the return of UNSAT. We intended to design the algorithm to quickly find ranges of exponents that satisfy the corresponding SMT equation. The remaining exponents that were excluded from the search set due to a timeout should be investigated further. The found SAT and UNSAT FP exponent intervals could be leveraged as threshold values to accelerate a complementary brute-force approach, as shown in Sect. 4.

Example Run of `SafeFloatZone` An exemplary run of the algorithm is depicted in Fig. 3. It shows the different iterations of the algorithm as stages of the execution. For each stage, the evaluated FP exponent intervals of single-precision FPs are shown. `SafeFloatZone` begins by examining the largest possible FP exponent interval, which is $[0, 254]$, and iteratively reduces its scope through the various stages. The interval to be analyzed in the next stage depends on the result obtained from the SMT solver: SAT, UNSAT, or timeout, for the interval of the current stage. In the first stage, if the problem is UNSAT or there is a timeout, the algorithm terminates. If the problem is SAT in the exponent interval $[0, 254]$, `SafeFloatZone` continues to stage 2. At each stage, different

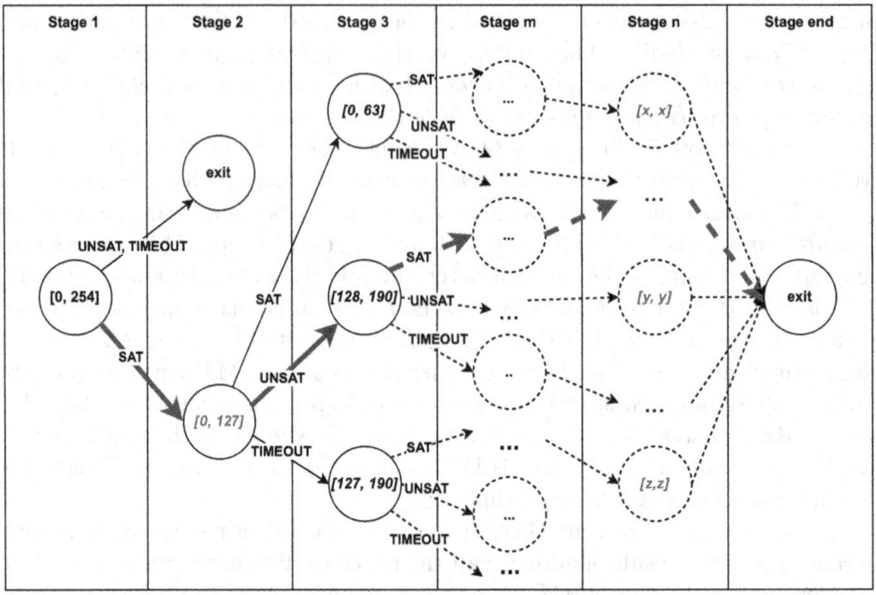

Fig. 3. Potential stages of `SafeFloatZone` examining exponent intervals

solver results lead to the analysis of different parts of the investigated FP exponent intervals until the upper and lower bounds of the interval become equal in the next-to-last stage. If, in stage 2, the problem is SAT within the interval $[0, 127]$, we continue with $[0, 63]$ in stage 3; if it is UNSAT then we test if the satisfying exponent might lie in the interval $[128, 190]$ (because in $[0, 254]$ it was SAT); and if there is a timeout, we continue with the interval $[127, 190]$, as we treat the occurrence of a timeout similar to UNSAT (except that the current upper bound is reused as new lower bound). From here on, at each stage, these three possible outcomes of the SMT analysis determine which interval to analyze in the succeeding stage. `SafeFloatZone` terminates once the upper and lower bounds of the processed interval in the last stage are equal, as demonstrated by the transition from stage n to stage *end*.

During the execution of `SafeFloatZone`, only one path from the start vertex, representing the initial FP exponent interval, to the final vertex, indicating the end of the algorithm, can be taken. An exemplary path through possibly analyzed FP exponent ranges is demonstrated by the thick, red arrows in Fig. 2. Note, that in this figure and throughout the entire paper, all shown exponents represent the actual stored values within the FP format, including the bias. Therefore, an exponent denoted with a value of 0 equates to an FP exponent of -127 once the bias is taken into account.

4 Case Study

Our goal is to evaluate SafeFloatZone's ability to automatically determine ranges of FP numbers based on FP exponents that lead to correct or imprecise results when submitted to a FP function written in C. We compare its performance against a purely brute-force method and conduct a combined approach by using the intermediate results of SafeFloatZone as initial and potential end values for the brute-force technique.

4.1 Overview

As exemplary single precision FP implementation, we used an approximation for the sine (*sinf*) function taken from the *Cephes* single library [1]. We designed a test suite in C to validate the FP function by inserting an assertion to confirm that its mathematical characteristics are maintained. In detail, the analyzed C function shall possess the following property, with ϵ representing the maximal tolerated absolute rounding error. For this exemplary evaluation we chose $\epsilon := 0.1$ to find input values that lead to a deviation of 10%.

$$\text{assertion\_sinf}: x \notin \{NaN, \pm infinity\} \implies abs(sinf(x)) \leq 1.0 + \epsilon \quad (1)$$

As shown before in Fig. 2, the C source files with the FP function and the test suite are translated into SMT equations supporting the FP theory using CBMC. Subsequently, we apply SafeFloatZone to these SMT formulas by employing various SMT solvers and analyze the returned FP exponent intervals.

In comparison, the C sources are additionally compiled with an enumeration routine that verifies the specified assertion through executing the function with each possible FP value. This algorithm terminates once a first counterexample for the assertion has been obtained. The interval comprising all FP values from the start of the search up to the occurrence of the identified counterexample shall be deemed safe input for the FP function.

We deliberately ignored any recommended limit on the input values submitted to the examined function to ensure these are detected by SafeFloatZone or by enumeration independently. For demonstration purposes, we evaluated both approaches using only positive FP values. Nevertheless, SafeFloatZone can also handle negative FP values, as the exponent representation is the same for both positive and negative numbers. Next, we present the key results of applying SafeFloatZone and compare them with those obtained using enumeration. For performing the evaluation of SafeFloatZone and brute-force approaches, a machine with an Intel i7-12700KF processor and 32 GB of memory was used.

4.2 Evaluation

In Table 1, the FP exponent ranges identified by SafeFloatZone are summarized. It shows the potential of various SMT solvers used by SafeFloatZone to detect potential violations of the stated assertion. The columns categorize the results by the solvers used, whereas the rows display the SAT, UNSAT, and timeout intervals, as well as the total number of solver calls and the overall time taken. Each cell placed in either the SAT, UNSAT, or timeout row presents all the searched FP exponent intervals along with the corresponding solving time, depending on the result returned by the solver. The number of solver calls indicates how often the solver was executed on the given intervals, corresponding to the aggregate of all FP exponent intervals submitted to the solver. The values in the total time row reflect the duration `SafeFloatZone`, in conjunction with the corresponding solver, took to iterate over and reason about the intervals.

Table 1. FP exponent intervals for the property $abs(sinf(x)) \leq 1 + \epsilon$

	bitwuzla		CVC5		Z3		MathSAT	
SAT	0.17 s	[0,254]	1.73 s	[0,254]	1.48 s	[0,254]	0.47 s	[0,254]
	0.45 s	[128,190]	1.05 s	[190,222]	2.65 s	[127,190]	0.55 s	[128,190]
	0.06 s	[128,159]	0.01 s	[190,206]	174.97 s	[127,158]	0.71 s	[128,159]
	0.11 s	[151,155]	0.01 s	[190,198]	4.07 s	[150,154]	0.49 s	[151,155]
	0.01 s	[151,153]	0.01 s	[190,194]	156.48 s	[150,152]	0.02 s	[151,153]
	0.01 s	[151,152]	0.01 s	[190,192]	121.17 s	[151,151]	5.97 s	[151,152]
	83.1 s	[151,151]	0.04 s	[190,191]				
			9.5 s	[190,190]				
UNSAT	15.42 s	[0,127]	43.67 s	[0,127]	[]		50.78 s	[0,127]
	247.44 s	[128,143]					312.93 s	[128,143]
timeout	600.01 s	[144,151]	600.01 s	[128,190]	600.01 s	[0,127]	600.02 s	[144,151]
					600.01 s	[127,142]	600.01 s	[151,151]
					600.01 s	[142,150]		
					600.01 s	[150,151]		
solver calls	10		10		10		10	
total time	946.76 s		656.48 s		2860.89 s		1571.96 s	

Each interval displayed in the UNSAT row is guaranteed to contain only FP exponents for which all corresponding FP numbers do not violate the assertion, and are therefore deemed safe for use in the analyzed function. For determining the lowest FP exponents whose FP numbers would violate the stated assertion, one should consider the FP exponent interval in the last line of the cells within the SAT row. In contrast, the interval in the first line of these cells is typically of a larger size and ensures that there exists at least one FP value with an exponent within this range that violates the assertion.

`SafeFloatZone` initially submits to the solver an interval starting with the minimal and ending with the largest exponent, encompassing the entire range of possible FP exponents. If the solver returns a timeout for this specific first interval, it becomes impossible to further reason about any other sub-intervals, and `SafeFloatZone` is consequently terminated.

Table 2 presents the results of using either a brute-force approach exclusively or in combination with `SafeFloatZone`. The first column displays the outcome of using brute-force alone, the subsequent ones show the results of brute-force initialized with the first FP value that lies outside of the UNSAT FP exponent intervals obtained by SafeFloatZone. In the top two rows, the value of the counterexample and its exponent are shown. The following rows show either the runtime of the brute-force approach alone or together with the time needed to obtain the threshold values using SafeFloatZone. The last two rows show the total calls to the investigated FP function, and the inaccurately computed result of the *sinf* function.

Table 2. Enumeration of FP input values for property $abs(sinf(x)) \leq 1 + \epsilon$

	brute-force starting from 0.0	brute-force starting from 2.0	brute-force starting from 131072.0
first found counterexample	32421038.0	32421038.0	32421038.0
FP exponent of counterexample	151	151	151
time brute-force	54.16 s	3.01 s	1.05 s
total time	54.16 s	18.6 s	264.59 s
number of iterations	1274501719	200759895	66542167
returned sinf value	-1.11	-1.11	-1.11

If SafeFloatZone successfully identifies unsatisfiable FP exponent intervals, but there also exist intervals for which a timeout was reached, the runtime to brute-force these remaining intervals—and consequently, the total number of iterations—can be drastically reduced. However, this requires waiting until SafeFloatZone either terminates or outputs its first unsatisfiable intermediate results. In cases where SafeFloatZone is not able to identify any unsatisfiable FP exponent ranges, the brute-force approach cannot be expedited.

Table 1 shows the intervals of FP exponents analyzed for determining whether the associated FP values would violate the assertion stated in *assertion_sinf*. By using the *bitwuzla* and *MathSAT* SMT solvers, it was possible to find an UNSAT interval that guarantees that all FP numbers with an exponent in the interval of $[0, 143]$ can be submitted to the *sinf* function, ensuring the result respects the assertion. *CVC5* could identify the smaller exponent range of $[0, 127]$ as UNSAT. However, *z3* could not detect any UNSAT FP exponent interval. Additionally, *bitwuzla* and *z3* identified the smallest FP exponent interval of $[151, 151]$, and *MathSAT* retrieved a slightly larger interval of $[151, 152]$, both of which are guaranteed to contain FP values that violate the given assertion. Conversely, *CVC5* could determine the smallest FP exponent interval of $[190, 190]$ to include FP values representing counterexamples. However, several intervals are present for which all applied solvers could not find a solution within the provided timeout. Without any further investigation, it remains uncertain whether these FP exponent intervals might contain FP numbers that would make the output of *sinf* violate the stated assertion.

On the other hand, Table 2 shows the results of performing different kinds of brute-force approaches. The approach starting brute-forcing from the smallest positive FP value 0.0 took 54.52s to find the first counterexample that lead the *sinf* function to return a wrong value. The *sinf* function was executed with 1,274,501,719 different FP numbers until a violation of the assertion was detected. The FP exponent of this counterexample lies also within the smallest FP exponent interval that `SafeFloatZone` identified by using the *bitwuzla*, *z3*, and *MathSAT* solver. Considering the order of `SafeFloatZone` processing the intervals, the fastest available intermediate results containing an UNSAT interval, could be obtained after around 15.59s when using *bitwuzla*. When leveraging the first FP value succeeding this specific interval (2.0) as start for the brute-force method, brute-forcing took 3.01s and required 200,759,895 iterations. The total time for this method, which combines brute-force with the first intermediate results delivered by `SafeFloatZone`, was close to 18.6s. This represents only 34.34% of the time that the brute-force method required, starting from the FP value 0.0. The next intermediate result which includes the UNSAT interval [128, 143], is provided by `SafeFloatZone` after 263.54s using the *bitwuzla* SMT solver. When utilizing the first FP number following this interval (131072.0) as start value, brute-forcing alone took 1.05s and performed 66,542,167 executions of the *sinf* function with distinct FP values. The total time for this combined approach was around 264.59s which corresponds to 488.53% of employing brute-force from 0.0.

4.3 Strengths and Limitations

Overall, the presented FP exponent intervals obtained by using `SafeFloatZone` are a helpful indicator to quickly determine which ranges of FP values should and which should not be submitted to the analyzed function.

Additionally, `SafeFloatZone` could also be used with shorter timeout values, such that only few intervals are labelled as SAT or UNSAT, whereas the majority will remain uncertain due to more timeouts. Still, these few determined exponent ranges might already serve as valuable input to significantly reduce the runtime of the brute-force approach as shown in Table 2.

The quality of `SafeFloatZone`'s outcome strongly depends on the results of the initial iterations; such that if a timeout occurs during the analysis of the first exponent interval, the whole analysis by `SafeFloatZone` yields no valuable results. However, due to its compatibility with the SMTLIB2 format, `SafeFloatZone` can utilize any SMT solver that adheres to the standard and can handle the FP theory. Employing multiple solvers, and thus diverse solving strategies, may enhance the likelihood of identifying more SAT or UNSAT FP exponent intervals in total, and particularly in determining whether the initial interval is SAT or UNSAT. Additionally, this enables `SafeFloatZone` to employ the current state-of-the-art SMT solvers and seamlessly integrate newly developed solutions.

`SafeFloatZone` relies on CBMC to generate the SMT equations, where the bounded model checking routine makes the processing of loop iterations difficult. Therefore, the number of loop iterations as well as the recursion depth in the processed C programs have to be bounded.

One also has to consider that the performed analysis only validates whether the specified assertions are respected. For instance, the FP exponents identified by SafeFloatZone for which *assertion_sinf* holds may still contain FP numbers that could lead to false or imprecise results of the *sinf* implementation with regard to the mathematical sine function. Nevertheless, this is not a limitation of SafeFloatZone itself; rather, it requires the user to specify the intended behavior through adequate assertions which should be analyzed.

5 Related Work

In [26] the authors propose a tool to leverage the KLEE symbolic execution framework to generate full test coverage for FP programs. The authors use a real-world library for trigonometric functions and generate coverage based on analysis using the STP SMT solver as backend. The approach uses iterative deepening of abstractions and compares the results to a reference implementation. This might be interesting to identify unsafe domains in our approach, i.e., using this tool in parallel to an SMT solver, because it might be more effective in finding SAT instances. If the instance is UNSAT or the approach takes too long due to a lot of deepening, the result of the SMT solver can be used.

There exist different approaches for analyzing FP program apart from SMT solvers. Colibri [20] and ObjCP-FP [27] are based on constraint programming and enforce high level reasoning as much as possible. This can often scale better than bit-blasting SMT solvers, in particular for non-linear properties. Such solvers could also be used in our approach as alternative to SMT solvers. We found that the combination with other datatypes like arrays and bitvectors is currently better handled by SMT solvers, so we would need to find ways to separate the problems into the different theories and only pass the pure FP value. A similar approach would be to use Gappa [15] which is based on using interval arithmetic to solve FP problems separately and propagate the results to SMT solvers dealing with other datatypes.

Proving properties about FP programs is challenging due to the large possible state space and the complexity involved in encoding the IEEE754 format. Approaches like SPARK also use strategies based on automatic SMT solvers [17] to prove properties about programs. Similar approaches have been proposed [11] for the correct-by-construction B method [4] which uses refinement to derive a correct program from a specification. In this approach, specific proof obligations are generated depending on whether real numbers or IEEE754 numbers are used. These proof obligations could also be used as input to our approach in order to refine the bounds of input values, guaranteeing safe domains for FP functions.

Herbgrind [25] instruments binaries to detect potential FP errors by performing the same FP calculations with higher precision. This dynamic analysis further enables characterizing inputs that lead to FP inaccuracies. However, this approach may produce false positives. Additionally, the input characterization relies on well-chosen, representative inputs provided by the developer. Herbie [23] is a tool that employs heuristics to identify and rewrite expressions that result in FP rounding errors. Evaluating Herbie with our approach could be interesting to explore if the suitable FP input range for the analyzed functions could be extended. In general, dynamic approaches do not scale effectively due to their nature of performing recalculations in higher precision.

6 Conclusion and Outlook

We demonstrated the potential of `SafeFloatZone` to determine safe FP intervals that guarantee a given FP algorithm to perform as specified. This provides developers of embedded software with a fully automatic process to verify whether the expected properties hold for an implemented FP algorithm.

In particular, this could significantly enhance the safety of embedded systems that utilize FP computations to control critical processes. The novel approach of `SafeFloatZone` is the application of binary-search to efficiently iterate through the possible FP intervals by focusing on the FP exponent. This allows to obtain sub-intervals that are proven to contain either valid or invalid input for the analyzed FP function even if FP exponent intervals exist for which the solver could not find a solution in the given timeout duration. We envision this approach as a method that can be used in conjunction with other techniques, such as brute-force, intensive testing, or other formal methods.

For the future, we aim to evaluate the ability of `SafeFloatZone` to analyze the implementation of double precision FP algorithms. The total number of all possible `double` values is fundamentally larger than for single precision. Therefore, brute-forcing approaches do not scale well for analyzing double-precision FP functions. Additionally, we see potential to enhance the current, partly linear binary-search process by splitting the FP exponent intervals into several independent ranges that can be submitted to and solved by multiple solvers running in parallel. Furthermore, the binary search algorithm of `SafeFloatZone` could be extended for multidimensional searches, e.g., by applying multidimensional binary search trees [8], thereby enabling the analysis of FP functions with more than one FP input value.

References

1. Cephes. https://www.netlib.org/cephes/
2. Frama-C - Framework for Modular Analysis of C programs. https://frama-c.com/
3. A formal model of IEEE floating point arithmetic. https://www.isa-afp.org/entries/IEEE_Floating_Point.html (2013)
4. Abrial, J.R., Hoare, A., Chapron, P.: The B-Book (1996)
5. Barbosa, H., et al.: CVC5: a versatile and industrial-strength SMT solver. In: Proceedings of TACAS. Springer LNCS (2022). https://doi.org/10.1007/978-3-030-99524-9_24
6. Barrett, C., Fontaine, P., Stump, A.: The SMT-LIB Standard (2011)
7. Baudin, P., Bobot, F., Correnson, L., Dargaye, Z., Blanchard, A.: WP Plug-in Manual (2010)
8. Bentley, J.L.: Multidimensional binary search trees used for associative searching. Commun. ACM **18**(9), 509–517 (1975)

9. Bertholon, G., Martin-Dorel, É., Roux, P.: Primitive Floats in Coq. In: Proceedings of ITP (2019)
10. Borges, M., Phan, Q.S., Filieri, A., Păsăreanu, C.S.: Model-counting approaches for nonlinear numerical constraints. In: Proceedings of NFM. LNCS, Springer (2017). https://doi.org/10.1007/978-3-319-57288-8_9
11. Burdy, L., Dufour, J.L., Lecomte, T.: The B method takes up floating-point numbers. In: Embedded Real Time Software and Systems (ERTS2012). Toulouse, France (2012)
12. Chilenski, J.J., Miller, S.P.: Applicability of modified condition/decision coverage to software testing. Softw. Eng. J. **9**(5), 193 (1994)
13. Cimatti, A., Griggio, A., Schaafsma, B.J., Sebastiani, R.: The MathSAT5 SMT Solver. In: Proceedings of TACAS. LNCS, Springer (2013). https://doi.org/10.1007/978-3-642-36742-7_7
14. Cousot, P., et al.: Varieties of static analyzers: a comparison with ASTREÉ. In: Proceedings of TASE. IEEE (2007)
15. De Dinechin, F., Lauter, C.Q., Melquiond, G.: Certifying floating-point implementations using Gappa (2008). https://doi.org/10.48550/arXiv.0801.0523
16. de Moura, L., Bjørner, N.: Z3: an efficient SMT solver. In: Ramakrishnan, C.R., Rehof, J. (eds.) Proceedings of TACAS. LNCS, Springer (2008). https://doi.org/10.1007/978-3-540-78800-3_24
17. Fumex, C., Marché, C., Moy, Y.: Automating the Verification of Floating-Point Programs. In: Proceedings of VSTTE. Springer LNCS (2017). https://doi.org/10.1007/978-3-319-72308-2_7
18. Goldberg, D.: What every computer scientist should know about floating-point arithmetic. ACM Comput. Surv. **23**(1), 5–48 (1991)
19. Kroening, D., Tautschnig, M.: CBMC–C Bounded Model Checker: (Competition Contribution). In: Proceedings of TACAS. Springer (2014). https://doi.org/10.1007/978-3-642-54862-8_26
20. Marre, B., Bobot, F., Chihani, Z.: Real behavior of floating point numbers. In: Proceedings of the SMT Workshop (2017)
21. Monniaux, D.: The pitfalls of verifying floating-point computations. ACM Trans. Program. Lang. Syst. **30**(3), 1–41 (2008)
22. Niemetz, A., Preiner, M.: Bitwuzla. In: Proceedings of CAV. LNCS, vol. 13965. Springer (2023). https://doi.org/10.1007/978-3-031-37703-7_1
23. Panchekha, P., Sanchez-Stern, A., Wilcox, J.R., Tatlock, Z.: Automatically improving accuracy for floating point expressions. SIGPLAN Not. **50**(6), 1–11 (2015)
24. Rümmer, P., Wahl, T.: An SMT-LIB Theory of Binary Floating-Point Arithmetic ∗ (2010)
25. Sanchez-Stern, A., Panchekha, P., Lerner, S., Tatlock, Z.: Finding root causes of floating point error. SIGPLAN Not. **53**(4), 256–269 (2018)
26. Schumann, J., Schneider, S.A.: Automated testcase generation for numerical support functions in embedded systems. In: Proceedings of NFM. Springer LNCS (2014). https://doi.org/10.1007/978-3-319-06200-6_20
27. Zitoun, H., Michel, C., Michel, L., Rueher, M.: An efficient constraint based framework for handling floating point SMT problems (2020). http://arxiv.org/abs/2002.12441

Radar Object Detection on a Vector Processor Using Sparse Convolutional Neural Networks

Daniel Köhler[1,2(✉)], Frank Meinl[2], and Holger Blume[1]

[1] Institute of Microelectronic Systems, Leibniz University Hannover, Hanover, Germany
[2] Cross-Domain Computing Solutions, Robert Bosch GmbH Leonberg, Leonberg, Germany
daniel.koehler2@de.bosch.com

Abstract. Autonomous driving systems require performant and reliable perception, though they only possess limited computational resources, which places a high priority on the efficiency of the underlying algorithms. Radar sensors play an important role in this context, because they provide data in the form of sparse point clouds, which can be stored and processed in a condensed and efficient manner. However, this sparsity is often overlooked in the design of perception algorithms, such as convolutional object detection networks. In this work we investigate how sparse submanifold convolutions can be used to exploit this sparsity to drastically reduce the computational complexity of a CNN-based radar object detector. To this end, we propose an efficient implementation of submanifold convolutions on a vertical vector processor architecture called V^2PRO, which is emulated on an FPGA board. Benchmarks on the public nuScenes dataset and an internal dataset show, that the sparse models provide competitive detection performance, while achieving average speedups of up to 27x over their dense counterparts on the considered vector processor. Finally, the sparse model deployed on the FPGA is integrated into a measurement vehicle with three front-facing high-resolution radars, to demonstrate real-time online radar object detection running at 15 Hz.

Keywords: Radar object detection · Perception · Sparse CNN · Vector Processor · Neural network accelerators · FPGA

1 Introduction

Environmental perception, such as detecting other road users, is an essential task for autonomous vehicles. Radar sensors play an important role in this context, due to their robustness against adverse lighting and weather, as well as their comparably low cost. In general, radar object detection models can be categorized into two groups based on their type of input data. Spectrum-based

L. Carro et al. (Eds.): SAMOS 2024, LNCS 15226, pp. 138–154, 2025.
https://doi.org/10.1007/978-3-031-78377-7_10

approaches use the raw spectral data or parts of it [17], which still includes all noise components of the signal and thus imposes large memory and bandwidth requirements. In contrast, point clouds (PC) provide a more condensed input representation of the radar data, that typically reduces the size by several orders of magnitude. Furthermore, it is more robust to sensor modifications, because most of the hardware-dependent signal processing tasks have already been executed, which facilitates generalization across different sensor types.

Models that receive the radar PC as input can be divided into point-based methods that directly operate on the irregular point cloud data structure, such as graph neural networks [23], PointNets [2] or networks using kernel point convolutions [18] and grid-based methods that convert the PC into regular feature maps. Previous research has shown that grid-based object detectors, which apply convolutional neural networks (CNN) to a grid representation of the radar PC, outperform purely point-based models [25]. However, these approaches tend to overlook the inherent sparsity of feature maps after grid rendering, which yields great potential for reducing the computational complexity and memory requirements. Thus, we investigate how this sparsity can be exploited by means of submanifold sparse convolutions (SubMConv) [5] in a CNN-based radar object detector. For this purpose, we benchmark dense and sparse network architectures on the public nuScenes dataset and an internal dataset to demonstrate that the models based on SubMConv provide a competitive detection performance.

Furthermore, we propose an efficient implementation of SubMConv on a flexible vector processor architecture called V^2PRO. An evaluation on a field programmable gate array (FPGA) emulating the V^2PRO shows that large inference speedups averaging up to 27x, can be achieved with the proposed implementation. Lastly, the runtime-optimized sparse object detector is deployed in a measurement vehicle to realize an online radar object detection system running at 15 Hz on the considered vector processor.

2 Related Work

A comprehensive overview of the various approaches to radar-based object detection can be found in [21, 28]. Several works in this context [10, 11, 20] evaluate the inference speed of the underlying models and achieve real-time capable performance. However, these evaluations are typically based on powerful server-grade GPUs, which are often unavailable on mobile platforms due to space and power constraints. We therefore aim at real-time performance on an embedded platform by reducing the algorithmic complexity. This can be achieved by leveraging the inherent sparsity of radar data by means of sparse convolutions. To this end, [19] uses 3D sparse convolutions to reduce the memory requirements of detection backbones for the K-Radar dataset. In [7] a network based on SubMConv is applied to process point clouds obtained by fusion of camera and radar sensors. [15] proposes a hybrid object detection architecture, that combines SubMConv with kernel point convolutions and exploits the dualism between point clouds and sparse feature maps. In contrast to this previous work, we quantify the effects of retaining sparsity in CNNs on the detection performance by comparing equivalent dense and sparse architectures and focus on the efficient implementation of SubMConv.

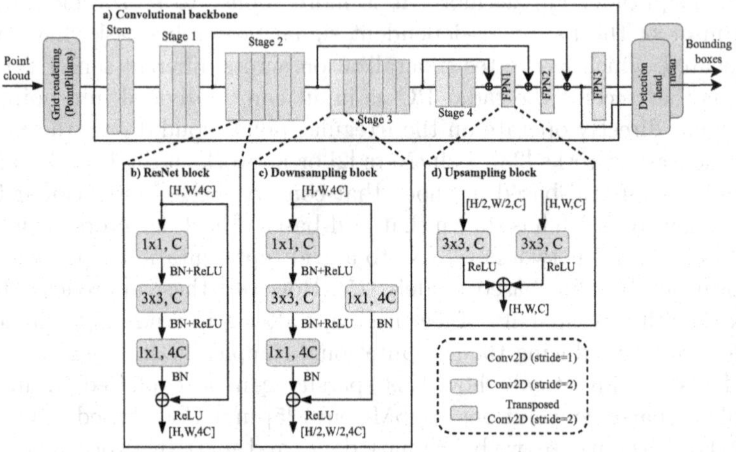

Fig. 1. Overview of the radar object detection model. a) Convolutional backbone consisting of a residual network (ResNet) and feature pyramid network (FPN). b) Bottleneck residual block. c) Residual block with strided convolutions for downsampling. d) FPN block using strided transposed convolutions for upsampling.

While there are dedicated accelerators for sparse convolutions, such as [13], we select a platform that is able to compute both sparse and dense networks to perform a fair comparison on the same hardware. The embedded V^{2}PRO architecture uses a vertical vectorization concept, which achieved good performance in a benchmark against GPUs for regular dense CNNs [24]. Due to its flexible indirect addressing [3], which allows for vectorized gather-scatter accesses in the individual processing lanes, it is also a promising candidate for the implementation of SubMConv.

3 Method

3.1 Object Detection Model

A common approach for radar object detection is to apply convolutional neural networks to a bird's eye view (BEV) representation of the radar point cloud. We use the architecture from [25], which is shown in Fig. 1. It takes as input a point cloud $\mathcal{P} = \{p_0, \ldots, p_{n-1}\}$ with n points $p \in \mathbb{R}^{C_{in}}$, that consist of Cartesian coordinates x, y, z, radial velocity v_r and radar cross section σ.

Based on their x/y-coordinates the points are rendered into a 2D grid defined by a field of view and cell size s_0, using the PointPillars [12] encoder. For this purpose, the points are first transformed into a higher-dimensional feature space by means of a 1D convolutional layer. Subsequently, features of points within the same grid cell are aggregated via max-pooling. The resulting BEV feature map is fed into the backbone (Fig. 1.a), that consists of a residual network (ResNet) similar to [27] and a feature pyramid network (FPN) [14].

The ResNet comprises a stem with two convolutional layers and four residual stages, each composed of several residual bottleneck blocks (Fig. 1.b). At the beginning of each stage, a residual block with strided convolutions (Fig. 1.c) is used, to downsample the input feature map. Consequently, the network contains feature maps at the initial scale s_0 after grid rendering and four downsampled scales $s_i = s_0/2^i$. The subsequent FPN, is connected to the outputs of each residual stage and upsamples the feature maps by means of strided transposed convolutions (Fig. 1.d). Finally, class-specific convolutional detection heads connected to one of the last two blocks of the FPN are used to predict class scores and bounding box parameters.

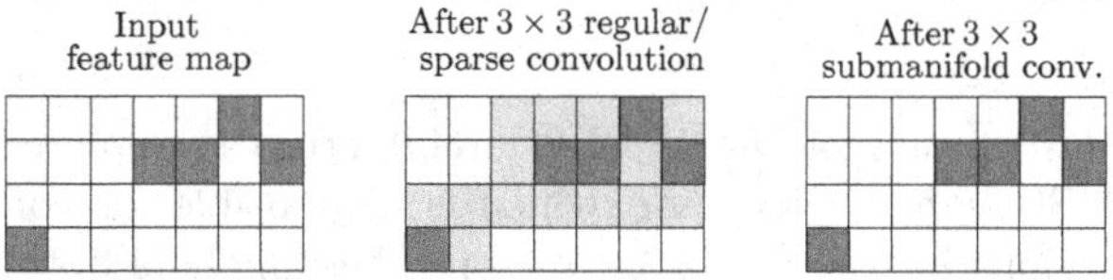

Fig. 2. Feature maps illustrating the dilation of features after a regular dense or sparse 3 × 3 convolution, and the maintained sparsity after a 3 × 3 submanifold convolution.

In order to exploit the sparsity of radar point clouds in this CNN-based architecture, we replace all convolutional layers with submanifold sparse convolutions (SubMConv) [5]. This type of convolution differs from regular sparse convolutions, in that all pixels in the output feature map, that do not correspond to an active (non-zero) pixel in the input feature map, are set to zero. This is visualized in Fig. 2 and has the useful property that it prohibits the dilation of features and maintains the sparsity irrespective of the depth of the neural network.

3.2 Hardware Architecture

The vertical vector processor architecture considered in this work, called V^2PRO [24], is used as an accelerator for digital signal processing and machine learning applications. In contrast to common horizontal SIMD (single input multiple data) architectures [8,22], which process multiple smaller data paths in parallel within a single processing element, the V^2PRO uses a vertical vectorization scheme [26]. More specifically, individual vector elements are processed sequentially in one of several processing lanes of the V^2PRO, which allows for flexible vector lengths. Thus, parallelization can be achieved by exploiting inter-lane data-level parallelism, i.e. performing computations with different data in the individual lanes.

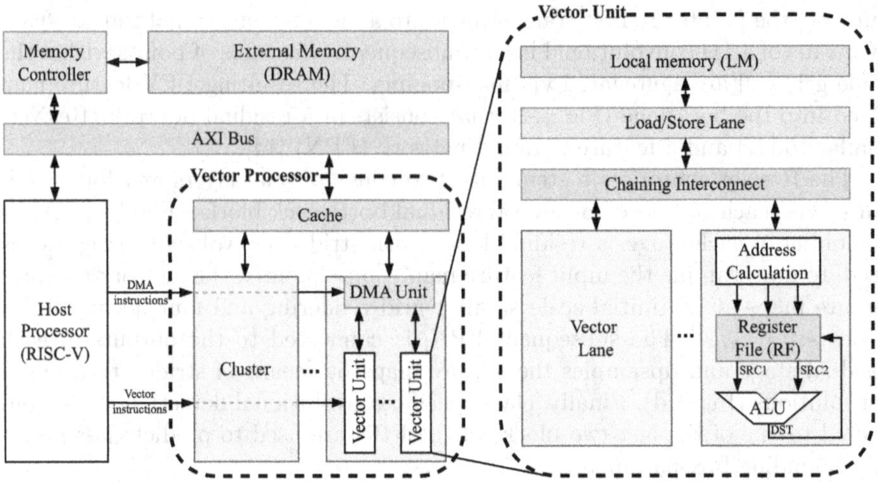

Fig. 3. Overview of the V²PRO hardware architecture.

The general structure of the V²PRO architecture is depicted in Fig. 3. It consists of a RISC-V host processor, which is responsible for control flow and provides instructions for the vector processor. These include both DMA (direct memory access) instructions, that specify data transfers between the vector processor and an external DRAM, as well as vector instructions defining the operations to be performed. The vector processor itself is structured in a hierarchy of clusters, units and lanes. Each cluster has a DMA unit that can access the external memory via an intermediate cache to load and store data into or from the associated vector units. For this purpose, each unit features a shared local memory connected to the DMA unit and a dedicated Load/Store lane (LS lane) that is responsible for exchanging data with the vector lanes. The vector lanes are the actual processing elements of the vector processor and consist of address calculation units, a register file (RF) and an arithmetic logic unit (ALU). The ALU supports fixed-point arithmetic for word widths of up to 24 bits and offers a 48-bit wide accumulator register. Distinct RF Addresses for the two source operands (SRC1, SRC2) and the destination (DST) of an operation are computed by the address calculation units, which offer a 3D addressing mode with fixed strides α, β, γ and offset δ encoded in the vector instruction

$$a(x, y, z) = \alpha \cdot x + \beta \cdot y + \gamma \cdot z + \delta \tag{1}$$

where $x \in [0, x_{end}]$, $y \in [0, y_{end}]$, $z \in [0, z_{end}]$ are nested iterators that allow to specify individual RF addresses a for each vector element. The parameters x_{end}, y_{end} and z_{end} are also encoded in the instruction and define the total vector length of $(x_{end} + 1) \cdot (y_{end} + 1) \cdot (z_{end} + 1)$.

Besides this register-direct addressing mode, the V²PRO also features an indirect addressing mode [3], in which the offset δ in Eq. 1 is no longer encoded in the instruction, but chained from a neighboring lane or the local memory via the LS lane. This is achieved by using the chaining network that connects the lanes in a unit with each other and allows to use different offsets for each vector element. The indirect addressing mode is the basis for the implementation of SubMConv on the V^{2}PRO, as it enables gather/scatter access patterns to the RF, which are required to efficiently implement sparse operations.

3.3 Implementation

In this section the implementation of SubMConv on the V^{2}PRO is explained in detail. First, the memory layout and segmentation of sparse feature maps is described and how the mapping between active input and output pixels is realized with a rulebook. Finally, the dataflow and parallelization of the computation on the V^{2}PRO is illustrated. A description of the regular dense convolutions and the PointPillars grid rendering can be found in [3] and is omitted here.

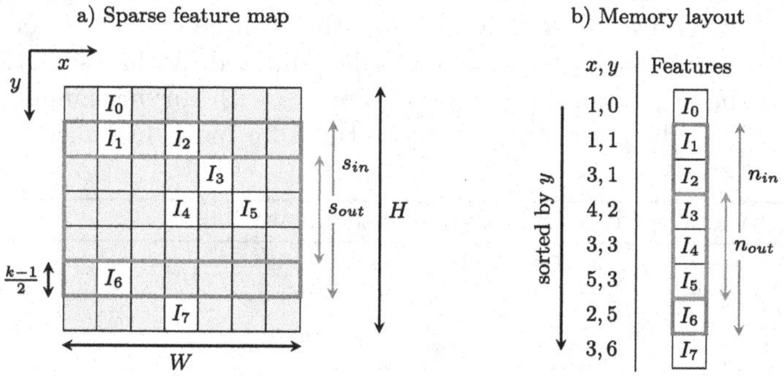

Fig. 4. a) Output segment (orange) with s_{out} rows and corresponding padded input segment (blue) with s_{in} rows for a convolution with kernel size $k = 3$. b) Corresponding memory layout of the cell-wise features and number of active cells n_{out} and n_{in} for output and input segment. (Color figure online)

Dynamic Segmentation. Figure 4 shows the data format of sparse feature maps for SubMConv and how they are segmented, such that the necessary input data for the computation of a segment is available. The segmentation serves two purposes. On the one hand, it allows to distribute the computation onto the parallel processing lanes, and on the other hand, it ensures that the required data fits into the corresponding local memories and register files.

The output segments are dimensioned such that at least one, but potentially several, rows of the $H \times W$ feature map are computed at once. This row-wise segmentation simplifies locating all required pixels at the segment borders within the receptive field of the convolution by simply loading the neighboring rows. More specifically, for a convolution with kernel size k the segment is padded with the adjacent $(k-1)/2$ rows at both sides. This is visualized in Fig. 4.a) for a

3×3 convolution. Note that a column-wise segmentation of the computation is possible in the same way.

The features of active cells in a sparse feature map are stored sequentially in memory, with the constraint that they are ordered along the y axis, as shown in Fig. 4.b). Placing this constraint on the memory layout has the advantage that pixels of the output segment and the required padding are located in contiguous memory regions. Consequently, loads and stores of segments can be encoded with a single cache-friendly DMA transfer of size n_{in} and n_{out} respectively. This segmentation approach minimizes the control overhead for the host processor at the cost of potentially loading some pixels that are not actually required for the computation of the output segment (e.g. I_1 and I_6).

Using a fixed number of rows s_{out} per segment leads to a high variance in the number of active cells n_{out} per segment, as the radar locations are not uniformly distributed over the field of view. More precisely, the point density is particularly high at small distances and close to the boresight of the radar. This high variance in the number of active pixels imposes two challenges. On the one hand it reduces the number of rows that can be processed per segment, since the maximum possible number of cells is limited by the capacities of LM and RF. On the other hand, processing segments with varying numbers of cells n_{out} in parallel leads to different execution times for individual vector lanes and potential stalls.

Algorithm 1: Greedy K-way dynamic segmentation

Input: Number of segments $K \in \mathbb{N}$, cells per row $N_r \in \mathbb{N}^H$
Output: Cells per segment $N_s \in \mathbb{N}_0^K$

```
N_s[i] ← 0, i ∈ {0, ..., K − 1};
T ← ⌈(1/K) Σ_{i=0}^{H} N_r[i]⌉; // target number of cells per segment
s ← 0; // current segment
n ← 0; // number of cells in current segment
for i ← 0 to H − 1 do
    n ← n + N_r[i];
    if |T − n| > |T − (n + N_r[i + 1])| or i = H − 1 then
        N_s[s] ← n;
        n ← 0;
        s ← s + 1; // next segment
    end
end
```

Thus, the number of rows s_{out} is determined dynamically during runtime for each sample and may differ for each individual segment, to account for the data-dependent point densities. Finding an optimal partitioning, such that the number of cells n_{out} per segment is as similar as possible is a special case of the NP-hard multiway number partitioning problem [6] with the additional condition that the order of rows and their number of cells may not be changed.

We benchmarked two different approximative algorithms for the solution of this problem on the datasets described in Sect. 4.1. Firstly, a greedy strategy shown in Alg. 1 with linear time complexity $\mathcal{O}(H)$ and secondly a dynamic programming (DP) approach using $\mathcal{O}(KH^2)$. The evaluation showed that the greedy algorithm produces similar results and is an order of magnitude faster than the DP approach. Therefore, the greedy approach is used in the following.

Rulebook. In the following, we describe how the computation of SubMConv is realized on the V^{2}PRO. Let W be the kernel of size $k^2 \times C_{in} \times C_{out}$, I the input feature map of size $N \times C_{in}$ and O the resulting output feature map of size $N \times C_{out}$, where N is the number of active cells and C_{in}/C_{out} are the number of input/output channels. To implement the computation, a rulebook R of size $N \times k^2$ is created, that provides a mapping between input pixels, weights and output pixels, as shown in Fig. 5.a). Each row of the rulebook specifies the input pixels that an output pixel depends on, while the column indicates the corresponding kernel weight. In the actual implementation, the rulebook does not store the features directly, but their respective RF addresses. This allows to store the input segment I_s as one sequential vector (see Fig. 4) in the RF and gather the required element via the indirect addressing described in Sect. 3.2 for each computation step.

Entries of the rulebook that do not correspond to an active input cell, point to a zero-initialized location in the RF, such that the corresponding weight is multiplied with zero and does not contribute to the convolution result. While this approach leads to redundant calculations, it ensures that the same number of operations is performed per output pixel, which significantly simplifies the parallelization, as vector instructions will have the same length and can be broadcasted to all lanes. Each spatial scale and type of SubMConv (regular, strided and transposed) present in the corresponding neural network requires a distinct rulebook. Consequently, for the model described in Sect. 3.1 five rulebooks are required for the regular SubMConv, four for the downsampling stages and three for the upsampling stages.

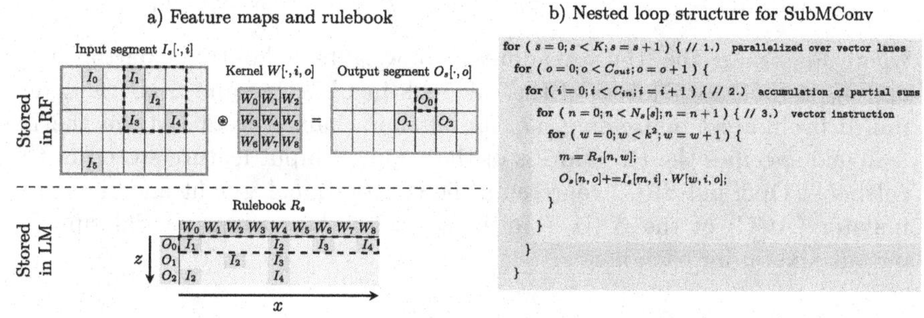

Fig. 5. Example for the computation of SubMConv with the corresponding rulebook and loop structure.

Dataflow. The computation of SubMConv is described by the nested loops in Fig. 5.b) and performed with an output-stationary dataflow, i.e. the partial sums of the accumulation over the input channels remain in the RF. The mapping of the nested loops onto the hardware is divided into three parts.

1. The outer two loops (blue) are parallelized over the vector lanes and iterate over the K segments obtained via dynamic segmentation and the C_{out} output feature map channels. First, all output channels of a specific segment s are distributed. If the number of vector lanes exceeds the number of output channels, the next segment will be scheduled in parallel on the remaining lanes. This mapping strategy allows to multicast the input feature maps I_s and rulebooks R_s to all lanes computing the same segment s, while only the convolution weights $W[\cdot, i, o]$ have to be unicasted to the respective lane.
2. The next loop (green), i.e. the accumulation of partial sums over the input channels C_{in}, is performed sequentially in hardware. Following the output-stationary dataflow, the partial sums for each output channel are stored in the RF of the respective vector lane.
3. The two innermost loops (orange) are encoded in a single multiply-accumulate vector instruction of form

$$\underbrace{\mathrm{RF}\left[a_{\mathrm{DST}}(x,y,z)\right]}_{\mathrm{DST}=O_s[n,o]} \leftarrow \underbrace{\mathrm{RF}\left[a_{\mathrm{SRC1}}(x,y,z)\right]}_{\mathrm{SRC1}=I_s[m,i]} \cdot \underbrace{\mathrm{RF}\left[a_{\mathrm{SRC2}}(x,y,z)\right]}_{\mathrm{SRC2}=W[w,i,o]} + \mathrm{ACC} \quad (2)$$

with $x \in [0, k^2-1]$ iterating over the kernel weights, $y = 0$ and $z \in [0, N_s[s]-1]$ iterating over the cells of segment s. The corresponding operand addresses with their strides α, β, γ and offsets δ calculated according to Eq. 1 are

$$\begin{aligned}
a_{\mathrm{SRC1}}(x,y,z) &= \mathrm{LM}[a_{\mathrm{LS}}] & \alpha &= 0, \beta = 0, \gamma = 0\ , \delta = \mathrm{LM}[a_{\mathrm{LS}}] \\
a_{\mathrm{SRC2}}(x,y,z) &= x + \delta_W & \alpha &= 1, \beta = 0, \gamma = 0\ , \delta = \delta_W \\
a_{\mathrm{DST}}(x,y,z) &= z + \delta_O & \alpha &= 0, \beta = 0, \gamma = 1\ , \delta = \delta_O \\
a_{\mathrm{LS}}(x,y,z) &= x + k^2 \cdot z + \delta_R & \alpha &= 1, \beta = 0, \gamma = k^2, \delta = \delta_R
\end{aligned} \quad (3)$$

where δ_W, δ_O are the RF base addresses of weights and outputs/partial sums and δ_R is the base address of the rulebook in LM. Operand SRC1 is determined by indirect addressing, i.e. its offset is chained from LM via the LS lane and specifies the RF address of the required input feature stored in the rulebook. Operand SRC2 represents the convolutional weight and the accumulator (ACC) of the ALU is initialized with the current partial sum for output pixel n for each new z.

3.4 Neural Network Compiler

To map the radar object detection models onto the V^{2}PRO, its dedicated neural network compiler [4] is utilized. For this purpose, it is extended to support SubMConv using the proposed implementation and other operations required by the sparse CNNs, such as addition and activation functions for sparse feature maps. The Python frontend of the compiler takes a TensorFlow model and in a first step searches the underlying graph for optimizable patterns. For the models considered in this work, this includes the folding of batch normalization into convolutional layers [9] and fusing activations with their preceding layer to reduce memory transfers.

Subsequently, a fixed-point analysis based on a calibration dataset is performed to quantize the model for deployment on the V^{2}PRO (16-bit quantization is used here). The optimized and quantized network is then exported in an intermediate C++ representation, which is parsed layer-wise by the backend, to segment the computation and generate a scheduling of segments onto the vector lanes. The result of this process is an executable binary for the RISC-V host processor, that contains the required vector and DMA instructions and a second binary containing the quantized weights.

4 Experiments

The evaluation of dense and sparse radar object detection networks and their implementation on the V^{2}PRO is structured in two parts. First, the detection performance for both network variants is compared on two different datasets. The second part of the evaluation focuses on the runtime improvements that can be achieved by leveraging the proposed implementation of SubMConv on the V^{2}PRO architecture.

4.1 Datasets and Detection Performance

The public nuScenes dataset [1] provides a large collection of multi-modal sensor data from urban driving scenarios. The radar point clouds in nuScenes are captured with three front and two rear mounted radar sensors and are known to be extremely sparse [10,18,23,25]. This leads to only a very few or no reflections for many objects and limits the achievable detection performance for most classes. Thus, we aggregate radar point clouds over 500 ms (typically corresponds to six measurements per sensor), to enhance the point density and only focus on objects of class *Car* for our evaluation on nuScenes.

To determine the influence of SubMConv on the detection performance of multi-class models, we consider a second non-public dataset (referred to as internal dataset in the following) containing diverse urban and rural traffic scenarios recorded by a measurement vehicle equipped with three high-resolution front radars. The object detection models on this second dataset are trained to predict objects of classes *Car*, *Truck*, *Pedestrian* and *Bicycle*.

Table 1 shows the field of view in which objects are predicted and the resolution of the initial feature map after grid rendering for both datasets. The field of view takes the positioning of radars into account, as the nuScenes dataset features sensors in both front and rear direction, while the internal dataset only uses front sensors. Furthermore, a smaller cell size of 0.25 m is used for the internal dataset, as the point cloud density is higher, although no time aggregation is used. This also becomes evident in Fig. 6, which shows statistics for the number of input points, point cloud density and sparsity for both datasets. The total number of points of the radar measurements in nuScenes averages 1343 points and is higher than the average of 1039 points in the internal dataset due to the higher number of sensors and time aggregation. However, the average point cloud density of 0.16 points/m^2 on the internal dataset is nearly twice as large as the 0.09 points/m^2 of nuScenes, because of the smaller area covered by the field of view and the higher resolution of the radar sensors.

Table 1. Field of view w.r.t the vehicle coordinate frame, cell size and resolution of the initial feature map after grid rendering and time aggregation interval for both datasets.

	Field of view				Initial	Initial	Time
Dataset	x_{min}	x_{max}	y_{min}	y_{max}	cell size s_0	resolution	aggregation
nuScenes	−60 m	60 m	−60 m	60 m	0.5 m	240×240	500 ms
Internal	0 m	80 m	−40 m	40 m	0.25 m	320×320	none

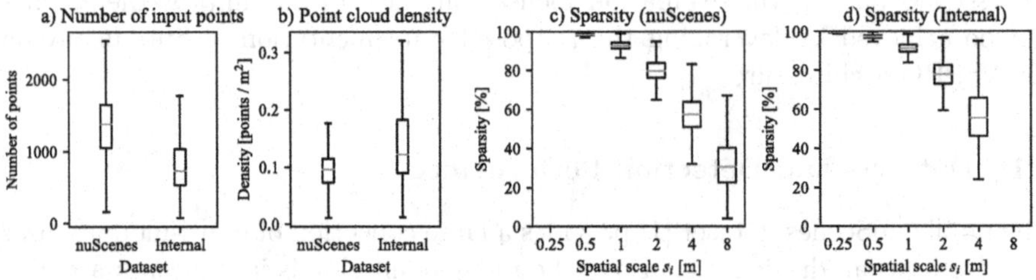

Fig. 6. Statistics for the validation sets of nuScenes and the internal dataset. a) Number of input points; b) Point cloud density, given by dividing the number of points by the area of the respective field of view (see Tab. 1); c-d) Sparsity, given by the ratio of active cells to the total number of cells for the different spatial scales s_i in the networks.

The sparsity statistics in Fig. 6.c-d) illustrate the motivation for using sparse CNNs for radar object detection. In particular, feature maps at the first three spatial scales exhibit very high sparsity and show great potential for reducing the computational effort by the use of sparse convolutions. For example, the average sparsity on the first spatial scale s_0 is 98.53 % for nuScenes and 99.45 % for the internal dataset. At each subsequent scale the sparsity decreases, as the feature map resolution decreases and the spatial extent of the feature map cells increases. On the final scale, this results in an average sparsity of 31.72 % for nuScenes and 55.98 % for the internal data set.

The detection performance is quantified in terms of mean average precision (mAP) as defined in the nuScenes detection benchmark [1]. More specifically, the average precision (AP) is computed for four different matching thresholds $\{0.5, 1, 2, 4\}$ meters between ground truth and predicted objects for each class, by integrating over the precision-recall curve. The class-specific mAP values are obtained by averaging over the AP values for all four matching thresholds, while the total mAP is calculated by averaging over mAP values for all predicted classes.

Table 2 shows the class-specific and general mAP values of the dense and sparse networks for both datasets. In order to reduce the influence of model initialization and training stochasticity on the results, five models are trained per network variant (i.e. each row in the table) and the averaged metrics are listed. It becomes evident that the sparse network variants using SubMConv provide a competitive detection performance to their dense equivalents. For nuScenes, the sparse network with a *Car* mAP of 23.30 % performs even slightly better than the dense network with 22.34 %. A possible explanation for this slight performance improvement might be, that in the sparse network objects are only predicted for feature map cells containing a corresponding radar location. In contrast, the dense detection heads generate object hypotheses for every feature map cell, which can lead to a higher number of false positives or inaccurate predictions.

Table 2. Performance of dense and sparse radar object detection networks in terms of mean average precision (mAP) for the considered classes *Car*, *Truck*, *Pedestrian*, *Bicycle* and number of parameters and operations. Only the operation count for the dense model is listed, as it is data-dependent and varies for the sparse model.

Dataset	Type	mAP [%]					Parameters	Operations
		Total	*Car*	*Truck*	*Ped.*	*Biycle*		
nuScenes	dense	22.34	22.34	-	-	-	1.99 M	7.93 G
	sparse	**23.30**	**23.30**	-	-	-		
Internal	dense	31.80	**51.17**	25.22	39.90	**10.89**	0.81 M	15.59 G
	sparse	**32.54**	49.31	**26.18**	**45.64**	9.01		

The multi-class evaluation on the internal dataset shows a similar tendency, as the mAP averaged over all classes is slightly higher for the sparse models 32.54 %, than for their dense counterparts with an mAP of 31.80 %. The individual class-specific mAP values show small differences between both network variants, with the dense networks performing better for the *Car* and *Bicycle* classes and the sparse networks performing better for the *Truck* and *Pedestrian* classes. For the latter, a quite significant absolute improvement of 5.74 % can be observed, leading to the overall better mAP of sparse CNNs on this dataset.

4.2 Runtime

The second aspect of the evaluation focuses on the runtime improvements, that can be achieved by leveraging the proposed implementation of SubMConv on the V^2PRO architecture. The planned target platform is an application-specific integrated circuit (ASIC) for which we perform a prototypic evaluation on an `Aldec TySOM-3A-ZU19-EG` FPGA board. For this purpose, a comparably small configuration of the V^2PRO with hardware support for indirect addressing [3] and eight clusters consisting of eight vector units with two processing lanes is emulated on the programmable logic. Consequently, the system has 128 parallel lanes which are clocked at 400 MHz, resulting in a peak performance of 51.2 GOP/s. The RISC-V host processor has a clock frequency of 200 MHz.

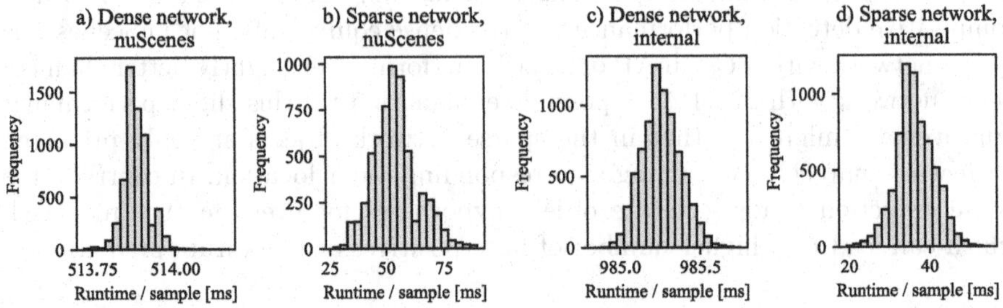

Fig. 7. Runtime comparison of dense and sparse radar object detection networks on the V^2PRO for a-b) nuScenes and c-d) the internal dataset.

The dense and sparse network variants, including grid rendering, convolutional backbone and detection heads, are mapped onto the hardware using the extended N^2V^2PRO framework [4] described in Sect. 3.4. Their runtime is measured using integrated hardware performance counters of the RISC-V host processor. The preprocessing steps for the sparse CNNs, including the dynamic segmentation and generation of rulebooks, are implemented on the `ARM Cortex-A53`.

The histograms in Fig. 7 show the varying runtime for each sample in the validation set of nuScenes and the internal dataset. In general, the observed variance in runtime is much smaller for the dense networks than for the sparse networks. This is due to the fact, that only the runtime of the PointPillars grid rendering depends on the number of input points, while the backbone and detection heads have a data-independent constant runtime. For nuScenes the dense network takes on average 513.9 ms to compute, whereas the sparse networks achieve a speedup of 10x with an average runtime of 53.9 ms. On the internal dataset, the dense networks take longer to compute with an average runtime of 985.3 ms, due to the higher feature map resolutions (see Tab. 1), which contributes quadratically to the runtime. This is not reflected in the runtime of the corresponding sparse CNN as its computational complexity does not depend on the feature map resolution, but rather the number of active cells. As a result, the corresponding sparse CNN takes on average 36.4 ms, resulting in a speedup of a factor 27. For the dense models a utilization of about 31 % of the peak performance is achieved, which corresponds to 16 GOP/s. This can be improved in future work by optimizing the mapping strategy of the neural network compiler for both dense and sparse models for memory-bound layers. These are typically layers with low arithmetic intensity that perform only few operations per loaded data word. For instance, the element-wise additions in the skip connections of the network can be fused into preceding layers to eliminate data transfers and increase the performance.

Further improvements to the SubMConv implementation could be achieved by enabling the LS lane to simultaneously read the rulebook and chain the required input features to the vector lane ALUs. This could avoid loading features into the RF prior to computation at the cost of additional hardware resources, e.g. an additional read port to the LM or a dedicated rulebook buffer.

5 Vehicle Demonstrator

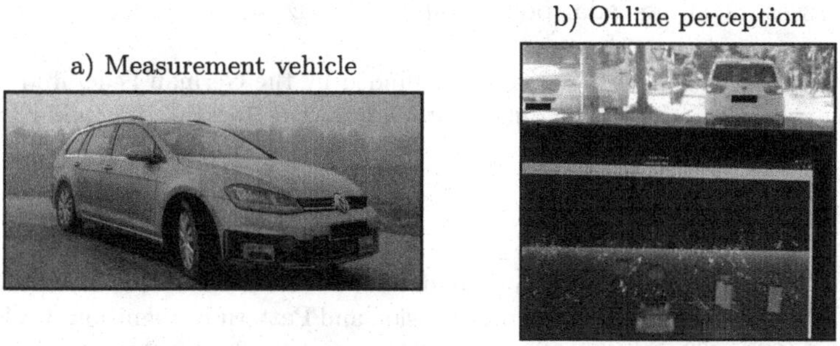

Fig. 8. a) Vehicle demonstrator with three front-facing high-resolution radars. b) Visualization of the radar point cloud (color encodes radial velocity) and detected objects (blue: *Car*, red: *Pedestrian*) in the vehicle. (Color figure online)

The sparse models evaluated in Sect. 4 are deployed into the same measurement vehicle that was used to record the internal dataset (see Fig. 8.a). For this purpose, the FPGA board emulating the V^2PRO was mounted in the vehicle and connected to its network. The communication between radar sensors and vector processor is realized with the robot operating system (ROS) [16] via Ethernet. A ROS node is implemented on the ARM cores of the FPGA board, which receives the aggregated point cloud of all three radar sensors, performs the necessary preprocessing including dynamic segmentation and rulebook generation, and reads back the predicted bounding boxes from the DRAM. The radar point cloud and predicted objects are visualized on a display (see Fig. 8.b). The implemented perception system is capable of processing the point clouds produced at a rate of 15 Hz in real-time without dropping frames.

6 Conclusion

In this work, we investigate how SubMConv can be used to exploit the sparsity of radar point clouds and reduce the computational effort of grid-based object detectors, paving the way for fast and real-time capable perception. A benchmark between dense and sparse architectures with identical network structure on nuScenes and an internal dataset demonstrates that this can be achieved without sacrificing detection performance. The sparse models exhibit comparable mAP scores and even outperform the dense models on the internal dataset for the *Pedestrian* class.

Furthermore, we propose an efficient rulebook-based implementation of SubMConv on the V^2PRO vector processor, which utilizes its indirect addressing mode to realize the mapping between input and output pixels. Runtime evaluations on an `Aldec TySOM-3A-ZU19-EG` FPGA board emulating the V^2PRO show that the sparse detectors achieve an average speedup of 10x for nuScenes. On the internal dataset, the speed improvement is even larger, averaging 27x. The fast inference of the proposed sparse model is used to deploy online object detection, that processes incoming radar point clouds at 15 Hz, into a measurement vehicle.

Acknowledgment. This work was partly funded by the German Federal Ministry of Education and Research (BMBF) under project number 16ME0379 (ZuSe-KI-AVF).

References

1. Caesar, H., et al.: nuScenes: a multimodal dataset for autonomous driving. In: 2020 IEEE/CVF Conference on Computer Vision and Pattern Recognition (CVPR), pp. 11618–11628 (2020). https://doi.org/10.1109/CVPR42600.2020.01164
2. Danzer, A., Griebel, T., Bach, M., Dietmayer, K.: 2D car detection in radar data with PointNets. In: 2019 IEEE Intelligent Transportation Systems Conference (ITSC), pp. 61–66 (2019). https://doi.org/10.1109/ITSC.2019.8917000
3. Gesper, S., et al.: A novel chaining-based indirect addressing mode in a vertical vector processor. In: To be published in International Conference on Embedded Computer Systems: Architectures, Modeling and Simulation (2024)
4. Gesper, S., et al.: N2V2PRO: neural network mapping framework for a custom vector processor architecture. In: 2023 IEEE 13th International Conference on Consumer Electronics - Berlin (ICCE-Berlin), pp. 94–99 (2023). https://doi.org/10.1109/ICCE-Berlin58801.2023.10375652, ISSN: 2166-6822
5. Graham, B., Engelcke, M., Maaten, L.V.d.: 3D semantic segmentation with submanifold sparse convolutional networks. In: 2018 IEEE/CVF Conference on Computer Vision and Pattern Recognition, pp. 9224–9232 (2018). https://doi.org/10.1109/CVPR.2018.00961, ISSN: 2575-7075
6. Graham, R.L.: Bounds on multiprocessing timing anomalies. SIAM J. Appl. Math. (1969). https://doi.org/10.1137/0117039
7. Hwang, J.J., et al.: CramNet: camera-radar fusion with ray-constrained cross-attention for robust 3D object detection. In: Computer Vision – ECCV 2022, pp. 388–405 (Oct 2022)
8. Intel: Intel advanced vector extensions 10. Doc. Nr: 355989-001US (2023)
9. Jacob, B., et al.: Quantization and training of neural networks for efficient integer-arithmetic-only inference. In: 2018 IEEE/CVF Conference on Computer Vision and Pattern Recognition (CVPR), pp. 2704–2713. IEEE Computer Society, Los Alamitos, CA, USA (2018). https://doi.org/10.1109/CVPR.2018.00286
10. Köhler, D., et al.: Improved multi-scale grid rendering of point clouds for radar object detection networks. In: 2023 26th International Conference on Information Fusion (FUSION), pp. 1–8 (2023). https://doi.org/10.23919/FUSION52260.2023.10224223

11. Kosuge, A., Suehiro, S., Hamada, M., Kuroda, T.: mmWave-YOLO: a mmWave imaging radar-based real-time multiclass object recognition system for ADAS applications. IEEE Trans. Instrum. Meas. **71**, 1–10 (2022). https://doi.org/10.1109/TIM.2022.3176014
12. Lang, A.H., et al.: PointPillars: fast encoders for object detection from point clouds. In: IEEE/CVF Conference on Computer Vision and Pattern Recognition (CVPR) (2019)
13. Lee, M., et al.: Spade: Sparse pillar-based 3D object detection accelerator for autonomous driving. In: 2024 IEEE International Symposium on High-Performance Computer Architecture (HPCA), pp. 454–467 (2024). https://doi.org/10.1109/HPCA57654.2024.00041
14. Lin, T.Y., et al.: Feature pyramid networks for object detection. In: 2017 IEEE Conference on Computer Vision and Pattern Recognition (CVPR), pp. 936–944 (2017). https://doi.org/10.1109/CVPR.2017.106
15. Lippke, M., et al.: Exploiting Sparsity in Automotive Radar Object Detection Networks (Aug 2024). https://doi.org/10.48550/arXiv.2308.07748
16. Macenski, S., Foote, T., Gerkey, B., Lalancette, C., Woodall, W.: Robot Operating System 2: design, architecture, and uses in the wild. Sci. Robot. **7**(66), eabm6074 (2022). https://doi.org/10.1126/scirobotics.abm6074
17. Meyer, M., Kuschk, G., Tomforde, S.: Graph convolutional networks for 3D object detection on radar data. In: 2021 IEEE/CVF International Conference on Computer Vision Workshops (ICCVW), pp. 3053–3062 (2021). https://doi.org/10.1109/ICCVW54120.2021.00340
18. Nobis, F., Fent, F., Betz, J., Lienkamp, M.: Kernel point convolution LSTM networks for radar point cloud segmentation. Appl. Sci. **11**(6), 2599 (2021). https://doi.org/10.3390/app11062599
19. Paek, D.H., Kong, S.H., Wijaya, K.T.: K-Radar: 4D radar object detection for autonomous driving in various weather conditions (2022). https://doi.org/10.48550/ARXIV.2206.08171
20. Popov, A., Gebhardt, P., Chen, K., Oldja, R.: NVRadarNet: real-time radar obstacle and free space detection for autonomous driving. In: 2023 IEEE International Conference on Robotics and Automation (ICRA), pp. 6958–6964 (2023). https://doi.org/10.1109/ICRA48891.2023.10160592
21. Scheiner, N., Kraus, F., Appenrodt, N., Dickmann, J., Sick, B.: Object detection for automotive radar point clouds – a comparison. AI Perspect. **3**(1), 1–23 (2021). https://doi.org/10.1186/s42467-021-00012-z
22. Stephens, N., et al.: The ARM scalable vector extension. IEEE Micro **37**(2), 26–39 (2017). https://doi.org/10.1109/MM.2017.35
23. Svenningsson, P., Fioranelli, F., Yarovoy, A.: Radar-PointGNN: graph based object recognition for unstructured radar point-cloud data. In: 2021 IEEE Radar Conference (RadarConf21), pp. 1–6 (2021). https://doi.org/10.1109/RadarConf2147009.2021.9455172, ISSN: 2375-5318
24. Thieu, G.B., et al.: ZuSE Ki-Avf: application-specific AI processor for intelligent sensor signal processing in autonomous driving. In: 2023 Design, Automation & Test in Europe Conference & Exhibition (DATE), pp. 1–6 (2023). https://doi.org/10.23919/DATE56975.2023.10136978, ISSN: 1558-1101
25. Ulrich, M., et al.: Improved orientation estimation and detection with hybrid object detection networks for automotive radar. In: 2022 IEEE 25th International Conference on Intelligent Transportation Systems (ITSC), pp. 111–117 (2022). https://doi.org/10.1109/ITSC55140.2022.9922457

26. Weißbrich, M., García-Ortiz, A., Payá-Vayá, G.: Comparing vertical and horizontal SIMD vector processor architectures for accelerated image feature extraction. J. Syst. Architect. **100**, 101647 (2019). https://doi.org/10.1016/j.sysarc.2019.101647
27. Yang, B., Luo, W., Urtasun, R.: PIXOR: real-time 3D object detection from point clouds. In: Proceedings of the IEEE Conference on Computer Vision and Pattern Recognition (2019)
28. Yao, S., et al.: Radar-camera fusion for object detection and semantic segmentation in autonomous driving: a comprehensive review. IEEE Trans. Intell. Veh. **9**(1), 2094–2128 (2024). https://doi.org/10.1109/TIV.2023.3307157

Optimizing QAM Demodulation with NEON SIMD and Algorithmic Approximation Techniques

Ilias Papalamprou[1(✉)], Giorgos Armeniakos[1], Ioannis Stratakos[1], George Lentaris[1,2], and Dimitrios Soudris[1]

[1] National Technical University of Athens, Athens, Greece
[2] University of West Attica, Athens, Greece
{ipapalambrou,armeniakos,istratak,dsoudris}@microlab.ntua.gr, glentaris@uniwa.gr

Abstract. In any telecommunication system, it is crucial to have a high-performance receiver to meet the desired requirements. However with the newer protocols demanding high order constellations, the demodulation process in the receiver becomes a bottleneck. To facilitate the implementation of telecommunication systems on embedded platforms, in this work we explore optimizations to the QAM demodulation, by applying SIMD operations with the NEON engine along with algorithmic approximation techniques. We implement a NEON-based Demodulator using the Approximate LLR algorithm, while we also propose an approximate method for QAM16/QAM64 that focuses on one quadrature for calculating the required Euclidean distances, along with the respective NEON accelerator. We perform a trade-off analysis between system's BER and execution time of the Demodulator and the receiver module for the base and approximate implementations, while also exploring the impact of different bit widths and precision in computations. We demonstrate that our approximate technique can achieve ×18–×37 speedup over the original algorithm without BER deviations on uncoded channels, while the use of LDPC is also examined.

Keywords: SIMD · NEON · QAM · Demodulation · Approximation

1 Introduction

In most digital telecommunication systems, hardware-based processing blocks within the Physical (PHY) Layer play a critical role, directly impacting overall system performance and reliability [6]. Recognizing their inherent limitations and methods to enhance both functionality and performance is crucial. This necessity becomes more pronounced with the increasing adoption of Software Defined Radio (SDR) technology across various applications [1].

L. Carro et al. (Eds.): SAMOS 2024, LNCS 15226, pp. 155–166, 2025.
https://doi.org/10.1007/978-3-031-78377-7_11

SDR systems replace traditional hardware components with software and/or hardware/software implementations, offering enhanced flexibility and adaptability through easily modifiable radio behavior via software updates. A representative example of such a framework is the open-source GNU Radio [3], which includes various signal processing blocks capable of emulating different communication protocols. While its primary focus is on testing telecommunication scenarios in realistic communication links, it lacks on software optimizations that might lead to increased throughput, rate or performance.

Most of the recent research works focus on optimizing fundamental modules, such as: 1) Transmitter (TX), 2) Channel, and 3) Receiver (RX), with great focus given on the RX, since it demands the highest computational resources, owing to the intricate Digital Signal Processing (DSP) algorithms employed for data processing. Specifically, the RX is responsible for reversing the TX operation on the received signal transmitted over a noisy channel, involving demodulation and decoding to recover the original data. Among these tasks, demodulation of received symbols stands out as one of the most computationally intensive processes in the RX, alongside Channel Decoding. Indicatively, as we demonstrate in a software-based telecommunication processing pipeline with QAM64 and LDPC Decoder, the Demodulator block accounts for 20%–30% of the total execution time in RX, making it one of the bottlenecks for achieving the high throughput required for several scenarios (e.g., satellite communications). While several research efforts have focused on enhancing RX's execution time through hardware acceleration features of CPUs, such as Intel's AVX512 Extensions [7] and algorithmic optimizations in various demodulation algorithms [11,13], none have applied optimizations across different layers of abstraction.

To this end, through this work, we examine and combine for the first time both algorithmic optimizations and software acceleration techniques in telecommunication applications. Specifically, targeting embedded ARM-based devices, we implement an accelerator for the Approximate LLR algorithm, utilizing Single Instruction Multiple Data (SIMD) operations provided by the NEON engine [12]. Furthermore, we propose a novel approximate algorithm for the LLR calculation in the Demodulator for both QAM16 and QAM64 schemes. This algorithm focuses solely on one quadrature, thus reducing the required computations while still maintaining almost the same output quality compared to the conventional method. Finally, by using different bit precisions in the computations, we examine different trade-offs between the execution time and the overall accuracy of the system. Our evaluation shows that the proposed algorithmic approximation along with its NEON-based implementation, achieves $\times 2$–$\times 4$ speedup depending on the modulation type, over the original NEON-based LLR algorithm. Additionally, the approximate NEON demodulator exhibits identical Bit Error Rate (BER) performance for uncoded data, while the scenario of using encoded data (e.x. using LDPC) is also examined.

2 Related Work

In the field of software based digital communication systems, extensive research has been conducted in recent years. Authors in paper [5] proposed a software optimized digital communication transceiver for the DVB-S2 protocol, that leverages parallel processing as well as Single Instruction Multiple Data (SIMD) operations of general-purpose processors. This implementation is based on the telecommunication library AFF3CT [4], which also utilizes multi-threaded and multi-core execution, as well as task level pipelining for the different transceiver modules. Other works like [16], focus on ultra low power and resource constrained devices, where an Internet-of-Things (IoT) oriented SDR platform was introduced. Software-based computations were implemented for the selected protocols (LoRa and Sigfox) on the ARM Cortex-M4 microcontroller, along with a hardware-based module for the RF front-end. Extensive research has been conducted on creating a software-based testbed for designing latest generation network protocols. The methodologies outlined in papers [8,9] introduce a framework capable of supporting Single-Input Single-Output (SISO) and Multiple-Input Multiple-Output (MIMO) communication schemes at over-the-air interface. These approaches involve accelerating multiple algorithms on servers, through the utilization of SIMD techniques Intel CPUs provide.

Regardless of the extensive software optimizations for telecommunication systems, the continuous scale of network protocols keep increasing the demand for higher computational resources. Specifically, in order to meet performance requirements, constellation dimensions are also scaling, with some reaching as high as QAM4096. However this scaling increases the complexity and the computational resources required to implement the algorithms [15]. In particular, the Demodulator in the RX, due to use of high order constellations introduces a large overhead in processing the received symbols. Therefore, over the years various approximation techniques have been explored to optimize the demodulation process by reducing the required arithmetic operations. For example, authors in [11] proposed a simplified approach for calculating the LLR in 8-PSK and 16-PSK schemes. Their work reduces the needed calculations by dividing the constellation into smaller segments and calculating the LLR values there, since it requires fewer adjacent symbols. Researchers in [13] also focused on the demodulation of APSK constellations and proposed a method with decreased complexity. They are based on the piecewise form of the LLR calculation, in order to compute the number of required Euclidean distances in a limited region.

The approaches, although aiming at more efficient demodulation techniques, they only simulate the accuracy of the algorithms without optimizing them for deployment in an embedded system. On the other hand, our work distinguishes and presents a cross-layer optimization approach, providing a software accelerated demodulation implementation, that targets ARM-based processors equipped with NEON technology, along with a novel approximate QAM demodulation method. Furthermore, our work is protocol-independent and can be effective for both terrestial and non-terrestial networks that support these modulation schemes.

3 QAM Demodulation

In digital communication systems, QAM modulation involves converting a binary sequence into the complex plane (I, Q), where'I' represents the in-phase component and'Q' represents the quadrature component of the transmitted signal. Upon receiving the signal, the receiver must reverse this transformation, a process known as *Demodulation.* This operation is responsible for undoing the modulation process. Next, we will briefly discuss the two main categories of demodulation algorithms.

- ***Hard-Decision*** algorithms determine the reference constellation symbol with the minimum distance from the received symbol. Upon finding this reference symbol, its binary code is then employed to demodulate the received symbol.
- ***Soft-Decision*** algorithms, on the other hand, do not produce a set of binary values as a result. Instead, their operation revolves around generating a metric known as the Log-Likelihood Ratio (LLR). This metric is calculated for each bit in the binary code of every symbol and represents the logarithm of the probability that '0' was transmitted over to the probability that '1' was transmitted for a received symbol.

In this work, our focus centers in the field of *Soft-Decision* algorithms. The initial LLR algorithm, known as Exact LLR (abbreviated as ELLR thereafter), assumes equal probability for all received symbols, and calculates the LLR value in an AWGN channel [10] using Eq. 1. Given the computational complexity of logarithmic and exponential operations, researchers have sought simpler alternative forms, leading to the development of Approximate LLR (referred to as ALLR). Unlike the ELLR equation, which considers all constellation points, the computation of the ALLR is simplified. It involves using only the nearest constellation point to the received sample, considering either'0' or'1' at that specific bit position. As defined in [10], the ALLR of bit b is given by Eq. 2.

$$L_b = \log\left[\frac{\Pr(b=0|r)}{\Pr(b=1|r)}\right] = \ln\left\{\frac{\sum_{s\in S_0} e^{-\frac{1}{\sigma^2}[(x-s_x)^2+(y-s_y)^2]}}{\sum_{s\in S_1} e^{-\frac{1}{\sigma^2}[(x-s_x)^2+(y-s_y)^2]}}\right\} \tag{1}$$

$$L_b = -\frac{1}{\sigma^2}\left\{\max_{s\in S_1}\left[(x-s_x)^2+(y-s_y)^2\right] - \max_{s\in S_0}\left[(x-s_x)^2+(y-s_y)^2\right]\right\} \tag{2}$$

where (x, y) are the received (I, Q) symbol coordinates, $s_{x,y}$ is the reference constellation symbol and σ^2 is the noise variance. For the rest of this paper we consider and examine the ALLR demodulation based on Eq. 2 as our target algorithm for acceleration.

3.1 SIMD-Based ALLR

Examining Eq. 2 indicates the possibility of parallelization capabilities, enabling the calculation of multiple arithmetic operations per LLR value. On ARM-based embedded devices, the NEON engine emerges as a promising solution to accelerate applications. NEON is a general–purpose SIMD engine, that extents the ARM instruction set. It works seamlessly with its own independent datapath pipeline and register file and is able to perform packed SIMD processing that act upon vectorized data (it's registers are vectors of elements of the same data type). This capability is that we aim to leverage in this study to compute multiple arithmetic operations in parallel. Furthermore, we introduce a generic procedure suitable for various modulations, including QAM16/64/256/512/1024, with no customization needed per modulation.

In Fig. 1 we present the original NEON-based ALLR demodulator we developed. In order to ensure that we have a uniform range of results across multiple data ranges, we normalize the computed Euclidean distances, using the Euclidean distance of the input symbol from the first point of the constellation. Furthermore, our NEON-based accelerator is designed to support different I/Q input widths (8/16-bit), as well as varying precision (16/32-bit) for the multiplication with the constant α $(= -1/\sigma^2)$. Moreover, the 16-bit multiplication is implemented using the `vqdmulhq_n_s16()` intrinsic since it can handles overflows internally [2], while for the multiplication with 32-bit of precision we implemented a custom function to deal with it (Fig. 1(b)). Specifically, we overcome possible overflows by following these steps: 1) split a single input vector into two vector with half the size 2) perform the multiplication in each new vector separately with 32-bit precision, and 3) convert the result back to 16-bit by selecting which bits to keep. Furthermore, to find the maximum of each Euclidean distance a maximum-tree structure was developed, that uses a single intrinsic to obtain the maximum of a vector, while also using previously calculated comparison results to reduce the complexity.

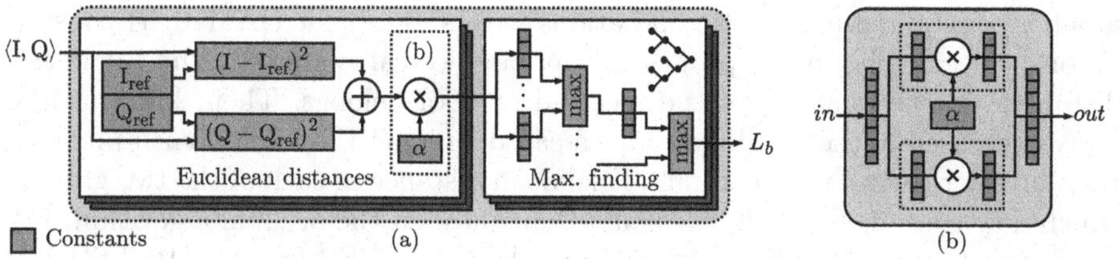

Fig. 1. (a) ALLR NEON Demodulator; (b) Custom multiplication module.

Next, we present an initial evaluation of our NEON-ALLR demodulator for all combinations of input widths and multiplication precision for various QAM modulations.

3.2 Initial Exploration

The execution time as well as the BER performance for each Demodulator configuration is examined, with the details for the setup listed in Sect. 4. From Fig. 2

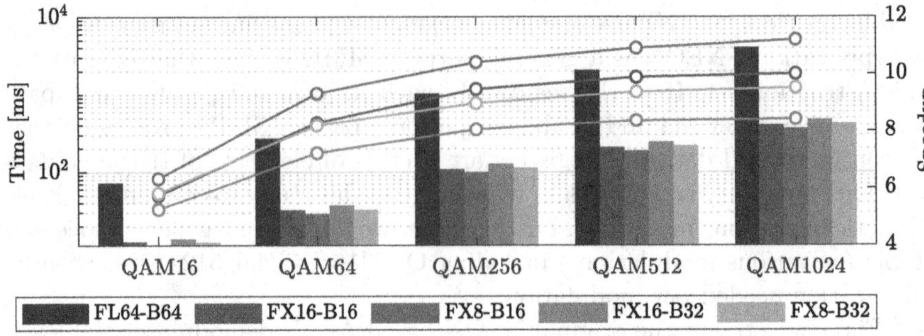

Fig. 2. Execution Time performance of ALLR NEON Demodulator.

we can observe the acceleration using NEON over the original floating-point implementation (denoted as FL64-B64). We note that for better visualization of the data due to the large execution time difference between the constellations, the left y-axis is in logarithmic scale. By observing the right y-axis plot lines that refer to the speedup of each NEON implementation over the baseline model, we notice that as the QAM constellation increases, the use of the NEON engine becomes more efficient, resulting in an exponential increase in speedup until a saturation point is reached. While a speedup of up to $\times 11$ was achieved, further performance gains were explored by applying algorithmic optimizations along with SIMD acceleration to the original Approximate LLR algorithm.

3.3 Proposed Approximate QAM Demodulation

Additional optimizations were applied to the original Eq. 2, in order to reduce the number of required arithmetic operations with support for QAM16/64 constellations. Specifically, in the proposed approach we calculate only the Euclidean distances on the quadrature the received symbol belongs. Then, knowing the Gray code used in the constellation, we can define the'1' and'0' in each bit position, in order to find the maximum Euclidean distance in each of the two groups, which now contain $1/4$ of the elements than those in the original algorithm. For bits located in two specific digit positions (LSB-1 & MSB for QAM16, LSB-3 & MSB for QAM64) in any quadrature mapped with Gray code, we observe that there is only'1' or'0' as a possible bit value, thus $s \notin S_0$ or $s \notin S_1$ respectively. Therefore if we refer back to Eq. 2, one of the two sets for finding the maximum Euclidean distance is empty ($S_0 = \emptyset$ or $S_1 = \emptyset$). In our preliminary approach, in order to avoid this indeterminate form we relied only on the available distances and assumed that the maximum Euclidean distance of the empty set is a constant value c. Even though we evaluated different values for c, including $c = 0$ and $c = -\infty$ (where $-\infty$ refers to a large negative number), this technique resulted in significantly elevated LLR Mean Relative Error (MRE) values and a noticeably deviated BER. Therefore for the cases where $S_0 = \emptyset$ or $S_1 = \emptyset$, a different methodology had to be applied to replace the maximum value of non-

Table 1. Demodulation arithmetic operations per symbol

Module	Operation	QAM16		QAM64	
		Base	Approx.	Base	Approx.
Euclidean distance	Mul.	48	18	192	54
	Add./Sub.	48	18	192	54
Max. finding	Comparisons	42	16	186	64

existing elements. As a solution we utilized two additional Euclidean distances $d(s, s_c)$, one for each scenario: whether none'1' or none'0' are present. The supplementary calculations are performed by selecting a predetermined symbol from the neighboring quadrature with coordinates $(s_{x,c}, s_{y,c})$. After exploring various combinations, we identified that selecting the symbol closest to the center of the axis from the diagonally adjacent quadrature performs with the least MRE. We note that different methods could possibly be applied, like selecting each time randomly or in a cyclic pattern the symbol. Equation 3 describes the above mentioned procedure for calculating the LLR $L_{b,apx}$ where b is the current bit position and Q_i is the quadrature the received symbol belongs, with $i = 1, \ldots, 4$. Furthermore, Table 1 shows the computational complexity difference over the original ALLR calculation.

$$L_{b,apx} = L_{b,s \in Q_i} + \begin{cases} 0 & S_0 \neq \emptyset \text{ and } S_1 \neq \emptyset \\ -\frac{1}{\sigma^2}[(s - s_{x,c})^2 + (s - s_{y,c})^2] & S_0 = \emptyset \text{ or } S_1 = \emptyset \end{cases} \tag{3}$$

NEON Implementation: An accelerator for the proposed approximate demodulation algorithm is developed for NEON, with the architecture shown in Fig. 3. In order to efficiently use SIMD operations, the reference Euclidean distances used for normalization are calculated in parallel for multiple symbols. Additionally for the implementation of the smaller QAM16 constellation, I/Q coordinates are packed in a single vector, while this is complemented by the according access pattern in the array that contains the reference I/Q values (Fig. 3(b)). Similarly to the NEON Demodulator analyzed in Sect. 3.1, multiple implementations were examined regarding bit precision. Specifically, 16/32-bit multiplication precision is supported using the same module of Fig. 1. Regarding the input bit width, for the QAM16 constellation due to the small number of parallelizable calculations with SIMD instructions, the 8-bit vectors are not used efficiently, therefore we only examined 16-bit input. For the larger QAM64 constellations however we implemented both 8-bit and 16-bit input width. Hence in total we have two different configurations for QAM16 and four different configurations for QAM64. Furthermore, the Maximum finding of the Euclidean distances reuses the aforementioned tree-based structure, tailored for the new dimensions of the sets.

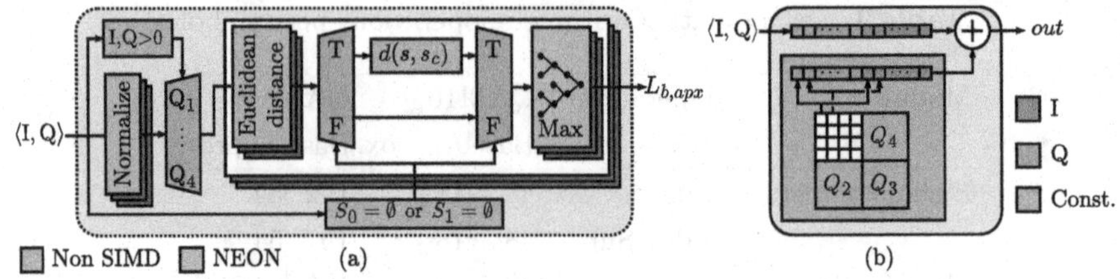

Fig. 3. (a) Proposed NEON demodulation; (b) Access Pattern for I and Q values.

4 Evaluation

This section presents the experimental results of the different Demodulator implementations, focusing on the execution time as well as the BER performance. The functions of the telecommunication processing pipeline are developed in C++, while the experiments were conducted on the Zynq Ultrascale+ MPSoC ZCU106 evaluation board, which features a quad-core ARM A53 processor clocked at 1GHz and 4GB of DDR4 RAM. Regarding the operating system we opted for Ubuntu 20.04.6 LTS (aarch64) with kernel 5.4.0-1015-xilinx-zynqmp, while for code compilation we relied on GCC (g++ version 9.4.0). All the subsequent implementations were compiled using the `-O3 -march=native` flag. The experimental telecommunication processing pipeline used is presented in Fig. 4, where an AWGN channel model is used. We examined the performance of the RX in two configurations: 1) *Without Forward Error Correction (FEC)*: Uncoded transmission and the classification of the output bit b_i was performed by comparing the sign of the calculated LLR value: $b_i = 0, \text{if } LLR < 0$ or $b_i = 1, \text{if } LLR \geq 0$, and 2) *With FEC*: LDPC for encoding/decoding with a fixed coding rate of 3/4 through all simulation runs. We also note that each simulation run consists of 32 blocks with 64800 symbols in each one, with the execution time calculated from taking the average of the blocks.

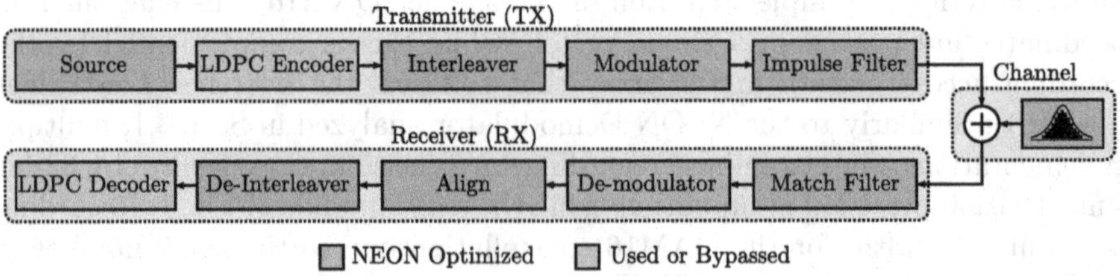

Fig. 4. Experimental telecommunication Chain

Table 2 shows the execution time of the NEON-based Demodulator as well as the whole RX in the different configurations, where we can observe the impact on acceleration when using our approximate approach. Although the 16-16 combination outperforms the other configurations our selected implementation is the

16–32, since it still offers sufficient acceleration gains and as we will analyze, it exceeds the others in terms of BER.

Table 2. NEON Demodulator Execution Time (ms)

Conf.*	QAM16						QAM64					
	Demod.		RX-I†		RX-II‡		Demod.		RX-I†		RX-II‡	
	Base	Apprx.	Base	Apprx.	Base	Apprx.	Base	Apprx.	Base	Apprx.	Base	Apprx.
16-16	10.81	3.91	16.84	9.94	522.88	531.72	32.60	5.95	41.81	15.17	861.87	798.06
16–32	10.89	3.86	16.91	9.87	553.99	548.33	32.68	6.96	41.88	16.18	855.58	814.48
8–16	8.93	-	14.96	-	538.55	-	26.07	6.41	35.29	15.63	814.73	779.13
8–32	9.64	-	15.67	-	533.46	-	28.88	7.10	38.10	16.32	836.33	832.87

* I-M: I: Input bits; M: Mul. precision † RX w/o FEC. ‡ RX w/ LDPC at 5 iter.

In Fig. 5 the BER results of the most representative configurations are presented. The 8-bit input width configurations are not included, since they offer comparable speedup but worse BER performance. For comparing the base and approximate NEON demodulation, we used the default floating point implementation, while we also compared the performance along the theoretical BER values (denoted as "Theoretical Reference") in an AWGN channel for uncoded data, which are calculated using equations stated in [14].

In an uncoded channel, regarding both the QAM16 and QAM64 constellations, the NEON-based ALLR and the proposed approximate Demodulator closely follow the BER curve of the floating-point model as well as the theoretical estimation, while the 16–32 configuration achieves the best BER performance. When using LDPC encoder/decoder for the base QAM16/QAM64 demodulation, the NEON-based ALLR shows similar BER with the base floating point model, while the best results are obtained with the 16–32 configuration. The proposed approximation, when using LDPC presents deviations in the BER curves compared to the baseline model. Specifically the QAM64 performs worse as opposed to the smaller QAM16. Upon analysis of the relative error of the approximated LLRs compared to the original values, the loss of accuracy occurs due to the points where an additional Euclidean distance from an adjacent quadrature is required.

Figure 6 shows the execution time of the Demodulator and the RX for the two most representative configurations (16-16 and 16–32) regarding accuracy versus acceleration trade off. Due to the sufficient acceleration and best BER performance, the 16–32 configuration was finally selected. Additionally we note that for all listed results, the higher speedup is observed for QAM64. Referring to Fig 6a, 6d where the execution time of only the Demodulator is presented, for the NEON-based ALLR we observe a speedup of ×6.41–×7.92 over the original floating-point implementation. Furthermore the proposed approximation approach features a ×18.11–×37.19 acceleration over the baseline implementation, thus improving the execution time of the base algorithm in NEON by a factor of

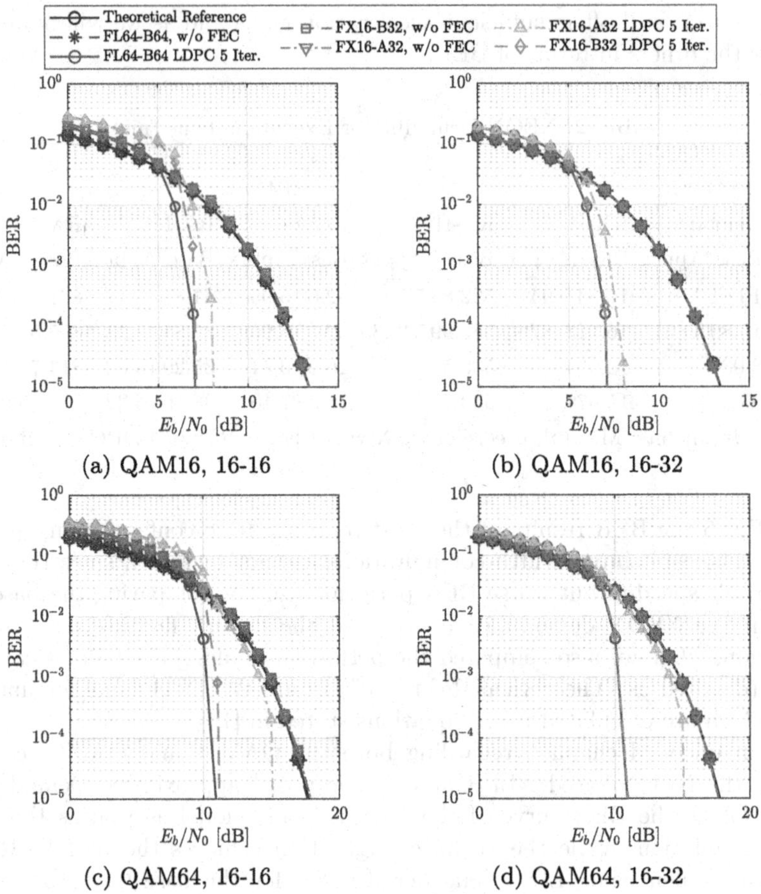

Fig. 5. BER Analysis

×2.83–×4.7. Afterwards we examine the effect of the accelerated Demodulator to the whole RX system, where apart from the LDPC decoder we also include the execution time of the de-interleaver (in row by column configuration) and the alignment block. In Fig. 6b, 6e where we have uncoded data, the Demodulator occupies most of the execution time and the proposed approximate Demodulator improves the RX's execution time by a factor of ×6.79–×15.23, while the ALLR in NEON obtains a speedup of ×4.17–×6.19. When using LDPC decoder at 5 iterations, as seen in Fig. 6c and Fig. 6f, the decoder bottlenecks the RX's performance. The impact of this block is significant, to the extend that the NEON-ALLR achieves speedup of ×1.1–×1.27, while the proposed approximate Demodulator achieves acceleration of ×1.11–×1.34 over the baseline model. Without loss of generality and as a proof of concept we consider 5 iterations for the LDPC decoder, since after conducting offline exploration and evaluating dif-

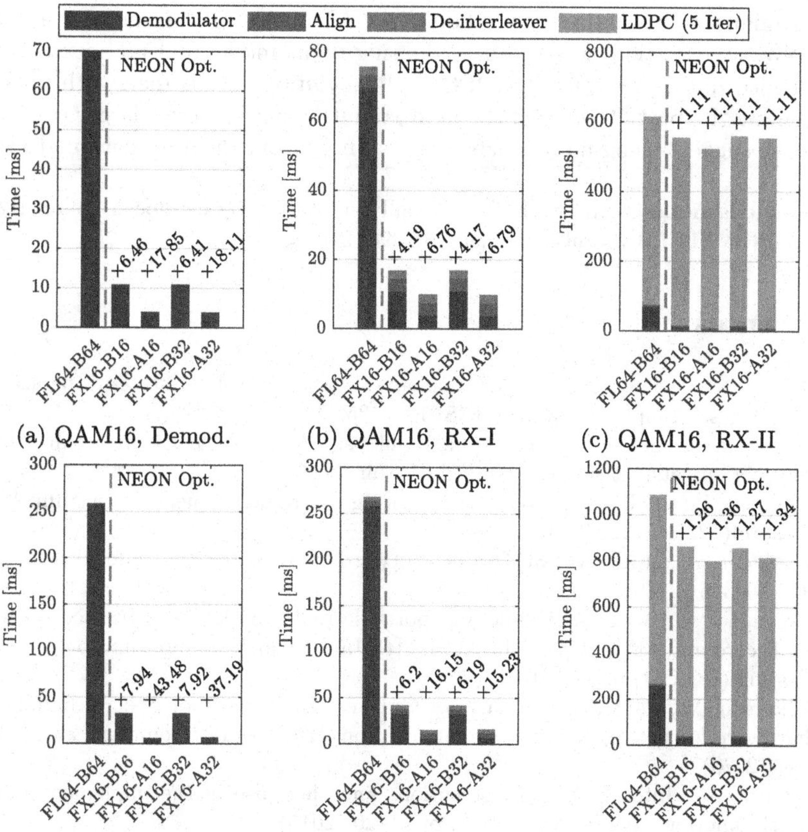

(a) QAM16, Demod. (b) QAM16, RX-I (c) QAM16, RX-II

(d) QAM64, Demod. (e) QAM64, RX-I (f) QAM64, RX-II

Fig. 6. Execution time for different configurations

ferent iteration settings, the BER performance was sufficient. However, we note that for a more robust system, the number of iterations might be increased.

5 Conclusions

This work presented an accelerator for the QAM Demodulation function utilizing SIMD operations provided by the NEON engine featured in ARM processors. Two different algorithms are utilized: a baseline LLR soft-demodulation algorithm along with a proposed approximate approach of the same algorithm. Furthermore various configurations are presented for each accelerator, regarding the input bit-width and the multiplication precision. We examine the different Demodulator implementations based on their execution time in a telecommunication processing pipeline with or without FEC, while we explore the accuracy performance throught the BER metric. Our findings reveal that our proposed approximation demodulation method for QAM16/QAM64 is promising, with ×19–×39 acceleration over the base floating-point model and no accuracy loss in uncoded data. When using LDPC BER deviations are higher, with QAM16 performing the best. To extend the approximation approach for larger constellations, we suggest using more Euclidean distances from the adjacent quadrature.

Acknowledgments. This work was partially supported by European Union H2020 project PRIVATEER (grant agreement 101096110).

References

1. Akeela, R., Dezfouli, B.: Software-defined radios: architecture, state-of-the-art, and challenges. Comput. Commun. **128**, 106–125 (2018)
2. ARM: Arm neon intrinsics guide. https://developer.arm.com/architectures/instruction-sets/intrinsics. Accessed 25 Mar 2024
3. Blossom, E.: GNU radio: tools for exploring the radio frequency spectrum. Linux J. **2004**(122), 4 (2004)
4. Cassagne, A., et al.: AFF3CT: a fast forward error correction toolbox! SoftwareX **10**, 100345 (2019)
5. Cassagne, A., et al.: A flexible and portable real-time DVB-S2 transceiver using multicore and SIMD CPUs. In: 2021 11th International Symposium on Topics in Coding (ISTC), pp. 1–5. IEEE (2021)
6. Chamola, V., Patra, S., Kumar, N., Guizani, M.: FPGA for 5G: re-configurable hardware for next generation communication. IEEE Wirel. Commun. **27**(3), 140–147 (2020)
7. Cornea, M.: Intel AVX-512 instructions and their use in the implementation of math functions. Intel Corporation, pp. 1–20 (2015)
8. Filo, M., Xia, Y., Nikitopoulos, K.: SACCESS: towards a software acceleration framework for 5G radio access networks. In: 2021 IEEE International Mediterranean Conference on Communications and Networking (MeditCom), pp. 318–323. IEEE (2021)
9. Georgis, G., et al.: SWORD: towards a soft and open radio design for rapid development, profiling, validation and testing. IEEE Access **7**, 186017–186040 (2019)
10. Hamkins, J.: Performance of low-density parity-check coded modulation. In: 2010 IEEE Aerospace Conference, pp. 1–14. IEEE (2010)
11. Olivatto, V.B., Lopes, R.R., de Lima, E.R.: Simplified LLR calculation for DVB-S2 LDPC decoder. In: 2015 IEEE International Conference on Communication, Networks and Satellite (COMNESTAT), pp. 26–31. IEEE (2015)
12. Reddy, V.G.: Neon technology introduction. ARM Corporation **4**(1), 1–33 (2008)
13. Sandell, M., Tosato, F., Ismail, A.: Efficient demodulation of general APSK constellations. IEEE Signal Process. Lett. **23**(6), 868–872 (2016)
14. SIMONS, M., Alouini, M.: Digital communication over fading channels: a unified approach to performance analysis (2000)
15. Singya, P.K., Shaik, P., Kumar, N., Bhatia, V., Alouini, M.S.: A survey on higher-order QAM constellations: Technical challenges, recent advances, and future trends. IEEE Open J. Commun. Soc. **2**, 617–655 (2021)
16. Xhonneux, M., Louveaux, J., Bol, D.: A Sub-mW Cortex-M4 microcontroller design for IoT software-defined radios. IEEE Open J. Circuits Syst. (2023)

A Novel Chaining-Based Indirect Addressing Mode in a Vertical Vector Processor

Sven Gesper[1(✉)], Daniel Köhler[2,3], Gia Bao Thieu[1], Jasper Homann[1], Frank Meinl[3], Holger Blume[2], and Guillermo Payá-Vayá[1]

[1] Chair for Chip Design for Embedded Computing, Technische Universität Braunschweig, Braunschweig, Germany
s.gesper@tu-braunschweig.de

[2] Institute of Microelectronic Systems, Leibniz University Hannover, Hannover, Germany
daniel.koehler2@de.bosch.com

[3] Cross-Domain Computing Solutions, Robert Bosch GmbH Leonberg, Leonberg, Germany

Abstract. Efficient processing architectures for irregular data patterns require vector element addressing with flexible indices. Therefore, state-of-the-art SIMD vector extensions implement gather and scatter instructions for indexed addressing of data in memory. In vertical vector processors, different data is processed sequentially in parallel lanes and can be exchanged via chaining. This paper proposes an extension of such chaining mechanisms in a vertical vector processor architecture (V2PRO) to flexibly chain not only data but also address offsets between vector lanes. The indirect addressing enables vector access patterns with irregular strides for both register file and memory. The extension has a low hardware overhead of +4.8 % lookup tables and +1.8% registers on a Xilinx Ultrascale+ FPGA. A runtime evaluation for two applications from computer vision, namely Deformable Convolutions and point cloud encoding with PointPillars, demonstrates speedups of at least an order of magnitude with the proposed extension.

Keywords: Vector Processor Architecture · Indirect Addressing Mode · Computer Vision · Radar Object Detection

1 Introduction

Numerous applications in scientific computing require indexed memory accesses to efficiently operate on irregular data structures, such as graphs or sparse matrices and tensors. Providing hardware support for vectorized indexed reads (gather) and writes (scatter) can significantly improve the performance of such applications and help to minimize control and instruction overhead.

Therefore, many modern SIMD (single input multiple data) extensions, such as AVX512 [9], feature specialized instructions for gather-scatter addressing.

S. Gesper and D. Köhler: The first two authors contributed equally to this work.

L. Carro et al. (Eds.): SAMOS 2024, LNCS 15226, pp. 167–182, 2025.
https://doi.org/10.1007/978-3-031-78377-7_12

These instructions typically involve a base address and a vector of offsets to define the addresses of individual vector elements. In this context, a distinction between memory-based and register-based scatter-gather addressing is often made. While the former can be used to implement vectorized loads from and stores to the main memory, the latter is used to permute data in registers, e.g., to align subwords into a suitable form for SIMD processing.

This work investigates how both memory- and register-based scatter-gather operations can be integrated into a vertical processor architecture. Here, vertical vectorization [23] refers to the sequential processing of vector elements encoded in a vector instruction. Data-level parallelism in vertical architectures is achieved by executing the same vector instruction in multiple processing elements with different data. This differs from the more common horizontal SIMD scheme, which groups multiple smaller data paths into a single processing element and processes them in parallel.

The considered architecture is called V^2PRO (vertical vector processor) [15,21] and consists of multiple parallel processing vector lanes with individual register files. The vector lanes are grouped into vector units with a shared memory that can be accessed via a dedicated load-store lane (L/S lane). Each vector unit features a chaining interconnect, allowing the exchange of data between its lanes. This work is focused on how the interconnect can be extended to not only chain data, but also address offsets that can be used to implement an indexed gather-scatter addressing mode for both local memory and vector lane register files. This new indirect addressing mode allows the encoding of complex operations, that combine gather-reads and/or scatter-stores with arithmetic or logic operations, in a single vector instruction.

The proposed chain-based indirect addressing mode is evaluated with two applications in terms of required hardware resources and performance gain. The first application is the Deformable Convolution [4] used in convolutional neural networks for object detection. The second application is the PointPillars encoder [12], which is used to transform point clouds into two-dimensional feature maps in the context of radar and lidar object detection.

To summarize, the contributions of this work are:

- Extending a vertical vector processor architecture with an indirect addressing mode for both, memory- and register-based gather-scatter access, by utilizing the existing chaining system between vector lanes.
- Increasing the flexibility of the processor architecture by adding support for complex operations, that combine indexed addressing with arithmetic or logic operations.
- Evaluating the proposed chaining-based addressing mode extension in terms of required hardware resources and performance gains on two exemplary applications that utilize memory- and register-based gather-scatter addressing.

This paper is organized as follows: In Sect. 2, related parallel vector processing architectures are presented, focusing on vector addressing modes. Section 3 describes the V^2PRO architecture and the proposed chaining-based addressing mode extension. The evaluation of the proposed addressing mode (using two use cases) is described in Sect. 4. Finally, the conclusion is drawn in Sect. 5.

Table 1. Operand addressing modes for RISC, SIMD, and the V^{2}PRO architecture. RF refers to the register file and MEM to the memory. Data gather modes are shown in (d) for memory and in (f) for register-file accesses. For the scatter addressing mode, the address is calculated as in the gather mode. The δ represents chained data from a neighboring lane in (d), (e), and (f).

Addressing Mode	**RISC** e.g. 32-bit	**SIMD** e.g. 4 x 32-bit = 128-bit	**(Vertical) Vector Processor V²PRO** e.g. x∊[0..x$_{end}$], y∊[0..y$_{end}$], z∊[0..z$_{end}$]

(a) Instruction-Encoded Data	Operand = Immediate	for(i = 0; i < 4; ++i){
		Operand[i] = Immediate
		}
			for(i ∊ (x, y, z)){
			Operand[i] = Immediate
			}

(b) Register Data	Operand = RF[addr]	for(i = 0; i < 4; ++i){
		Operand[i] = RF[addr + i]
		}
			for(i ∊ (x, y, z)){
			Operand[i] = RF[Address(x,y,z)]
			}

(c) Memory Load Data	Operand = MEM[RF[addr]]
	Operand = MEM[RF[addr] + Immediate]
		for(i = 0; i < 4; ++i){
		Operand[i] = MEM[RF[addr] + i]
		}
			for(i ∊ (x, y, z)){
			Operand[i] = MEM[Address(x,y,z)]
			}

(d) Memory Gather Data		for(i = 0; i < 4; ++i){
		Operand[i] = MEM[RF[addr + i]]
		}
			**for(i ∊ (x, y, z)){
			Operand[i] = MEM[Address(x,y,z) + δ[i]]
			}**

(e) Register Gather Data		for(i = 0; i < 4; ++i){
		Operand[i] = RF[RF[addr + i]]
		} // Permute
			**for(i ∊ (x, y, z)){
			Operand[i] = RF[Address(x,y,z) + δ[i]]
			}**

(f) Chaining Data (Neighbor Unit)			**for(i ∊ (x, y, z)){** // δ[i] is chained from neighbor lane **Operand[i] = δ[i] }**

re-use of data chaining (f) during vector address calculation

2 Related Work

Common Reduced Instruction Set Computers (RISC) commonly use a register file to fetch operands as inputs for the execution of arithmetic operations. The respective register address is typically encoded in the executed instruction (see Table 1.b). Data transfers between the register file and the memory can also be performed using pointers and an offset address (or immediate). A pointer is an address commonly stored in a register of the register file (see Table 1.c). This technique is called register indirect addressing and allows data processing from arbitrary address sequences by performing address or pointer arithmetic (using the arithmetic instructions). Besides the register indirect addressing mode, compile-time constants can be encoded as immediate values in the instruction, as shown in Table 1.a for RISC.

Data parallel SIMD instructions enable higher performance due to the parallel processing of multiple subwords. Examples of such instructions can be found in vector instruction set extensions, like Intel's Advanced Vector Extensions (AVX) [1,5], the RISC-V 'V' extension [16], or ARM's Scalable Vector Extension (SVE) [20]. The data processing mostly uses a dedicated vector register file (Table 1.b) or addresses the external memory via SIMD Load/Store instructions (Table 1.c). The SIMD instruction performs parallel operations on multiple elements of the vector. For non-sequential data access patterns, SIMD Load and Store units can implement extended addressing modes to access data with constant strides. The stride and offset parameters for the accesses are typically stored in registers or given as immediate values in the instruction. Providing hardware support for vectorized indexed reads (gather) and writes (scatter) can significantly improve the performance of applications that require irregular data access patterns. These instructions use an index vector to modify the load address of individual vector elements and gather them into the vector register file (see Table 1.d). The processed vector results are stored back to irregular positions in external memory by corresponding scatter instructions. For the realization of the scatter and gather element indices, vector registers with index sequences are referenced and used to modify the address of each vector element memory address.

Typical examples for these instructions are the gather operations `vgatherdps` and `vgatherqps` in AVX10 [8] (based on the AVX2 [7]) or the RISC-V vector extension addressing modes [16]. They specify a base address (or register) and a vector with packed indices or strides to address data in memory in any order. Both examples utilize the indirect addressing method for element addressing during access to the memory in Load/Store instructions. Some other instructions can reorder data in the register file, like compress or vector-gather instructions (`vrgather`), as specified in RISC-V [16] (Table 1.e).

Vertical vector processor architectures [23], work on SIMD vectors as well. The hardware is structured in parallel units and can utilize Load-/Store (L/S) units for accessing the external memory. The vectors of the SIMD instructions are processed sequentially in time and produce one element after the other, which allows element-wise address modifications. Hardware implementations of vertical vector processors can be found in the VESPA [25], VEGAS [3], VENICE [18], or MXP [19]. The implemented operand addressing modes use stridden, 2D, and 3D data access patterns, and show improved processing performance of regular data processing. In Table 1.a-f, the implemented operand addressing mode in the V^2PRO architecture is described with a loop of three iterator variables (i.e., x, y, z). This complex addressing mode is explained in detail in next section. In general, the sequential execution scheme implemented by vertical vector processor architectures allows the chaining of processed data between vector lanes, as shown for operand data in Table 1.f. For irregular data access patterns that require indirect addresses, dedicated hardware units are commonly added to fetch data from external memory with a vector register for memory access indices (e.g., in the successor to Cray-1 [17], the Cray X-MP [13]). This work proposed a novel chaining-based technique for indexed vector operand addressing from the memory or the register file by using the data (i.e., target operands) chained from other vector lanes as an offset address during the operand address computation (see Table 1.d-e).

3 Hardware Architecture and Extension

The vector processor used in this work is named V^2PRO and is part of the interdisciplinary project ZuSE-KI-AVF [21]. It implements a purely vertical vector processing architecture, controlled by a RISC-V processor, and features a scalable number of parallel vector lanes. The processing vector lanes are grouped in units with a shared local memory that can be accessed via a dedicated Load-Store vector lane (L/S lane).

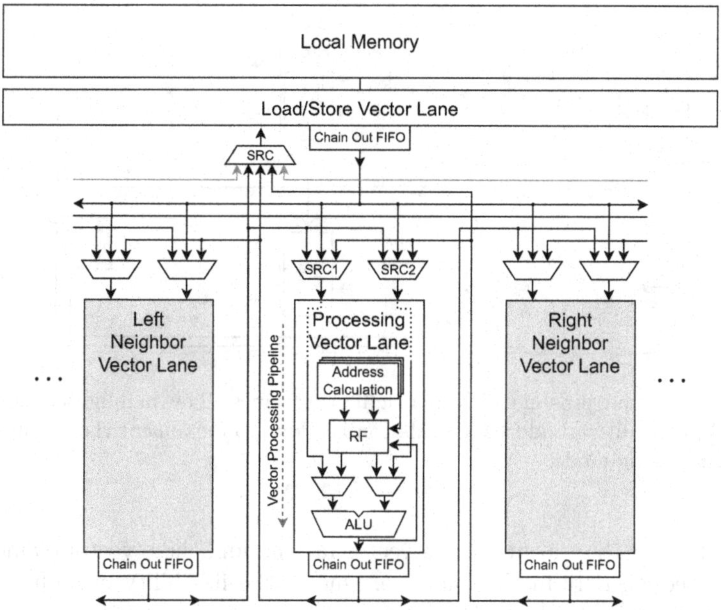

Fig. 1. Overview of a vector unit and the chaining network, that connects the output FIFOs of each vector lane with the input multiplexers of other vector lanes. Additionally, a Load/Store vector lane is used to access the local memory.

To process data from the local memory, the L/S lane loads a vector of elements and pushes it to an output queue called chaining FIFO (First-In-First-Out Memory). Following the sequential processing in the vertical vectorization scheme, one element per cycle is read and pushed to this chaining FIFO. Similarly, the processing lanes can push their output vectors into a chaining FIFO to send data to other processing lanes or to the local memory through the L/S lane.

The vector instructions define two input operands (i.e., SRC1 and SRC2) that can be selected from the chaining FIFOs by multiplexers. An interconnect network links the FIFOs to the input multiplexers of all vector lanes in the same vector unit. Consequently, data can be flexibly chained between one or multiple vector lanes. This concept is visually depicted in Fig. 1, illustrating the interconnect network between input operand multiplexers and the chaining FIFOs in processing and load/store (L/S) lanes. In the case of store vector instructions, the L/S lane selects chained data from one of the processing lanes' output chaining FIFOs and writes it to the local memory.

The pipeline of the vector lanes consists of a vector element address calculation unit, register file access, an input multiplexer, the arithmetic-logic unit (ALU) and a write-back. Each vector element is stored in a register of the register file. Therefore, in contrast to other vertical vector architectures, a vector operand is composed of several vector elements located in any position of the vector reg-

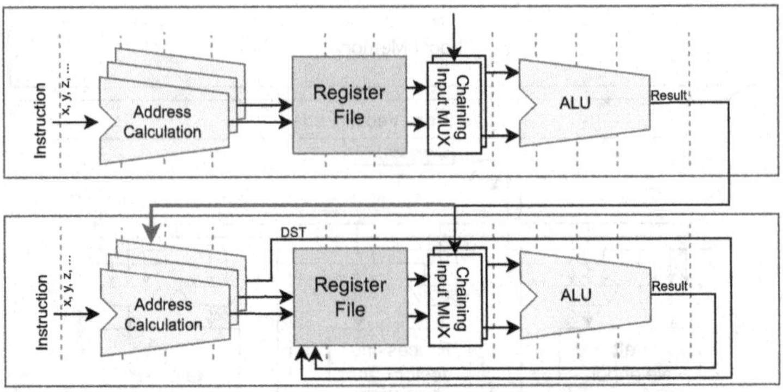

Fig. 2. Vector lane pipeline of two neighboring lanes. The highlighted connection between ALU result and address calculation is added to implement the chaining-based indirect addressing mode.

ister file. During the execution of a vector instruction, these vector elements are processed sequentially in this pipeline. Due to the flexibility of addressing the different register (elements) of the register file and the long pipeline, write-after-read conflicts (i.e., data hazards) could happen within the same vector operation if the same register addresses are used as an operand and target element. These hazards are not handled by means of a forwarding mechanism or bubble insertion and, therefore, these conflicts should be detected and resolved during the application software programming. However, stalls of the vector lane pipeline occur when the output chaining FIFO is full and no data can be written to the memory. The same happens when vector instruction operands are chained from an empty chaining FIFO. These stalls hold the stages until FIFO space or data becomes available.

Figure 2 shows the vector lane pipeline with the chaining connection to a neighboring lane. To implement the proposed indirect addressing, the highlighted connection (in red) that can forward chained data to the address calculation unit was added. With this modification, the source and destination operands can indirectly address the register file by using the chained data as address offset. This is similarly implemented for the L/S lane such that the local memory can also be accessed with chained address offsets. It is worth mentioning that the read of the chaining FIFO in the addressing stage of the pipeline adds a new stall condition to the vector lane pipeline.

The regular register file addresses for the vector elements of an input operand are determined by the equation shown in Fig. 3 where x, y, and z represent the vector iterators within the specified ranges: $x \in [0, x_{\text{end}}]$, $y \in [0, y_{\text{end}}]$, and $z \in [0, z_{\text{end}}]$. The total vector length of the instruction becomes $(x_{end}+1)\cdot(y_{end}+1)\cdot(z_{end}+1)$. The operand parameters α, β, and γ determine the multiplied stride factors, while δ is the operand address offset. With the instruction parameters x_{end}, y_{end}, z_{end}, the addresses of the vector operands elements are defined. For example, to address the first block of a sliding 3×3 window from a 4×6 input

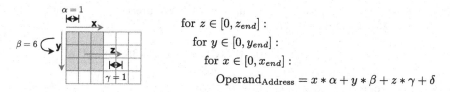

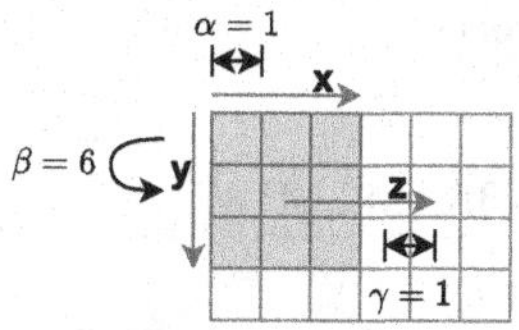

$$
\begin{aligned}
&\text{for } z \in [0, z_{end}] : \\
&\quad \text{for } y \in [0, y_{end}] : \\
&\quad\quad \text{for } x \in [0, x_{end}] : \\
&\quad\quad\quad \text{Operand}_{\textbf{Address}} = x * \alpha + y * \beta + z * \gamma + \delta
\end{aligned}
$$

Fig. 3. The vector operand address calculation. δ is the memory address offset of the first pixel. Each operand (SRC1, SRC2, and DST) encodes α, β, γ, and δ individual. On the left, an example of a 3×3 sliding window is given.

image (stored line-based sequentially in the vector register file, shown in Fig. 3), the encoding of a corresponding vector operand should set the following complex addressing parameters: $x_{\text{end}} = 2$, $y_{\text{end}} = 2$, $z_{\text{end}} = 3$, $\alpha = 1$, $\beta = 6$, $\gamma = 1$, and $\delta =$ image offset.

With the proposed chaining-based indirect addressing extension, the offset parameter δ no longer has to be encoded as a constant in the instruction, but can also be obtained via the chaining connection. Consequently, the offset can change for each vector element. This allows the implementation of gather and scatter instructions by using two vector lanes. For gathering indirectly addressed elements, the offset parameter δ of the input source operand is determined by a dynamically calculated value. For scattered vectors, the offset parameter δ of the destination address can be set to address the element indices from the chaining source. Besides the processing vector lane, the L/S lane can use this indirect addressing when accessing the local memory.

From a hardware perspective, the proposed chaining-based indirect addressing mode in the vertical vector processor requires a third stall condition for the pipeline and an additional input for the offset parameter to the address calculation unit. The Vivado FPGA synthesis tool utilizes DSP (digital signal processing) slices for implementing the ALU and address calculation units, block RAM (BRAM) for the register files and local memory, and configurable logic blocks (CLB) for the control logic, pipeline, and chaining registers. In Table 2, the resource requirements on an `XCZU19-EG-FFVB1517` FPGA with and without the proposed chaining-based indirect addressing mode are shown for a vector unit consisting of two processing lanes, a L/S lane, a local memory and the chaining interconnect. It can be seen, that the proposed chaining-based indirect addressing introduces only a small area overhead (+4.8% LUTs and +1.8% Registers). The frequency (400 MHz) is not affected by the indirect addressing extension.

4 Case Studies

In this section, the benefits of the proposed chaining-based indirect addressing mode are evaluated based on two exemplary algorithms from the field of computer vision and radar object detection. For this purpose, the runtime of respective baseline implementations is compared against implementations that

Table 2. Resource utilization of a vector unit with two processing lanes on a Xilinx Ultrascale+ `XCZU19-EG-FFVB1517`.

	CLB LUTs	CLB Registers	BRAM	DSP
Pipeline without indirect addressing	2787	4007	8	16
Pipeline with indirect addressing	2922 (+4.8%)	4078 (+1.8%)	8	16

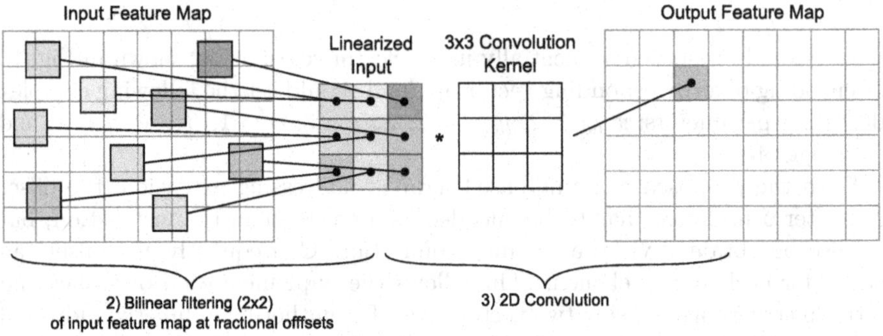

Fig. 4. Exemplary Deformable Convolution. The input is addressed with offsets and gets bilinear filtered (see algorithm step 2). The following convolution (step 3) produces the output pixel in the output feature map.

leverage the new offset chaining hardware feature. The benchmark is performed on an `Aldec TySOM-3A-ZU19-EG` FPGA board that emulates a V^{2}PRO architecture with eight clusters consisting of eight vector units with two processing lanes each, resulting in a total of 128 parallel lanes. The clock frequencies are $200MHz$ for the RISC-V host processor and $400MHz$ for the vector processor. The DMA access to the cached external memory is clocked at $200MHz$. The runtime is measured using hardware performance counters implemented on the RISC-V.

4.1 Deformable Convolution

Deformable Convolutions [4] improve the accuracy of CNNs by adaptively sampling distant points of an input feature map. Initially, a standard convolutional layer computes offsets within the input feature map. Introduced with Deformable Convolutions v2 [27], an additional sigmoid-activated mask value is utilized for scaling. These offsets are then used to sample the locations of the input feature map for a 2D convolution (see Fig. 4). Additionally, as the offset convolution produces non-integer locations in the input feature map, a bilinear filter is used to subsample the input.

For the implementation of the deformable convolution, three steps are performed, based on the implementation described in [14]:

1. First, a common convolutional layer calculates the offset and mask values. This is implemented via vector instructions, where the first source operand addresses the input locations from local memory (chained input data from the L/S lane), while the second operand is used to address and reuse the convolution kernel stored in a vector lane's register file. The following formula shows the computation of the 2D convolution on the vector processor. The vector operand addresses are calculated according to Fig. 3 with the iterators x, y, and z. The kernel size ($\text{Kernel}_{\text{Xlen}}$) defines the stride for the register file address in SRC2 and gets multiplied by the input pixel data (SRC1) via chaining from the L/S lane (see Eq. 1).

$$\underbrace{\text{RF}[z]}_{\text{DST}} \leftarrow \underbrace{\text{RF}[z] + \underbrace{\delta[\text{LS}]}_{\text{SRC1}} \cdot \underbrace{\text{RF}[\text{Kernel}_{\text{Base}} + x \cdot 1 + y \cdot \text{Kernel}_{\text{Xlen}}]}_{\text{SRC2}}}_{\text{Multiply-Accumulate / 2D-Convolution}} \tag{1}$$

   The output channel count during this processing step is 3 times the kernel size, as the input offset is encoded in x and y direction, and an additional mask value is set for each kernel coefficient.
2. As the previously calculated offsets are non-integer numbers, the second step applies bilinear filtering to the calculated offset/pixel positions in the input feature map to produce the input data for the final convolution (see Fig. 4.2). For this pixel deformation, the vector processor uses the proposed indirect addressing to select the 2×2 region at the offset position of the input pixels, as the offsets are dynamically calculated in the first step. The fractional part of an offset value in the x- and y-direction are represented by x_{frac} and y_{frac}. They are used as the factors for the bilinear filtering in the corresponding 2×2 input block ($I_{2 \times 2}$), which is determined by the integer part of the offset value. Each bilinear filtered input ($F(x, y)$) can be computed by a multiply-accumulate instruction:

$$F(x,y) = \begin{bmatrix} I_{x,y} & I_{x+1,y} & I_{x,y+1} & I_{x+1,y+1} \end{bmatrix} \begin{bmatrix} (1-y_{\text{frac}}) \cdot (1-x_{\text{frac}}) \\ (1-y_{\text{frac}}) \cdot x_{\text{frac}} \\ y_{\text{frac}} \cdot (1-x_{\text{frac}}) \\ y_{\text{frac}} \cdot x_{\text{frac}} \end{bmatrix} \tag{2}$$

   To calculate the bilinear filtering with a vector instruction, Lane 0 chains the previously calculated offset values to the L/S lane, which uses the offset to load the correct 2×2 input block dynamically (see Eq. 3 and 4). Lane 1 applies the MAC operation of Eq. 2 required for the bilinear filtering (see

Eq. 5) and generates linearized data for the final part of the algorithm.

$$\text{Lane 0}: \ \delta[\text{L0}] \leftarrow \underbrace{\text{RF}[z]}_{\text{4x indices}} \tag{3}$$

$$\text{L/S Lane}: \ \delta\,[\text{LS}] \leftarrow \underbrace{\text{LM}[\underbrace{\delta[\text{L0}]}_{\text{SRC1}} + \underbrace{(x \cdot 1 + y \cdot \text{Input}_\text{w})}_{\text{SRC2}}]}_{2 \times 2 \text{ block of Input with indexed offset}} \tag{4}$$

$$\text{Lane 1}: \ \underbrace{\text{RF}[z]}_{\text{DST}} \leftarrow \underbrace{\text{RF}[z] + \underbrace{\delta[\text{LS}]}_{\text{SRC1}} \cdot \underbrace{\text{RF}\,[\text{Factor}_{2\times 2}]}_{\text{SRC2}}}_{\text{Bilinear-Filtering } (2\times 2)} \tag{5}$$

3. The final step multiplies and accumulates the previously deformed input and produces the output feature maps of the deformable convolution (see Fig. 4.3). It can be seen as a simple matrix multiplication because the input deformation took place in the second step and was stored linearly. Equation 6 shows the multiply-accumulate operation for this processing step.

$$\underbrace{\text{RF}[i]}_{\text{DST}} \leftarrow \underbrace{\text{RF}[i] + \underbrace{\delta[\text{LS}]}_{\text{SRC1}} \cdot \underbrace{\text{RF}[\text{Coeff} + i]}_{\text{SRC2}}}_{\text{Multiply-Accumulate}} \tag{6}$$

To evaluate the implementation of the Deformable Convolution using the proposed indirect addressing technique, an implementation of the Deformable Convolution without indirect addressing is chosen as a baseline. Instead of dynamically loading the deformed input pixels through the indirect addressing feature, the offsets were set by the RISC-V processor in the form of constants in the load vector instructions in step 2 (i.e., vector load operations for 2×2 blocks with immediate encoded offsets). However, this approach has multiple limitations that can be avoided by using the proposed indirect addressing feature. The first limitation is the broadcast of vector instructions, as the same offset gets issued to all parallel vector units. Therefore, all units will load the same input channel position and only process different output channels (with indirect addressing, different input channels can be processed on different vector units). As a second limitation, there are short vectors with a length of only 4 (each bilinear filtering uses 4 positions around the current offset). With indirect addressing, several 2×2 blocks can be encoded in a single vector instruction. Furthermore, cache synchronization is required, because the offsets previously calculated in the vector processor need to be accessed by the RISC-V.

In both cases (RISC-V-based and indirect addressing implementation), each vector unit loads more data than it processes during the deform step. The local memory that contains the input feature map is sampled using the calculated offsets and, therefore, must hold a larger region than the processed segment (padded by the maximum allowed offset). The implemented maximal offset influences the required data loads. In the following evaluation, the maximal offset is set to 8

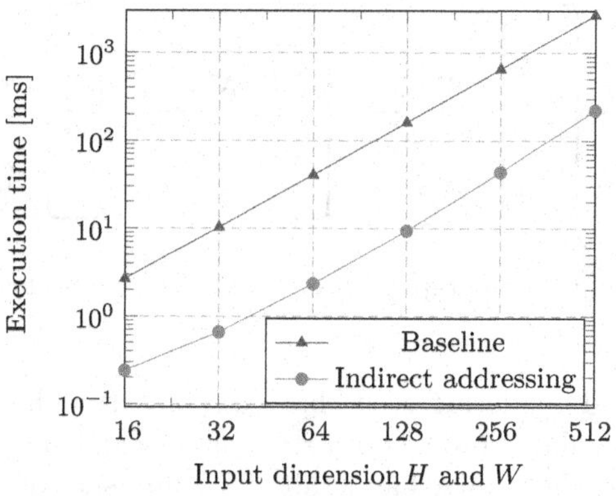

Fig. 5. Execution time (in milliseconds, logarithmic scale) of the complete Deformable Convolution for height H and width W ranging from 16 to 512.

which influences the total accuracy of a Faster R-CNN (trained for COCO) by less than 1%.

Comparing RISC-V-based and indirect addressing implementation, the average vector length for Load instructions executing the deformable convolution increased from 9.83 to 70.97 vector elements if the proposed indirect addressing feature is used. The relative amount of Load instructions was reduced from 82.26% to 34.47%. The calculation of this average includes all three steps of the implementation and differs slightly for different input dimensions, as the underlying segmentation is generated by the neural network conversion framework (N^2V^2PRO) [6]. Using indirect addressing results in fewer, but longer vector instructions with several offsets, instead of more instructions with a shorter vector length of 4 (for bilinear filtering at the position of a single calculated offset). The total execution time of the deformable convolution layer is reduced with the indirect addressing possibility by a factor ranging from 11.18 to 17.25 (at 8 input channels and 8 output channels) against the implementation with a RISC-V-based offset parameterization. In Fig. 5, the execution times of the RISC-V-based and the indirect addressing implementation are shown for different input feature map dimensions (the input- and output channel count is 8) with an average time reduction factor of 14.74. Here is to mention, that the transfers for the implementation with indirect addressing cannot be completely overlapped with the data processing and therefore they have an influence on the performance gain. This can be seen in the non-linear speedup behavior in Fig. 5 for small input dimensions.

4.2 PointPillars

The second case study originates from lidar- and radar-based object detection using point clouds. Many architectures in this context apply convolutional neural networks (CNNs) to the input point cloud's 2D or 3D grid representations. This

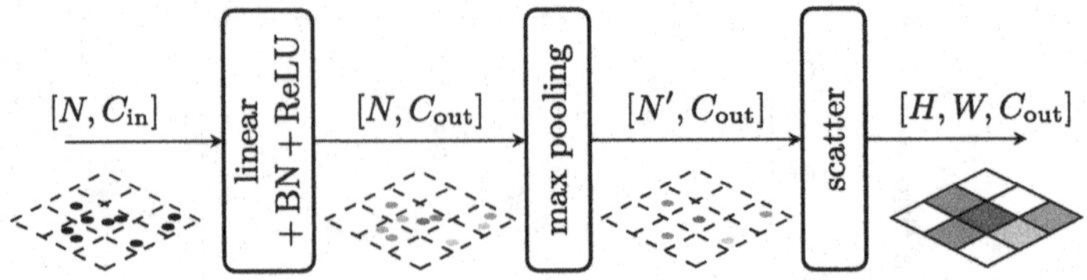

Fig. 6. Computation graph of the PointPillars point cloud encoder.

requires a prior grid rendering step that converts irregular and unstructured point clouds into regular grid-like data structures. Typically, this is achieved by point cloud encoders that utilize handcrafted features such as intensity or density maps [2, 24] or learnable feature extractors consisting of small neural networks [11, 12, 22, 26].

This use case focuses on PointPillars [12], which is a prominent example for learnable encoders that convert point clouds into 2D bird's eye view (BEV) grids. The computation graph of the encoder is visualized in Fig. 6. As input, it receives a point cloud $\mathcal{P} = \{x_0, \ldots, x_{N-1}\}$ consisting of points $x_i \in \mathbb{R}^{C_{in}}$ with Cartesian coordinates x, y, z and further application-specific features such as reflectance or radial velocity. The encoder output is given by a dense BEV grid $\mathcal{G} \in \mathbb{R}^{H \times W \times C_{out}}$ with specified height H, width W and number of output feature channels C_{out}.

First, the point-wise input features are transformed into a higher dimensional feature space $\mathbb{R}^{C_{out}}$ by means of a linear layer (1D convolution) followed by batch normalization (BN) and ReLU activation. Subsequently, each point is projected into the output grid based on its respective x and y coordinates. In order to obtain N' cell-wise features max-pooling is applied to aggregate features of multiple points within the same grid cell. Finally, the cell-wise features are scattered into the dense output tensor of shape $[H, W, C]$.

Implementing PointPillars on the V^{2}PRO architecture is challenging for several reasons. The regular memory access patterns, that can be realized with the addressing scheme in Fig. 3 are not well suited for the point-wise computations required by PointPillars. On the one hand, this is due to the variable number of non-empty grid cells and points per cell, which impede the use of fixed vector lengths for max-pooling. On the other hand, the algorithm requires a scatter operation, that moves data based on a set of addresses and realizes irregular access patterns, in order to transfer cell-wise features into the dense output grid. Without the proposed indirect addressing mode this kind of data rearrangement operation can not be vectorized efficiently in the processing lanes of the V^{2}PRO.

For these reasons, the max-pooling and scatter operation in Fig. 6 are delegated to the RISC-V host processor in the baseline implementation. Consequently, only the linear layer, BN and ReLU activation are computed in parallel on the processing lanes. For this purpose, the BN is folded into the preceding linear layer by updating its convolutional weights [10]. The linear layer itself is implemented using the multiply-accumulate operation of the V^{2}PRO in a simi-

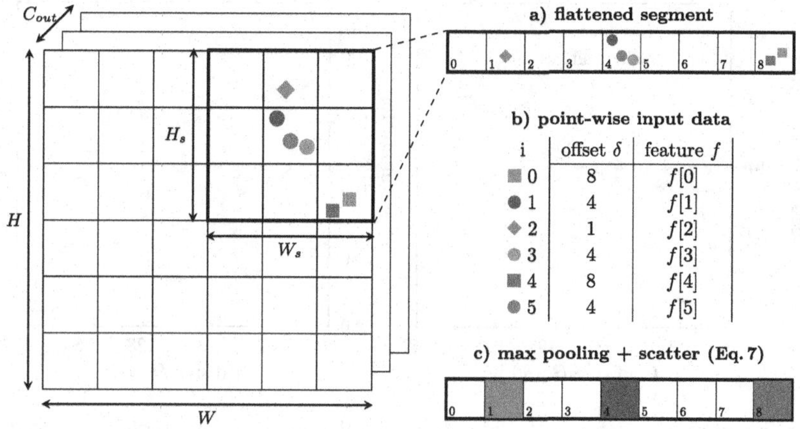

Fig. 7. Segmentation and data format for the indirect addressing implementation of PointPillars.

lar manner to the 2D convolution described in the previous section. A detailed description of the operation is omitted here, as it is identical for both implementations and not affected by the indirect addressing mode extension.

The indirect addressing implementation leverages the proposed offset chaining mechanism to perform the complete computation including max-pooling and scatter operations directly in the processing lanes. To parallelize the computation and fit the required input data into the register files of individual processing lanes, the computation is subdivided into evenly sized segments with dimensions $H_s \times W_s \times 1$ as shown in Fig. 7. Each segment is computed in a fused manner on a specific vector lane, such that all operations in Fig. 6 are performed subsequently without transferring intermediate results back to the main memory.

The input data for a segment comprises two arbitrarily ordered vectors, that contain feature and offset values for each point within the segment as shown in Fig. 7.b. Here, the offset values $\delta \in \{0, \ldots, H_s \cdot W_s - 1\}$ represent both the cell index of points in the flattened segment (see Fig. 7.a) and the register file (RF) address that stores the feature value of the corresponding cell. After initializing the features of all cells with zero, the cell-wise max pooling and scattering can be realized with a single vector instruction. For this purpose, both the first input vector (SRC1) and the destination vector (DST) use the offset values chained from local memory by the L/S lane to indirectly address the RF

$$\underbrace{\mathrm{RF}\,[\delta[i]]}_{\mathrm{DST}} \leftarrow \max(\underbrace{\mathrm{RF}\,[\delta[i]]}_{\mathrm{SRC1}}, \underbrace{f[i]}_{\mathrm{SRC2}}) \tag{7}$$

where the current maximum value of the cell (SRC1) specified by offset $\delta[i]$ is compared against the current point-wise feature $f[i]$ read from the RF (SRC2) and the resulting maximum is written back (DST). The result of this operation is the corresponding segment of the dense output tensor as depicted in Fig. 7.c.

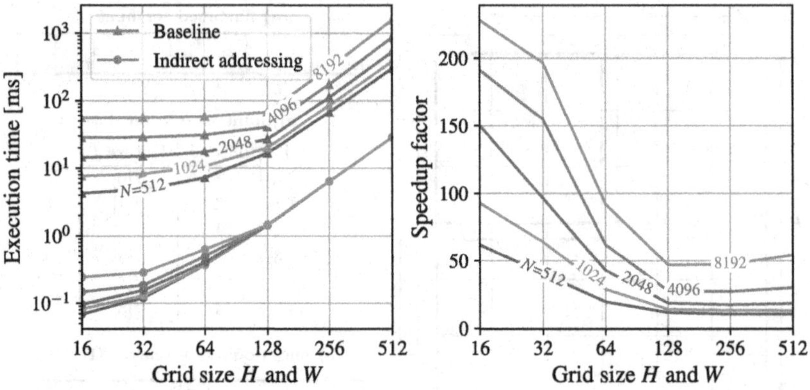

Fig. 8. Execution time for both PointPillars implementations and achieved speedup of the indirect addressing implementation over the baseline for $C_{in} = 5$ input features, $C_{out} = 64$ output features and different parametrizations of grid sizes $H \times W$ and number of input points N.

To compare both implementations and investigate their scalability the runtime is measured for different grid dimensions H and W ranging from 16 to 512, while the number of input points is varied between 512 and 8192 points. The results of this evaluation are shown in Fig. 8. It becomes evident, that the implementation with indirect addressing reduces the runtime by at least one order of magnitude compared to the baseline for all parametrizations. For smaller grid sizes, in particular grid sizes smaller than 128, even larger speedups of up to a factor of 230 can be observed. This is due to the fact that for these rather small grid sizes the point-wise processing of convolution, max pooling and scattering operations accounts for a large proportion of the total runtime.

For larger grid sizes, the computation becomes memory-bound, as the runtime is dominated by memory transfers required to write the dense output tensor back to the main memory. In this memory-bound region, the speedup achieved by the indirect addressing variant converges to a factor of 10 for 512 points and a factor of 50 for 8192 points.

5 Conclusion

In this work, we investigate how the vertical vector processor architecture V^{2}PRO can be extended by a chaining mechanism for address offsets. This mechanism allows the implementation of an indirect addressing mode that can realize flexible irregular access patterns for the individual register files and local memories in each unit of the vector processor.

The additional hardware resources required for this increased flexibility are relatively small. On a `XCZU19-EG-FFVB1517` FPGA, only 135 additional LUTs (+4.8%) and 71 registers (+1.8%) are required to implement a vector unit composed of two processing lanes and one L/S lane with support for indirect addressing. The critical path is not affected by the indirect addressing extension.

The proposed hardware extension allows the processing of long vertical vector instructions with irregular access patterns, which can significantly reduce the control overhead for the RISC-V host processor. Its benefits are assessed in the context of two exemplary applications from the computer vision domain, that use indexed address patterns. For the Deformable Convolution, which requires sampling from the input feature map based on data-dependent offsets, indirect addressing of the local memory can be used to achieve speedups of up to factor 17.25. For the PointPillars encoder, which converts irregular point clouds into regular grid-like data structures, the indirect addressing is used to scatter and pool point-wise features in the register file. The speedup for this application ranges from a factor of 10 for relatively small point clouds of 512 points to a factor of 50 for larger point clouds of 8192 points.

In summary, the proposed indirect addressing mode for the V^2PRO architecture has a relatively small hardware footprint and enables large performance gains for applications that profit from more flexible and irregular addressing patterns.

Acknowledgment. This work was partly funded by the German Federal Ministry of Education and Research (BMBF) under project number 16ME0379 (ZuSe-KI-AVF).

References

1. Amiri, H., Shahbahrami, A.: SIMD programming using Intel vector extensions. J. Parallel Distrib. Comput. **135**, 83–100 (2020). https://doi.org/10.1016/j.jpdc.2019.09.012
2. Chen, X., Ma, H., Wan, J., Li, B., Xia, T.: Multi-view 3D object detection network for autonomous driving. In: Conference on Computer Vision and Pattern Recognition (CVPR). pp. 6526–6534. IEEE (2017), ISSN: 1063-6919
3. Chou, C.H., Severance, A., Brant, A.D., Liu, Z., Sant, S., Lemieux, G.G.: VEGAS: soft vector processor with scratchpad memory. In: Proceedings of the 19th ACM/SIGDA International Symposium on Field Programmable Gate Arrays. ACM (2011)
4. Dai, J., et al.: Deformable convolutional networks. In: International Conference on Computer Vision, pp. 764–773. IEEE (2017)
5. Dolbeau, R.: Theoretical peak FLOPS per instruction set: a tutorial. J. Supercomput. **74**(3) (2018)
6. Gesper, S., et al.: N^2V^2PRO: neural network mapping framework for a custom vector processor architecture. In: 13th International Conference on Consumer Electronics - Berlin (ICCE-Berlin), pp. 94–99. IEEE (2023)
7. Intel: Intel architecture instruction set extensions programming reference. Doc. Nr: 319433-016 (2013)
8. Intel: Intel Advanced Vector Extensions 10. Doc. Nr: 355989-001US (2023)
9. Intel: Intel architecture instruction set extensions and future features. Doc. Nr: 319433-051 (2023)
10. Jacob, B., et al.: Quantization and training of neural networks for efficient integer-arithmetic-only inference. Tech. rep. (2017). http://arxiv.org/abs/1712.05877

11. Köhler, D., Quach, M., Ulrich, M., Meinl, F., Bischoff, B., Blume, H.: Improved multi-scale grid rendering of point clouds for radar object detection networks. In: 26th International Conference on Information Fusion (FUSION), pp. 1–8 (2023)
12. Lang, A.H., Vora, S., Caesar, H., Zhou, L., Yang, J., Beijbom, O.: PointPillars: fast encoders for object detection from point clouds. IEEE/CVF Conference on Computer Vision and Pattern Recognition (CVPR) (2019)
13. Lewis, J.G., Simon, H.D.: The impact of hardware Gather/Scatter on sparse Gaussian elimination. SIAM J. Sci. Stat. Comput. **9**(2), 304–311 (1988). https://doi.org/10.1137/0909019
14. MMCV Contributors: OpenMMLab Computer Vision Foundation (2018). https://github.com/open-mmlab/mmcv
15. Nolting, S., Giesemann, F., Hartig, J., Schmider, A., Paya-Vaya, G.: Application-specific soft-core vector processor for advanced driver assistance systems. In: 27th International Conference on Field Programmable Logic and Applications (FPL) (2017)
16. RISC-V: Vector extension 1.0 (2023). https://github.com/riscv/riscv-v-spec/
17. Russell, R.M.: The CRAY-1 computer system. Commun. ACM **21**(1), 63–72 (1978). https://doi.org/10.1145/359327.359336
18. Severance, A., Lemieux, G.: VENICE: a compact vector processor for FPGA applications. In: International Conference on Field-Programmable Technology. IEEE (2012)
19. Severance, A., Lemieux, G.G.: Embedded supercomputing in FPGAs with the VectorBlox MXP matrix processor. In: International Conference on Hardware/Software Codesign and System Synthesis (CODES+ ISSS). IEEE (2013)
20. Stephens, N., et al.: The ARM scalable vector extension. IEEE Micro **37**(2), 26–39 (2017)
21. Thieu, G.B., et al.: ZuSE-Ki-Avf: application-specific AI processor for intelligent sensor signal processing in autonomous driving. In: 2023 Design, Automation & Test in Europe Conference & Exhibition (DATE). IEEE (2023)
22. Ulrich, M., Braun, S., Köhler, D., Niederlöhner, D., Faion, F., Gläser, C., Blume, H.: Improved orientation estimation and detection with hybrid object detection networks for automotive radar. In: 25th International Conference on Intelligent Transportation Systems (ITSC), pp. 111–117. IEEE (2022)
23. Weißbrich, M., García-Ortiz, A., Payá-Vayá, G.: Comparing vertical and horizontal SIMD vector processor architectures for accelerated image feature extraction. J. Syst. Archit. **100** (2019)
24. Yang, B., Luo, W., Urtasun, R.: PIXOR: real-time 3D object detection from point clouds. In: IEEE Conference on Computer Vision and Pattern Recognition (2019)
25. Yiannacouras, P., Steffan, J.G., Rose, J.: VESPA: portable, scalable, and flexible FPGA-based vector processors. In: International Conference on Compilers, Architectures and Synthesis for Embedded Systems. ACM (2008)
26. Zhou, Y., Tuzel, O.: VoxelNet: end-to-end learning for point cloud based 3D object detection. In: IEEE Conference on Computer Vision and Pattern Recognition (2017)
27. Zhu, X., Hu, H., Lin, S., Dai, J.: Deformable ConvNets v2: more deformable, better results. In: Proceedings of the IEEE/CVF Conference on Computer Vision and Pattern Recognition, pp. 9308–9316 (2019)

AutoSync Framework for Expressing Synchronization Intentions in Multithreaded Programs

Jasmin Jahić[1(✉)] and Matheus Bortoloti[2]

[1] University of Cambridge, Cambridge, UK
jj542@cam.ac.uk
[2] University of Kaiserslautern, Kaiserslautern, Germany

Abstract. To find concurrency bugs in multithreaded software and to be able to reconstruct synchronisation bottlenecks, it is necessary to understand concurrency-related aspects of such programs (shared variables, used synchronisation mechanisms, synchronisation intentions). However, static and dynamic analysis approaches (including the hybrid ones) either overapproximate their results, or are prone to missing some concurrency-related aspects. As a consequence, testers and software architects have to work in the dark when trying to choose tools for finding concurrency bugs and when trying to optimize multithreaded programs to take full advantage of parallel computing potential of multicore processors. To solve this problem, we suggest to divide the activities around synchronisations into two parts. In the first part, developers should only specify high-level intentions regarding access to shared variables. In the second part, it should be possible to automatically transfer these intentions to concrete programming-language specific synchronisation mechanisms. To enable this solution, we have developed the AutoSync framework that provides interfaces for specifying high-level synchronisation intentions and then automatically maps these to optimal synchronisation mechanisms (e.g., locks). AutoSync by design avoids concurrency bugs and is able to provide to architects information about program's concurrency-related aspects so they can perform necessary optimisations.

Keywords: Multicore · Multithreaded · Concurrency · Synchronisation · Parallelisation

1 Introduction

To harvest computing parallelism of multicore processors for reducing execution time of individual programs [21], software developers are forced to partition programs into multiple threads. As long as the concurrent threads of a program do not share mutable program states, threads can execute safely without synchronisation. However, once there is a need for threads to communicate their results or intermediate states, then there is a need to synchronise their access to shared mutable states (i.e., shared variables, in the rest of the text).

L. Carro et al. (Eds.): SAMOS 2024, LNCS 15226, pp. 183–198, 2025.
https://doi.org/10.1007/978-3-031-78377-7_13

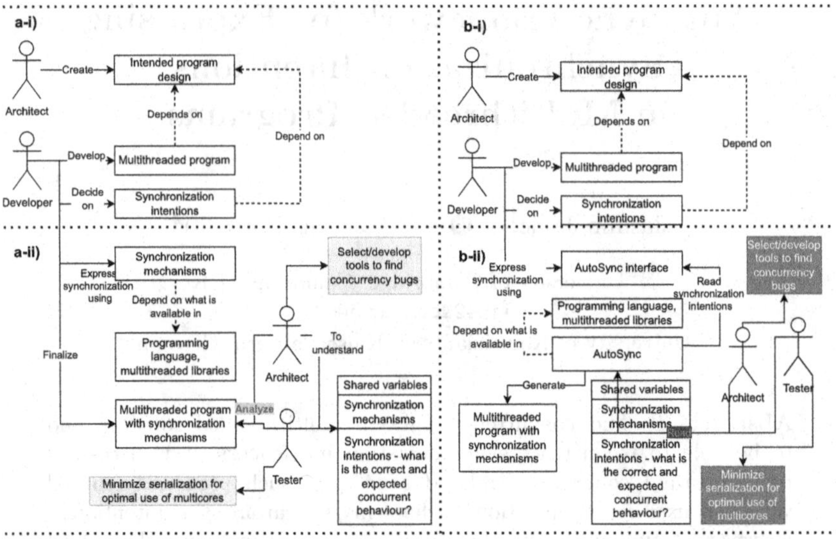

Fig. 1. Designing, developing, and testing of multi threaded software: a) Common approach and challenges (in yellow); b) Our approach and solutions (in green) (Color figure online)

Improper synchronisation leads to *concurrency bugs* and *issues with performance*, something that remains a challenge to this day. To understand why, let us observe a process for developing standard multithreaded software (Fig. 1-a). Software architects design such software to maximize parallelisation and work with developers on intended synchronisation between threads. Developers implement synchronisation intentions using synchronisation mechanisms available in the language of the program. This is already a limiting factor, as developers need to constrain their synchronisation intentions and try to fit them into code according to the available synchronisation mechanisms (e.g., sometimes a mutex is the perfect fit for synchronisation, but sometimes developers have more complex synchronisation intentions). This is already critical because the improper use of synchronisation mechanisms can lead to concurrency bugs (e.g., improper use of mutex leads to deadlocks). However, the true problems begin when testers and architects try to understand multithreaded software to test it and optimize it, respectively (Fig. 1-aii). To do so, architects and testers need to somehow reverse engineer shared variables, synchronisation mechanisms, and synchronisation intentions from the code. The prospect of reconstructing concurrency aspects from software is quite bleak. Static analysis, theoretically, can reconstruct all these aspects, but is prone to overapproximation [7]. Dynamic analysis can be more precise, but tends to miss some aspects (it often requires a huge number of runs to detect all concurrency aspects of a program) [2] [10] [11] [14]. Hybrid analysis (static+dynamic) is able to improve analysis precision, but is not able to solve all of these challenges. If testers and architects are not able to understand concurrency aspects of multithreaded programs, how can they select or develop tools for finding potential concurrency bugs and minimize improper use of synchronisation mechanisms that leads to the serialization (outsides of heuristic approaches [12])? Concurrency bugs appear only under specific interleaving of instructions between different threads. Netzer and Miller proved that computing event orderings in multithreaded software is an *NP-hard* problem [17]. For n threads and i number of instructions, equation $2^{n \cdot i}$ defines the number of possible event orderings. Performance of concurrent software is in particular sensitive to the serialization. For example, Hennessy and Patterson [6] have demonstrated that in a case of a 64-processor configuration, where only 1% of the code is serialized, the speedup is about 35 (instead of the ideal 64 times).

Therefore, the research question we address is: **How to reverse-engineer concurrency-related aspects of multithreaded programs (shared variables, used synchronisation mechanisms, synchronisation intentions) to be able to eliminate concurrency bugs and maximize parallelism?**

To address this research question, we suggest to separate the problem of programming concurrent software into two parts (Fig. 1-b). In the first part, developers should be able to express their high-level intentions regarding the synchronisation of concurrent threads. In the second part, it is necessary to use those intentions and automatically translate them into source code using existing programming synchronisation mechanisms. By doing this, we clearly decouple specification of the synchronisation intentions from the actual implementation. Effectively, by design we eliminate any possibility to introduce implementation concurrency bugs, because developers do not program synchronisation mechanisms anymore. To do this automatically, we have developed a framework for expressing synchronisation in multithreaded programs - AutoSync (the framework is publicly available[1]). Our framework integrates with a programming language in which developers create their programs and offers a set of high-level synchronisation intentions that developers can use (e.g., read a variable with the intention to update it). AutoSync analyses their intentions and generates the code using synchronisation mechanisms in the concrete programming language (e.g., locks in C). It does so in a way to choose optimal synchronisation mechanisms considering the whole program, while at the same time it is able to avoid classical pitfalls of synchronisation such as deadlocks. If some of the intentions that developers express are contradictory, it can warn them. Consequently, AutoSync has information about all shared variables in software and all used (generated) synchronisation mechanisms (there is no need anymore to do any reverse engineering analysis). Besides eliminating the need for finding concurrency bugs, AutoSync indicates mutually exclusive parts of concurrent software that lead to serialization. As such, it is very convenient as the first step before visualisation of concurrency, which software architects can use to reason about how to optimize the software (e.g., reduce the number of shared variables, move them to other parts of the program, or change the number of threads). The only constraint that AutoSync has is that developers must access all shared variables

[1] https://github.com/matheusbortoloti/AutoSync.

only through AutoSync interfaces. The evaluation results show that AutoSync does not introduce any performance overhead, while providing these benefits: i) keeps the full overview of concurrency-related aspects of multithreaded programs (suitable for visualization) and ii) eliminates concurrency bugs by design.

The rest of this paper is structured as follows. In Sect. 2, we discuss approaches that try to solve this problem (documentation discipline in Agile teams, static and dynamic analysis, approaches for finding concurrency bugs). In Sect. 3, we introduce our approach, and then we introduce its implementation (in Sect. 4). In Sect. 5, we present evaluation of AutoSync with SPLASH-3 benchmark, and finally we conclude in Sect. 6.

2 Related Work

When it comes to understanding concurrency-related aspects of multithreaded programs, one way to deal with the inability to reverse engineer concurrency-related aspects of multithreaded programs is to enforce documentation discipline during development [9] (e.g., whenever a developer introduces a shared variable or a synchronisation mechanism, they need to document it).

There exist several approaches that try to identify shared memory and used synchronisation mechanisms in software [5] [15] [16] [20]. However, they suffer from the limitations of static and dynamic analysis. Static analysis takes as input a static representation of a piece of software and reasons about its properties without running it (e.g., by using *abstract interpretation* [4]). However, most of the interesting questions that exist with regard to software are *not decidable*. Therefore, static analysis has to make overapproximations and use a combination of analyses (e.g., path sensitivity and type analysis) to produce more complete but less precise results (e.g., to reduce the number of false warnings). *Dynamic analysis* executes the software and uses an execution trace as input for the analysis. However, according to Dijkstra [3]: "Program testing can be used to show the presence of bugs, but never to show their absence!".

While there are numerous approaches for finding concurrency bugs [13] [20], this task still remains a challenge in practice [8]. To understand why, let us observe an example in Fig. 2. Although the two examples (a) and b)) follow the same synchronisation pattern to a shared variable, it is obvious that the example in Fig. 2-b has a potential bug (atomicity violation type of a concurrency bug). In Fig. 2-b, thread t1 first creates an object, releases a lock on it, and after some time acquires the lock again to invoke a method on the object. If thread t2 executes between these two operations, then it will delete the object from memory. Consequently, t1 will generate a NULL pointer exception. The question is, how to detect such bug, when in the case of Fig. 2-a, the same access and synchronisation pattern do not introduce any bugs [15]. Furthermore, let us observe the example in Fig. 2-c). What is the correct synchronisation? Did the developers originally plan to use lock1 or lock2 when accessing shared variable *account*? As Herb and Larus [22] have noticed, "*the relationship between a lock and the data that it protects is implicit, and it is preserved only through*

```
a) t1:
     lock1.lock()
     account = account + 100;
     lock1.unlock()
     ...
     lock1.lock()
     account = account + 200;
     lock1.unlock()

   t2:
     lock1.lock()
     account = account - 10;
     lock1.unlock()
```

```
b) t1:
     lock1.lock()
     object = new ObjectClass();
     lock1.unlock()
     ...
     lock1.lock()
     object.method1();
     lock1.unlock()

   t2:
     lock1.lock()
     delete(object);
     object = NULL;
     lock1.unlock()
```

```
c) t1:
     lock1.lock()
     account = account + 100;
     lock1.unlock()
     ...
     lock2.lock()
     account = account + 200;
     lock2.unlock()
```

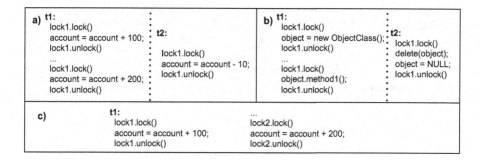

Fig. 2. a) No concurrency bugs; b) Atomicity violation; c) Improper use of locks.

programmer discipline. A programmer must always remember to take the right lock at the right point before touching shared data. Conventions governing locks in a program are sometimes written down, but they're almost never stated precisely enough for a tool to check them ". The question is, how will testers or testing tools know what was the original intention? Access to shared variables in most of the programming languages available today is without any interfaces. Hence, if one developer in any thread introduces an improper synchronisation when accessing a shared variable, all accesses to that shared variable in all other threads might be affected. Because of the lack of access interfaces [8] and because concurrency bugs appear only under specific interleaving of instructions between different threads, a bug might remain unnoticed for years!

Besides finding concurrency bugs, it is quite important to understand design of the concurrent software, so architects can reason about their performance. Blocking synchronisation between threads leads to serialization of execution, and as a consequence has a negative impact on performance of such software. Visualization of software is a good tool to reason about such properties of concurrent software [18]. However, here we again have the same problem as in the case of finding concurrency bugs. It is not possible to have a proper visualization of concurrency aspects of multithreaded software without proper information about synchronisation mechanisms, shared variables, and synchronisation intentions.

3 AutoSync Framework

When developing multithreaded software with AutoSync (Fig. 3), developers use AutoSync ***interfaces*** to express their high level intentions instead of using specific synchronization mechanisms available in the concrete programming language. This decouples ***synchronization intentions*** (we discuss the logic behind synchronization intentions present in AutoSync interface in Sect. 3.1) from a concrete ***implementation*** of multithreaded programs. The main and only assumption in the case of AutoSync is that developers must access all shared variables only through AutoSync interfaces (Sect. 3.2). Once developers

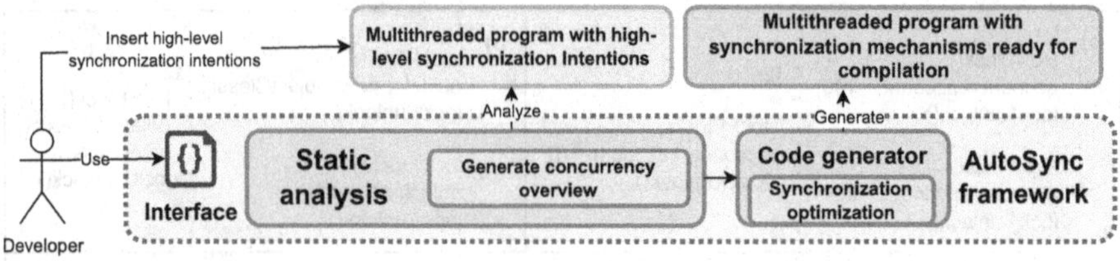

Fig. 3. Overview of the components in the AutoSync framework.

write their multithreaded program using the high-level synchronization provided in the AutoSync ***interface***, their work is done.

To produce source code that compiles, AutoSync uses ***static analysis*** to identify ***AutoSync interfaces with synchronisation intentions*** in the multithreaded program (it is straightforward and not complicated as the general static analysis due to the well-defined interfaces). The output is a ***concurrency overview*** of the program. This overview contains data about threads, their shared variables, operations on those shared variables, and any dependencies between shared variables (e.g., to compute shared variable var1 it is necessary to use shared variable var2). Even when using AutoSync, developers still can express intentions that are contradictory to each other. However, contrary to other tools that require very complex and slow static analysis (or exhaustive analysis of execution traces), AutoSync has explicit access to all synchronization intentions. Therefore, it can ***identify inconsistencies*** in developers' intentions.

Next, AutoSync runs a ***code generator*** to identify ***optimal*** synchronization between threads. One of the common challenges in multithreaded programs is that developers synchronize operations that do not require synchronization. For example, two threads modify a variable var. After some time, developers change the program so that only the main thread initializes the variable var, and the two threads only read it. If this is not transparent to developers who maintain those threads (and in most cases this is not transparent due to the challenges with analyzing source code as discussed in the Sect. 1), then threads block each other and serialize their execution when there is no need to do so.

Finally, ***code generator*** creates a multithreaded program with the synchronization in the targeted programming language. In Sect. 3.3, we discuss the static analysis and code generation. Let us illustrate this flow using an example in C programming language. Consider the following piece of code found inside a thread which has multiple runtime instances:

```
pthread_mutex_lock(&lock1);
   v++;
pthread_mutex_unlock(&lock1);
```

In the original code above, the variable v is expected to be shared between several threads. Furthermore, developers must remember that whenever they access the variable v, they always have to use lock *lock1*. *All* developers working with the variable v must be aware of this dependency. Architects and testers on the other hand have to either find a way to learn about this dependency from the developers or have to rely on documentation. Otherwise, it is impossible to reconstruct this relationship between the code (use *lock1* when accessing variable v). The best they can do is to assume this relationship based on some heuristic. We can refactor the code above using AutoSync interface, as specified below:

```
iAutoSyncReadToUpdate(&newV, &v,sizeof(newV), syncIntention);
    newV++;
iAutoSyncUpdate(&v, &newV, sizeof(newV), syncIntention);
```

In the case of the code that is using AutoSync interface, we express our intention to read and update the variable v. We point to it using a local variable $newV$, operate on it, and use another interface to update the shared variable v. This offers several advantages. Developers do not have to remember which lock is associated with which variable - AutoSync will generate the appropriate synchronization for them. If some developers change other threads such that they stop using the variable v and only this thread is using it, then no synchronisation will be generated. Finally, we can express additional synchronisation intentions using the final argument *synchIntention* in the interface (see Sect. 3.2 for more details). This approach does not only save time and avoids concurrency bugs by design, it also allows for various optimizations. Depending on synchronization intentions, some complex yet highly efficient synchronization mechanisms might be appropriate (e.g., data structures such as rings). While a developer who has only insight in their threads might miss to notice this, pattern matching in AutoSync ***code generator*** might be able to identify this automatically.

3.1 Logic Behind Synchronization Intentions

All high-level synchronisation intentions can be reduced to the following basic intentions. A thread can: i) use (read) data produced by (written) other threads, ii) produce (write) data to be used by other threads, iii) wait for an event produced by other threads, or iv) generate an event on which some other thread might be waiting (e.g., wake some thread so it can continue with the execution). Any complex synchronisation intention can be described with the combination of these intentions. E.g., a thread reads shared variable of the program, uses it to compute another variable of the program, and upon completing that operation informs all other threads to continue. Obviously, developers can implement this using several programming synchronisation mechanisms (e.g., mutex, barriers, conditional variables). But, there is a gap between these synchronisation intentions and programming synchronisation mechanisms. Synchronisation mechanisns available in programming language are fit for specific communication patterns (very limited, predefined, bugs-prone, and rigid synchronization intentions). Instead, let us discuss high-level synchronisation intentions that developers of multithread programs really need.

Access to a Single Shared-Variable: The simplest, yet the most often misunderstood intention in concurrent software is about atomicity of certain code sections. A common pattern in multithreaded programs is the *read-modify-write* (RMW) construct. In the RMW pattern, a developer intents to have mutual exclusion of code sections in different threads - i.e., atomic execution of these code sections. However, developers often focus on synchronisation of small critical sections (e.g., by using a mutex) and lose the overview of the full program. Therefore, it can happen that multiple threads exercise an interleaving where that is not allowed, leading to an atomicity violation.

Access to a Shared Data Structures: Data structures (e.g., structures in C, classes in object oriented programming) can comprise data elements that are either: i) fully independent of each other, or ii) have some logical dependencies. In the first case, it is possible to observe access to each individual element of a data structure as an access to a single shared-variable. Therefore, it is necessary to make synchronisation between threads on the level of the data structure field. In the second case, when there are logical dependencies between data structure elements, it is necessary to update all of them atomically. Therefore, it is necessary to make synchronisation between threads on the level of the data structure.

Access to a continuous Data in Memory: This is a well-known pattern where threads access limited sections of a (very) long continuous data allocated in memory. A common example of this pattern is slicing an array into subsections, where each thread is accessing only specified subsection. In this way, threads operate on isolated data subsections and they do not need to synchronise their data access. An inadequate synchronization would prevent parallel processing.

Shared Constants: Constants in multithreaded programs reflect a one-time write, many times read pattern. These constants (either single variables of whole data structures) are in the most cases initialised before threads are even created.

3.2 AutoSync Interface

The AutoSync interface comprises a set of methods and custom data types. Here, we present them using C programming language:

```
--- ---
typedef struct xAutoSyncIntentionsStruct {
void* pvDependsOn[MAX_DEPENDENCIES];
bool bConstantInitByMain; bool bSlicedArray;
uint64_t uiFirstAccess; uint64_t uiLastAccessM;
} const xIntent;

typedef int8_t xAutoSyncEvent;

iAutoSyncCreate(void);
iAutoSyncDestroy(void);
```

```
iAutoSyncRead(void* lV, void* sV, size_t s, xIntent i);
iAutoSyncWrite(void* sV, void* lV, size_t s, xIntent i);

iAutoSyncReadToUpdate(void* lV, void* sV, size_t s, xIntent i);
iAutoSyncUpdate(void* sV, void* lV, size_t s, xIntent i);

iAutoSyncSharedVarAsArg(void* sV);

iAutoSyncProceedOnEvent(xAutoSyncEvent e, uint8_t uiNoOfThreads);
--- ---
```

Here follows the explanation of the AutoSync interfaces. Each interface is defined to represent a basic synchronization intention (e.g., iAutoSyncRead to read a shared variable).

In addition to the basic synchronization intentions, structure *xAutoSyncIntentionsStruct* contains additional information about synchronization intentions. In cases when a developer operates on shared variables that depend on other variables (e.g., variables need to be updated simultaneously, or up to date value of one variable should be used when calculating another), developers can specify those dependencies in *pvDependsOn* adding all shared-variables that depend on one another. Field *bConstantInitByMain* in *xAutoSyncIntentionsStruct* is used to convey an intent about accessing a shared variable initialized by the main thread (before other threads are created). When accessing a succession of a continuously allocated data in memory, developers indicate their intention using *bSlicedArray*. In that context, fields *uiFirstAccess* and *uiLastAccessM* serve to determine the boundaries related to this access.

In the case of the *read* interface, *lV* is the address of a local variable where the content of the shared-variable is copied to. In the case of the *write* interface, *lV* is the address of a local variable that contains the value to be written to the shared-variable. At the same time, *sV* is the shared-variable itself.

Finally, *e* represents an event and *uiNoOfThreads* is the number of threads that must wait for this event.

Interfaces for Accessing a Single Shared Variable: Sometimes, it is just necessary to read or write to a shared variable. In such cases, a thread simply updates a shared variable (e.g., handling sensors data) or uses a shared variable to compute some local results. Therefore, AutoSync prescribes the following interface - *iAutoSyncRead* and *iAutoSyncWrite*.

Interfaces for Updating a Shared Variable Based on its Previous Value: In cases when a thread uses one shared variable to compute another, or updates a shared variable based on its previous value, there is a need to understand the scope of such critical section. Therefore, developers need ways to explicitly specify what they plan to do. The interface has been designed in a way that the intention behind the critical section is clear: it starts with the interface *iAutoSyncReadToUpdate* and finishes with *iAutoSyncUpdate*. By introducing the local variable in between (*lV*), this enables developers to construct clear transactions and only commit them when they are done with processing the shared variables (solving the problem we introduced in the Sect. 1).

Interfaces for Accessing a Shared Data Structure: In this case, it is necessary for developers to specify if some data structure elements depend on other elements of that data structure. To access the elements of these structures, developers use standard read, write, or update interfaces. However, if accessing data structure elements with dependencies to other elements, then developers need to populate *pvDependsOn* field of the *xAutoSyncIntentionsStruct* structure. If that is not the case, then they access those elements as any other regular access.

Interfaces for Accessing Continuous Data in Memory: The sliced array is a good example for this interface. In order to access a sliced array, developers can use the same interfaces that they would use for regular shared variables. The only difference is in the intention passed as argument (*xAutoSyncIntentionsStruct*). When accessing this type of data, developers need to set *bSlicedArray* to *true*, and initialize *uiFirstAccess* and *uiLastAccess.*

Interfaces for Accessing a Constant Initialized by the Main Thread: When accessing this type of a shared variable, developers can use the same interfaces that they would use for regular shared variables. The only difference is in the intention passed as argument (*xAutoSyncIntentionsStruct*). When accessing this type of data, developers need to set *bConstantInitByMain* to *true.*

Interfaces for Accessing Shared-Variables Through a Pointer: AutoSync contains an interface (*iAutoSyncSharedVarAsArg*) to indicate that a given shared pointer is being used as an argument to a function and can, therefore, be read or written inside that function. This interface exists to warn programmers about passing shared variables through a pointer.

Interfaces for Proceeding on an Event: AutoSync has an interface (iAutoSyncProceedOnEvent) to wait for a specific event before proceeding. Developers also need to specify the number of threads that need to reach this event.

Finally, **iAutoSyncCreate** is responsible for initializing the synchronization and any other startup code required by the framework. This interface should be called before any AutoSync interfaces. Consequently, **iAutoSyncDestroy** is responsible for releasing the resources allocated during the startup phase.

3.3 Static Analysis and Code Generator

Static analysis component of the AutoSync framework has a mission to find AutoSync interfaces used in the code and reconstruct information from them. It also has a task to identify all threads in the code (thread libraries use standard interfaces to create and destroy threads, hence identifying them is mostly straightforward). The static analysis generates a human-readable file containing a concurrency overview in JSON format. To do this, static analysis constructs an *Abstract Syntax Tree* (AST) of the source code. It writes a JSON file with threads of the program, number of instances of each thread, shared variables used by every thread and their types, operations that each thread performs on its shared variables, and associates every access to a shared variable with its respective synchronization intention.

Code generator in AutoSync takes as input the JSON file created by the static analysis component and the source code with the high-level synchronisation mechanisms. This component is then responsible for synthesizing the synchronisation mechanisms automatically and placing them in the correct position and context inside the source code. As output, it produces new source code files by replacing the AutoSync interfaces with proper synchronisation mechanisms. It also generates a static library with framework's startup and cleanup code.

The code generator contains optimization algorithms that try to find an optimal set of synchronization mechanisms using all the intentions and information from the static analysis. These algorithms are described in our code repository, and describing them would be a separate research question. However, for the sake of completeness of this paper, we will describe a few simple algorithms. The trivial use case for the generation of synchronization mechanisms is when the intentions data structure (*xAutoSyncIntentionsStruct*) has not been filled at all. In that case, the simplest synchronisation-generation algorithm assumes that the program under analysis has no special constructs that allow any optimisations. Thus, the code generator will employ a strict locking policy, meaning that it will assign a lock to every shared-variable. On the other hand, if any dependency is indicated via the field *pvDependsOn* in the *xAutoSyncIntentionsStruct*, it will apply a more optimized lock assignment strategy: all shared-variables that depend on one another will be associated with the same lock.

More complex optimizations would analyze type of the access to shared variables, instances of access, position of the access in the AST, etc. Based on these, the code generator would use more advance synchronisation mechanisms that perform the most efficiently considering the intentions passed by developers and considering the overall context of the whole program.

4 Implementation

In this section, we explain the implementation of the conceptual framework (Fig. 4) introduced in Sect. 3. We have implemented AutoSync interface in C

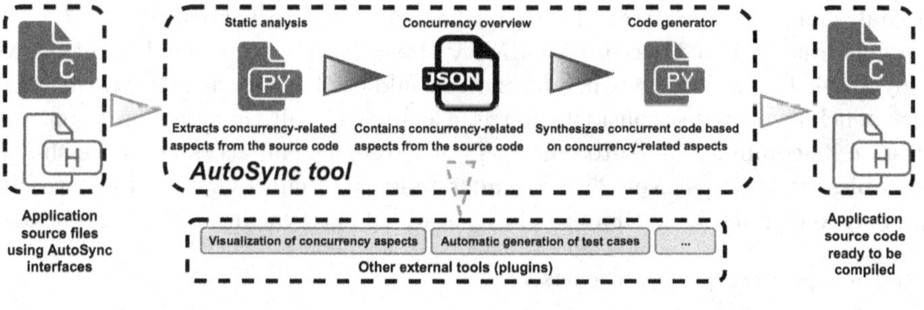

Fig. 4. Implementation of the AutoSync framework.

programming language, using POSIX pthreads. Static analysis and code generator components are implemented in Python. Communication between the static analysis and the code generator works through a JSON file. This file represents overview of concurrency properties of a multithreaded program and as such can be used by third party tools for visualization, automatic generation of tests cases, and similar activities. To implement static analysis, we have used a Python library ***pycparser***[2]. This library is able to parse pre-processed C code into an *Abstract Syntax Tree* (AST).

5 Evaluation

5.1 Setup

To evaluate AutoSync, we chose a multithreaded FFT (Fast Fourier Transform) application from the SPLASH-3 benchmark [19]. SPLASH-3 is an enhancement of the SPLASH-2 [24], which has been used for almost three decades as one of the most popular benchmarks for concurrent and parallel applications. **FFT** is a 1-D version of the radix-$\sqrt{n}$ six-step FFT algorithm described in [1], which is optimized to minimize inter-processor communication [24]. We configured FFT to use 12 887 045 176 data points and 512 cache lines. The original code contains 917 LOC and 36 shared-variables. The program uses one lock, and seven barriers. All shared variables are gathered in a single data structure. When it comes to synchronisation intentions, developers use read-modify-write shared-variable pattern and some threads wait until other complete specific action.

To identify shared variables, synchronisation mechanisms, and the intentions behind the synchronisation mechanisms from the code, it took us around 30 h of manual work. In order to evaluate our approach, we've decided to rewrite the FFT example using the AutoSync framework (the coding part was straighforward). After we have refactored the whole program using AutoSync, we executed both the original SPLASH version and the AutoSync version, and compared the execution time and the memory footprint. We have averaged the execution time because the single measurements have shown some discrepancy among them. Hence, we executed each program six times and we have used the average of all measurements. To measure the memory footprint, we used **Valgrind's**[3] [23] tool called ***massif***[4]. The tool keeps track of all memory allocated during program execution and gives a detailed report when the program is finished.

One criticism (**a threat to validity**) towards this paper could be that we only applied it to a single benchmark. We could easily refute this by stating that the benchmark under consideration is a complex multithreaded program and despite its complexity - AutoSync was able to replace all accesses to the shared variables. It took us over 25 h to understand the benchmark, and eventually, we had to contact its authors to clarify some of the synchronisation intentions.

[2] https://pypi.org/project/pycparser/.
[3] https://valgrind.org/.
[4] https://valgrind.org/docs/manual/ms-manual.html.

We tried to apply our framework to another multithreaded program *netdedup*[5]. However, after investing over 20 h into trying to understand its synchronisation intentions and not getting too far, we gave up. This situation strongly demonstrates why it is important to have an approach such as the AutoSync.

5.2 Results

After replacing all accesses to global variables with AutoSync interfaces, we have identified the following. The program uses more global variables than what was actually needed. The JSON file generated by AutoSync's static analysis reported several variables that were global, but have been used only locally. Hence, we changed the scope of those variables from global to local, improving the code quality without compromising its functionality. This led to a better design of the program by decreasing its complexity (in multithreaded software the complexity grows exponentially with the number of shared variables).

Table 1. Measurements for the original SPLASH FFT program and its version rewritten with AutoSync.

Version	Average execution time (s)	Memory consumption (Bytes)	LOC	Shared variables
SPLASH	26.5	12 887 045 280	917	39
AutoSync	25.8	12 887 045 176	1107	21

Table 1 shows average execution time, memory consumption, lines of code, and the number of shared variables considering the original FFT program and its version rewritten using AutoSync. From these, we concluded the following:

1. Regarding the *execution time*, the *AutoSync* version performs almost identical to the original one. Originally, there were a few synchronisation mechanisms that were actually not required, because the shared memory accesses were already correct-by-design (e.g., only one thread accessing a protected variable). In the *AutoSync* version, we have removed these mechanisms.
2. There is no benefit or drawback of using *AutoSync* when it comes to *memory footprint.* The memory footprint is almost identical in both versions.
3. Using *AutoSync* increases the lines of code (LOC) when comparing with the SPLASH version. This is not necessarily a drawback, because in this case having more LOC improves considerably the code readability which, in turn, will decrease the maintenance and debugging time.
4. Using *AutoSync* resulted in a decrease of the number of shared variables. This result is strongly related to reducing the complexity of a program and to its potential for concurrency bugs to emerge. Thus, this reduction can be considered a benefit from using the developed framework.

[5] https://github.com/cirosantilli/parsec-benchmark/tree/master/pkgs/netapps/netdedup.

In summary, the evaluation shows that the *AutoSync* version performs as good as the original version, so the question is **what is the real benefit from using AutoSync**? In principle, AutoSync could generate optimized synchronisation for the program under test. This was not the case for the FFT. However, we also demonstrated that AutoSync did not introduce any overhead. When it comes to the benefits, *AutoSync* version of the program now contains a concurrency overview in a JSON file. At the beginning of the analysis, it took us around 25 h to understand the FFT program (shared variables, synchronisation mechanisms, synchronisation intentions). Programs developed with AutoSync provide these information out of the box in a JSON file. This, in return makes the work easier for developers, testers, and architects who all need these information in order to do their job.

Furthermore, *AutoSync* forces developers to systematically reason about synchronisation and interaction between threads. It forces them to think about the high-level intentions, and as a consequence it can lead to simplification of multithreaded programs (as we have seen in the case of FFT, through the reduction of the number of shared variables). Another benefit of using *AutoSync* is the potential elimination of over-constrained or superfluous synchronisation mechanisms. This is achieved in two different ways. First, the expression of high-level synchronisation intentions already forces developers to be more careful and scrupulous about the real need behind shared variables. Second, the *AutoSync* static analysis is already able to automatically detect conflicting synchronisation intentions. Moreover, manual analysis of the concurrency-related information file can lead to new insights towards the concurrency design, resulting in the elimination or optimization of synchronisation. The biggest benefit of them all that we see with AutoSync is the avoidance of concurrency bugs by design. With AutoSync, as long as developers have clear synchronisation intentions, they cannot introduce concurrency bugs. With this, the finding of concurrency bugs is moved away from developers who write code to developers who develop the AutoSync tool. Compared to the existing approaches, AutoSync has all the necessary information to make informed conclusions about potential concurrency bugs and warn developers about their potentially contradictory synchronisation intentions. The evaluation shows that *AutoSync* is mature to handle synchronisation in very complex multithreaded programs such as FFT.

6 Conclusion and Future Work

Dealing with concurrency in multithreaded software is a challenging tasks. Even when there are just two threads with more than one shared variable, developers quickly become overwhelmed with the complexity and possible execution combinations. Developers have intentions about synchronising their software. However, they often make mistakes when trying to express those intentions using synchronisation mechanisms that are available in various programming languages. Even when they do so, reverse engineering of their implementation and understanding implemented concurrency aspects is a hard task.

That is why we have decided to enable developers to express their high-level intentions using AutoSync interfaces, and then map those interfaces to concrete synchronisation mechanisms. This divides the problem into two parts, where developers do not have to worry about concrete implementation of the synchronisation. Consequently, AutoSync eliminates concurrency bugs by design while keeping a full overview of concurrency-related aspects of multithreaded programs, which is in particular suitable for visualization of concurrency.

The evaluation shows that *AutoSync* is mature to handle synchronisation in a very complex benchmarking multithreaded program. It does so without introducing an overhead, with the benefit of improved readability of the code, reduction of complexity, and the ability to provide precise and complete overview of concurrency-related information about the program (shared variables, used synchronisation, synchronisation intentions) without complex static analysis.

In future, we plan to expand our optimisation algorithms, introduce interfaces for other programming languages, introduce new synchronisation intentions, and integrate AutoSync in compilers.

References

1. Bailey, D.H.: FFTs in external or hierarchical memory. J. Supercomputing, 23–25 (1990)
2. Bianchi, F., Margara, A., Pezze, M.: A survey of recent trends in testing concurrent software systems. IEEE Trans. Software Eng. (99), 1–1 (2017)
3. Buxton, J.N., Randell, B. (eds.): Software Engineering Techniques: Report of a Conference Sponsored by the NATO Science Committee, Rome, Italy, 27-31 Oct. 1969, Brussels, Scientific Affairs Division, NATO (1970)
4. Cousot, P., Cousot, R.: Abstract interpretation: past, present and future. In: Proceedings of the Joint Meeting of the Twenty-Third EACSL Annual Conference on Computer Science Logic (CSL) and the Twenty-Ninth Annual ACM/IEEE Symposium on Logic in Computer Science (LICS), pp. 2:1–2:10. CSL-LICS '14, ACM, New York, NY, USA (2014)
5. Dinning, A., Schonberg, E.: Detecting access anomalies in programs with critical sections. SIGPLAN Not. **26**(12), 85–96 (1991)
6. Hennessy, J.L., Patterson, D.A.: A new golden age for computer architecture. Commun. ACM **62**(2), 48–60 (2019). https://doi.org/10.1145/3282307
7. Hind, M.: Pointer analysis: haven't we solved this problem yet? In: Proceedings of the 2001 ACM SIGPLAN-SIGSOFT Workshop on Program Analysis for Software Tools and Engineering, pp. 54–61. PASTE '01, Association for Computing Machinery, New York, NY, USA (2001)
8. Jahić, J., Bauer, T., Kuhn, T., Wehn, N., Antonino, P.O.: FERA: a framework for critical assessment of execution monitoring based approaches for finding concurrency bugs. In: Arai, K., Kapoor, S., Bhatia, R. (eds.) Intelligent Computing, pp. 54–74. Springer International Publishing, Cham (2020). https://doi.org/10.1007/978-3-030-52249-0_5
9. Jahić, J., Doganci, V., Gehring, H.: CASA: an approach for exposing and documenting concurrency-related software properties. In: Orailoglu, A., Reichenbach, M., Jung, M. (eds.) Embedded Computer Systems: Architectures, Modeling, and Simulation, pp. 139–154. Springer International Publishing, Cham (2022). https://doi.org/10.1007/978-3-031-15074-6_9

10. Jahic, J., Jung, M., Kuhn, T., Kestel, C., Wehn, N.: A framework for non-intrusive trace-driven simulation of manycore architectures with dynamic tracing configuration. In: Colombo, C., Leucker, M. (eds.) Runtime Verification, pp. 458–468. Springer International Publishing, Cham (2018). https://doi.org/10.1007/978-3-030-03769-7_28
11. Jahić, J., Kuhn, T., Jung, M., Wehn, N.: BOSMI: a framework for non-intrusive monitoring and testing of embedded multithreaded software on the logical level. In: Proceedings of the 18th International Conference on Embedded Computer Systems: Architectures, Modeling, and Simulation, pp. 131–138. SAMOS '18, Association for Computing Machinery, New York, NY, USA (2018)
12. Jannesari, A.: Detection of high-level synchronization anomalies in parallel programs. Int. J. Parallel Program. **43** (2014)
13. Lamport, L.: Time, clocks, and the ordering of events in a distributed system. Commun. ACM **21**(7), 558–565 (1978)
14. Lee, E.: The problem with threads. Computer **39**(5), 33–42 (2006)
15. Lu, S., Tucek, J., Qin, F., Zhou, Y.: AVIO: detecting atomicity violations via access-interleaving invariants. IEEE Micro **27**(1), 26–35 (2007)
16. Miné, A., et al.: Taking static analysis to the next level: proving the absence of run-time errors and data races with astrée. In: 8th European Congress on Embedded Real Time Software and Systems (ERTS 2016). Toulouse, France (2016). https://hal.archives-ouvertes.fr/hal-01271552
17. Netzer, R.H., Miller, B.P.: On the complexity of event ordering for shared-memory parallel program executions. In: In Proceedings of the 1990 International Conference on Parallel Processing, pp. 93–97 (1990)
18. Pourjafarian, M., Jahic, J.: Archvimp – a framework for automatic extraction of concurrency-related software architectural properties. In: 50th International Conference on Parallel Processing Workshop. ICPP Workshops '21, Association for Computing Machinery, New York, NY, USA (2021)
19. Sakalis, C., Leonardsson, C., Kaxiras, S., Ros, A.: Splash-3: a properly synchronized benchmark suite for contemporary research. In: 2016 IEEE International Symposium on Performance Analysis of Systems and Software (ISPASS), pp. 101–111 (2016). https://doi.org/10.1109/ISPASS.2016.7482078
20. Savage, S., Burrows, M., Nelson, G., Sobalvarro, P., Anderson, T.: Eraser: a dynamic data race detector for multithreaded programs. ACM Trans. Comput. Syst. **15**(4), 391–411 (1997)
21. Sutter, H.: The free lunch is over: a fundamental turn toward concurrency in software. Dr. Dobb's J. **30**(3), 202–210 (2005)
22. Sutter, H., Larus, J.: Software and the concurrency revolution: Leveraging the full power of multicore processors demands new tools and new thinking from the software industry. Queue **3**(7), 54–62 (2005)
23. Vlahović, T., Mišić, M., Tomašević, M., Karadžić, A., Rikalo, A.: Extending valgrind framework with the MIPS MSA support. In: 2017 Zooming Innovation in Consumer Electronics International Conference (ZINC), pp. 47–51 (2017)
24. Woo, S., Ohara, M., Torrie, E., Singh, J., Gupta, A.: The splash-2 programs: characterization and methodological considerations. In: Proceedings 22nd Annual International Symposium on Computer Architecture, pp. 24–36 (1995)

HyRPF: Hybrid RRAM Prototyping on FPGA

Daniel Reiser[1(✉)], Johannes Knödtel[1], Liliia Almeeva[2], Jianan Wen[3], Andrea Baroni[3], Miloš Krstić[3,4], and Marc Reichenbach[1]

[1] University of Rostock, Rostock, Germany
daniel.reiser@uni.rostock.de
[2] Brandenburg University of Technology, Cottbus, Germany
[3] IHP Leibniz Institut für innovative Mikorelektronik, Frankfurt (Oder), Germany
[4] University of Potsdam, Potsdam, Germany

Abstract. This work presents HyRPF, a hybrid approach for simulating RRAM-based memory blocks and registers on FPGAs. HyRPF combines the accuracy and speed of physical prototypes with the scalability and cost-effectiveness of computer simulations. Our approach is implemented in the form of advanced IP blocks, which facilitate rapid prototyping of computer architectures that integrate RRAM memory. These blocks are intended to replace existing memory seamlessly, allowing for quick implementation of system designs and tests while also addressing critical challenges such as functional and non-functional device properties. Statistical models are utilized to account for various temporal and non-temporal variabilities and environmental conditions, including temperature influences. Additionally, energy consumption estimates can be conducted. The performance of our approach is validated by simulating register files and caches within a RISC-V processor architecture. The evaluation shows that HyRPF achieves functional accuracy comparable to purely software-based solutions and faithfully reproduces all essential properties of RRAM devices with minimal resource utilization, while outperforming them in terms of simulation speed and achieving a performance faster than real-time. HyRPF has the potential to significantly accelerate the development and testing of RRAM-based systems, providing researchers and engineers with a versatile and easy-to-use tool that balances accuracy and efficiency.

Keywords: RRAM · Prototyping · FPGA · Variability Modelling

1 Introduction

In recent years, Resistive Random-Access Memories (RRAMs) have emerged as a pivotal technology in enhancing computer systems, offering significant improvements in performance and energy efficiency across numerous applications. Their versatility enables them to serve in various roles: from denser alternatives to SRAM and DRAM, to non-volatile memory elements integrated within systems,

L. Carro et al. (Eds.): SAMOS 2024, LNCS 15226, pp. 199–215, 2025.
https://doi.org/10.1007/978-3-031-78377-7_14

and even as computational elements in crossbar configurations. Across these diverse applications, RRAMs consistently demonstrate the potential to surpass traditional memory technologies in efficiency and performance. However, the integration of RRAMs into computer systems presents a set of challenges that extend beyond those encountered with conventional memory technologies. The development process must rigorously address both functional properties, such as the impact of variability on stored data, and non-functional properties, including latency and the energy consumption of programming and reading operations.

One approach to developing and prototyping RRAM-based systems involves incorporating actual RRAM devices with Field-Programmable Gate Arrays (FPGAs). This method allows for direct assessment of both functional and non-functional characteristics but demands considerable effort in setting up and executing tests, alongside offering limited adaptability for varying applications. Given these complexities, the creation of device models that can seamlessly integrate into design workflows emerges as a beneficial strategy. Nevertheless, crafting such models represents a significant challenge: they must detail the devices' behavior with sufficient accuracy while remaining computationally efficient to facilitate rapid development cycles from design to evaluation.

Striking an optimal balance between detailed representation and swift execution involves designing and prototyping architectures that integrate RRAM devices on FPGAs through the application of RRAM emulation modules. Despite the advantages, the field lacks accessible intellectual property (IP) blocks that quickly and accurately emulate both the functional and non-functional properties of RRAM devices. Although our previous work [16] addressed parts of this gap specifically for in-memory computing by proposing analog emulation blocks for RRAM-based crossbar circuits on FPGAs, the current work expands on this idea by introducing an extremely resource-efficient, fast, and scalable model for the digital domain. This model focuses on the utilization of RRAM devices as multi-level storage cells capable of directly replacing traditional memory devices in a prototyping environment. Specifically, we explore the implementation of RRAM-based flip-flops (FFs) and memory arrays, delineating their potential to revolutionize memory storage and access paradigms. Our approach falls between physical prototypes and pure simulation, combining the positive properties of both. Figure 1 shows a diagram that outlines our approach.

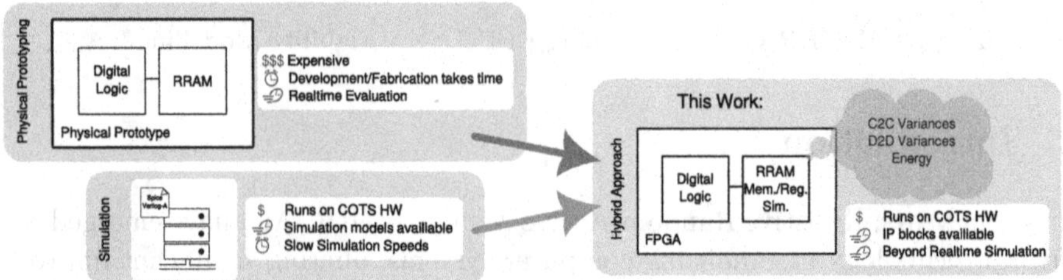

Fig. 1. Comparison of proposed approach to regular methods.

This work makes several contributions to the field of RRAM integration and system-level prototyping. Specifically:

- A comprehensive analysis of existing platforms for RRAM device prototyping, identifying key requirements for functional correctness and high emulation speed essential for our model.
- The development of IP blocks for emulating RRAM-based flip-flops and memory arrays. These modules are designed with a digital interface to ensure ease of use and minimize complexity, making them ideal for rapid prototyping of extensive system designs. Beyond serving as building blocks for constructing larger systems, they enable detailed evaluation of functional properties including performance across variable environmental conditions and non-functional properties, such as latency and power consumption.
- A demonstration of the functional correctness and emulation speed of our model through the design of a RISC-V Central Processing Unit (CPU) that incorporates both RRAM-based CPU registers and a RRAM-based cache using our developed modules.

2 Related Work

In the quest to harness the full potential of RRAM technologies, researchers and engineers employ a variety of approaches to understand the behavior and capabilities, as well as explore and simulate systems including these memory devices. In the following we aim to put our work into the context of prior approaches. The exploration of RRAM devices can be broadly categorized into three main types: simulation, physical hardware prototypes and hybrid approaches. Each category embodies a distinct methodology with its inherent advantages, limitations, and areas of application, offering a spectrum of tools for handling RRAM-based hardware designs.

Simulation Approaches provide a flexible and scalable option for investigating RRAM technologies with a comparatively low barrier to entry. Simulations are typically slower in execution time, but they are also less expensive and require less time and effort to setup than physical prototypes. Simulations enable the detailed study of RRAM characteristics and behaviors under a vast array of conditions without the need for physical fabrication. RRAM simulations can be further divided into three sub-categories:

Device-Level Models focus mainly on simulating individual RRAM devices and their transient behavior. Physical models aim to capture the fundamental physical phenomena that govern the operation of RRAM devices, such as ion migration and filament formation. They provide deeper insights into device operation and can be used for developing memristive devices or peripheral circuitry. One of the most influential physical models is the Stanford PKU model [4]. Behavioral Models on the other hand, abstract the device operation to capture the essential input-output relationships and dynamic responses of RRAM devices without delving into the underlying physical mechanisms. This approach is particularly useful for high-level design and analysis. A popular behavioral model is for example the VTEAM model [5].

Circuit-Level Models provide a more abstract description by combining the properties of specific circuit components. One widely known circuit-level model is *NVSim* [1]. This tool offers a simple method for estimating the performance and energy consumption of different non-volatile storage devices. However, it is restricted to specific circuit types, such as caches.

System-Level Models broaden the scope of RRAM simulation models by considering the integration of the devices into larger systems and abstracting away the analog behavior of the devices. This approach is crucial for evaluating the performance, power consumption, and overall feasibility of RRAM-based systems, including memory arrays and computing architectures. Examples of such models are [6,10,11].

Among these contributions, two papers from our group, [10,11], hold particular relevance to the current work. In [11], we tackled the critical issue of RRAM conductance drift, a subtle yet impactful phenomenon leading to the gradual degradation of stored information. This exploration shed light on an often-neglected aspect of RRAM non-ideality, highlighting its significance in the long-term reliability of RRAM-based systems. Building upon this foundation, [10] introduced ReSS, a comprehensive SystemC-based framework tailored for simulating system-level aspects of RRAM memories and its integration into larger systems. The simulation outcomes derived from these studies serve as foundational references and benchmarks for the IP blocks discussed in the current work.

Physical Hardware Prototypes are the concrete manifestation of RRAM technologies. This method involves fabricating and testing RRAM devices or arrays directly, which provides valuable insights into their real-world performance, reliability, and integration challenges with existing systems. Physical hardware is by construction accurate and experiments can be carried out in real time. Despite its advantages, this method has a very high barrier to entry. Time-consuming setups and high costs may not always be feasible for early-stage exploration or for studying a wide range of device configurations and material compositions. Examples for these approaches are [3,7,12].

Hybrid Approaches involve embedding a simulation of an RRAM component within a traditional prototyping platform, such as an FPGA. These approaches uniquely blend flexibility, high accuracy, and reduced simulation time. By merging the key advantages of other classes of approaches, hybrid approaches offer a comprehensive solution, which is why they were selected for the concept and implementation discussed in this paper.

NORM [13] aimed to establish an FPGA-based emulation framework for energy-harvesting, memory-based intermittent computing systems. It focused on emulating RRAM device non-volatility, incorporating energy estimation and backup strategies for state preservation. Despite its innovative approach, it was hindered by resource inefficiency due to the extensive use of control blocks for activity counters and power-down emulation, without considering device variability. Tolba et al. explored an FPGA-based simulation [14] of a binary convolutional neural network (BCNN) utilizing memristor-based XNOR gates for MNIST number recognition. Although pioneering, this application-specific model demanded significant resources and did not consider essential device characteristics. Luo et al. addressed the prohibitive costs of CPU-based software simulations of memristor-based chips by developing a fast, relatively accurate FPGA emulator for neuromorphic hardware [8]. This alternative significantly outpaced software simulations but faced scalability limitations due to considerable allocation of chip resources.

One notable gap in current research on hybrid approaches is the lack of consideration of device variabilities, a critical hurdle in the integration of RRAM technologies. Variability, such as imposed by time-independent device to device (D2D) and by time-dependent cycle to cycle (C2C) variations for example, poses significant challenges for the consistent performance and reliability of RRAM systems. In a previous work, we discussed modeling variabilities in RRAM device conductance and number of RRAM programming pulses on an FPGA [16]. However, we have only considered RRAMs in a crossbar configuration for analog in-memory calculation of matrix-vector multiplications. In this work, we focus on modeling memory cells with digital interfaces for direct integration into existing computer architectures and workflows. This approach enables the development of more efficient and scalable models and facilitates the practical exploration of different RRAM-based systems in cooperation with other system building blocks. It ensures that different types of device variabilities are comprehensively addressed and that system-level mitigation strategies can be developed during prototyping.

A summary of the findings of this section reveals that hybrid approaches offer low integration complexity and accuracy comparable to that of pure simulation approaches, while delivering a simulation speed that is as high as or surpasses real-time execution. This balance is achieved without incurring high costs, extended development times, and adaptability challenges associated with physical prototypes, positioning hybrid methodologies as a compelling alternative for RRAM technology development and evaluation. In comparison to literature and our previous work, our hybrid model HyRPF presented in the following aims to introduce ease of usability, scalability, universal applicability for RRAM as digital memory, the inclusion of real-world variability, straightforward evaluation of different environmental conditions, and extreme resource efficiency to this category of approaches.

3 Methodology

The objective of this work consists in implementing the RRAM models already used in our SystemC framework ReSS [10] on FPGAs by means of RRAM emulation blocks so they can be used in a prototyping environment and directly interact with other system components in real time. These models have a generic interface that enables the direct input of measurement data, such as from IHP devices [11]. The models have undergone evaluation against real measurements of RRAM devices and have accurately reproduced their behavior. The two blocks that will be implemented are designed to have minimal resource consumption, be user-friendly, and allow for the evaluation of non-functional properties, specifically energy consumption and latency. The blocks will cover RRAM-based flip-flops with a digital interface, and RRAM memory banks.

3.1 Preconditions and Simplifications

To achieve our goal of minimizing resource consumption, it is necessary to integrate prior knowledge in a clever manner. To function as a drop-in replacement for classic memory, RRAM-based flip-flops and memory blocks must have a digital interface. Functional errors can be analysed by a change in the expected bit pattern. To achieve this, the emulated block must simulate all the variabilities that can occur in combination. However, it is important to note that these errors are only visible to the user when attempting to read out the devices. Therefore, the programming phase of the RRAM devices does not need to be considered separately in this case. Instead, the variabilities that occur during this phase should be simulated alongside all other variabilities. To accurately estimate the latency and energy consumption, it is necessary to log all read and write accesses.

3.2 RRAM-Based Flip-Flop Model

Taking into account the previously established principles, we have created a design for the RRAM-based flip-flop emulation block. The data width of the emulated flip-flop is given by the number of states to be stored inside the RRAM cell. For the sake of clarity, we will assume 4 stored states and 2 bits in the following. However, all models presented here can be parameterized and can also be simulated with a different bit width. Each bit pattern of input data is encoded by a conductance state of the RRAM. We designate the states used here as L0 (50 μ S), L1 (100 μ S), L2 (150 μ S) and L3 (200 μ S).

A block diagram for our emulated RRAM-based flip-flop is shown in Fig. 2a. The module includes a clock port, a data input and output, and a write-enable signal, similar to conventional flip-flops. Additionally, it has an extra port for the input of a randomly generated value. The data to be written is stored in a buffer and used as input for a multiplexer. This multiplexer selects the state transition table corresponding to the targeted conductance state. The state transition table determines the probability for a targeted RRAM state to be classified as the correct state or misclassified as any of the other states. We will explain how we derived this table from RRAM variability models in the next section. In each clock cycle, a new entry is randomly selected from the table to emulate the stochastic nature of different variability phenomena inside the RRAM (such as C2C). This way a Monte-Carlo-Simulation is realized and the output value determined is sent to the data output port.

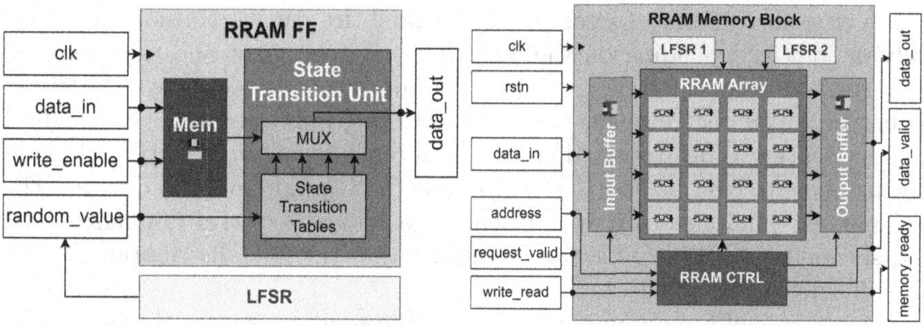

(a) RRAM-based Flip-Flop (b) RRAM-based Memory

Fig. 2. Block diagrams of the implemented emulation blocks.

3.3 Random Value Generation

One of the least hardware-demanding approach to pseudo-random number generation is the linear feedback shift register (LFSR). By propagating the data through the sequence of one-bit registers with XOR gate feedback at certain positions, the LFSR outputs the numbers in a manner resembling a seemingly random and independent sequence [9]. The period of the LFSR sequence returning to the default position is dependent on the bit width of the module. The number of entries in the state transition table of our RRAM emulation module and the resolution of the mapped probability distribution are also determined by the data width of the LFRS in our design.

For our emulation blocks, one LFSR module can be used to deliver a random value for all simulated memory cells or several LFSR modules can be used for different memory cells. Randomizing the bit order of the LFSR output value for different emulation blocks can make sure that the sequence of output states is different for each emulated block, even if the same value is stored in the cells and the same LFSR is used. For larger designs, it is advisable to use multiple LFRs with varying initial values.

It is important to mention that the LFSR used for our emulation design can be replaced by any (pseudo-)random number generator (e.g. proprietary IP cores or any other soft- or hardware based blocks). For the simulation on an FPGA, however, the LFSR probably offers the best design compactness.

3.4 From Statistical Model to State Transition Table

Rather than investing time and resource into emulating the conductance value of the RRAM devices and its variability distributions as well as the ADC functionality on the FPGA itself, we can use a priori knowledge to transfer this information into a simple look up table.

Our statistical model of RRAM behavior utilizes a generic interface to define conductance probability distributions extracted from measurements of real devices for different target states. Variabilities can be considered individually or jointly depending on the underlying measurement and the evaluation goal. For a more detailed description of the functionality, please refer to [10,11]. To ensure a compact implementation in FPGAs, it is necessary to include all the variabilities to be examined in the measurements and final statistical model. For instance, to consider both cycle-to-cycle (C2C) and device-to-device (D2D) variabilities simultaneously, it is essential to measure several different devices over several read and write cycles. To ensure that the final distribution includes the influence of both factors.

An example of a random distribution of the conductance for the target state L0 is shown in Fig. 3. The line plot describes the random distribution. The borders of the areas below the curve are defined by the ADC thresholds. The percentage of area occupied by each color corresponds to the probability of the L0 state being evaluated as the respective marked state. It is 70% likely to be correctly classified as state L0 in this case, while misclassification as state L1 would occur in 23% of cases.

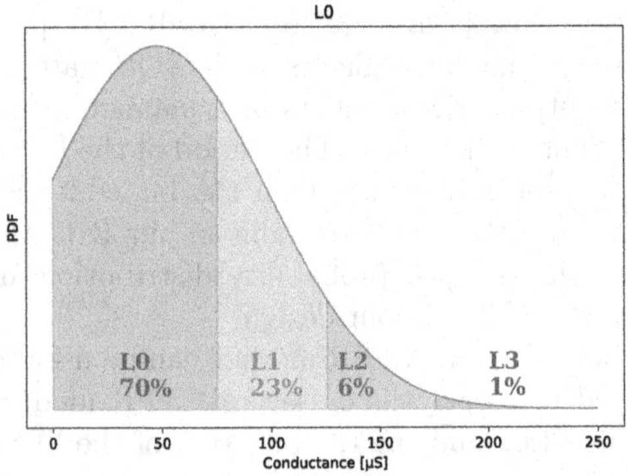

Fig. 3. Examplary plot of a probability density function (PDF) for the conductance distribution of the L0 state. (Illustrative example, not the actual distribution used.)

These transition probabilities are a combined representation of the RRAM device and ADC behaviour. They are transferred to the state transition table, and the probabilities for the other three states are added. Table 1 shows an overview of the three state transition tables used in this work. The transition probabilities of the three tables listed include all measurable variabilities of the RRAM devices that were programmed with the *Mixed*-programming algorithm [11]. The time of measurement is 24 h after programming. The three tables differ in the temperatures of the devices, which are 25 °C, 85 °C and 125 °C. The left side of the table shows the relative transition probabilities, the right side shows the values transferred to the state transition table for a 7-bit random number.

Some important conclusions can be drawn from these tables alone. For example, it can be seen that the misclassification probability increases as the temperature rises. And also that the misclassification as a neighboring state is the most probable. However, the tables also show that the L3 state (highest conductance target) is the least susceptible to variability and that the L2 state at high temperatures is the state to which other states most frequently transition. The fact that these properties are recognizable in the table is a good prerequisite for ensuring that the simulated models later reproduce a behavior that corresponds to the real RRAM devices. These state transition tables are integrated into the design at synthesis time. By reconfiguration or resynthesis, different variabilities resulting from different environmental conditions can be investigated.

Table 1. Transition Table for Conductance distributions of four different conductance target states at 25 °C, 85 °C and 125 °C 24 h after programming.

Temp.			Relative Result Input State				7 Bit LFSR Input State			
			L0	L1	L2	L3	L0	L1	L2	L3
25°C	Output	L0	99.80%	1.57%	0.00%	0.00%	127	2	0	0
		L1	0.20%	98.42%	4.55%	0.00%	0	125	6	0
		L2	0.00%	0.01%	95.45%	0.00%	0	0	121	0
		L3	0.00%	0.00%	0.00%	100.0%	0	0	0	127
85°C	Output	L0	85.31%	4.45%	0.00%	0.00%	108	6	0	0
		L1	14.68%	92.17%	4.12%	0.00%	19	117	5	0
		L2	0.01%	3.38%	95.88%	0.01%	0	4	122	0
		L3	0.00%	0.00%	0.00%	99.99%	0	0	0	127
125°C	Output	L0	68.49%	5.85%	0.00%	0.00%	87	7	0	0
		L1	30.95%	77.08%	3.62%	0.00%	39	98	5	0
		L2	0.56%	17.05%	96.23%	4.97%	1	22	122	6
		L3	0.00%	0.03%	0.15%	95.03%	0	0	0	121

3.5 RRAM-Based Memory Block Model

The block diagram for our RRAM based memory block is shown in Fig. 2b. Here an array of RRAM based flip-flop emulation blocks is assembled to an array and additionally input and output buffer, as well as a control module with a finite state machine is implemented. This allows different input and output data widths to be realized. The interface is extended by an address port, a read and write selection port and handshake signals. In addition, several LFSRs are instantiated, which alternately generate the random values of the individual emulated RRAM cells. In addition to controlling the correct cells in the array and handling the handshake signals, the RRAM control unit can also count the individual accesses in order to be able to perform an energy and latency estimation later.

3.6 Specification of the Implemented Blocks

Table 2 lists the specifications of the two implemented emulation blocks including all components introduced in the previous section. The synthesis target was a Xilinx ARTIX-7 (7A100TCSG324) FPGA, and the software used was Xilinx Vivado version 2023.1. The specifications were determined by averaging over several synthesis runs with different numbers of RRAM flip-flops or different memory sizes of the RRAM memory block. The duration needed to simulate one read or write access to one RRAM-based FF or one row of the RRAM-based Memory depends on the frequency with which the blocks are implemented. The read operation for the memory block needs two cycles, due to control overhead when reading multiple RRAM cells in parallel. The utilized resources are given as the mean per emulated RRAM device. The resource usage scales linearly with the number of simulated RRAM devices and Table 2 can be used to estimate it for specific memory sizes. Simulating different numbers of target conductance states stored in the RRAM cells is easily possible by adding different numbers of entries in the transition table. However, while the resource utilization is asymptotically linear to the amount of target conductance states, it only increases in multiples of N (depending on the LUT size of the FPGA). The values given in the table are for the simulation of four target states. The interface, designed by us, allows for straightforward simulation of different operation conditions (such as different temperatures, different points in time after programming the devices, influence of radiation etc.). For each environmental condition, a new transition table must be generated. This will not impact the resource utilization as long as the number of target conductance states and the number of simulated devices remain constant. It is evident that the implementation is highly resource-efficient, allowing for emulation of even the largest designs.

Table 2. Properties of the implemented IP-Blocks including all components. Average over the number of simulated cells and multiple synthesis runs. For RRAM devices with 4 target conductances states.

IP	$f_{\max}$	Simulation Duration		Resources per cell	
		Read	Write	FF	LUT
RRAM FF	470 MHz	2 ns	2 ns	2.1	4.9
RRAM Memory Block	200 MHz	10 ns	5 ns	2.4	9.8

4 Evaluation

In the following, we want to investigate whether our emulation modules fulfill our requirements in terms of functional correctness reproducing real RRAM properties and high execution speed. As an evaluation scenario, we have opted for the integration of RRAM-based register files and RRAM-based cache into a RISC-V CPU. The HyRPF IP blocks synthesized on an Xilinx ARTIX-7 FPGA. The data read and written to the RRAM-based register files and cache was extracted from the QEMU simulation of a RISC-V CPU. It was fed to the RRAM simulation blocks inside a behavioural VHDL simulation to facilitate the evaluation of the large amount of data without the need for a complex evaluation setup. Future work will include the implementation of a complete design, including the HyRPF IP blocks, a RISC-V core, and all the required peripheral components on the same FPGA. This will require significant implementation overhead, and without new results regarding the RRAM model itself, it was considered out of scope for this work.

4.1 Processor Emulation

To thoroughly evaluate our approach, we designed two comprehensive datasets that serve as a foundation for analysis. The first dataset captures the dynamics of register contents across a diverse suite of test applications executed on an emulated RISC-V CPU. Simultaneously, the second dataset focuses on the behavior of cache hierarchies. By tracing cache interactions, across the same set of test applications, this dataset sheds light on memory access patterns and their implications for our simulation. Both datasets were generated using instrumentation techniques on the QEMU platform. The detailed methodology used to generate these datasets will be elaborated in the following.

Register Traces. QEMU, a well-established emulator, employs a Just-In-Time (JIT) approach for emulation. This process involves translating target platform code into an immediate representation (IR), which is then converted into code executable on the host platform. For our experiments, we modified this translation process from target code to IR. Specifically, after the instruction translation, we analyzed the IR to identify any register usage, subsequently generating code to log all read and write operations. Figure 4 illustrates this process. Each log entry records the registers involved, the type of access (read or write), and the associated data. This detailed tracking was accomplished by directly modifying the QEMU source code. We opted for this approach because, at the time of our research, QEMU's plugin API did not offer the necessary functionality to examine the IR thoroughly or to insert arbitrary IR.

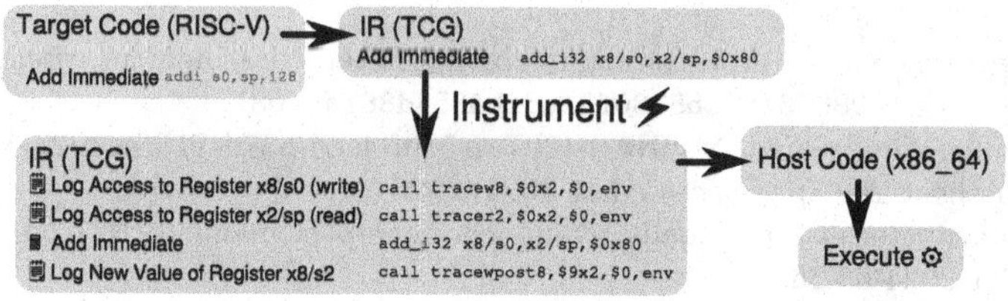

Fig. 4. Operation principle of the register tracing

Cache Traces. Building on the previously described modifications to the QEMU emulator, our approach also leveraged QEMU's extensible plugin API, despite its limitations, to extend our dataset focused on cache behavior. Specifically, we adapted the existing cache plugin, a tool primarily designed to track cache hit rates under varying cache configurations. This cache plugin was adapted to not only monitor hit rates but also to log accesses to both tags and data memories. This was crucial for our analysis, as it allowed us to obtain a more granular view of cache operations, beyond mere hit and miss rates. For the cache configurations, we selected parameters that represent a range of different, real-world CPUs that have been taped out. This selection was guided by the aim to cover a cache designs of CPUs with different performance targets and to ensure the relevance and applicability of our findings to existing hardware. The specific cache configurations chosen for our study are detailed in Table 3.

To ensure our evaluation encompassed a wide range of computational behaviors and workloads, we selected a diverse set of applications by utilizing benchmark suites known for their broad coverage across various computing domains. These included Embench, Coremark, STREAM, and Dhrystone. Each suite brings its unique set of characteristics and challenges, allowing us to rigorously test and demonstrate the capabilities of our approach. The Embench suite was particularly notable in our selection due to its composition of different applications from varied domains, presented as separate programs. This diversity makes Embench especially valuable for assessing the adaptability and performance of our simulation across a wide spectrum of application behaviors. Such a range ensures that our findings are not limited to a specific type of workload but are indicative of the performance across different computing workloads. Our experiments were conducted on an architecture modeled after a 32-bit RISC-V with IMC extensions. Therefore only integer registers were considered.

Table 3. Cache Configurations used in Experiments (Size in KiB, Line Width in Bytes)

Arch.	L1						L2		
	I			D					
	Assoc.	Line Width	Size	Assoc.	Line Width	Size	Assoc.	Line Width	Size
Ariane	4	16	16	8	16	16	4	64	64
SiFive U74	2	64	32	4	64	32	8	64	128
SiFive P550	4	64	32	4	64	32	8	64	256

Sources:
https://github.com/openhwgroup/cva6/blob/master/core/include/ariane_pkg.sv at Commit `86e1408666eb62b5380f31edfb4354d887a81087`
https://sifive.cdn.prismic.io/sifive/b4f3f7c7-560f-4ecd-857d-715cc6be237b_p550-8mc-data-sheet-2022.pdf accessed at 2024-03-26
https://starfivetech.com/uploads/u74mc_core_complex_manual_21G1.pdf accessed at 2024-03-26

4.2 Functional Correctness

We have selected five different algorithms from the benchmark suites to test the functional correctness of our modules. These are representative of various application areas, such as applications with many main memory accesses (Stream), crypto algorithms (Nettle AES), applications with tight loops (Matmul), parsing of data structures (PicoJPEG) and sorting algorithms (WikiSort). Table 4 shows the number of read and write accesses to the RISC-V registers that we were able to extract with the help of our previously described modifications to QEMU. We examined the execution of these algorithms on a RISC-V CPU with RRAM-based registers. In doing so, we benefited from the easy interchangeability of the RRAM variability models that our implementation offers and were able to examine each algorithm under 25°C, 85°C, and 125°C RRAM temperature. Thus, predictions on system reliability can be made for a extended temperature ranges, such as required in the automotive industry [15].

Table 4. Amount of data written to and read from the RRAM-based registers of the RISC-V CPU and estimated register-access energy.

Algorithm	Write Amount [MB]	Read Amount [MB]	Register Access Energy [MB]
Stream	1.2	2.0	0.28
Embench Matmul	9.3	18.5	2.2
Embench Nettle AES	16.5	22.5	3.8
Embench PicoJPEG	11.3	19.7	2.64
Embench WikiSort	4.5	7.3	1.04

Figure 5 shows the result of our investigations in comparison between the VHDL model for FPGAs (HyRPF) implemented here and our SystemC framework (ReSS), which has already been validated against real measurements. The resulting bit-error-rate (BER) per CPU register is shown for both. The absolute difference in percentage points between the BERs obtained is also shown. The result reveal that with increasing temperature the BER in the registers increase. With the highest BER at 125°C for the Embench Nettle AES algorithm occurring in register 3 and being about 20%. However, the average BER for all registers at 25°C is less than 1%. For a 32-bit register, this corresponds to less than 1 bit error on average. This is easily correctable even with a very simple error correction code (ECC), such as a Hamming code [2]. For higher temperatures more sophisticated ECCs, such as Bose–Chaudhuri–Hocquenghem (BCH) could be applied to handle BERs up to 20%. However, the result also shows that both our VHDL modules and the SystemC framework always deliver almost the same results. With a maximum deviation of 4% points and an average deviation below 1% point. This shows that the requirements for the functional accuracy of the model are met. In addition, both the SystemC framework and our VHDL modules can be used to estimate the energy required to access the registers for the individual algorithms. As both are based on the same energy model [10] and have simulated the same number of accesses, the results are exactly the same. They are also shown in Table 4.

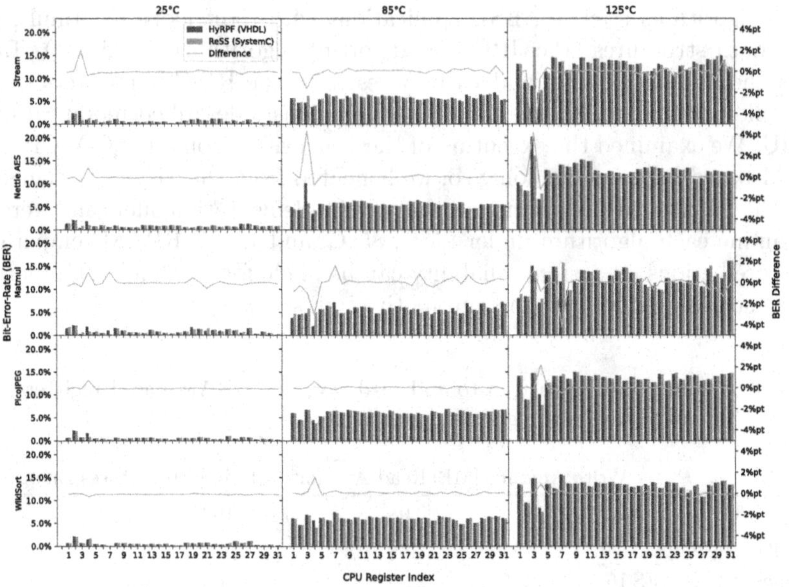

Fig. 5. Bit-error-rate (BER) for different RISC-V CPU registers and different algorithms. Shown for three different temperatures. Compared between our HyRPF modules implemented here and the ReSS framework implemented in SystemC [10,11].

4.3 Execution Speed

To evaluate whether our implemented modules provide an advantage in terms of speed, we compared the execution time of read and write accesses for different RRAM-based RISC-V cache configurations. For this purpose, we analyzed the same algorithms from the previous section using our adapted QEMU environment and investigated the required cache accesses to the L1 instruction and data caches (L1I, L1D) and the L2 cache. Figure 6 shows how long it takes to execute or simulate these accesses with our hybrid approach, with our SystemC simulator and in real life for real devices, divided into write (W) and read (R) accesses.

The RRAM devices are programmed using the incremental step pulse with verify algorithm (ISPVA) algorithm. For the duration of the real programming and the real readout, we have assumed average values of the access times, which we have presented in [16]. We ran our SystemC based ReSS framework on a server with an AMD EPYC 9654 CPU and measured the execution time. The cycle count required by our HyRPF module, which was implemented with a clock frequency of 150 MHz, was derived from the VHDL simulation. The figure shows that our HyRPF approach has the lowest execution time across all cache configurations and algorithms. Especially for write accesses, there is an average speedup of 1200×, since the actual programming of the RRAM devices currently takes a relatively long time. An average speedup of 7.5× can also be achieved for read accesses. This means that our implementation consistently achieves a speed that is faster than real time. Our SystemC-based framework can simulate write accesses faster than real time, but drops off for read accesses and is slower here. Using our HyRPF modules, a speedup of 8× to 23× for writes and 140× to 600× for reads can be achieved compared to ReSS, depending on the simulated cache size and algorithm.

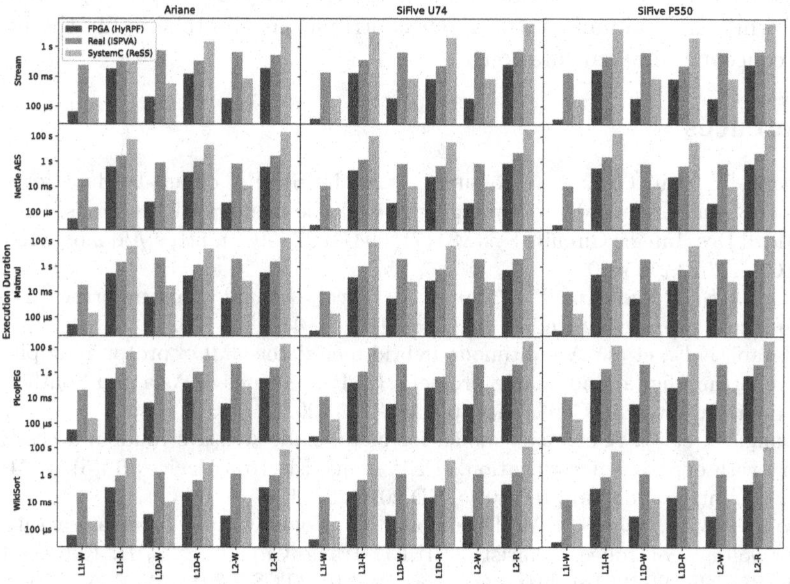

Fig. 6. Execution duration of the access to the RRAM-based cache for different RISC-V CPU cache configs and different algorithms. Compared between our HyRPF modules implemented here, the ReSS framework implemented in SystemC [10,11] and the programming and reading duration of actual RRAM devices. Logarithmic representation.

5 Conclusion

In this work, we advanced the integration and prototyping of RRAM technologies into larger computer systems, achieving significant progress in several areas. Our main contribution is the introduction of an RRAM model for FPGAs that provides high functional accuracy and simulation speed surpassing even real device prototyping. The model was implemented as emulation blocks for RRAM-based flip-flops and RRAM-based memory banks. This streamlines the prototyping process while allowing thorough evaluation of performance under varying environmental conditions. In addition, non-functional characteristics such as power consumption can now also be taken into account. Our approach has been applied to designing and evaluating a RISC-V CPU that integrates RRAMs as registers and cache, demonstrating the functional correctness and efficiency of our model. This method not only surpasses the simulation speed of traditional approaches, but also provides insight into energy consumption, emphasizing the practical relevance of our contributions and their potential to accelerate the adoption of RRAM technology. Essentially, our work provides the RRAM research and development community with tools and methodologies that bridge the gap between theoretical exploration and practical application, taking into account critical factors such as device variability and energy efficiency. By improving simulation speed while maintaining accuracy, our contributions aim to simplify the process from concept to implementation.

References

1. Dong, X., Xu, C., Xie, Y., Jouppi, N.P.: NVSIM: a circuit-level performance, energy, and area model for emerging nonvolatile memory. IEEE Trans. Comput.-Aided Des. Integr. Circuits Syst. **31**(7), 994–1007 (2012). https://doi.org/10.1109/TCAD.2012.2185930
2. Garani, S.S., Nadkarni, P.J., Raina, A.: Theory behind quantum error correcting codes: an overview. J. Indian Inst. Sci. **103**(2), 449–495 (2023)
3. Harabi, K.E., et al.: A multimode hybrid memristor-CMOS prototyping platform supporting digital and analog projects. In: Proceedings of Asia and South Pacific Design Automation Conference, pp. 184–185 (2023)
4. Jiang, Z., et al.: A compact model for metal-oxide resistive random access memory with experiment verification. IEEE Trans. Electron Devices **63**(5), 1884–1892 (2016). https://doi.org/10.1109/TED.2016.2545412
5. Kvatinsky, S., Ramadan, M., Friedman, E.G., Kolodny, A.: VTeam: a general model for voltage-controlled memristors. IEEE Trans. Circuits Syst. II: Express Briefs **62**(8), 786–790 (2015). https://doi.org/10.1109/TCSII.2015.2433536
6. Lee, M.K.F., et al.: A system-level simulator for RRAM-based neuromorphic computing chips. ACM Trans. Archit. Code Optim. (TACO) **15**(4), 1–24 (2019)
7. Liu, Q., et al.: 33.2 a fully integrated analog reram based 78.4 tops/w compute-in-memory chip with fully parallel mac computing. In: 2020 IEEE International Solid-State Circuits Conference (ISSCC), pp. 500–502. IEEE (2020)
8. Luo, T., et al.: An FPGA-based hardware emulator for neuromorphic chip with RRAM. IEEE Trans. Comput.-Aided Des. Integr. Circuits Syst. **39**(2), 438–450 (2018)
9. Mukherjee, N., Rajski, J., Mrugalski, G., Pogiel, A., Tyszer, J.: Ring generator: an ultimate linear feedback shift register. Computer **44**(6), 64–71 (2011). https://doi.org/10.1109/MC.2010.334
10. Reiser, D., Chen, J., Knödtel, J., Baroni, A., Krstic, M., Reichenbach, M.: Design and analysis of an adaptive radiation resilient RRAM subsystem for processing systems in satellites. In: Memory-centric Computing for Data-Intensive Workloads in Design Automation for Embedded Systems (2024)

11. Reiser, D., et al.: Technology-aware drift resilience analysis of RRAM crossbar array configurations. In: 2023 21st IEEE Interregional NEWCAS Conference (NEWCAS), pp. 1–5 (2023). https://doi.org/10.1109/NEWCAS57931.2023.10198076
12. Roy, S., et al.: Toward a reliable synaptic simulation using Al-doped HfO2 RRAM. ACS Appl. Mater. Interfaces **12**(9), 10648–10656 (2020)
13. Ruffini, S., Caronti, L., Yıldırım, K.S., Brunelli, D.: Norm: an FPGA-based non-volatile memory emulation framework for intermittent computing. ACM J. Emerg. Technol. Comput. Syst. (JETC) **18**(4), 1–18 (2022)
14. Tolba, M.F., Halawani, Y., Saleh, H., Mohammad, B., Al-Qutayri, M.: FPGA-based memristor emulator circuit for binary convolutional neural networks. IEEE Access **8**, 117736–117745 (2020)
15. Watson, J., Castro, G.: A review of high-temperature electronics technology and applications. J. Mater. Sci.: Mater. Electron. **26**, 9226–9235 (2015)
16. Wen, J., et al.: Cycle-accurate FPGA emulation of RRAM crossbar array: efficient device and variability modeling with energy consumption assessment. In: Latin American Test Symposium (LATS) 2024 (2024)

GLoRia: An Energy-Efficient GPU-RRAM System Stack for Large Neural Networks

Rafael Fão de Moura(✉), Michael Jordan, and Luigi Carro

Informatics Institute - Federal University of Rio Grande do Sul - Porto Alegre, Porto Alegre, Brazil
{rfmoura,mgjordan,carro}@inf.ufrgs.br

Abstract. While the potential of in-memory RRAM computation for achieving energy-efficient NNs is recognized, concerns persist about its relative scalability to support modern NNs with billions of parameters. In this context, this paper presents GLoRia, a GPU-RRAM architecture and associated software stack to handle these limitations. We strategically identify the optimal NN layers for RRAM acceleration, enhancing the scalability of RRAMs for complex NN architectures and reducing energy consumption. We validate our approach using practical large CNN and GPT models, showing a 6.4× decrease in energy consumption, without compromising inference accuracy, thanks to the proposed strategy.

Keywords: Neural Networks · Resistive RAM · Scalability

1 Introduction

Neural Network (NN) models have grown in size and complexity across various application domains [13]. However, this growth introduces notable performance and energy challenges for current available architectures due to the core operation of NNs, which involves matrix-vector multiplication (MVM) and the constant transfer of weights over memory channels [16]. To overcome these inefficiencies, Computing-in-memory (CIM) architectures have been proposed, which use resistive memories store NN weights as the conductance of the memory cell, enabling in-place multiplication/summation in constant time.

Single- or many-core CIM chips, utilizing Resistive RAM (RRAM), Phase-change memory (PCM), and Magneto-resistive RAM (MRAM) technologies, have been developed [4,11]. These chips include integrated data conversions and activation functions, showcasing competitive energy efficiency at 10 $TOPS/W$. The largest to date, a 64-core chip based on 256×256-sized PCM crossbar arrays from IBM [11], has a capacity of up to 4M weights, making it suitable primarily for smaller networks like ResNet-9. Despite technological advancements, analog CIM architectures are unlikely to significantly increase their capacity due to substantial space requirements for peripherals, hardware imperfections, and

L. Carro et al. (Eds.): SAMOS 2024, LNCS 15226, pp. 216–229, 2025.
https://doi.org/10.1007/978-3-031-78377-7_15

fabrication costs [16]. Figure 1 illustrates the scalability issue in resistive NN accelerators, as the model size of current NNs surpasses the storage capacity of chips. As crossbar arrays become larger and more densely integrated, disturbances caused by random noises and parasitic voltage drop emerge, exacerbating the problem and making the CIM approach less attractive than expected.

Despite efforts to reduce NN model sizes [9], they still occupy hundreds of megabytes, creating a 10^5 gap compared to current CIM implementations. For large models like GPT-3, ranging from 125 million to 175 billion parameters, analog CIM can still enhance energy efficiency and execution time if smartly designed. Achieving scalability requires combining analog CIM (weight stationary due to low endurance and high write costs) with other non-stationary approaches. Heterogeneous GPU/RRAM architectures, initially proposed for hybrid NN training [8], offer a promising solution to efficiently handle large-scale inference while addressing scalability, endurance, and energy efficiency challenges. However, the NN-Hardware co-design and mapping decision for the N layers of a model onto such a heterogeneous system poses a challenge. With up to $O(2^N)$ offloading configuration combinations, a brute-force search for the optimal mapping is computationally infeasible for most networks. This raises the question of finding rapid mapping solutions that maximize the benefits of both approaches.

To harness the potential of RRAM devices for modern NNs, we propose a solution that closes the gap between RRAM chips' storage capacity and the increasing demand for large NN models. Our solution, named GLoRia, is a GPU-RRAM architecture with an associated software stack designed to address these limitations. GLoRia includes a CAD flow for selecting and allocating the most advantageous RRAM-accelerated layers to run large NN models in RRAM/GPU heterogeneous 3D architectures. Therefore, we make the following contributions:

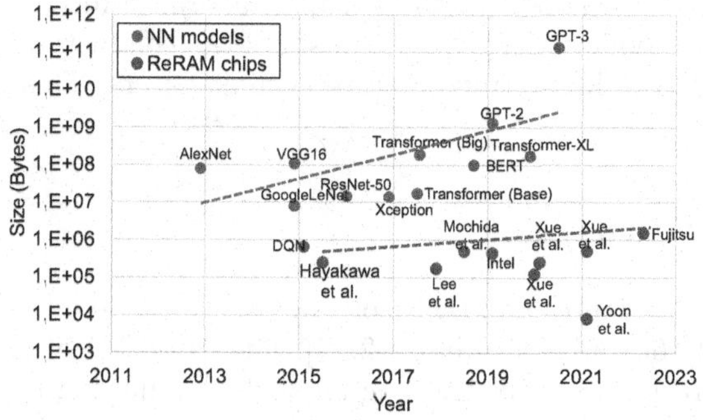

Fig. 1. Size growth comparison of state-of-the-art NN models and fabricated RRAM chips over the years.

- We show that offloading strategies for GPU-RRAM systems are mandatory to address the scalability issue found in the disparity in size between NN models and available RRAM;
- We introduce a lightweight ($O(N)$) method to determine the best NN layers for RRAM offloading and show a mapping approach that improves data locality and reduces communication between GPUs and RRAM;
- We evaluate our solution over a mixed architecture with 3D-stacked RRAM chips integrated to a GPU. Our experiments show that our approach stays only 3.75% behind an optimal exhaustive solution ($O(2^N)$) in FPS. Compared to state-of-the-art GPU-RRAM solutions, we achieve up to 6.4x energy reduction.

2 Background

RRAM cells store data using the resistance-switching properties of a filament between two electrodes. The memory state is determined by the presence of this filament and read by measuring current. To use RRAM for synaptic weights in the CIM architecture, floating-point weights must be normalized, converted into integers, and mapped to conductance levels, as illustrated in Fig. 2-Ⓐ. For instance, with 3-bit precision, weights are normalized to integers from 0 to 7, then mapped to 3-bit conductance levels. A weight like "+0.8906" would be normalized to 7 and mapped to the corresponding RRAM cell.

After mapping, the dot product for each NN neuron can be computed within the synaptic array, as illustrated in Fig. 2-Ⓑ, enabling rapid and efficient MVM operations with $O(1)$ time complexity [4]. Ideally, the conductance range of an RRAM cell is 0 to $2^b - 1$, with b being the number of bits. However, current RRAM implementations can't achieve this range due to limitations in the minimum conductance level. To address this, dummy columns with middle conductance levels (g_{mid}) are added to the synaptic arrays. Subtracting the dummy outputs from each synaptic array column shifts the conductance range to zero-centered at $[-1, +1]$, eliminating off-state current effects. This is illustrated in Fig. 2-Ⓒ.

3 Related Work

RRAM-based architectures and their software stack are popular for accelerating both inference [3,16], and NN training [2,17]. The REGENT architecture [7] handles the backward phase of the training algorithm (requiring high precision) on GPUs, similar to [12]. However, both works [7,12] sacrifice performance, as a significant portion of NN execution is done by GPUs rather than RRAMs. RRAMs are more efficient than GPUs in implementing the vector dot-product, the core computation during NN processing [6]. To address this, the GRAMARCH architecture [8] was proposed. However, these works do not address the scalability challenges of RRAM in their designs, and most assume ideal operating conditions and infinite RRAM chip capacity.

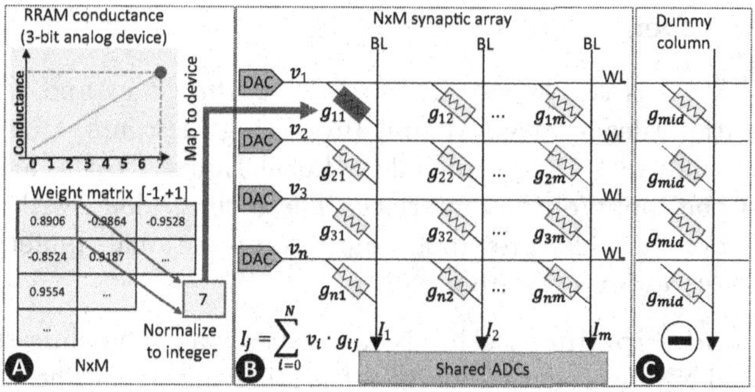

Fig. 2. a) Physical model of conductive filament-based ReRAM cell, b) Mapping weight to synaptic device conductance, c) Parallel dot-product implemented in a ReRAM crossbar, and d) Introducing dummy column to cancel out the off-state current effects.

Some solutions attempted to address the gap size using unary, binary, or ternary representations of NNs [1,9]. However, these approaches come with a notable drawback: a decrease in NN accuracy due to the use of encoding schemes with fewer bits for representing synaptic weights. Additionally, these techniques have a limited impact (up to 8 times) on reducing NN size, which falls short of effectively addressing the actual gap size of 10^5. Other efforts employ transformation and pruning techniques to tackle the gap size problem as well [4]. While pruning and transforming NNs lead to improved accuracy and reduction in model size, pruning for RRAM faces the challenge of not fragmenting weight matrices to avoid sparse MVM. This limitation hinders these techniques from significantly reducing NN size.

Our Contributions: Our work differs from the previous by providing an orthogonal heuristic to select the best-fit layers to execute in the RRAM accelerator, which can be used combined with any NN model reduction technique.

4 Architecture Specification

Figure 3 depicts the GPU-RRAM architecture. The configuration consists of two flat layers of RRAMs and GPUs connected in a 3D arrangement. To accommodate the size difference between RRAM and GPU tiles, RRAM tiles are grouped with one GPU tile to create a 3D structure known as a *Vault*. Vertical connections within each Vault are established using Though Silicon Vias (TSV).

4.1 GPU Layer

Each GPU tile consists of a GPU core (an SM in NVIDIA terms) with its private L1 cache and a portion of the Last-Level Cache (LLC). RRAMs are cost-effective for MVM operations compared to GPUs. However, GPUs provide a high-precision computing platform scalable for deeper NN models. In this architecture, GPUs manage layers not offloaded to RRAM.

4.2 RRAM Layer

The RRAM layer has two types of tiles: *Computation tiles* and *Buffer & I/O tiles.* Computation tiles have MVM Unit Processing Elements (PEs) and analog ReLU units. Buffer & I/O tiles include a Local Buffer, DACs, and ADCs for buffering and the input/output interface. These tiles, along with the routing system, are programmable, providing ample computational, buffering, control, and wiring resources for software use.

Data Flow and Pipeline. Each NN layer serves as a pipeline stage. In the RRAM-mapped NN layer, data undergoes the following steps: The current input, sourced from the Local Buffers marking the temporal barrier, initiates layer processing. DACs convert the input into the analog domain. The analog data is directed to MVM Unit PEs, simultaneously performing dot-product operations. MVM results are then fed to ReLU units for analog nonlinear computations if required. In cases of vertical splitting of large MVM operators, accumulation of partial results from each RRAM tile may be necessary to produce the final result. To address this, the last tiles are designated as *Accumulation Tiles*, while others are *Linear Tiles.*

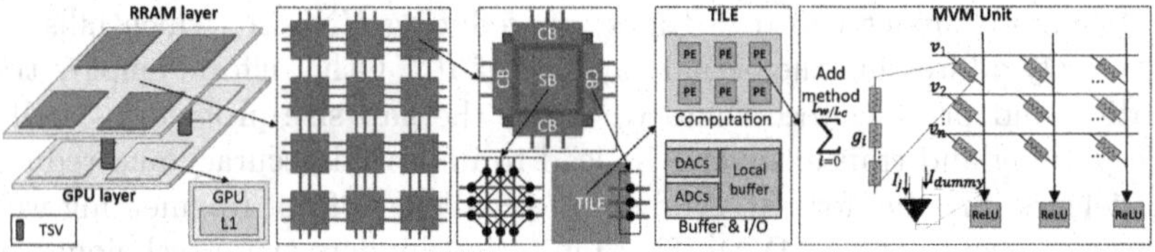

Fig. 3. GPU-RRAM architecture overview: tiles are connected through the reconfigurable wiring network.

On Linear Tiles, MVM Unit results bypass ReLU and proceed directly through the reconfigurable wiring network before transmission. On Accumulation Tiles, MVM computation occurs simultaneously with that on Linear Tiles. Instead of transmitting partial results immediately, the controller awaits incoming partial sums from the wiring network. Upon arrival, the controller accumulates them with local partial results, and the accumulated results pass through ReLU units to produce the final output. The outputs from ReLU units are converted back into the digital domain using ADCs.

Routing Architecture. We employ an island-style reconfigurable routing architecture to connect Computation and Buffer & I/O tiles. This design diverges from memory buses and Network-on-Chip (NoC) systems found in other NN accelerators. Instead of reusing physical channels for different types of traffic, this routing architecture designates separate channels for each signal during configuration. It also incorporates a fixed runtime data path aligned with NNs' fixed topology. In contrast to bus and NoC approaches, where the worst communication latency is uncertain, the reconfigurable routing architecture allows for the calculation of the critical path latency in advance.

In our design, tiles are Configurable Logic Blocks (CLBs) connected to the wiring network via Connection Boxes (CBs), and various wiring segments are linked through Switch Boxes (SBs). Routing architectures typically consume a significant portion of the chip area, a concern amplified in an NN accelerator design due to increased fan-in/outs in the RRAM tiles compared to standard programmable devices. To mitigate this overhead, we use RRAM cells to construct CBs and SBs, minimizing their occupied area. The connections within SBs and CBs are determined by the resistance of the RRAM cells: high resistance means no connection between corresponding segments, while low resistance allows the signal to pass. Figure 3 illustrates this routing architecture with SBs and CBs positioned over the CLBs (tiles), and tiles connect to the wiring network through the CBs on all four sides.

Buffer & I/O Tiles. Our architecture includes ADCs and DACs for I/O handling and a Local Buffer, acting as the temporal barrier within the pipeline. The Local Buffer consists of two types of memories: a memory buffer using Dynamic RAM (DRAM) and a cache memory relying on Static RAM (SRAM). We assume that on-chip memory is sufficient to store all synaptic weights of NN layers mapped to the RRAM accelerator. Off-chip memory access is only required for fetching input data and storing output data for each tile. To optimize memory access, we configure the cache to hold necessary input/output data for a single Computation tile. We also group weight tensors sharing the same input onto one Computation tile, allowing these weight kernels to share the memory buffer, reducing communication and energy consumption.

Computation Tiles. Computation tiles are composed of MVM Units followed by analog ReLU units. Figure 3 illustrates the MVM Unit on the rightmost side. Each MVM Unit has a square RRAM array that stores the synaptic weights and does dot products simultaneously, as Sect. 2 explains. Following the dot product, ReLU units carry out nonlinear calculations for each NN layer. To ensure the signal between PEs remains unaffected, a voltage follower op-amp circuit grounds the BLs and separates them from nearby PEs.

RRAM technology is limited in producing cells with a specific range of conductance, typically 2-bit or 3-bit cells. Due to this constraint, some implementations use multiple RRAM crossbars to combine weight bits and execute shift-and-add operations to obtain final results. However, linear scaling of this approach may introduce unwanted ADC and DAC steps or noise into the signal. To address this, we adopt the Add method [5] to represent weight bits. This method adds several memory cells with lower levels to create a weight with higher levels. Generally, if the RRAM crossbar cells have L_c levels, and the NN weights need to be represented with L_w levels, where $L_c < L_w$, then $\lceil L_w \div L_c \rceil$ RRAM cells are necessary to represent the target weight.

5 System Stack

Figure 4 illustrates the system stack and CAD flow for the GPU-RRAM architecture. The CAD flow is designed inspired on compilers, with three main parts: Front-end (A), Middle-end (B), and Back-end (C). Each part is denoted by colored boxes: blue for the Front-end, green for the Middle-end, and orange for the Back-end. Intermediate data from CAD modules is shown in gray boxes.

5.1 Front-End

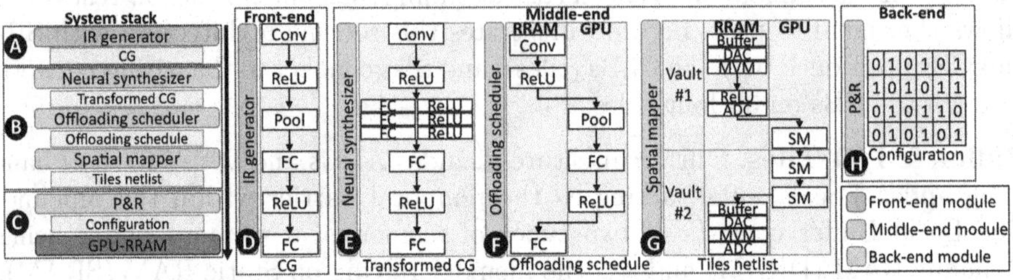

Fig. 4. System stack of GPU-RRAM architecture and its associated CAD flow.

IR Generator. The IR generator transforms a NN model into an architecture-agnostic Intermediate Representation (IR) format, shown in Fig. 4-(D). This generator produces a computational graph (CG) representing the NN model, featuring tensor operations and their relationships. We use the Open Neural Network Exchange (ONNX) format to represent the CG, initiating the process with a PyTorch NN model description and employing PyTorch's built-in export function to create the corresponding ONNX CG.

5.2 Middle-End

Neural synthesizer Our RRAM tiles efficiently handle MVM with ReLU functions. For operations beyond MVM and ReLU, the neural synthesizer (Fig. 4-(E)) adjusts the CG to match hardware capabilities by designing specialized structures with MVM and ReLU units. These structures enable the performance or approximation of other operations using multi-layer perceptrons (MLPs).

Offloading Scheduler. Figure 4-(F) shows the Offloading scheduler, which goal is to efficiently use RRAMs while minimizing overall NN processing costs. The layer offloading problem is modeled as the classical assembly line scheduling problem with a variation to handle the RRAM capacity issue. This manufacturing problem involves transferring parts between stations along an assembly line, sharing features and problem definition with the layer offloading problem. The objective is to minimize the total cost of building the entire product by determining which station (NN layer) to select from assembly line 1 (GPU layer) and assembly line 2 (RRAM layer), considering data transfer between the two assembly lines. To handle the capacity issue of RRRAMs, we enhance the Assembly Line Scheduling Problem solution to incorporate a 0/1 Knapsack solution. Like the Knapsack problem, the solution entails selecting a subset of NN layers to run on RRAM accelerators, with the goal of maximizing performance or minimizing energy consumption within the RRAM's capacity.

Algorithm 1 outlines a dynamic programming solution for solving an assembly line scheduling problem with a knapsack-like constraint. The objective is to find the minimum cost or time to assemble a product on one of two assembly lines (line#1 and line#2), considering processing times at different stations, transfer times between assembly lines, and a weight constraint. This dynamic programming approach has a time and space complexity of $O(W * N)$. Since W is a constant value, time and space complexity can be defined as $O(N)$, which is much faster than the brute force approach of evaluating all possible combinations (2^N), especially for larger N values.

The algorithm takes as inputs:

- N: Number of layers (stations).
- e: 2D array denoting execution cost at each NN layer on each assembly line. $e[0][i]$ is the processing time of layer i on line#1 (GPU), and $e[1][i]$ is the processing time on line#2 (RRAM).
- t: 2D array representing transfer time between assembly lines for each NN layer. $t[0][i]$ is the transfer time from line#1 to line#2 of layer i, and $t[1][i]$ is the transfer time from line#2 to line#1 of layer i.
- W: Integer denoting the maximum weight (capacity) constraint for products on line#2 (RRAM).
- $weight$: Array representing the weight of each NN layer.

Two 2D arrays, $dp1$ and $dp2$, with dimensions $(N + 1) \times (W + 1)$ store the dynamic programming solution: the minimum cost for each layer and product weight combination. Both arrays are initially filled with values of infinity to represent an uninitialized state. The first row of $dp1$ and $dp2$ is initialized for the base case, setting the cost to 0 for the initial state with no visited stations. The code then enters a nested loop, iterating over layers and product weights, calculating the minimum cost for assembling products on both assembly lines ($dp1[i][w]$ and $dp2[i][w]$) at each station and weight combination For assembly line 1 (GPU), it computes the minimum time by considering staying on line#1 ($dp1[i-1][w] + e[0][i-1]$) or switching from line#2 (RRAM) to line#1 ($dp2[i-1][w] + t[1][i-1] + e[0][i-1]$).

For assembly line 2 (RRAM), two options are considered: If the product's weight at the current station is less than or equal to the current weight capacity ($weight[i-1] \leq w$), it calculates the time based on staying on line#1 ($dp1[i][w]$), staying on line#2 ($dp2[i-1][w - weight[i-1]] + e[1][i-1]$), or switching from line#1 to line#2 ($dp1[i-1][w-weight[i-1]]+t[0][i-1]+e[1][i-1]$). Otherwise, if the product's weight exceeds the current capacity, it stays on line#1 ($dp1[i][w]$).

Algorithm 1: Offloading scheduler algorithm

Data: N, e[][], t[][], W, weight[]

Result: NN mapping to GPUs and RRAMs with minimal cost

for $i \leftarrow 1$ *to* $N + 1$ **do**

  for $w \leftarrow 1$ *to* $W + 1$ **do**

    $$dp1[i][w] \leftarrow min\begin{pmatrix} dp1[i-1][w] + e[0][i-1], \\ dp2[i-1][w] + t[1][i-1] + e[0][i-1] \end{pmatrix}$$

    if $weight[i-1] \leq w$ **then**

      $$dp2[i][w] \leftarrow min\begin{pmatrix} dp1[i][w], \\ dp2[i-1][w - weight[i-1]] + e[1][i-1], \\ dp1[i-1][w - weight[i-1]]+ \\ t[0][i-1] + e[1][i-1] \end{pmatrix}$$

    else

      $dp2[i][w] \leftarrow dp1[i][w]$

return $min(dp1[N][w], dp2[N][w])$

After processing all stations and weight capacities, the code determines which assembly line (line#1 or line#2) has the minimum cost to complete the product and returns this value.

Spatial Mapper. The Spatial Mapper in the middle-end aims to organize consecutive layers spatially while minimizing communication. Using the example in Fig. 4-Ⓖ, the Convolution layer (Conv) and ReLU are assigned to RRAM tiles on Vault1. Consequently, IFMs and OFMs related to Conv and ReLU are stored and accessed within Vault1. For the next layer, Pool, assigned to a GPU tile, optimal memory access occurs if assigned to Vault1, leveraging quick access through vertical links within the vault. Assigning Pool to a different vault would require inter-vault links, potentially slowing down memory access due to the longer path and increased communication time.

To ensure spatial locality and minimize communication overheads, we employ an affinity-based mapping approach using the FFD algorithm [14]. The FFD algorithm is commonly applied to solve the bin-packing problem. In this context, NN layers (items) are assigned to computing vaults (bins) to minimize fragmentation between consecutive layers and optimize overall execution time, similar to addressing the fragmented bin-packing problem.

Our custom FFD algorithm sequentially assigns layers (items) to vaults (bins), starting with the largest layer and progressing to smaller ones. Initially, the algorithm attempts to place a layer in a vault with sufficient computational resources (RRAMs or GPUs) to accommodate the entire layer without fragmentation. If no vault can hold the entire layer, the algorithm divides the layer into smaller fragments and attempts to place these fragments in available vaults. This process continues until all layers are assigned, beginning with the largest and proceeding to smaller ones [14]. The algorithm also considers *affinity*, indicating a preference for placing a layer in a vault partially occupied by a previous layer.

Affinity for mapping the current layer (i) to a vault (k), where k ranges from 1 to p (the total number of available vaults), is calculated using the following formula:

$$Affinity_{i,k} = \begin{cases} \frac{1}{V1} & \text{if i-1 is mapped to k} \\ 0 & \text{otherwise} \end{cases} \quad (1)$$

Each layer selects the best available vault based on affinity and availability. In cases where multiple layers show non-zero affinity for a particular vault (i.e., mapped partially or entirely on the same vault), the subsequent layer prioritizes mapping to the vault with the highest affinity and minimal interference from other layers. We modified the FFD algorithm to handle this conflict. After mapping to the optimal vault, affinities are recalculated based on the updated availability of computing resources. This approach maintains spatial locality among consecutive layers, ensuring that smaller layers can be mapped to their preferred vaults.

5.3 Back-End

Placement and Routing (P&R). The final step involves placing all tiles from the list onto physical units (Fig. 4-Ⓗ). Subsequently, the configuration of CBs and SBs in the routing architecture connects the function blocks according to the netlist's topology. We utilize the well-established Versatile Place and Route (VPR) tool-chain, employing a simulated annealing (SA) algorithm for placement and Dijkstra's shortest path for routing to minimize critical path latency.

6 Results

6.1 Evaluation Methodology

Simulation Environment. We used the NeuroSim [15] simulation framework within a PyTorch wrapper to simulate in-situ analog computing for inference accuracy. NN layers not designated for RRAM execution run on an Nvidia Geforce RTX 3080 GPU, with performance and energy metrics extracted using the Nvidia Nsight tool. The framework employs an analytical model of RRAM crossbar computation to report energy, area, and timing for NN layers offloaded to the RRAM.

We utilize the power, area, and timing model of RRAM crossbar and the Op-Amp from [4] to design the MVM Unit. The RRAM accelerator capacity is set to 8MB, aligning with state-of-the-art fabricated chips. To ensure all components share the same technology, we scale certain circuit parameters (e.g., transistor sizes) to be compatible with the 32 nm model. Each RRAM cell, with four bits (16 available conductance levels), represents an 8-bit weight value using the add method with 16 cells. The RRAM sub-array size is configured as 128×128. The ReLU unit, ADC, and DAC models are sourced from a fabricated chip [10]. Local buffer sizes and the number of DACs/ADCs are adjusted to match the throughput of the Computation tiles. NN weights undergo quantization to 8-bit under the WAGE8 format before being mapped to device conductance values. We employ Gaussian noise for device variation with the normal distribution of device error with mean zero. A Monte Carlo simulation in LTSPICE yielded variations of 0.2% for RRAM cells, 0.3% for op-amps, 0.1% for ReLU, and half LSB for AD-DA converters.

Table 1. Power and area breakdown of RRAM tiles

Component	Power (uW)	Area (um^2)	Quantity
Buffer & I/O tile	**34550.0**	**73213.0**	**1**
eDRAM;8kB	2098.0	4357.0	1
I/O Buffer;640B	652.0	1856.0	1
ADC;8 bits;1.3GSps	3100.0	1500.0	2
DAC;8bits;1.3GSps	200.0	500.0	128
Computation tile	**11904.0**	**9779.2**	**1**
RRAM XBAR 128×128	10.0	148.0	64
Op-amp	15.0	0.4	512
ReLU	7.0	0.2	512

Table 2. Top-one int8 inference accuracy, performance, and heuristics time comparison

NN	#Params	Dataset	Inference accuracy(%)		Performance (FPS)				Heuristic time	
			Software	GLoRia	GPU solo	Infinite RRAM	GPU-RRAM + oracle	GLoRia	Oracle	GLoRia
AlexNet	62M	UCF101	61.8	61.7	296	9951	7782	7622	272 s	8 s
ResNet18	11M	Kinetics-700	70.5	70.4	2159	5243	3156	3042	278509 s	19 s
VGG-16	138M	Kinetics-700	61.7	61.6	664	1490	1280	1233	96468 s	17 s
ResNet152	60M	UCF101	76.3	75.3	372	904	n/a	502	6×10^{40} days†	171 s
GPT3-Large*	760M	CoQA	65.2	64.3	5242	11008	n/a	6447	10^{39} days†	155 s

* The performance of GPT3 is measured in characters/second
† Estimated time to complete

Environment Characteristics. Table 1 presents the power and area breakdown of RRAM tiles: Buffer & I/O and Computation tile. Buffer & I/O tiles consist of 8 kB eDRAM and 640 B SRAM as Local Buffers, along with 128 ADC and 2 shared DACs. Computation tiles have four MVM Units, each containing 16x RRAM XBARs 128×128, 128 Op-amps, and 128 ReLU Units. The RRAM layer with 8 MB capacity supports 128 computation tiles, which one having 64 kB. A Vault is formed by grouping two Computation tiles, two Buffer & I/O tiles, and one GPU SM. The RTX 3080 GPU has 68 SMs, and all 128 RRAM tiles make up vaults with 64 of the 68 GPU SMs. The remaining four GPU SMs are not connected to the RRAM tiles. This tile dimensioning was determined experimentally as the most optimal for power efficiency and throughput.

Benchmarks Characterization. Table 2 shows the NN benchmarks used to evaluate this work. The *Software* column displays the accuracy of the NN models performing int8 inference on the RTX 3080 GPU. The *GLoRia* column displays the accuracy achieved by our system stack solution after retraining NN models with the simulation of the GPU-RRAM architecture, reaching near-optimal accuracy levels.

6.2 Offloading Strategy Analysis

To assess the effectiveness of the solutions generated by our system stack, Table 2 presents the performance, measured in Frames Per Second (FPS), and the time taken by GLoRia's heuristics to generate offloading and mapping schemes for various NN benchmarks. The columns include: *GPU Solo* for NNs running exclusively on the RTX3080 GPU, *Infinite RRAM* for a RRAM architecture without capacity restrictions, and *GPU-RRAM + oracle* for the offloading solution derived through exhaustive search, constrained by an 8MB RRAM capacity. *GLoRia* represents the offloading solution generated by our CAD flow, also adhering to the 8MB RRAM capacity limit in this study.

Our approach outperforms the *GPU Solo* scenario by up to 157%, showcasing significant benefits in efficiently offloading layers to the RRAM. Additionally, when compared to the Oracle, GLoRia shows only a slight performance degradation of 3.75%. Crucially, GLoRia achieves the offloading scheduling within a practical time frame, scaling linearly with the NN size ($O(N)$). In contrast, the exhaustive solution becomes impractical ($O(2^N)$) for deeper neural networks due to the combinatorial explosion in such cases.

Figure 5 illustrates the offloading schedule generated by our CAD flow for the VGG-16 NN and the GPU-RRAM architecture. This figure provides an in-depth evaluation of the proposed RRAM offloading and mapping strategy. The horizontal axis represents individual NN layers. On the left side of the chart, the execution time for each NN layer is broken down, with separate bars indicating RRAM, GPU, and Transfer time between RRAM and GPU components. The *Weight size* data series on the right of the chart shows sizes for each layer.

When analyzing the execution time and weights, one can observe a contrast between storage and computational requirements. The initial convolutional layers of VGG-16 use 0.028% of weight storage yet contribute 12.5% to the total computational workload. Conversely, the fully connected layers at the end of the NN exhibit the opposite pattern. They consume 89.3% of the total weight distribution but contribute only 0.8% to the computational demands. This imbalance presents a unique challenge when integrating RRAM crossbars, as these devices combine computation and storage at the same physical location. Our CAD flow leverages this imbalance with offloading and spatial mapping. Using our assembly line scheduling and knapsack-based offloading algorithm, we select the most advantageous layers for RRAM acceleration, resulting in significant performance gains. For the VGG-16 model, the offloading scheduler algorithm designates only four layers to run on the 8 MB RRAM. These layers represent just 5.7% of the total NN size but contribute to 70% of the total execution time (Fig. 6).

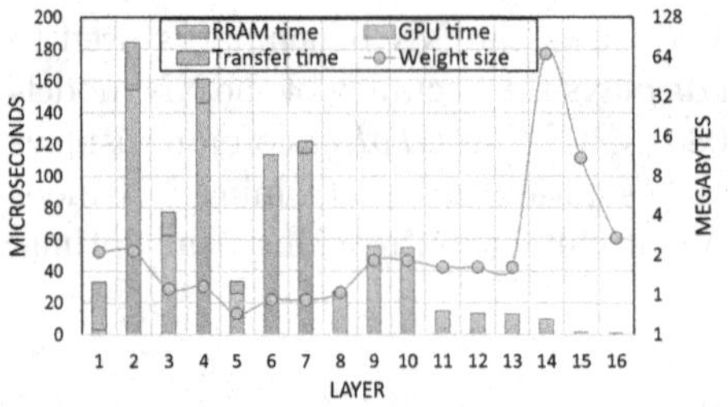

Fig. 5. NN layer offloading, execution time, and weight distribution of the VGG-16 NN.

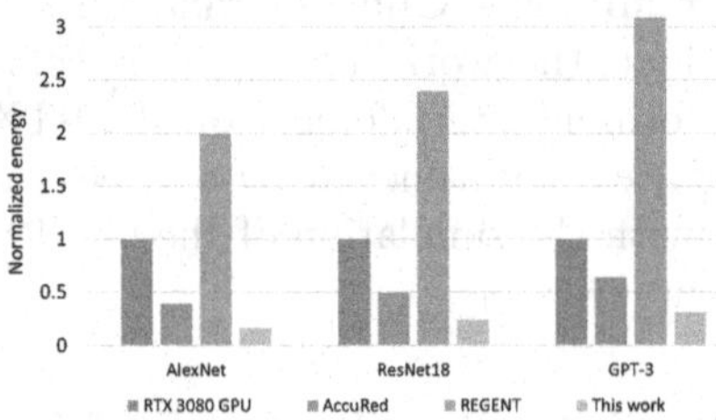

Fig. 6. Energy consumption comparison with related work.

6.3 Comparison over the State-of-the-Art

This Section evaluates the energy consumption of our approach over the state-of-the-art GPU-RRAM architectures. Figure 6 presents the normalized energy consumption comparison for the experimented scenarios. We compare our results to a GPU-only execution on an RTX 3080 GPU, and two GPU-RRAM related works: AccuRed [6] and REGENT [7]. By using the proposed architecture and CAD heuristics presented in this work, one can achieve energy reduction levels of 6.4x, 4.21x, and 3.26x for the AlexNet, ResNet18, and GPT3 NN compared to the RTX 3080 GPU, respectively. Regarding the solution's scalability, our approach scales better than the GPU-RRAM counterparts as the size of the NN model increases.

7 Conclusion

This work presents a GPU-RRAM architecture for NN acceleration and its associated system stack, which provides the best offloading schedule for NN layers between both RRAM and GPU, efficiently tackling the scalability challenges found in RRAM accelerators. Our results show that our approach stays only 3.75% behind an optimal exhaustive solution ($O(2^N)$) in FPS, bringing huge advantages in energy consumption over the state-of-the-art.

References

1. Arka, A.I., et al.: Performance and accuracy tradeoffs for training graph neural networks on ReRam-based architectures. IEEE VLSI **29**(10), 1743–1756 (2021)
2. Cheng, M., et al.: Time: a training-in-memory architecture for RRAM-based deep neural networks. IEEE TCAD **38**(5), 834–847 (2018)
3. Chi, P., et al.: Prime: a novel processing-in-memory architecture for neural network computation in ReRam-based main memory. ACM SIGARCH **44**(3), 27–39 (2016)
4. Han, J., Liu, H., Wang, M., Li, Z., Zhang, Y.: Era-LSTM: An efficient ReRam-based architecture for long short-term memory. IEEE TPDS **31**(6), 1328–1342 (2019)

5. Ji, Y., et al.: FPSA: a full system stack solution for reconfigurable ReRam-based NN accelerator architecture. In: 24th ASPLOS, pp. 733–747 (2019)
6. Joardar, B.K., Doppa, J.R., Pande, P.P., Li, H., Chakrabarty, K.: Accured: High accuracy training of CNNs on ReRam/GPU heterogeneous 3-D architecture. IEEE TCAD **40**(5), 971–984 (2020)
7. Joardar, B.K., Li, B., Doppa, J.R., Li, H., Pande, P.P., Chakrabarty, K.: Regent: a heterogeneous ReRam/GPU-based architecture enabled by NOC for training CNNs. In: 2019 DATE, pp. 522–527. IEEE (2019)
8. Joardar, B.K., et al.: Gramarch: a GPU-ReRam based heterogeneous architecture for neural image segmentation. In: 2020 DATE, pp. 228–233. IEEE (2020)
9. Kim, H., et al.: ADC-free ReRam-based in-situ accelerator for energy-efficient binary neural networks. IEEE Trans. Comput. (2022)
10. Kull, L., et al.: A 3.1 mw 8b 1.2 gs/s single-channel asynchronous SAR ADC with alternate comparators for enhanced speed in 32 nm digital SOI CMOS. IEEE JSSC **48**(12), 3049–3058 (2013)
11. Le Gallo, M., et al.: A 64-core mixed-signal in-memory compute chip based on phase-change memory for deep neural network inference. Nat. Electron. 1–14 (2023)
12. Li, B., Doppa, J.R., Pande, P.P., Chakrabarty, K., Qiu, J.X., Li, H.: 3D-reg: a 3D ReRam-based heterogeneous architecture for training deep neural networks. ACM JETC **16**(2), 1–24 (2020)
13. Luo, T., et al.: Dadiannao: a neural network supercomputer. IEEE Trans. Comput. **66**(1), 73–88 (2016)
14. Menakerman, N., Rom, R.: Bin packing with item fragmentation. In: Dehne, F., Sack, J.-R., Tamassia, R. (eds.) WADS 2001. LNCS, vol. 2125, pp. 313–324. Springer, Heidelberg (2001). https://doi.org/10.1007/3-540-44634-6_29
15. Peng, X., et al.: DNN+ neurosim v2. 0: an end-to-end benchmarking framework for compute-in-memory accelerators for on-chip training. IEEE TCAD **40**(11), 2306–2319 (2020)
16. Shafiee, A., et al.: ISAAC: a convolutional neural network accelerator with in-situ analog arithmetic in crossbars. ACM SIGARCH **44**(3), 14–26 (2016)
17. Song, L., et al.: Pipelayer: a pipelined ReRam-based accelerator for deep learning. In: 2017 IEEE HPCA, pp. 541–552. IEEE (2017)

Evaluating the Impact of Racetrack Memory Misalignment Faults on BNNs Performance

Leonard David Bereholschi[1(✉)], Mikail Yayla[1], Jian-Jia Chen[1], Kuan-Hsun Chen[2], and Asif Ali Khan[3]

[1] TU Dortmund University, Dortmund, Germany
{leonard.bereholschi,mikail.yayla,jian-jia.chen}@tu-dortmund.de
[2] University of Twente, Enschede, The Netherlands
k.h.chen@utwente.nl
[3] Technical University of Dresden, Dresden, Germany
asif_ali.khan@tu-dresden.de

Abstract. Racetrack memory (RTM) is a promising non-volatile memory (NVM) technology that offers exceptional density, power and performance benefits over other NVM and conventional memory technologies. RTM cells have the unique capability of storing hundreds of data bits per cell and are equipped with one or more access ports. However, accessing data in an RTM cell requires the data to be *shifted and aligned* to an access port, introducing performance and energy overheads and potentially leading to *misalignment faults*. A misalignment fault occurs when after the shift operation, the desired data is not properly aligned to an access port and incorrect data is read from the RTM cell. Countermeasures have been proposed to mitigate the effects of these faults on applications' accuracy, albeit at the cost of increased overhead. There is potential to balance the trade-offs between acceptable drops in accuracy and enhancements in performance, especially in error-resilient applications such as *Binarized Neural Networks* (BNNs). However, there exists no tool that enables effective exploration of this design space and assess the potential trade-offs.

This paper introduces NetDrift, a framework which facilitates investigation into the impact of RTM misalignment faults on BNNs accuracy at finer granularities. It enables controlled error injection in selected BNN layers with varying fault rates and simulates the impact of accumulated errors in weight tensors of several BNN models (FashionMNIST, CIFAR10, ResNet18) stored in RTM. The framework allows for tuning reliability for performance and vice versa, providing an estimate of the number of inference iterations required for a BNN model to drop below a certain lower threshold, with no protection, limited protection, and full protection, along with the associated impact on performance. The tool is openly available on Github.

Keywords: Binarized neural networks (BNNs) · Racetrack memory · Reliability · Accuracy · Misalignment Faults

L. Carro et al. (Eds.): SAMOS 2024, LNCS 15226, pp. 230–245, 2025.
https://doi.org/10.1007/978-3-031-78377-7_16

1 Introduction

In recent years, machine learning has experienced remarkable progress, especially with the advancements in generative AI and large language models (LLM), revolutionizing numerous aspects of our lives[1]. However, the complexity of these models demands extensive computational and memory resources, exposing the limitations of traditional technologies and computing paradigms. On the computing front, innovative system designs such as Google's tensor processing units (TPUs) [12], domain-specific accelerators [1,2], near-memory, and in-memory computing systems [14], and chiplets [19] have been proposed to meet the compute demands. However, the memory subsystem unfortunately continues to rely on conventional SRAM and DRAM technologies, which face significant technological limitations. These technologies not only suffer from larger feature size but also exhibit substantial energy consumption [5]. To overcome these challenges, a multitude of novel nonvolatile memory (NVM) technologies including spin-transfer-torque memory (STT-RAM), phase-change memory (PCM), resistive RAM (ReRAM), magnetic RAM (MRAM), Ferroelectric FETs (FeFETs), and racetrack memory (RTM) have emerged [5]. Notably, RTMs stand out as particularly interesting, offering unprecedented densities and boasting latencies comparable to SRAM [4]. Since their inception in 2008 [21], RTMs have achieved substantial breakthroughs and have been deployed at various levels in the memory hierarchy [4].

Unlike conventional memory technologies, a single cell in RTM is a magnetic nanowire that can store hundreds of data bits, as illustrated in Fig. 2. Each RTM cell has one or more access ports (AP) that enable the read/write operations. During an RTM access, the desired data must be *shifted and aligned* to an AP position before it can be accessed. The shift operations not only impose performance and energy overhead but can also lead to potential *misalignment faults*, also referred to as position errors. Common position errors in RTM, such as stop-in-the-middle and out-of-step scenarios [26], occur when the adjacent domain, rather than the desired one, aligns with the AP position, resulting in the erroneous reading or writing of data.

RTM errors have been extensively studied and countermeasures like *position error correction codes* (PECCs) have been proposed to detect and correct misalignment faults [15,26]. However, these schemes incur significant latency and energy overhead of up to 2× [26]. For applications where a slight drop in accuracy is acceptable, this overhead can be significantly reduced by selectively applying PECCs to only critical application regions. For instance, in image and video processing, edge pixels hold more significance compared to areas where surrounding pixel values are uniform. Even if a pixel in these regions is erroneously read, the overall impact on the image remains minimal. Similarly, certain machine learning models like *Binarized Neural Networks* (BNNs) [11], where weights and activations are represented in 1-bit, exhibit outstanding tolerance to bit errors [6,8]. In such cases, the overhead of PECC schemes can be reduced by selectively

[1] https://github.com/LeonardDavid/NetDrift.

protecting sensitive regions (e.g. BNN layers). To achieve this, new simulation tools are needed that are capable of identifying such important regions through detailed analysis and characterization of BNNs at a finer granularity, and allow conducting design space exploration to strike a balance between accuracy and performance overhead.

To this end, this paper presents NetDrift, a framework that enables investigating the impact of RTM misalignment faults on the BNNs accuracy. The framework allows for different mappings of BNN weights to the RTM arrays, controlled error injection across various BNN layers with adjustable error rates, varying the RTM nanowire size, and simulating the accumulated error impact on the overall accuracy. Additionally, it evaluates the combined effects on accuracy and performance overhead incurred by a given PECC scheme, e.g., P-ECC, P-ECC-O [26], and GROGU [15], across three BNN protection levels – unprotected (no layers protected), partially protected (sensitive layers protected), and fully protected. We showcase the versatility of our framework by conducting thorough evaluations of RTM reliability and BNN performance across different RTM sizes, fault rates, datasets, and models.

The rest of the paper is structured as follows: Sect. 2 presents a background on RTMs, BNNs, and the state-of-the-art PECC schemes. In Sect. 3, we elaborate on our framework, including detailed descriptions of its individual modules. Section 4 presents our evaluation results and discussions, while Sect. 5 concludes the paper.

2 Background

This section provides background on BNNs, RTMs, misalignment faults and PECC schemes. Additionally, it presents a summary of the relevant state-of-the-arts and a motivational example to emphasize the finer granularity analysis.

2.1 Binarized Neural Networks

Binarized neural networks (BNNs) [11] are a resource-efficient variant of NNs, in which the weights and the activations are binarized into 1-bit representations. Unlike the full-precision NNs, where one matrix multiplication must be performed for computing the output of each neuron, BNNs apply bitwise operators for computing the outputs of neurons. Notably, BNNs achieve comparable accuracy to full-precision NNs and requires considerably less resources, e.g. [11] achieves in practice 23× inference time improvement, compared to baseline NNs.

We assume for a certain layer a weight matrix $\mathbf{W}$ with dimensions $(\alpha \times \beta)$, where α is the number of neurons and β the number of weights of a neuron. The input matrix $\mathbf{X}$ has dimensions $(\gamma \times \delta)$, where $\beta = \gamma$ and δ is the number of convolution windows in the input. We leave out any layer indices for brevity. Every convolution of a conventional NN can be mapped to this matrix notation. Unlike the full-precision NNs, where one matrix multiplication must be performed for computing the output of each neuron, we can simply apply XNOR

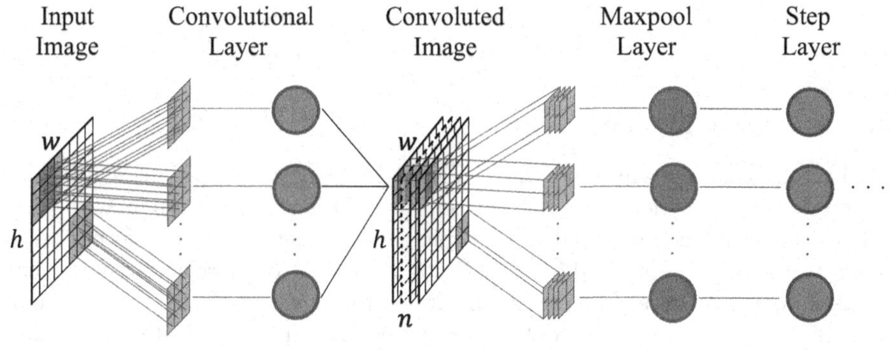

Fig. 1. Structure of a Convolutional BNN model demonstrating three major layer types: *Convolution*, *Maxpool*, and *Step* layer.

on the operands to compute the outputs.

$$2 \cdot \text{popcount}(XNOR(\mathbf{W}, \mathbf{X})) - \#bits > \mathbf{T}, \tag{1}$$

where $XNOR(\mathbf{W}, \mathbf{X})$ computes the XNOR of the rows in $\mathbf{W}$ with the columns in $\mathbf{X}$ (analogue to matrix multiplication), popcount counts the number of set bits in the XNOR result, $\#bits$ is the number of bits in the XNOR operands, and $\mathbf{T}$ is a vector of learnable threshold parameters, with one entry for each neuron. The thresholds are computed with the batch normalization parameters, i.e. $T = \mu - \frac{\sigma}{\psi}\eta$, where each neuron has a mean μ and a standard deviation σ over the result of the left side of Eq. (1), and ψ and η are learnable parameters (details about the batch normalization parameters can be found in [11,22]). Finally, the comparisons against the thresholds produce binary values.

Target BNN models: In this paper, we consider convolutional BNNs (Fig. 1) and a binarized version of a Residual Network (ResNet18). In a standard convolutional BNN, there are four fundamental types of layers: *convolutional*, *maxpool*, *step*, and *fully-connected.* The *convolutional* layer (Cχ) conducts a 2D convolution of the input with 3×3 filters, with χ representing the number of neurons in the layer. The *maxpool* layer (MPχ) downsamples inputs by selecting the maximum in a 2×2 window, with χ indicating its output size. A *step* layer (S) incorporates batch normalization [22] followed by a binary activation function. We use signed integers for the threshold values in the batch normalization, and apply Hard-Tanh as our binary activation function. The *fully-connected* layer (FCχ), connects all neurons in the current layer with those in the next layer and also uses binary weights. Additionally, a *flattening* layer (FLAT) reshapes high-dimensional matrices into lower-dimensional matrices (3D into 1D in our models).

We also use a Residual network (ResNet18) adapted for the binarized version of NNs. In addition to the aforementioned layers, it also contains shortcut connections that allow parameters to skip multiple layers inside *Skip-connection blocks* (SCBs), in order to reach deeper into the network. The main advantage of this structure is that it mitigates the effects of the vanishing gradient problem, enabling the model to be applied to more complex datasets [7,9].

2.2 Racetrack Memory

RTM is one of the many emerging NVM technologies that promises unprecedented density and energy benefits. A cell in RTM is a magnetic nanowire (also called track) that is composed of multiple tiny magnetic regions referred to as *domains*, which are separated by domain walls, and one or more access ports that are used to access data domains in the track, as shown in Fig. 2. Each domain in an RTM track represents a data bit and has its own magnetization direction. In order to access a domain in a track, a shift current is sent from one end of the track to shift the domains and align the corresponding data bit with a port position. To avoid data loss, each track has reserved domains at both ends of the nanowire that store data bits during the shift operation. The number of reserved domains in a track is dependent upon the number and position of access ports per track. In the case of evenly distributed access ports, the number of reserved domains is equal to the maximum shift distance. In this work, we assume one AP per track.

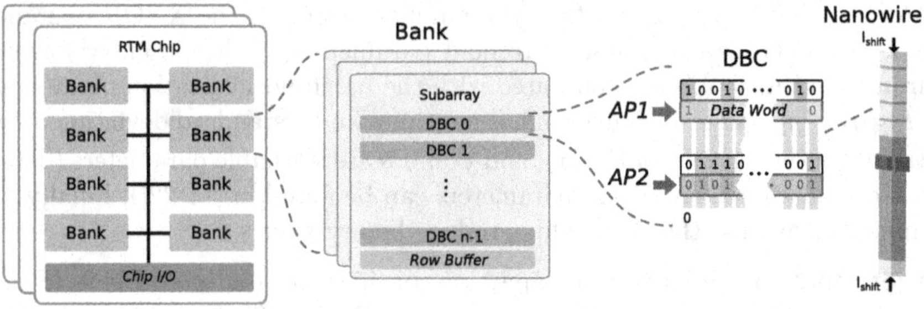

Fig. 2. RTM architectural overview

RTM, like other memory technologies, is organized into multiple banks, each containing one or more subarrays (see Fig. 2). Each subarray consists of one or more tiles, with each tile having multiple *domain wall clusters* (DBC). A DBC is a group of T nanowires, each containing K data domains (i.e., bits), and are equipped with one or more access ports for performing read/write operations. Typically, data is stored in a bit-interleaved manner across DBC tracks so that all T bits of a memory object can be accessed in parallel. To access a memory object, bits are shifted in a lock-step manner until they are properly aligned with the access port positions. Unlike domain wall RTMs, where data is stored in domains, the Skymiron-based RTM stores data in magnetic skyrmions and have been proposed as a more dense and more stable alternative [13]. However, due to the lack of its fault model, this work only focuses on domain walls. Nevertheless, the proposed framework is easily extendable to accommodate other fault models.

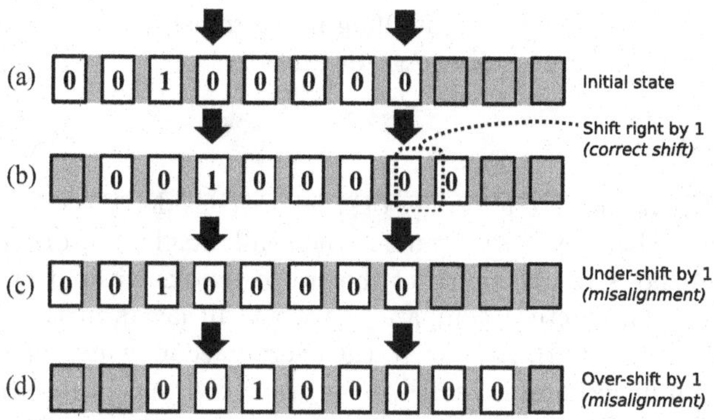

Fig. 3. Misalignment after a right shift by one position (a) Initial state before shifting (b) No error (c) Misalignment by one position (under-shift) (c) Misalignment by one position (over-shift). Adopted from [26].

2.3 Misalignment Faults

Misalignment faults (also known as position errors) may occur due to the fluctuation in the shifting current originated from variation in the operating conditions of the system or the non-linearities of the device itself [4]. The most common types of faults that can occur in an RTM are *stop-in-the-middle* and *out-of-step* misalignments. During an RTM access, the domain walls are shifted along the track until the desired location is reached. However, due to the aforementioned reasons, there exists certain probabilities that domains will be misaligned to the access ports. In the case of a stop-in-the-middle fault, which rarely occurs, the access port is aligned with a domain wall that separates two adjacent domains. The value read out is uncertain, it can either be random, or one of the values from the neighbouring domains. In the more common out-of-step misalignment, the domain is either under- or over-shifting by n positions, as illustrated in Fig. 3 for $n = 1$. Zhang et al. [26] characterized the misalignment probabilities as $P_1 = 4.55 \cdot 10^{-5}$ and $P_2 = 1.37 \cdot 10^{-21}$ for $n = 1$ and $n = 2$, respectively.

Conventional error correction codes are unfortunately not applicable to RTM misalignments because: (1) despite being correctable, misalignment faults may not always produce an immediate detectable error, (2) the misalignment fault changes the state of the entire nanowire, instead of a single bit. Many RTM-specific position error correction schemes are proposed of late. Zhang et al. [26] proposed P-ECC and P-ECC-O with various protection capabilities and overhead trade-offs. Ollivier et al. [20] proposed DECC to minimize the overhead of P-ECC and P-ECC-O by leveraging the transverse read access mode of RTM to quickly determine any potential misalignment. GreenFlag and Foosball make a correlation of the misalignment faults with the repeated and dropped bits in a communication channel and use VT codes to detect and correct RTM misalignment faults [3,17]. The most recent reliability technique, GROGU [15], proposed a novel scheme that is capable of handling misalignment by more positions with the least performance, area and energy overheads.

2.4 Motivation

To motivate the need for our framework, let us consider the example of binarized VGG7 and ResNet18 structures, where all weight tensors are stored in RTM. Figure 4 shows the accuracy of the two networks without employing any PECC scheme (unprotected) compared to when all layers in the networks are protected (fully-protected). As shown, the overall accuracy experiences a significant drop to an unacceptable level within just a few tens of iterations without protection. Conversely, with full protection, the networks maintain their baseline accuracy, albeit with an increase of, in some cases, over 100% performance overhead. The vast design space between these extremes offers opportunities to explore trade-offs in accuracy and performance. Our tool, as demonstrated in Sect. 4.4, reveals that selective protection of specific layers, identifiable using our framework through sensitivity analysis, can sustain accuracy for a longer duration with a 5–96% performance overhead (for ResNet18), depending on the nanowire size and the employed protection scheme (GROGU [15] in this case).

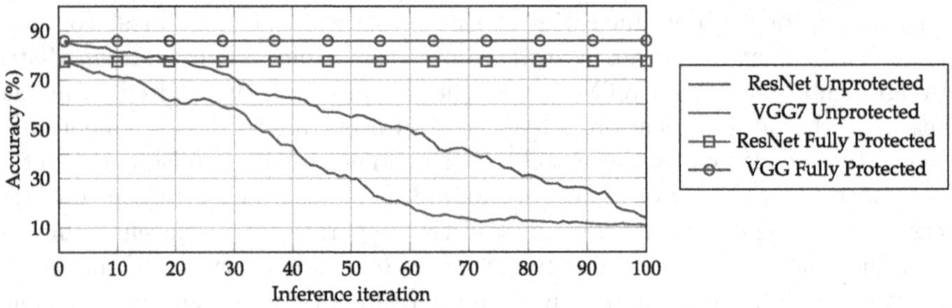

Fig. 4. Accuracy drop of ResNet and VGG7 models over time across inference iterations. The baseline accuracy is the same as in fully-protected configurations.

3 NetDrift Overview

This section presents our framework (NetDrift) which enables profiling BNNs on unreliable RTMs. Our framework is based on the SPICE-Torch error injection tool [25] that models injecting conventional memory faults, such as like bit-flips in BNN weights during inference and assessing their resilience. Contrary to existing frameworks for conventional permanent and transient faults, NetDrift specifically focuses on the RTM misalignment faults, comprising a mapping module, a fault injector, and accounting for parameters such as RTM track size and misalignment fault rate. Figure 5 illustrates a high-level overview of the operational steps of NetDrift.

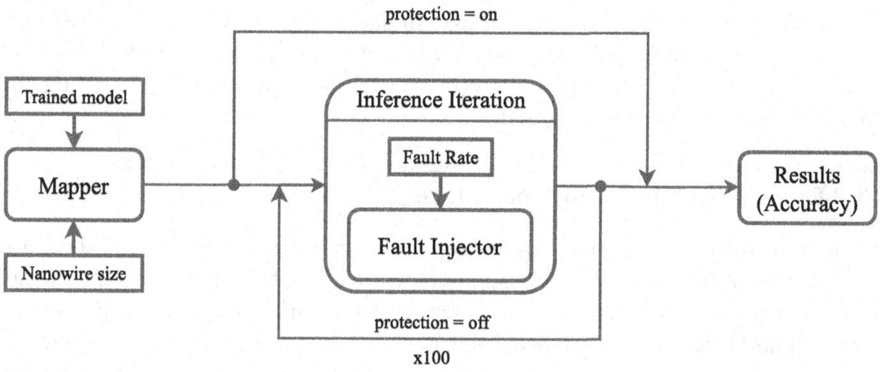

Fig. 5. A high-level overview of our NetDrift simulation framework.

3.1 Mapping of BNN Weights to RTM

We train different BNN models without any misalignments and map the weight tensors to RTM nanowires. The binary weight tensors (one per network layer) are split into blocks of size K, where K is the number of bits in the nanowire (typically $K \leq 64$). Hence, multiple nanowires are used to store a single weight tensor. The framework currently allows mapping the weight matrices to RTM in both row-major and column-major orders, but an arbitrary mapping can also be implemented. We assume a single access port per track, which requires resetting the AP to the beginning of the nanowire after every inference iteration. Nevertheless, the framework can also be used with the zig-zagged RTM accesses using two APs to avoid the long jumps after every iteration [18].

3.2 Fault Injection

We presume that all BNN weights are stored in RTM, and that an inference does not require any weight updates (i.e. write operations). In the course of an inference, the weights are fetched (i.e. read) from the memory, and each access mandates shifting the nanowire to the desired port position. The shift direction and distance depend upon the requested data and the current position of the AP. As input, the fault injector takes a fault rate and the BNN layers that need to be protected, along with the chosen PECC scheme. By default, the framework inserts faults in all layers and does not employ any protection. For each shift operation, the fault injector inserts a misalignment fault by one position, according to the provided fault rate. Note that while the fault injection rate governs the rate of fault injection, the control of under-shift and over-shift rates is not explicitly determined, following a uniform distribution.

Please note that, once a fault is injected, the values in the shifted nanowires remain misaligned so that the impact of faults is accumulated across multiple inference iterations. For example, if a nanowire in iteration i over-shifts by one position to the right, and the same nanowire in iteration $i + 1$ over-shifts to the right again, the overall misalignment accumulates to over-shift by *two* positions to the right. Conversely, subsequent misalignments, such as an over-shift followed by an under-shift (or vice versa), counteract each other, potentially bringing the nanowire back to the correct position.

3.3 Error Detection and Correction

NetDrift monitors the injected faults by the fault injector, along with the total shifts count, to estimate the performance overhead of the given PECC scheme. When protection is activated on a layer, the framework simulates the process as follows: The fault injector triggers as if it would inject a fault in the nanowire, tallying the fault count for the protection overhead estimation. However, no error is injected into the nanowire, thus necessitating no correction. For all correctable faults by the selected PECC, this yields similar outcomes to implementing the PECC scheme directly within the simulator.

3.4 Applicability to High-Precision Networks

This work is also applicable to high-precision neural networks. Here, we briefly explain how to modify the framework to implement and test such neural networks. First, the mapping module takes the weight matrices of the custom (trained) NN model along with the nanowire size, bit-slices them, and stores them in the RTM nanowires. The fault injector treats every nanowire independent and can be used out of the box without requiring any modifications. If needed, it can also be extended or used as a reference. In the provided GitHub repository (see link in the abstract), we explain how certain modules of the framework can be modified to achieve this. Finally, the accuracy of the framework in the presence of the misalignment faults is evaluated.

4 Evaluation

This section presents our experimental setup, including our datasets and BNN architectures. Additionally, it presents our evaluation results for conducting sensitivity analysis on various BNN models and our design space exploration to balance the accuracy and performance tradeoffs.

4.1 Experimental Setup

We use a Linux server with two GTX1080 cards, each having 8 GB of VRAM, to run our experiments. The server can handle four concurrent and independent runs. A run means executing a BNN model in our NetDrift framework for 100 consecutive inference iterations.

As explained in Sect. 3.2, the errors also accumulate over multiple inference iterations. In our evaluations, misalignment faults are accumulated over the course of 100 consecutive inference iterations. We focus only on the impact faults have on the accuracy of the models described in Sect. 4.2. The evaluated misalignment fault rates $p \in \{10^{-4}, 4.55 \times 10^{-5}, 10^{-5}\}$ are taken from [15,26]. The simulator generates results including details about each inference iteration, such as accuracy after each iteration and the total (accumulated) misalignment faults in each layer. Since the models have different sizes (as outlined in the following Sect. 4.2), *one* inference iteration takes on average 17 seconds for VGG3 (FMNIST), 39 seconds for VGG7 (CIFAR), and around 7 minutes for ResNet18 (ImageNette).

For error detection and correction, various PECC schemes are available, as discussed in Sect. 2.3, which can be used with NetDrift to estimate performance overhead. We use the state-of-the-art GROGU scheme [15] that operates by conducting a transverse read and a standard read operation to detect a misalignment by $\pm w$ positions, where w is the window size for the transverse read operation [15]. Assuming each of these read operations takes one cycle, fault detection requires two cycles and occurs after every shift operation in the protected layers. Upon detecting an error, GROGU proceeds with correction, involving shift and write operations. On average, GROGU typically requires around four cycles to correct a fault. While other schemes like P-ECC and P-ECC-O [26] exist, with varying detection and correction overhead cycle counts generally exceeding those of GROGU, in this section we focus exclusively on GROGU for the sake of brevity.

4.2 Datasets and BNN Models

We evaluate our framework on several commonly used datasets, for which we used BNN models based on VGG-type architectures [23] (in the case of CIFAR10 and Fashion-MNIST datasets) and ResNet18 for ImageNette.

Fashion-MNIST: The Fashion-MNIST [24] dataset consists of 70, 000 grayscale images and labels from 10 classes, representing different clothing articles. The size of each image is 28×28 pixels in 1 channel, with 0 representing the *brightest* and 255 the *darkest* values. We use 60, 000 images for training and the remaining 10, 000 for testing. Table 1.1 defines the BNN structure of the VGG3 model used for this dataset, using the notations from Sect. 2.1. The baseline accuracy for this model is 91.08%.

CIFAR10: The CIFAR10 [16] dataset contains 60, 000 colour images (3 channels), each with a size of 32×32. It is split into 50, 000 training and 10, 000 test images, which are classified in 10 different classes representing means of transportation (i.e. airplane, ship, truck, automobile) and animals (i.e. bird, cat, dog, deer, frog, horse). For this dataset we used a bigger VGG7 model, with its BNN structure illustrated in Table 1.2. It achieves a baseline accuracy of 85.82%.

ImageNette: ImageNette [10] is the subset of the larger ImageNet dataset. It classifies 10 various classes of 1000 images each, at a resolution of 64×64. Compared to the larger original dataset, ImageNette is more manageable and time efficient for running multiple inference iterations, necessary for our evaluations.

The BNN model used for the ImageNette dataset is a ResNet18 structure with a baseline accuracy of 77.50%, following the schematics of Table 1.3. It consists of convolutional layers, divided into multiple *Skip-connection blocks* (SCBs), which contain a shortcut connection that skips some of the layers inside the block. The blocks are made up of 4 convolutional layers, with the number χ after $SCB\chi$ denoting the amount of neurons in both of the convolutional layers.

Table 1. Structure of the BNN Models.

1. VGG3
In → C64 → MP14 → S → C64 → MP7 → S → FLAT → FC2048 → S → FC2048
2. VGG7
In → C64 → S → C64 → MP16 → S → C256 → S → C256 → MP8 → S → C512 → S → C512 → MP4 → S → FLAT → FC1024 → S → FC1024 → 10
3. ResNet18
In → C64 → SCB64 → SCB128 → SCB256 → MP2 → SCB512 → MP4 → FC10

4.3 Layer-Wise Sensitivity Analysis

To give an overview on the individual impact of each layer, we present the accuracy drops in a heatmap as Fig. 6, where darker reddish spots mean a bigger accuracy drop from the baseline. The rows represent the ordered layers of the evaluated model, while the columns denote different RTM nanowire sizes (varied from 2 to 64). The heatmap is generated as follows: For a given RTM nanowire size and a given fault rate, we inject faults in merely one layer (i.e., keeping all other layers protected) and observe the accuracy over 100 inference iterations. Each cell in the heatmap shows the accuracy after these 100 iterations. We repeat this experiment for each network layer (different rows), with different RTM nanowire sizes (columns) and different fault rates (different blocks in the heat map). This allows us to evaluate the sensitivity of each layer individually. Due to space constraints, we chose to only show the heatmaps for the VGG7 and ResNet18 models, with the realistic fault rates of $p \in \{10^{-4}, 4.55 \times 10^{-5}, 10^{-5}\}$.

Firstly, we can observe that, for smaller nanowire sizes, the probability of faults is smaller due to fewer shifts. For instance, when the nanowire has a size of 2 bits, the average accuracy drop across all layers is only around −1%. In most cases, this drop is deemed acceptable, thus obviating the need for error correction. However, common nanowire sizes tend to be 32 and 64, and using only two locations per nanowire significantly underutilizes the RTM. The accuracy drop increases, along with the increase of the nanowire sizes. For a nanowire size of 64, the accuracy drop can be as high as −75% (in VGG7) and −57% (in ResNet18) in selected layers, necessitating protection of RTM accesses.

Additionally, we also observe that certain network layers exhibit higher susceptibility to misalignment faults compared to others. The sensitivity of these layers varies across network models, yet the relative accuracy drop remains consistent for different block sizes, as illustrated in Fig. 6.

4.4 Design Space Exploration

Applying a PECC scheme can mitigate or even entirely prevent accuracy drops resulting from misalignment faults. However, this comes at the cost of performance overhead, namely an increase in inference execution time, as the employed PECC scheme requires a certain number of cycles to detect and correct misalignment faults. This subsection explores this design space by evaluating the following configurations and presenting results analysis.

a. VGG7 (CIFAR10)

Layer	10^{-4}						4.55×10^{-5}						10^{-5}					
	64	32	16	8	4	2	64	32	16	8	4	2	64	32	16	8	4	2
1	-0.40	-0.40	-0.51	-0.16	-0.45	-0.31	-0.42	-0.32	-0.13	0.00	-0.11	0.00	-0.13	-0.23	0.00	0.00	0.00	0.00
2	-69.8	-63.3	-45.9	-33.2	-11.1	-5.61	-62.1	-50.1	-30.2	-18.9	-5.87	-2.36	-19.8	-17.1	-4.00	-2.64	-0.53	-0.50
3	-67.4	-64.1	-53.3	-20.8	-7.07	-2.5	-65.7	-40.6	-28.9	-8.38	-2.38	-0.74	-16.2	-11.4	-2.91	-0.89	-0.90	-0.68
4	-75.8	-75.8	-74.4	-43.9	-15.5	-1.56	-75.8	-74.0	-37.3	-14.0	-2.35	-0.79	-44.4	-18.1	-5.45	-3.23	-0.50	-0.14
5	-65.2	-65.2	-58.7	-43.6	-12.3	-1.93	-59.9	-49.8	-29.3	-13.9	-2.94	-0.72	-22.9	-8.07	-2.75	-2.52	-0.46	-0.36
6	-75.8	-75.4	-62.0	-27.7	-5.37	-1.56	-75.7	-65.7	-31.5	-6.96	-2.42	-0.80	-24.7	-7.58	-3.87	-1.57	-0.57	-0.26
7	-75.8	-75.8	-67.7	-20.7	-2.93	-0.45	-75.8	-63.0	-19.4	-3.91	-0.77	-0.14	-18.4	-3.21	-1.01	-0.31	-0.15	-0.06
8	-34.7	-23.7	-20.3	-7.64	-1.58	-0.97	-20.3	-16.1	-7.96	-1.47	-0.84	-0.82	-6.52	-1.56	-0.54	0.69	-0.70	-0.41

b. ResNet18 (ImageNette)

Layer	10^{-4}						4.55×10^{-5}						10^{-5}					
	64	32	16	8	4	2	64	32	16	8	4	2	64	32	16	8	4	2
1	-0.53	0.02	-0.23	-0.60	0.00	0.11	-0.51	-0.46	-0.79	-0.63	-0.63	0.00	-0.71	-0.46	-0.63	-0.58	0.00	0.00
2	-10.4	-9.68	-8.26	-6.50	-3.62	-1.73	-9.47	-9.17	-6.75	-3.67	-1.78	-0.12	-5.60	-3.08	-2.29	-1.07	-1.04	-0.35
3	-12.0	-11.7	-11.3	-7.80	-2.63	-1.86	-9.73	-6.29	-4.20	-4.28	-1.60	-1.27	-6.26	-2.82	-0.61	-0.86	-0.96	-0.58
4	-30.5	-23.0	-22.5	-22.6	-5.07	-3.49	-29.7	-24.9	-4.74	-9.60	-1.50	-0.96	-11.9	-9.78	-2.65	-1.68	-0.58	-0.61
5	-12.9	-16.6	-13.4	-5.86	-5.07	-0.97	-20.7	-13.1	-6.32	-7.13	-5.12	-0.96	-3.28	-1.88	-1.30	-0.99	-0.74	-0.23
6	-57.0	-48.1	-47.7	-46.5	-16.9	-3.31	-48.6	-41.3	-33.6	-14.4	-5.27	-0.91	-40.5	-20.8	-7.13	-2.09	-0.71	-0.61
7	-52.1	-49.3	-45.2	-40.7	-13.7	-3.11	-51.4	-46.8	-29.8	-20.5	-4.94	-0.89	-32.2	-27.7	-6.70	-2.06	-1.47	-0.81
8	-19.1	-18.0	-16.3	-8.69	-3.47	-0.97	-11.9	-10.0	-7.59	-2.34	-0.99	-0.28	-8.68	-2.95	-1.45	-1.45	-0.33	0.00
9	-18.1	-17.1	-11.5	-6.78	-2.50	-1.07	-20.4	-9.83	-9.37	-1.98	-0.89	-0.30	-6.29	-2.29	-1.02	-0.12	-0.48	-0.18
10	-10.9	-7.19	-5.27	-4.87	-1.53	-0.13	-7.61	-7.00	-6.14	-1.93	-0.84	-0.23	-3.23	-2.60	-0.99	-0.89	-0.81	-0.38
11	-46.5	-42.7	-33.5	-19.6	-9.45	-1.15	-35.0	-28.3	-18.6	-6.82	-2.90	-0.51	-17.9	-7.33	-4.30	-1.35	0.05	-0.07
12	-12.5	-11.6	-9.27	-5.27	-1.53	-0.61	-12.4	-8.79	-5.30	-1.98	-0.74	-0.05	-5.17	-2.19	-1.30	-0.91	-0.35	-0.10
13	-8.53	-5.35	-4.77	-3.64	-1.38	-0.56	-6.04	-4.86	-2.42	-1.63	-0.71	-0.40	-2.88	-1.58	-0.28	-0.58	-0.33	-0.76
14	-9.56	-5.89	-3.80	-2.70	-0.33	0.08	-6.49	-5.88	-2.72	-0.61	-0.18	-0.48	-2.29	-1.07	-0.20	0.13	-0.43	-0.46
15	-7.82	-5.40	-5.00	-3.62	-1.28	-0.23	-5.78	-5.37	-2.95	-2.37	-0.96	-0.33	-1.81	-0.63	-0.56	-0.66	-0.74	-0.10
16	-52.8	-46.0	-36.2	-7.84	-5.73	-1.61	-44.7	-31.0	-17.6	-7.26	-2.72	-0.66	-18.8	-5.88	-2.67	-0.79	-0.79	-0.46
17	-45.2	-35.4	-25.6	-12.2	-3.82	-0.48	-34.9	-24.7	-13.7	-4.63	-1.63	-0.58	-11.6	-4.25	-1.42	-1.27	0.05	-0.33
18	-3.21	-2.06	-2.29	-1.38	-0.33	-0.41	-1.98	-1.75	-1.09	-0.48	-0.25	-0.23	-0.84	-0.18	-0.05	-0.53	-0.28	-0.07
19	-51.6	-40.3	-22.8	-9.30	-2.27	-0.46	-31.1	-21.5	-8.71	-2.06	-0.99	-0.18	-7.54	-2.77	-1.37	-0.02	-0.05	-0.10
20	-56.8	-51.3	-30.2	-7.31	-0.46	-0.20	-43.0	-31.8	-7.31	-0.18	-0.07	-0.02	-6.70	-0.48	0.00	0.05	-0.07	-0.15
21	-61.4	-62.1	-43.2	-25.0	-21.4	-2.93	-59.5	-55.5	-32.5	-14.2	-3.74	-1.07	-38.8	-3.95	-4.15	-2.04	-0.89	-0.76

Fig. 6. Heatmaps representing the accuracy drop each layer causes individually, for different block sizes and error rates. The baseline accuracy for VGG7 is 85.82% and for ResNet18 is 77.50%.

- *UNPROT:* This configuration is fully unprotected, where faults are injected into all network layers, and the accuracy results are reported.
- *EVEN:* In this configuration, protection is naively applied to all odd layers while leaving *even* layers unprotected, i.e., 50% of layers are protected.
- *EQUAL:* Similar to *EVEN*, this configuration also protects 50% of the layers. However, the layers are greedily selected based on their importance, i.e., based on the results of the sensitivity analysis in Sect. 4.3.
- *CUSTOM:* In this configuration, protection is exclusively applied to all critical layers—those with the most significant impact on accuracy—while leaving all other layers unprotected, usually $< 25\%$ of all layers.
- *FULL:* This configuration represents complete protection, maintaining baseline accuracy by protecting all layers.

For the RTM nanowire size of 32, Fig. 7 shows the accuracy drop across inference iterations for different BNN models and configurations. The red and blue lines are the same as in Fig. 4, namely the *FULL* configuration (maintaining baseline accuracy) and the *UNPROT* configuration, respectively. In all three models, the accuracy of the *UNPROT* configuration drops below 30% in less than 10 to 20 iterations. The *FULL* configuration maintains the baseline accuracy but at the cost of 87% and 109% performance overhead increase in ResNet and VGG, respectively.

To reduce this overhead, *EVEN, EQUAL* and *CUSTOM* selectively apply error protection to the network layers. The EVEN configuration slightly delays the accuracy drop but, since it is naively protecting network layers without considering their importance, in general it follows a similar trend as the unprotected configuration and increases the performance overhead by 51% (ResNet), and 105% (VGG), compared to the baseline *UNPROT*. The carefully chosen *EQUAL* configuration significantly delays the accuracy drop with a 72% increase in the overhead for ResNet, and only 6% for VGG. Note that while both *EVEN* and *EQUAL* protect the same number of layers, the overhead is different because the weight tensor sizes of the selected layers are varied, requiring different number of memory accesses, RTM shifts and misalignment. The *CUSTOM* configuration further reduces the accuracy drop: after 100 iterations, it is within 10% difference to the baseline, but at the cost of relatively higher performance overhead of 87% and 109% for ResNet and VGG respectively.

For RTM nanowire sizes 2 to 64, the accuracy after 100 inference iterations is reported in Table 2. Notably, for a nanowire size of two, the accuracy drop after 100 iterations is insignificant, especially in the VGG model. However, with increasing nanowire sizes, only the carefully protected configurations retain their accuracy and usability, while the accuracy in other configurations, such as *UNPROT* and *EVEN*, drops to unacceptable levels.

Analysis Summary: NetDrift simulates the impact of RTM misalignment faults on BNNs accuracy and enables balancing the tradeoffs between the accuracy drop due to misalignment faults and the performance overhead associated with PECC schemes. The framework allows for conducting sensitivity analyses on a given BNN model to identify crucial layers that have a substantial impact on

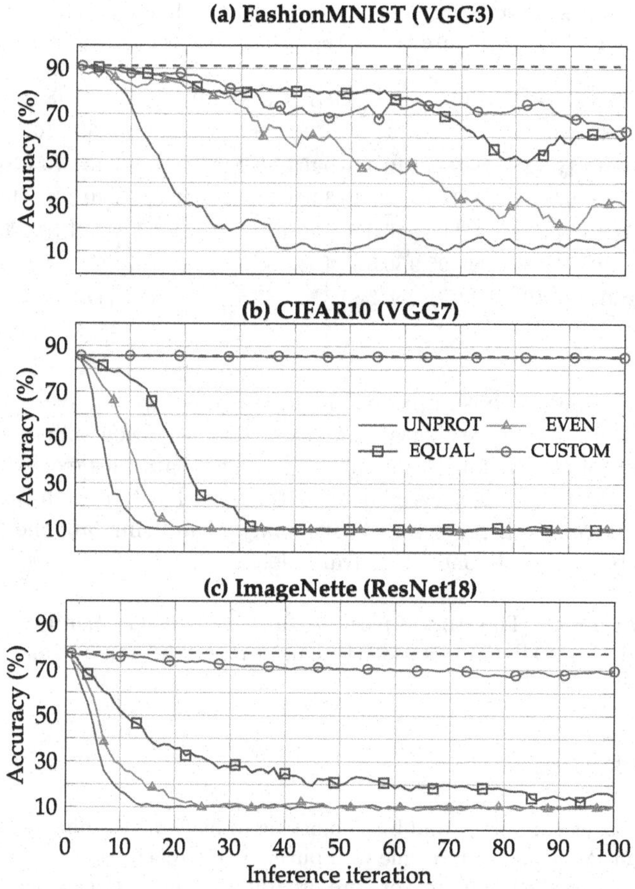

Fig. 7. Accuracy course over 100 inference iterations for different BNN models. The size of the nanowire tracks are 32 bits and the fault rate is $p = 10^{-4}$.

accuracy. Leveraging this information, selective application of error protection, such as in the *EQUAL* and *CUSTOM* configurations, becomes possible, enabling a collaborative reduction in both accuracy drop and performance overhead.

5 Conclusion

In this paper, we present NetDrift, a framework to simulate the effects of RTM misalignment faults on the accuracy of BNNs across multiple inference iterations. We evaluate various misalignment probabilities across different BNN models, exploring scenarios with no protection against misalignment faults, partial protection, and full protection. We show that NetDrift enables identifying critical network layers and exploring the trade-offs in accuracy and performance overhead. The framework also supports all necessary parameters to evaluate the

Table 2. Accuracies after 100 inference iterations, for different RTM nanowire sizes and configurations. The fault rate is $p = 10^{-4}$.

Model	VGG3 (FMNIST)						VGG7 (CIFAR10)						ResNet18 (ImageNette)					
Size	64	32	16	8	4	2	64	32	16	8	4	2	64	32	16	8	4	2
UNPROT	10.3	16.1	17.3	35.9	79.5	90.2	10.0	10.0	10.0	10.3	13.7	70.1	9.5	10.4	10.1	10.1	10.8	51.2
EVEN	20.7	30.2	67.4	81.8	88.0	89.7	9.9	10.3	10.0	11.8	34.5	76.6	9.3	10.3	10.3	10.2	24.0	51.6
EQUAL	38.3	60.1	54.0	74.0	90.1	90.5	10.0	10.0	10.4	29.4	63.5	79.4	9.8	15.1	18.7	25.5	55.1	73.5
CUSTOM	61.8	62.5	84.3	86.1	90.1	90.9	85.5	85.4	85.4	85.3	79.2	85.4	67.7	69.6	70.1	73.3	75.3	76.3
FULL	91.0	91.0	91.0	91.0	91.0	91.0	85.8	85.8	85.8	85.8	85.8	85.8	77.5	77.5	77.5	77.5	77.5	77.5

impact on the energy consumption and to optimise for it. We also illustrate that despite the inherent resilience of BNNs, their accuracy suffers significantly in the absence of PECC for misalignment fault probabilities exceeding approximately 10^{-5}. In the future, we plan to extend NetDrift to high-precision networks for more comprehensive sensitivity analysis and simulate the fault model of Skymiron-based RTMs once it is available.

Acknowledgements. This work is partially funded by the German Research Council (DFG) through the CO4RTM (450944241), OneMemory (405422836), and ARTS-NVM (502308721).

References

1. Reuther, A., et al.: Survey and benchmarking of machine learning accelerators. In: IEEE High Performance Extreme Computing Conference (HPEC), pp. 1–9 (2019)
2. Markidis, S., et al.: Nvidia tensor core programmability, performance & precision. In: IEEE International Parallel and Distributed Processing Symposium Workshops, pp. 522–531 (2018)
3. Archer, S., Mappouras, G., Calderbank, R., Sorin, D.: Foosball coding: correcting shift errors and bit flip errors in 3D racetrack memory. In: IEEE/IFIP International Conference on Dependable Systems and Networks (DSN), pp. 331–342 (2020)
4. Bläsing, R., et al.: Magnetic racetrack memory: from physics to the cusp of applications within a decade. Proc. IEEE **108**(8), 1303–1321 (2020)
5. Boukhobza, J., Rubini, S., Chen, R., Shao, Z.: Emerging NVM: a survey on architectural integration and research challenges. ACM Trans. Des. Autom. Electron. Syst. (TODAES) **23**(2), 1–32 (2017)
6. Buschjäger, S., et al.: Margin-maximization in binarized neural networks for optimizing bit error tolerance. In: Design, Automation and Test in Europe Conference and Exhibition (DATE), pp. 673–678 (2021)
7. He, K., Zhang, X., Ren, S., Sun, J.: Deep residual learning for image recognition. In: Proceedings of the IEEE Conference on Computer Vision and Pattern Recognition, pp. 770–778 (2016)
8. Hirtzlin, T., et al.: Outstanding bit error tolerance of resistive ram-based binarized neural networks. In: IEEE International Conference on Artificial Intelligence Circuits and Systems (AICAS), pp. 288–292 (2019)

9. Hochreiter, S.: The vanishing gradient problem during learning recurrent neural nets and problem solutions. Internat. J. Uncertain. Fuzziness Knowl.-Based Syst. **6**(02), 107–116 (1998)
10. Howard, J.: Imagenette. https://github.com/fastai/imagenette/ (2019). Accessed 25 Apr 2023
11. Hubara, I., Courbariaux, M., Soudry, D., El-Yaniv, R., Bengio, Y.: Binarized neural networks. In: Advances in Neural Information Processing Systems, pp. 4107–4115 (2016)
12. Jouppi, N.P., et al.: In-datacenter performance analysis of a tensor processing unit. In: International Symposium on Computer Architecture, pp. 1–12 (2017)
13. Kang, W., et al.: A comparative cross-layer study on racetrack memories: Domain wall vs skyrmion. J. Emerg. Technol. Comput. Syst. **16**(1) (2019)
14. Khan, A.A., De Lima, J.P.C., Farzaneh, H., Castrillon, J.: The landscape of compute-near-memory and compute-in-memory: a research and commercial overview. arXiv preprint arXiv:2401.14428 (2024)
15. Khan, A.A., Ollivier, S., Hameed, F., Castrillon, J., Jones, A.K.: Downshift: tuning shift reduction with reliability for racetrack memories. IEEE Trans. Comput. **72**(9), 2585–2599 (2023)
16. Krizhevsky, A.: Learning multiple layers of features from tiny images. Technical report (2009)
17. Mappouras, G., Vahid, A., Calderbank, R., Sorin, D.J.: Greenflag: protecting 3D-racetrack memory from shift errors. In: 2019 49th Annual IEEE/IFIP International Conference on Dependable Systems and Networks (DSN), pp. 1–12 (2019)
18. Multanen, J., Hepola, K., Khan, A.A., Castrillon, J., Jääskeläinen, P.: Energy-efficient instruction delivery in embedded systems with domain wall memory. IEEE Trans. Comput. **71**(9), 2010–2021 (2022)
19. Naffziger, S., et al.: Pioneering chiplet technology and design for the AMD EPYC™ and ryzen™ processor families: industrial product. In: ACM/IEEE International Symposium on Computer Architecture (ISCA), pp. 57–70 (2021)
20. Ollivier, S., Kline, D., Kawsher, R., Melhem, R., Banja, S., Jones, A.K.: Leveraging transverse reads to correct alignment faults in domain wall memories. In: International Conference on Dependable Systems and Networks, pp. 375–387 (2019)
21. Parkin, S., Hayashi, M., Thomas, L.: Magnetic domain-wall racetrack memory. Science **320**, 190–194 (2008)
22. Sari, E., Belbahri, M., Nia, V.P.: How does batch normalization help binary training? arXiv:1909.09139 (2019)
23. Simonyan, K., Zisserman, A.: Very deep convolutional networks for large-scale image recognition. In: International Conference on Learning Representations (2015)
24. Xiao, H., Rasul, K., Vollgraf, R.: Fashion-mnist: a novel image dataset for benchmarking machine learning algorithms (2017)
25. Yayla, M., Thomann, S., Wei, M.L., Yang, C.L., Chen, J.J., Amrouch, H.: HW/SW codesign for robust and efficient binarized SNNs by capacitor minimization. arXiv preprint arXiv:2309.02111 (2023)
26. Zhang, C., et al.: Hi-fi playback: tolerating position errors in shift operations of racetrack memory. In: 2015 ACM/IEEE 42nd Annual International Symposium on Computer Architecture (ISCA), pp. 694–706 (2015)

NanoSoftController: A Minimal Soft Processor for System State Control in FPGA Systems

Moritz Weißbrich(✉), Germain Seidlitz, and Guillermo Payá-Vayá

Chair for Chip Design for Embedded Computing, Technische Universität Braunschweig, Mühlenpfordtstraße 22-23, 38106 Braunschweig, Germany
{m.weissbrich,g.seidlitz,g.paya-vaya}@tu-braunschweig.de

Abstract. In many FPGA-based systems, only sequential system control structures modeled by finite state machines are actually required. In order to deal with complexity, design time, and verification issues, which are weaknesses of traditional hardware description languages, it may be preferred to describe the control flow behaviorally in software. However, it is reported that high-level synthesis for FPGA often generates inferior results in terms of resources and performance when translating software-style control flow description to hardware. In this paper, the NanoSoftController is proposed as an open-source soft processor, which is optimized for minimal and efficient logic resource usage on FPGA platforms. It is targeted at processing sequential finite state machine functionality in software, featuring a compact ISA for control flow in embedded systems and a tiny accumulator-based data path. Furthermore, an efficient mapping of memory to small distributed LUT RAM instances enables its use as a system state machine controller in even very resource-constrained FPGA designs, requiring only 104 slice LUTs and 76 slice registers in total. However, despite all optimizations, in a case study with high-level synthesis results of three reference software-style control applications, i.e., electronic door lock, smart glucose sensor, and sequential sensor network node, a better resource efficiency could not be shown. We evaluate the negative results and provide lessons we learned from them.

Keywords: Accumulator architecture · FPGA · High-level synthesis · Microcontroller · Programmable state machine · Soft processor

1 Introduction

Traditionally, FPGA-based control systems are defined using a hardware description language (HDL) such as Verilog or VHDL. While HDLs are considered as the "gold standard" for describing hardware implementations at register-transfer level (RTL), in many control applications, only some specific sequential finite state machine (FSM) control structures are actually required. HDLs offer large degrees of freedom, feature concurrent signal and data flow, and are not specifically designed to implement FSM models. Therefore, developers might be

L. Carro et al. (Eds.): SAMOS 2024, LNCS 15226, pp. 246–261, 2025.
https://doi.org/10.1007/978-3-031-78377-7_17

tempted to describe hardware behaviors that deviate from FSMs, leading to systems that are complex to prove, to document, and to maintain [18]. Furthermore, development time using HDL design entry can be significantly longer than describing control flow in a software programming language [9,15], which forces sequential FSM-like description by design.

On the one hand, in order to translate software describing a FSM behavior into a hardware circuit, *high-level synthesis* (HLS) approaches are a reasonable option. Design flows using HLS typically have a faster development time and smaller complexity at design time, since only the functional behavior needs to be described in, e.g., high-level C code. The selection of the underlying hardware architecture, timing behavior, etc., is left to the HLS tools. This also means that no HDL experience is required to implement hardware for an algorithm or application, enabling not only hardware engineers, but also the larger group of software developers to implement FPGA-based systems [2]. On the downside, it is reported that HLS solutions can achieve good results for regular data paths, however, may generate inferior results when it comes to control flow [15]. Recently, the authors of [5] mentioned that the use of HLS negatively impacted the implementation of a FPGA-based database accelerator, which could not meet the expectations of resource and performance requirements.

On the other hand, if the FSM behavior is described as software, a *soft processor* IP core is another option to implement the control flow on a FPGA. The FSM functionality is then directly executed as software, using the instruction-set architecture (ISA) of the soft processor. For this, FPGA vendors provide specific soft core IP, but also numerous alternatives of vendor-independent soft processors from the academic and open-source community can be found. As an example, the authors of [16,17] claim to have implemented one of the most resource-efficient soft processors based on an *accumulator machine* data path, optimized for ultra-low resource requirements to implement FSM and auxiliary system functionality on any small FPGA. In our previous work and ongoing research, the *NanoController* processor architecture is successfully applied as a minimal, yet fully programmable system state controller in ultra-low-power ASIC-based systems [19,21]. With the accumulator-based small data path and a compact 4-bit ISA designed for processing control flow, the complete data and control path fit into 219 standard gates of a 65 nm ASIC technology. Yet, this minimal architecture is fully programmable, enabling post-fabrication updates for the system control flow in smart ultra-low-power devices, e.g., electronic door locks in home automation, or implantable biomedical sensor systems.

In this work, we propose *NanoSoftController*, an open-source and free-to-use soft processor variant of the NanoController architecture, optimized for efficient use of FPGA resources, e.g., distributed LUT RAM. Admittedly, post-fabrication programmability is not a required key feature on FPGAs due to the inherent capability of reconfiguration. Nonetheless, the reported resource efficiency of accumulator architectures, the control-oriented NanoController ISA with previous convincing ASIC implementations, and the reported shortcomings of HLS-implemented control flow are encouraging arguments for *NanoSoftController*-based implementations of software-style FSMs on small FPGA devices.

However, in the evaluation of three application use cases of *NanoController*-based systems from our research, a higher resource efficiency compared to HLS-based implementations could not be shown. The contributions of this paper are:

1. Proposal of the *NanoSoftController* soft processor variant and description of the optimizations performed for FPGA to increase resource efficiency,
2. the evaluation of required resources and achieved maximum clock frequencies compared to hand-written VHDL implementations and HLS results of three application use cases, i.e., electronic door lock, glucose sensor, and sequential sensor network node,
3. and an examination of the negative results and lessons we learned.

This paper is structured as follows: In Sect. 2, related work on dedicated, soft processor-based and HLS-based FSM and control system implementation on FPGAs is presented. Section 3 contains the details of the proposed *NanoSoftController* and the optimizations performed for FPGA. For a set of three control applications, the implementation results are evaluated in Sect. 4 and compared with dedicated VHDL-based and HLS-based realizations. Section 5 concludes the paper and provides lessons learned from the results.

2 Related Work

In the following subsections, relevant related work to this paper is classified into three fields of research, i.e., *tools and methodologies* for FSM implementation onto FPGA, *minimal soft processors* for system control on FPGAs, and *high-level synthesis* of functional descriptions of FSMs.

2.1 Tools/Methodologies for FSM Implementation Onto FPGA

Tools and methodologies have been proposed to specifically map sequential FSMs onto programmable logic devices with simplified design entry and reduced complexity. A selection is shown in Table 1. In [14], the FSM behavior of an automotive window lift control application is entered as a graphical description using commercial tools, i.e., MATLAB StateFlow and Simulink. This enables designers not familiar with HDLs to implement and simulate FSMs at a high level of abstraction, which sets the focus on the functionality instead of the hardware realization. The generated implementation itself can follow different styles depending on the system requirements. This enables designers to explore a range of correct-by-construction implementation alternatives for FSMs, either as dedicated logic or based on a (soft) processor.

A second approach is to model FSM behavior as a textual description. A dedicated FSM modeling language inspired by the dot graph format is proposed in [18], which is significantly shorter than a VHDL description. With the tool approach called *aFSM* [11], it becomes possible to generate a hardware implementation of a FSM from a software description by using a MIPS assembly dialect, having 4.6x fewer code lines than the corresponding VHDL description

Table 1. Related tools/methodologies for FSM Implementation onto FPGA

Year/Ref.	FSM Source Description	Impl. Result	Impl. Style
2005 [14]	MATLAB StateFlow/ Simulink	Software (C/ binary code)	NoC of Xilinx MicroBlaze soft processors
2014 [10]	Simulink	Ada, C, VHDL codes	not specified
2017 [18]	Dedicated FSM modeling language	VHDL code	Dedicated logic (case...when structure)
2019 [11]	MIPS-based assembly dialect	VHDL code	Dedicated logic, Medvedev-style FSM (case...when structure)
2021 [12]	C code (for RISC-V target)	VHDL code	Dedicated logic, memory stack/heap-based FSM structure
this	*NanoController* assembly (current framework)	Software (binary code)	*NanoSoftController* soft processor

in a case study. The intended use case is to enable low-level programmers to offload control and communication state machines to FPGA-based systems. In follow-up work [12], this approach is extended to a HLS solution, where C code is compiled to assembly code for a RISC-V target, from which a dedicated FSM is generated via *aFSM*.

In this work, the *NanoSoftController* is proposed as a resource-efficient soft processor for FSM implementation on small FPGA devices, where the state machine functionality is programmed in assembly language and executed as software. Since the focus is on the controller architecture, other abstracted source entry methodologies found in the literature are considered out of the scope of this work and are left for future work on the *NanoSoftController* tool framework.

2.2 Minimal Soft Processors for System Control & Auxiliary Function FSMs on FPGAs

Table 2 summarizes related work on selected resource-efficient, recently proposed vendor-independent soft processors for system control FSMs and auxiliary functions. Vendor independence implies that the Xilinx MicroBlaze, for example, is excluded from the selection, as this processor IP is specifically designed for FPGA devices from Xilinx. *Lipsi* [16], *Leros* [17] as well as the proposed *NanoSoftController* belong to the class of *accumulator machines*, i.e., the ISA is designed to implicitly address an accumulator register in an instruction (1-address machine architecture). Compared to a typical RISC data path (3-address machine architecture), less resources are required for the implementation. *Lipsi* and *Leros* share a closely related instruction set, however, with different optimization goals. *Lipsi* implements a very small 8-bit data path, which can be fitted into 96 4-input LUTs and 1 block RAM instance on an Altera Cyclone IV FPGA [16]. *Leros* is targeted at executing compiled C code, and therefore features a 32-bit data path [17].

A different approach is applied in the *merv* soft processor [6]. Here, a full 32-bit RISC-V ISA is implemented, however, the data path units are serialized

Table 2. Related selection of minimal vendor-independent soft processors for system control & auxiliary function FSMs on FPGAs

Feature	Soft Processor/Ref. (Year)				
	Lipsi [16] (2018)	*Leros* [17] (2019)	*merv* [6] (2019)		*NanoSoftController* (**this**)
			Variant A	Variant B	
Data Path Architecture	8-bit Accumulator	32-bit Accumulator	32-bit RISC-V, serial ALU (1, 2, 4 or 8 bit)		7-bit Accumulator
IMEM Impl.	Single Block RAM	Block RAMs, not further specified	Separate (Harvard)	2 shared BRAM banks	Distributed RAM
DMEM Impl.					
Execution Paradigm	Sequential/ Multi-cycle	not specified	Sequential/Multi- cycle, Bit-serial		Sequential/ Multi-cycle
Instr. Width	8/16 bit (var.)	16 bit	32 bit		4/8/12 bit (var.)
Instruction Set	ALU (add, sub, and, or, xor, shift), direct/indirect load/store, cond./uncond. branches, IO	ALU (add, sub, and, or, xor, shift-right by 1), direct/indirect load/store, cond./uncond. branches	RISC-V (RV32I)		ALU (add, sub, cmp), direct load/store, single-instruction memory increment/ decrement/clear, cond. branch
Source Code Availability	Chisel (open-source[1])	Chisel (open-source[2])	MyHDL (not publicly available)		VHDL (open-source[3])

to a width between 1 and 8 bits and require multiple clock cycles to compute the result of a single instruction. This reduces the resource count at the trade-off of reduced instructions per cycle (IPC). *merv* is a recent successor of the older *SuperSmall* and *UltraSmall* MIPS implementations with bit-serial ALUs.[1,2,3]

Compared with the related architectures, the proposed *NanoController* soft processor follows the same optimization goals, but utilizes more aggressive compaction strategies on the ISA to further reduce the code size, memory requirements, and resource utilization. This includes a compact instruction set with 4-bit opcodes designed for FSM processing, variable-length operand encoding for minimal instruction lengths between 4 and 12 bits, reused operand and memory pointers between successive instructions, functional memory outputs, and a vector-based event trigger mechanism for compact interrupt handling and subroutines, all discussed in detail in [21].

2.3 High-Level Synthesis of FSMs

With constantly improving HLS solutions, it is feasible to program the behavior of a complex FSM in a high-level language like C, and then translate it to a dedicated logic circuit with no or minimum additional effort. In earlier works [4,13], control FSM functionality with explicit interface and state descriptions has been implemented in C and synthesized by Vivado HLS for FPGA. However, it is concluded that the non-concurrent control interfaces had a significant performance cost and resource overhead when implemented by HLS, which has mainly been used for regular, parallel data paths before. In [15], a detailed case study on a HLS-based FPGA implementation of a motion estimation algorithm is reported,

[1] https://github.com/schoeberl/lipsi.
[2] https://leros-dev.github.io/.
[3] https://github.com/tubs-eis/NanoController.

using two industrial synthesis tools, i.e., Vivado HLS and Catapult-C. For the complex control flow required within the algorithm, it is reported that the HLS implementation required 3-4x more resources than the VHDL reference and, therefore, had a lower quality of result. However, the development time in C was 3.5x faster, indicating a lower complexity of the design process.

In later works, HLS is applied to more sophisticated control and FSM designs. The authors of [1] have described a complete heterogeneous dual-core embedded processor in functional C code. The cycle behavior and implementation style of the processor are fully determined by the HLS tool. Also, some best practices of coding for HLS are presented, which support the claims from [15] about inefficient synthesis of control structures. In a recent literature survey [9], it is concluded that for a great majority of cases, the difference in FPGA resources between HLS and RTL-based implementations is small, which may be an indicator of the increasing maturity of HLS tools. It was observed that designers with limited HDL experience easily obtained better results with HLS, at only a third of the corresponding RTL design time and only half the RTL code size. The authors conclude that it becomes feasible to use HLS for non-performance-critical parts, and an optimized RTL description only for small cycle-critical parts. Therefore, a reasonable evaluation of the *NanoSoftController* should also consider HLS as a solution to implement FSMs from a software-style description.

3 FPGA Optimization of the NanoSoftController

The following section examines the individual components of the *NanoSoftController* architecture. The basic structure of the data path and control path has been inherited from the original NanoController architecture [21]. Optimizations have been made to the control path to increase the resource efficiency, as well as optimizations in the data and instruction memory implementation.

3.1 Data Path and Control Path

The entire structure of the *NanoSoftController* can be gleaned from Fig. 1. The NanoController architecture implements a multi-cycle 1-operand *accumulator machine* with a single adder unit and an *Accu* (`A`) register and is designed for minimum hardware resources. Data can be loaded into the data path through the *Operand* (`B`) register, which is either received from *data memory* or from an immediate value in the *instruction memory.* The constants 0/1, XOR and AND operations at the adder unit inputs enable, for example, clearing, subtraction, comparison, increment, and decrement operations. The `MEM_PTR` contains the pointer address for accesses to the data memory and holds it over multiple instructions, which enables re-accessing memory locations without further address encoding. This feature is exploited in the NanoController ISA for `MEM_PTR` and also for bit groups in the operand `B` register, in order to enable *variable-length operand encoding* for reduced instruction memory size. In order to further compact the code size, output signals for system control and address

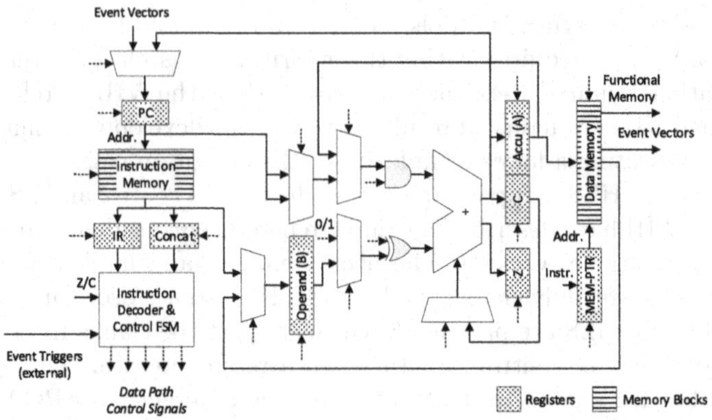

Fig. 1. Schematic block diagram of the *NanoSoftController* architecture.

vectors for interrupt events are directly generated from data memory locations, i.e., using a *functional memory* concept [7], so that no dedicated instructions are required. The registers `Z` and `C` store zero and carry flags, which are necessary for branch executions. The program counter `PC` is used as an address to load the *instruction register* (`IR`) from the instruction memory.

The control path consists of the multi-cycle instruction decoder & control FSM, which generates the required control signal sequences for the data path. Opcodes are loaded into `IR` in one machine cycle during the *fetch* phase. This is followed by the *register fetch* phase, in which instructions are interpreted and `B` or `MEM_PTR` register values are updated. Finally, the number of cycles in the multi-cycle *execution* phase depends on the complexity of the instructions.

For FPGA implementation, the data path from [21] has been implemented with a width of 7 bit for the applications evaluated in this work. The resource efficiency of the implementation has been checked for the Xilinx 7-Series slice architecture [23]. In particular, the mapping to available dedicated carry chain logic and the use of MUXF7/MUXF8 primitives for large multiplexer implementations was examined. Other FPGA-specific optimization potential was not identified in the data path without substantial structural changes to the NanoController architecture. For the control path, the generically configurable external event triggers have been reduced to just the required amount to minimize the required LUT and slice register resources.

3.2 Instruction Set Architecture (ISA)

The compact NanoController ISA consists of 16 different instructions, each encoded with 4 bits. A summary is provided in Table 3 and a detailed description can be found in [21]. Program code is currently written in architecture-dependent assembly language and translated to binary code using a customized assembler tool [22] adapted to the NanoController ISA. The instruction set has been laid out to efficiently encode state sequences in FSMs and control flow with the concept of functional memory. Therefore, only basic arithmetic operations using a

Table 3. Instruction set of the NanoController architecture.

Class	Mnemonic	Description
Arithmetic	ADDI	ADD Immediate to accumulator
	SUBI	SUBtract Immediate from accumulator
	CMPI	CoMPare Immediate with accumulator, set flags
Load/Store	LDI	LoaD Immediate into accumulator
	LD	LoaD from data memory
	ST	STore to data memory
	STL	STore to data memory at Last used address
SingleInstr.MemoryModify	LIS	Load-Increment-Store data memory
	LISL	Load-Increment-Store data memory at Last used address
	LDS	Load-Decrement-Store data memory
	LDSL	Load-Decrement-Store data memory at Last used address
	CST	Clear accumulator, STore to data memory
	CSTL	Clear accumulator, STore to data memory at Last used address
Branch	BNE	read flags, Branch if Not Equal zero
	DBNE	Decrement accumulator, Branch if Not Equal zero
Sleep	SLEEP	SLEEP until next wake-up trigger

single adder are included. The instructions `LIS`, `LDS` and `CST` handle incrementing, decrementing, and clearing of state values within single instructions, leading to compact code. The instructions `LISL`, `LDSL`, `CSTL` and `STL` contribute to code compaction as well, as they use the last memory address for incremental updates without further encoding. The instruction `SLEEP` halts program execution until either externally triggered or the internal RTC counter reaches the tick limit specified through functional memory.

All instruction opcodes serve as inputs to the control unit (CU) FSM, from which *control signals* (CS) are generated for the multi-cycle data path. The CS consist of 24 lines in the current implementation. Within these control lines, patterns of useful combinations can be potentially exploited for resource optimization. In order to optimize the CU for FPGA implementation, the internal binary state encoding of the *fetch*, *register fetch*, and *execute* phases of the multi-cycle execution is manually pre-selected for minimum resource requirements. Since the states only need to be encoded with two bits, all possibilities could be exhaustively tested to obtain the optimal encoding. For all other binary encodings, i.e., instruction opcodes and patterns of control line output combinations, the VANAGA framework has been applied to explore the design space of encoding solutions, which is described in detail in [20]. VANAGA uses the NSGA-II evolutionary algorithm to optimize sets of binary encoding for a specific metric, i.e., minimized FPGA LUTs and slice registers after implementation in this work.

3.3 Data and Instruction Memory

For the evaluated use cases in this work, the data storage capacity of the *NanoSoftController* is 16 7-bit wide entries, i.e., 112 bits only. Accordingly, the data storage will be implemented as distributed LUT RAM, as depicted in Fig. 2. Distributed memory can efficiently store a relatively small amount of data in LUTs, compared to, e.g., the rather large capacity of dedicated 18/36 kbit block

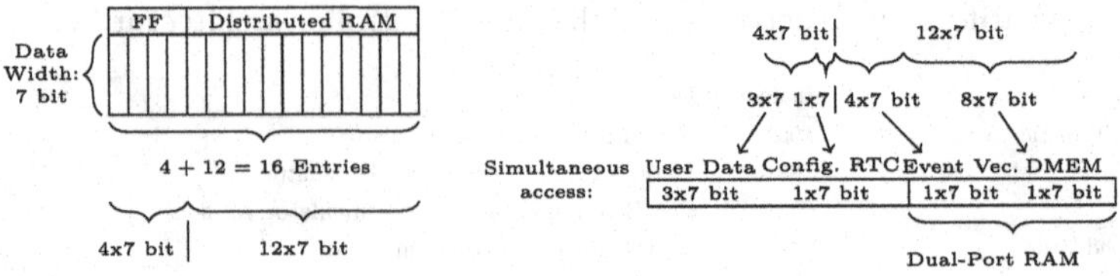

Fig. 2. Resource optimization of the data memory through the utilization of distributed LUT RAM

RAM resources in Xilinx 7-Series FPGAs [24], or an inefficient implementation using 112 slice registers. However, the utilization of distributed memory is subject to certain conditions. Firstly, writing to distributed memory must be synchronous, but reads can be asynchronous. Secondly, data can only be output in the read/write bit width simultaneously. It is possible to generate dual-port distributed RAM, i.e., two outputs can be simultaneously accessed via two different addresses. The depth and data width can be configured, with the depth ranging from 16 to 65536 entries and the data width ranging from 1 to 1024 bits [23].

The *NanoSoftController* data memory performs synchronous writes and asynchronous reads, satisfying the first condition. Furthermore, the data path logic only requires access to a single address, thus fulfilling the second condition in this context. The concept of functional memory outputs requires multiple locations to be read simultaneously. For event trigger handling, up to four jump vector addresses are currently reserved in the functional memory. However, there is no requirement for the event vectors to be simultaneously accessible due to sequential program execution and event handling. Simultaneous accessibility is only necessary for functional address locations of the configurable RTC and system control output, along with a single event vector. This makes it possible to integrate the data memory and parts of the functional memory within a single dual-port distributed memory with a depth of 16 entries and a data width of 7 bits, as illustrated in Fig. 2. The data required for the data path can be placed on the first output port, while the second output port can be utilized for accessing event vectors. With this memory layout, only 4 7-bit wide entries of functional memory need to be implemented as separately readable slice registers, i.e., 3×7 bit of user data and 1×7 bit of RTC configuration in Fig. 2, optimizing the resource requirements from 112 slice registers to 14 distributed dual-port RAM LUTs and 28 slice registers.

Similarly, due to its small size, the instruction memory is mapped to distributed LUT RAM instead of a register array or block RAM instance. Here, a single-port memory is sufficient, leading to a requirement of 8 distributed RAM LUTs for a total capacity of 512 bits in the required configuration for this work.

4 Evaluation

The scope of the evaluation is to quantify the proposed *NanoSoftController* in terms of resource requirements and maximum clock frequency when imple-

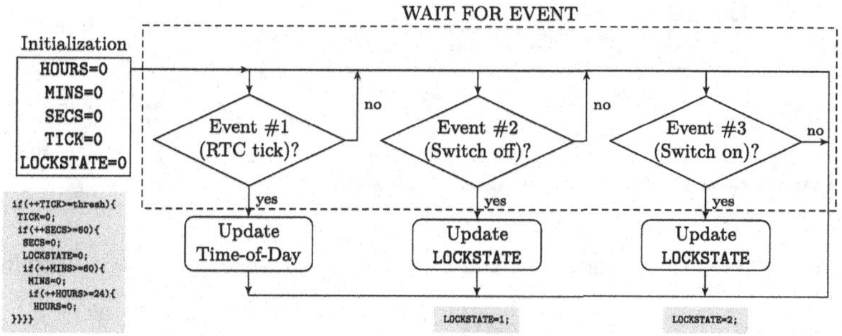

Fig. 3. Flow diagram of the Electronic Door Lock (EDL) application

mented on a Xilinx Artix-7 *xc7a35ti* FPGA. For this, three exemplary control applications have been selected from previous [19] and ongoing work that utilize ASIC implementations of the *NanoController* architecture, i.e., *Electronic Door Lock* (EDL) control, a state machine for a smart *Glucose Sensor* (GS) and the control flow for a *Sequential Sensor Network* (SSN) node. Each application has been implemented in three variants, i.e., hand-written VHDL code at RTL as a hardware designer's reference, a software implementation of the FSM in C for HLS, and a software implementation in *NanoController* assembly language to be directly executed on the *NanoSoftController*.

4.1 Exemplary Control Applications

In Fig. 3, the control flow of the *Electronic Door Lock* (EDL) FSM is depicted, which is part of a heterogeneous control system using the *NanoController* and a separately implemented general-purpose micro-controller (GPC). The system functionality is described in detail in [19]. On the one hand, real-time clock time-keeping functionality is implemented. Based on a reference tick signal (event #1), a time-of-day stamp, consisting of `HOURS`, `MINS`, `SECS`, and sub-second `TICK` outputs, is updated to sequence time-dependent actions on the GPC. On the other hand, the operation state of the EDL is influenced by the `LOCKSTATE` output. Event #3 is triggered by a proximity sensor when a RFID key card is presented to the EDL, switching on the GPC for encrypted RFID communication. Via event #2, the GPC can request to be switched off for energy efficiency. As shown by the explanatory code excerpts from the C implementation annotated in Fig. 3, the software implementations of this control application mainly consist of separated counter variables in a chain of `if`-clauses. An equivalent structure is also used for the VHDL hardware description.

The *Glucose Sensor* (GS) control application can be described as regular transitions of a FSM, as shown in Fig. 4. This control sequence is intended for a smart implantable biomedical device, consisting of three sensors, an ADC to digitize sensor samples, and a radio transmitter unit to send the sensor samples to the outer world. The first hardware implementation of such a demonstration

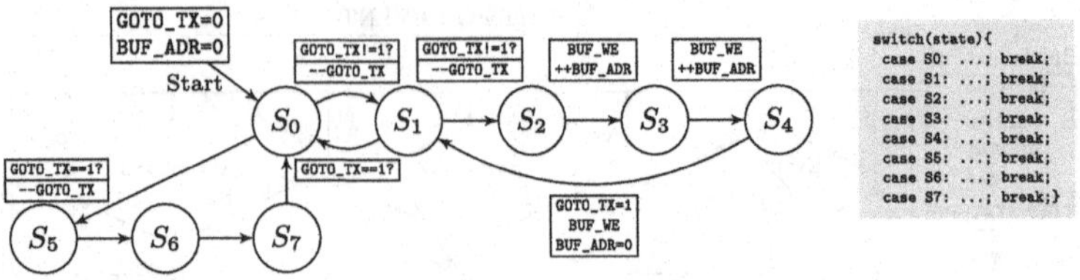

Fig. 4. State transition diagram of the FSM of the Glucose Sensor (GS) application

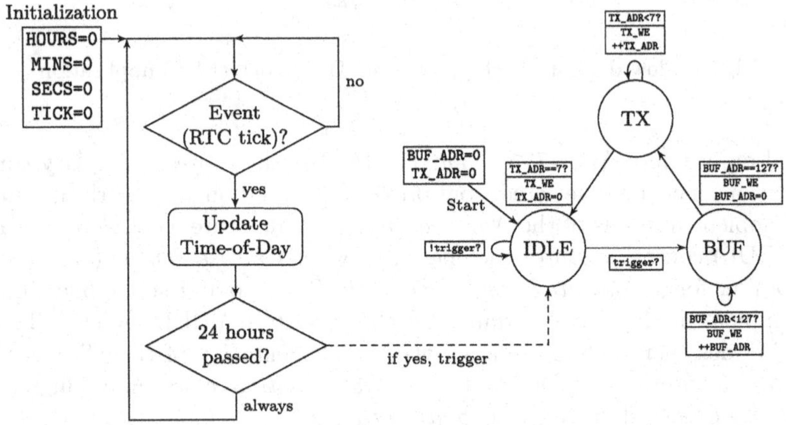

Fig. 5. Flow diagram and state transition diagram of the FSMs of the Sequential Sensor Network (SSN) application

system is presented in [8], and full-scale integration is the subject of current research. From each of the eight states S_0 to S_7, a set of control/enable signals is generated by functional memory. S_0 is the idle state, S_1 prepares the ADC, and S_2, S_3, and S_4 are used to digitize samples from the three sensors and store them in an addressable buffer. For this, buffer address and write enable outputs `BUF_ADR` and `BUF_WE` are generated. States S_5, S_6, and S_7 control the radio transmitter and are reached after sampling the sensors when `GOTO_TX` = `1`. In both FSM descriptions, VHDL and C, the eight states are defined as an enumeration type and evaluated by `case..when` and `switch..case` structures, respectively. The assembly implementation using the *NanoController* ISA makes use of the load-increment-store and load-decrement-store instructions on functional memory to effectively cycle through FSM states, and uses conditional branching with `SLEEP` termination to execute additional variable updates in each state.

In Fig. 5, the control flow of a use case in a distributed *Sequential Sensor Network* (SSN) of devices is depicted. A timestamp is updated analogously to the EDL application. After 24 h have passed, a series of sensor values is sequentially collected in a buffer with 128 locations, and a set of 8 values is transmitted afterwards. This use case represents two coupled state machines, merging the concepts from the EDL and GS applications, which increases the application complexity

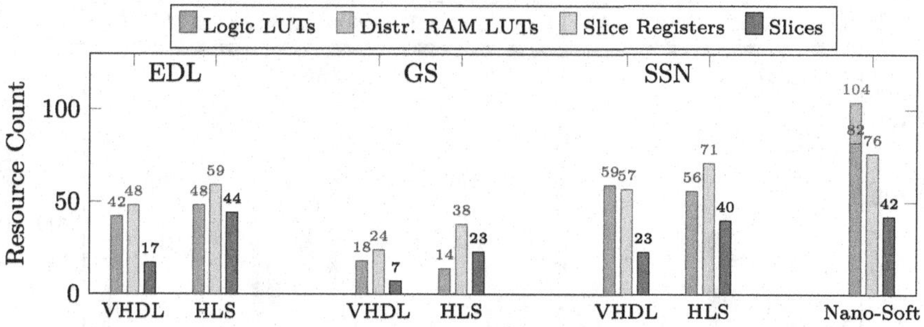

Fig. 6. Comparison of resource counts for resource-driven FPGA implementation of application cases (Xilinx Artix-7 *xc7a35ti* target)

to the limit of the resource-minimal instruction memory of the *NanoSoftController* implementation. More specifically, the parameters of this application have been tuned so that the program length completely fills the minimum capacity provided by distributed LUT RAM, i.e., 512 bits.

4.2 Comparison of Implementation Results

The RTL description of the three evaluation applications described in VHDL, as well as the *NanoSoftController* are implemented for the Xilinx Artix-7 *xc7a35ti* device using Vivado 2023.2. For HLS of the C implementations, Vitis HLS 2023.2 is used with the same target device and default implementation and optimization flow. To guide register optimization, the `bool` data type is applied for single control signals in the C code. Numeric types are described as 16 bit `unsigned short` instead of `unsigned int` whenever possible.

In Fig. 6, the required FPGA resources, i.e., LUTs, slice registers and occupied slices, are plotted. The timing constraints have been fully relaxed to a period of 1 µs to achieve the smallest implementation. In general, the dedicated VHDL implementation and the HLS result show different resource counts depending on the complexity of the application, with the GS FSM being the smallest and the SSN control flow requiring the most resources. Contrary to our initial expectation regarding control flow, the HLS solutions perform reasonably well compared to the VHDL implementation. The amount of LUTs is very similar, and the amount of registers required by the HLS solution is between 23 % and 58 % larger. This is mainly because C variables from the software description of the FSMs are not mapped to bit-optimized value ranges in hardware, as it is the case in the RTL description. The amount of slices required by HLS is also higher due to less dense logic packing. This could possibly be influenced by tuning the Vitis flow configuration, which, however, has not been the scope for this evaluation.

The *NanoSoftController* is implemented with the least parameterizable capacity of distributed RAM within 22 LUTs, i.e., 64 × 8-bit single-port instruction memory in 8 LUTs, and 16 × 7-bit dual-port data and functional memory in

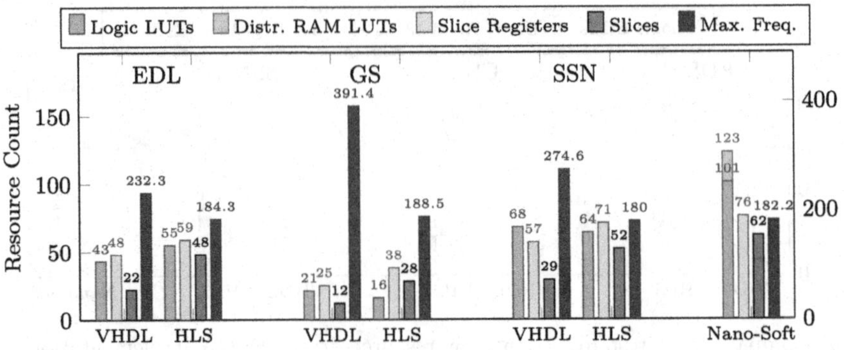

Fig. 7. Comparison of resource counts and maximum frequency for timing-driven FPGA implementation of application cases (Xilinx Artix-7 *xc7a35ti* target)

14 LUTs, and all applications fit within this memory amount. From our experience with optimizing standard cell ASIC implementations of the *NanoController*, we disabled ISA features and instructions not required in a specific application in order to reduce the complexity of the CU. However, a reduction of control logic LUT resources could not be achieved by this for the FPGA target, which is one of the lessons we learned for minimal soft controller architectures. Overall, despite the optimizations, the *NanoSoftController* is not more resource-efficient than the reference HLS results. 1.86x of the LUTs of the most complex SSN application is required due to overhead by data path, control path, and memories, although the amount of required registers is similar due to the minimal accumulator architecture.

In Fig. 7, resources and the maximum achieved clock frequency are plotted for timing-driven implementation. For this, the timing constraints were tightened until violations occurred, and the maximum clock frequency was determined from the worst negative slack of the critical path. In general, the same relations as for the resource-driven implementation can be observed, with slight absolute increases in the logic LUT count. The tightest execution time constraint is set by the GS application with a required state transition every 50 µs. Therefore, the minimum clock frequency of HLS solutions is 20 kHz (state transition possible every cycle) and 2 MHz for the *NanoSoftController* due to multi-cycle execution (max. 100 cycles for performing a state transition in GS application). For all implementations, these performance requirements are met. The clock frequency of HLS implementations saturates between 180 MHz and 190 MHz and does not reach the performance of the VHDL implementations. This is in agreement with recent observations of other authors [5], where HLS results did not meet the theoretically expected performance goals. It should be noted that the HLS frequencies are obtained best values for a single cycle of latency. Higher absolute clock frequencies could be achieved when allowing multiple cycles of latency, however, at the expense of massively increased LUT and register count. For the three applications, the higher clock frequencies did not compensate the increased latency and were therefore impractical. The *NanoSoftController* can reach a clock frequency of 182 MHz and is comparable to the HLS results, with 19 additional LUTs required, compared to the resource-driven *NanoSoftController.*

5 Conclusion and Lessons Learned

Designing FPGA-based control systems and FSM functionality at the software level, i.e., as program code, can have advantages in terms of complexity, development time, verification, and maintenance compared to traditional HDL-based descriptions. For the translation to hardware, HLS or soft processor architectures are viable options. In this paper, the *NanoSoftController* has been proposed, which is a very small, resource-efficient accumulator-based soft processor architecture derived from the *NanoController* architecture for ASIC targets [21], featuring a compact ISA designed for processing FSMs and control flow in general. Specifically, the architecture has been optimized to map as many memory components as possible to distributed LUT RAM to improve efficient resource usage. Overall, on a Xilinx Artix-7 FPGA, a total of 82 LUTs are used for logic, 22 LUTs for distributed memory, and 76 slice registers are used for the *NanoSoftController.* The LUT count is substantially less than reported for the tiny *Lipsi* accumulator-based soft processor for control flow (162 LEs) [16], but a direct comparison is not possible due to the different LUT architectures.

However, contrary to ASIC implementations, a minimal programmable architecture is not a prime necessity for post-fabrication adaptability, as FPGAs feature inherent reconfigurability. Therefore, for the use case of bringing software-implemented control flow to FPGAs, the results of dedicated solutions created by HLS also need to be taken into consideration. In related work, it is reported that HLS produces inferior results for control flow implementations in terms of resource efficiency and maximum clock frequency [5,15]. However, for the evaluation of three control application use cases from current *NanoController* research activities, i.e., electronic door lock, glucose sensor, and sequential sensor network, HLS implementation results proved reasonably well and achieved resource counts close to hand-written VHDL implementations. Therefore, an advantage in terms of resource efficiency could not be shown for the *NanoSoftController*, which requires 1.86x the amount of LUTs (including those LUTs used as distributed RAM) of the most complex HLS implementation of the evaluation. We take away the following lessons:

1. For the complexity and size of control flow envisioned for *NanoController*-based systems, the results of HLS-based implementations in terms of resource requirements are not as bad as reports from the literature suggest. A possible explanation is that the reports have been published some years ago, and HLS tools have been constantly improved since then. This outcome, however, could change with more complex application cases, to which *NanoController*-based systems have currently not been applied.
2. Opposed to our expectation from optimizing the architecture for standard cell ASIC technologies, control path specializations, e.g., removing unused

instructions from the CU decoder and binary re-encoding of opcodes, do not achieve a significant reduction in resource requirements on LUT-based FPGA targets. For the Xilinx Artix-7 FPGA architecture, most of the optimization potential was found to be in the efficient mapping of memory resources to distributed RAM, rather than in the packing of LUTs used for logic.

Nonetheless, we are convinced that the *NanoSoftController* still has a very low resource footprint and can be an interesting soft processor architecture for implementation on small, resource-constrained FPGA devices, e.g., the Cologne Chip GateMate FPGA [3] for applications with more complex control flow. Code compaction techniques, ISA customization concepts, and framework-based approaches to simplify control flow and FSM model entry for the *NanoController* architecture are subjects of current ongoing research. The *NanoSoftController* is open-source and free-to-use, whereas the application of commercial HLS solutions may have licensing issues. The hardware description and software toolchain are accessible via our GitHub repository (https://github.com/tubs-eis/NanoController).

Disclosure of Interests. The authors have no competing interests to declare that are relevant to the content of this article.

References

1. Ahmed, T., Sakamoto, N., Anderson, J., Hara-Azumi, Y.: Synthesizable-from-C embedded processor based on MIPS-ISA and OISC. In: 2015 IEEE 13th International Conference on Embedded and Ubiquitous Computing, pp. 114–123 (2015)
2. Canis, A., et al.: LegUp: an open-source high-level synthesis tool for FPGA-based processor/accelerator systems. ACM Trans. Embed. Comput. Syst. **13**(2) (2013)
3. Cologne Chip AG: GateMate FPGA (2024). https://colognechip.com/programmable-logic/gatemate/. Accessed 13 June 2024
4. Dahlstrom, J., Taylor, S.: Migrating an OS scheduler into tightly coupled FPGA logic to increase attacker workload. In: MILCOM 2013 - 2013 IEEE Military Communications Conference, pp. 986–991 (2013)
5. Drewes, A., Koppehel, M., Pionteck, T.: Dead-ends in FPGAs for database acceleration. In: Orailoglu, A., Jung, M., Reichenbach, M. (eds.) SAMOS 2021. LNCS, vol. 13227, pp. 493–504. Springer, Cham (2022). https://doi.org/10.1007/978-3-031-04580-6_33
6. Felton, C.L., Gilbert, B.K., Haider, C.R.: A parameterized and minimal resource soft processor for programmable logic. In: 2019 53rd Asilomar Conference on Signals, Systems, and Computers, pp. 1601–1605 (2019)
7. Halverson Jr., R., Lew, A.: An FPGA-based minimal instruction set computer. Technical report (1995)
8. Issakov, V., et al.: Fully autonomous system-on-board with complex permittivity sensors and 60 GHz transmitter for biomedical implant applications. In: 2020 IEEE Radio Frequency Integrated Circuits Symposium (RFIC), pp. 159–162 (2020)
9. Lahti, S., Sjövall, P., Vanne, J., Hämäläinen, T.D.: Are we there yet? A study on the state of high-level synthesis. IEEE Trans. Comput. Aided Des. Integr. Circuits Syst. **38**(5), 898–911 (2019)

10. Lanoe, M., Bordin, M., Heller, D., Coussy, P., Chavet, C.: A modeling and code generation framework for critical embedded systems design: from Simulink down to VHDL and Ada/C code. In: 2014 21st IEEE International Conference on Electronics, Circuits and Systems (ICECS), pp. 742–745 (2014)
11. Meyer, D., Eckert, M., Klauer, B., Haase, J.: HDL FSM code generation using a MIPS-based assembler. In: 2019 IEEE 28th International Symposium on Industrial Electronics (ISIE), pp. 1351–1356 (2019)
12. Meyer, D., Haase, J., Eckert, M., Klauer, B.: A modern approach to application specific processors for improving the security of embedded devices. In: IECON 2021 – 47th Annual Conference of the IEEE Industrial Electronics Society (2021)
13. Navarro, D., Lucía, O., Barragán, L.A., Urriza, I., Artigas, J.I.: Teaching digital electronics courses using high-level synthesis tools. In: 2013 7th IEEE International Conference on e-Learning in Industrial Electronics (ICELIE), pp. 43–47 (2013)
14. Paulsson, K., Hübner, M., Zou, H., Becker, J.: Realization of real-time control flow oriented automotive applications on a soft-core multiprocessor system based on Xilinx Virtex-II FPGAs. In: Proceedings of the International Workshop on Applied Reconfigurable Computing (ARC'05), pp. 103–110 (2005)
15. Schewior, G., Zahl, C., Blume, H., Wonneberger, S., Effertz, J.: HLS-based FPGA implementation of a predictive block-based motion estimation algorithm – a field report. In: Proceedings of the 2014 Conference on Design and Architectures for Signal and Image Processing (2014)
16. Schoeberl, M.: Lipsi: probably the smallest processor in the world. In: Berekovic, M., Buchty, R., Hamann, H., Koch, D., Pionteck, T. (eds.) ARCS 2018. LNCS, vol. 10793, pp. 18–30. Springer, Cham (2018). https://doi.org/10.1007/978-3-319-77610-1_2
17. Schoeberl, M., Petersen, M.B.: Leros: the return of the accumulator machine. In: Schoeberl, M., Hochberger, C., Uhrig, S., Brehm, J., Pionteck, T. (eds.) ARCS 2019. LNCS, vol. 11479, pp. 115–127. Springer, Cham (2019). https://doi.org/10.1007/978-3-030-18656-2_9
18. Vandeportaele, B.: A finite state machine modeling language and the associated tools allowing fast prototyping for FPGA devices. In: 2017 IEEE International Workshop of Electronics, Control, Measurement, Signals and Their Application to Mechatronics (ECMSM) (2017)
19. Weißbrich, M., Blume, H., Payá-Vayá, G.: A silicon-proof controller system for flexible ultra-low-power energy harvesting platforms. In: 2022 11th International Conference on Modern Circuits and Systems Technologies (MOCAST) (2022)
20. Weißbrich, M., Moreno-Medina, J.A., Payá-Vayá, G.: Using genetic algorithms to optimize the instruction-set encoding on processor cores. In: 2021 10th International Conference on Modern Circuits and Systems Technologies (MOCAST) (2021)
21. Weißbrich, M., Payá-Vayá, G.: NanoController: a minimal and flexible processor architecture for ultra-low-power always-on system state controllers. In: Orailoglu, A., Reichenbach, M., Jung, M. (eds.) SAMOS 2022. LNCS, vol. 13511, pp. 103–119. Springer, Cham (2022). https://doi.org/10.1007/978-3-031-15074-6_7
22. Williams, A.: Universal cross assembler (2015). https://github.com/wd5gnr/axasm. Accessed 13 June 2024
23. Xilinx: 7 Series FPGAs configurable logic block (UG474) (2016). https://docs.amd.com/v/u/en-US/ug474_7Series_CLB. Accessed 13 June 2024
24. Xilinx: 7 Series FPGAs memory resources (UG473) (2019). https://docs.amd.com/v/u/en-US/ug473_7Series_Memory_Resources. Accessed 13 June 2024

Author Index

L. Carro et al. (Eds.): SAMOS 2024, LNCS 15226, pp. 263–265, 2025.
https://doi.org/10.1007/978-3-031-78377-7

Printed in the United States
by Baker & Taylor Publisher Services